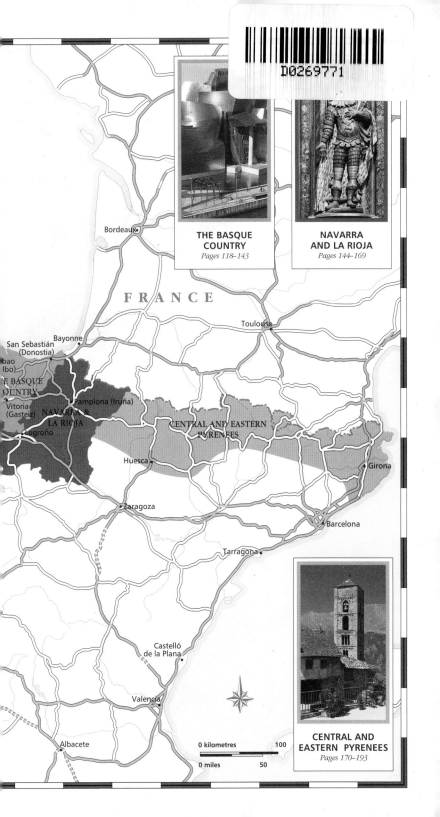

**THE BASQUE
COUNTRY**
Pages 118–143

**NAVARRA
AND LA RIOJA**
Pages 144–169

FRANCE

Bordeaux

Toulouse

Bayonne

San Sebastián
(Donostia)

bao
lbo)

E BASQUE
OUNTRY

Vitoria
(Gasteiz)

NAVARRA &
LA RIOJA

Pamplona (Iruña)

Logroño

CENTRAL AND EASTERN
PYRENEES

Huesca

Girona

Zaragoza

Barcelona

Tarragona

Castelló
de la Plana

Valencia

Albacete

**CENTRAL AND
EASTERN PYRENEES**
Pages 170–193

| 0 kilometres | 100 |
| 0 miles | 50 |

D0269771

EYEWITNESS TRAVEL

NORTHERN SPAIN

EYEWITNESS TRAVEL

NORTHERN SPAIN

AGNIESZKA DREWNO, ZUZANNA JAKUBOWSKA,
RENATA SZMIDT

LONDON, NEW YORK,
MELBOURNE, MUNICH AND DELHI
www.dk.com

Produced by Hachette Livre Polska sp. z o.o., Warsaw, Poland

SENIOR GRAPHIC DESIGNER
Paweł Pasternak

CONTRIBUTORS
Agnieszka Drewno, Zuzanna Jakubowska,
Renata Szmidt, Carlos Marrodán Casas

CARTOGRAPHY
Magdalena Polak

PHOTOGRAPHERS
Dorota and Mariusz Jarymowicz

ILLUSTRATORS
Michał Burkiewicz, Paweł Marczak

EDITOR
Maria Betlejewska

TYPESETTING AND LAYOUT
Elżbieta Dudzińska

Reproduced by Colourscan, Singapore.
Printed and bound in China by Toppan Printing Co.
(Shenzhen Ltd.)

First published in Great Britain in 2007
by Dorling Kindersley Limited
80 Strand, London WC2R 0RL

Copyright ©2007 Dorling Kindersley Limited, London
A Penguin Company

ISBN 978 1 4053 1788 7

Front cover main image: La Ainsa in the Pyrenees

◁ Vineyards near the Miño river in Galicia

CONTENTS

HOW TO USE THIS
GUIDE **6**

**A tympanum of the Iglelsia de
San Saturnino in Pamplona**

INTRODUCING
NORTHERN SPAIN

**Fishing boats in the port of Luarca
on the Asturian coast**

The town of Laspuña near Ainsa, surrounded by imposing massifs

A figure in the Iglesia de Santa María del Palacio in Logroño

Sculpted figures in the portal of San Bartolomé in Logroño

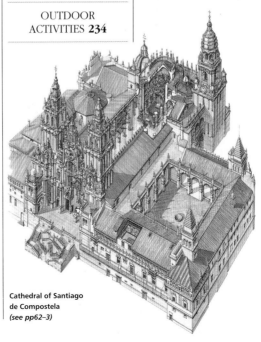

Cathedral of Santiago de Compostela
(see pp62–3)

HOW TO USE THIS GUIDE

This guide will help you get the most from your stay in Northern Spain. It provides both expert recommendations and detailed practical information. The guide maps the region and sets it in its historical and cultural context. The important sights are described, with maps, photographs and illustrations. Suggestions for food, drink, accommodation, shopping and activities are given, as well as tips on everything from the Spanish telephone system to travelling to and getting around the region.

NORTHERN SPAIN REGION BY REGION

In this guide, Northern Spain has been divided into five regions, each of which has its own chapter. A map of these regions can be found inside the front cover of the book. The most interesting places to visit in each region have been numbered and plotted on a Regional Map.

Each area of Northern Spain can be quickly identified by its colour coding.

1 Introduction
The history and character of each region is described here, showing how the area has developed over the centuries and what it has to offer the visitor today.

A locator map shows the region in relation to the rest of Northern Spain.

Highlight special or unique aspects of a particular sight.

2 Regional Map
This gives an illustrated overview of the whole region. All the sights are numbered, and there are also useful tips on getting around by car and public transport.

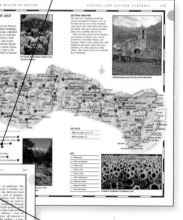

Features give information on topics of each particular region.

3 Detailed information
All the important towns and other places to visit are described individually. They are listed in order, following the numbering on the Regional Map. Within each town or city, there is detailed information on important buildings and other major sights.

4 Major towns *All the important towns and other places to visit are described individually. They are listed in order, following the numbering on the map. Within each town or city, there is detailed information on important buildings and other major sights.*

A Visitors' Checklist gives contact points for tourist and transport information, plus details of market days and local festival dates.

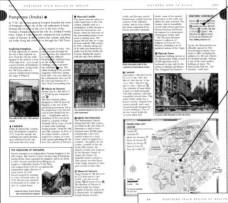

The town map shows all major through-roads as well as minor streets of interest to visitors. All the sights are plotted, along with the bus and train stations, parking, tourist offices and churches.

A suggested route for a walk covers the most interesting streets in the area.

5 Street-by-Street Map *Towns or district of special interest to visitors are shown in detailed 3D, with photographs of the most important sights, giving a bird's-eye view of the area.*

For all the top sights, a Visitors' Checklist provides the practical information you will need to plan your visit.

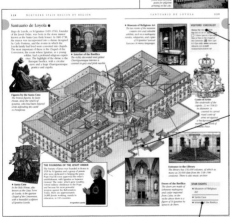

6 Top sights *These are given two or more pages. Important buildings are dissected to reveal their interiors.*

Stars indicate the works of art or features that no visitor should miss.

INTRODUCING
NORTHERN SPAIN

Putting Northern Spain on the Map

The area described in this guide comprises the autonomous regions of Northern Spain – Galicia, Asturias, Cantabria, the Basque Country, Navarra and La Rioja – as well as the Central and Eastern Pyrenees, which lie in Aragón and Catalonia respectively. Northern Spain's varied coastline borders the Atlantic Ocean. The country's most northerly point, the headland of Estaca de Bares, is in Galicia.

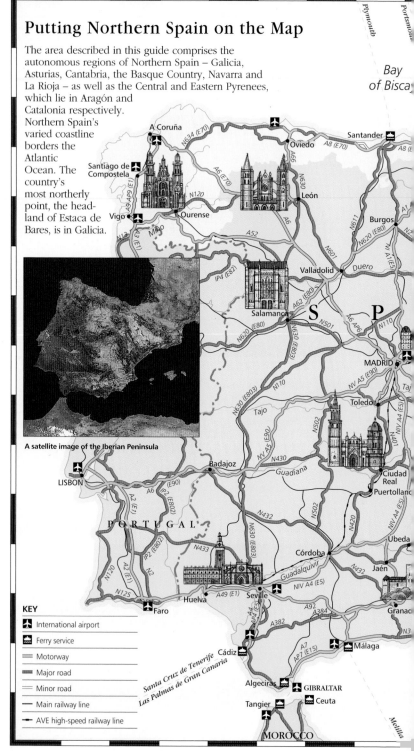

A satellite image of the Iberian Peninsula

KEY

✈	International airport
⛴	Ferry service
▬	Motorway
▬	Major road
═	Minor road
—	Main railway line
⬝	AVE high-speed railway line

◁ *The Environs of Bilbao 1918*, by Benjamin Palencia

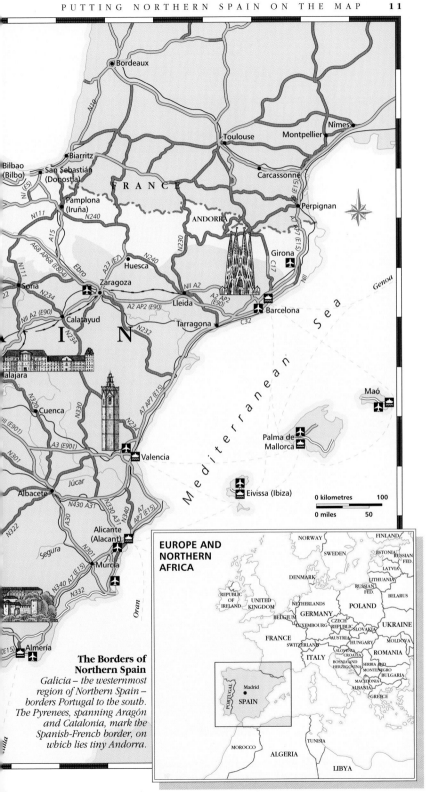

The Borders of Northern Spain

*Galicia – the westernmost
region of Northern Spain –
borders Portugal to the south.
The Pyrenees, spanning Aragón
and Catalonia, mark the
Spanish-French border, on
which lies tiny Andorra.*

**EUROPE AND
NORTHERN
AFRICA**

DISCOVERING
NORTHERN SPAIN

A capital in San Juan de la Peña

Green Spain, as it's often known, offers images very different from those of Mediterranean Spain: lush forests and deep-green valleys, soaring high mountain scenery, and Spain's most dramatic coastline, with fiords and giant cliffs – as well as exquisite beaches – facing the Atlantic surf. The north has some of Spain's most special cultures, in Celtic Galicia and the unique ways of the Basques, and remarkable architecture, from early Christian chapels to Bilbao's modern Museo Guggenheim. And it has superb food, whether harbourside seafood or refined Basque cuisine, and many of Spain's finest wines. Here is a guide to the region's highlights.

A stone cross on the Costa da Morte, in northwestern Galicia

GALICIA

- **Santiago de Compostela**
- **Rugged coastlines**
- **Miño & Ribeira wine valleys**

The greenest and wettest region of all, Galicia, just north of Portugal, has always lived a little apart from the rest of Spain. At its heart is fascinating **Santiago de Compostela** *(see pp60–5).* A focus for pilgrims since the early Middle Ages, the city is centred on a magnificent Gothic cathedral. To the west the coast is broken up by the **Rías Baixas** *(see p67),* beautiful fiord-like inlets lined by fine beaches and picturesque fishing villages. Just to the north is the Costa da Morte ("Coast of Death"), an awesome stretch of wild,

rocky coast so-named because of the many ships wrecked here over centuries.

Inland, Galicia has a soft green landscape of hills, woods, remote-feeling, utterly tranquil villages and charming towns lost in the past. Loveliest of all are the exquisite valleys of the **Miño and Ribeiro region** *(see pp70–1),* winding, sometimes extraordinarily steep clefts that produce excellent wines to go with Galicia's celebrated fish and seafood.

ASTURIAS AND CANTABRIA

- **Spectacular Picos de Europa**
- **Beautiful Costa Verde**
- **Oviedo's ancient churches**
- **Cuevas de Altamira**

Straddling the border between these two regions, the **Picos de Europa** *(see pp100–3)* form one of Spain's most spectacular mountain ranges,

a knot of towering summits between plunging gorges and valleys sheltering idyllic mountain villages. A paradise for walkers and climbers, coloured by dazzling sprays of gentians and narcissi, the Cantabrian mountains are also home to some of Europe's rarest wildlife, such as chamois and brown bears *(see pp26–7).*

The two regions offer the north coast's best beaches along the **Costa Verde** *(see p85),* in fine arching bays between red-roofed villages and massive cliffs topped by verdant meadows.

Their long human history has left many treasures too, such as the pre-Romanesque churches of **Oviedo** *(see pp92–3)* or extraordinary **Santillana del Mar** *(see pp106–7)* – almost a whole town of 16th-century mansions. Just nearby are the **Cuevas de Altamira**, with some of the greatest prehistoric cave paintings in the world *(see pp108–9).*

Lago Enol in the Picos de Europa, a high massif of wild beauty

The titanium façade of the Museo Guggenheim in Bilbao

THE BASQUE COUNTRY

- **Museo Guggenheim**
- **San Sebastián's beaches and its old town**
- **Picturesque harbours**
- **Bergara & the countryside**

The Basque people's many idiosyncrasies – in language, architecture, music, social life, food and more – give this region a special flavour. The stunning ultra-modern **Museo Guggenheim** has helped rejuvenate **Bilbao** and drawn a new wave of visitors to appreciate the city and its vibrant street life *(see pp122–7)*. Stately **San Sebastián** *(see pp132–5)* is very different. Gastronomic capital of northern Spain and an elegant resort of the 19th century, it has a superb beach on a perfectly curved bay, and a charming old town full of lively bars, ideal for sampling *pintxos* – the Basques' celebrated style of *tapas*. Between the two cities, the Basque Coast has rugged green crags and lofty headlands with fabulous views, sheltering never-crowded beaches and colourful fishing towns that sometimes climb straight up the flanks of the cliffs. For lovers of rural quiet, the

Basque countryside is fascinating to explore, with historic towns such as **Bergara** *(see p137)* and forest valleys dotted with stone farmhouses.

NAVARRA AND LA RIOJA

- **The Pyrenean valleys**
- **Pamplona & San Fermín**
- **The Rioja winelands**
- **Burgos & its cathedral**

Though part-Basque, the ancient kingdom of Navarra has its own marked character. In the north are wooded mountain valleys and glittering, fast-flowing rivers that rise up to historic passes over the Pyrenees like **Roncesvalles** *(see p150)*, lined with delightful villages of stone houses with whitewashed walls and flower-filled balconies. In the

middle of the province is its ancient capital, **Pamplona**, founded by the Romans and famous for its bullrunning festival of San Fermín each July *(see pp154–5)*. A must for wine-lovers is a visit to the vineyards of southern Navarra, which combine with those in **La Rioja** province to form Spain's most celebrated wine region *(see pp164–5)*. A short detour away is **Burgos** – the grand old capital of Castile, with its dramatic Gothic cathedral *(see pp166–9)*.

CENTRAL AND EASTERN PYRENEES

- **Parque Nacional de Ordesa**
- **San Juan de la Peña**
- **Parc Natural de Aigüestortes**
- **Romanesque architecture**

The highest part of the Pyrenees is in Aragón, particularly in and around **Ordesa National Park** *(see pp182–3)*, an awe-inspiring alpine landscape of towering walls of rock, plunging waterfalls and flowers. The mountains are great for outdoor activities. Below, stone villages cling to spectacular locations, but the best sight is the **Monasterio de San Juan de la Peña**, built against a massive rock screen *(see pp176–7)*. Further east in Catalonia the mountains surround pristine, sparkling lakes in the **Parc Natural d'Aigüestortes** *(see p188–9)*. Amid the superb scenery are gems of early Romanesque architecture, from churches in the remote **Vall de Boí** *(see p189)* to the mountain town of **Ripoll** *(see p192)*.

The Monasterio de San Juan de la Peña in the Pyrenees

A PORTRAIT OF NORTHERN SPAIN

*S*pain's diversity is evident in its northernmost part, the source of many of the country's oldest and most fascinating traditions. The peoples of the north speak three languages – Galician, Basque and Catalan – as well as Spanish. And instead of sun-browned southern plains there are thickly wooded hills, facing a misty Atlantic Ocean.

Northern Spain is, above all, extremely lush and green, with pockets of abundance like the winelands of Galicia and La Rioja. Thanks to the steepness of its mountains and their proximity to the Atlantic, it gets plenty of rain, so much of the region is carpeted with woodland or rich pasture. Yet it is sufficiently far south for the weather to be often warm and mild.

Red peppers drying in the sun

The north was the only part of Spain not conquered by the Moors in the Middle Ages, and some of its peoples even resisted the Romans. The Basques are the longest-established people in Europe, having already been in their green mountain home for centuries when the Romans encountered them around 200 BC. The Celtic Galicians are only relative newcomers by comparison. The other communities of the north took shape after the influx of the Moors into Spain in AD 711, when retreating Christians took refuge in the northern mountains. The tiny principalities and dukedoms formed in the valleys of Asturias and the Pyrenees were the cradles of the later states – Castile, Aragón, Catalonia – that eventually spread south to defeat the great Moorish kingdoms of Spain.

For centuries the regions west of Navarra were linked by the *Camino de Santiago*, the road to one of Europe's greatest pilgrimage sites, the

The busy harbour in A Coruña, one of Galicia's major cities

◁ **Graus – a village and monastery at the foot of massive rocks**

The landscape near Fuente Dé in the Picos de Europa

shrine of St James at Santiago de Compostela. The abundant traffic along the *camino* during the Middle Ages encouraged the growth of striking cities with magnificent Gothic architecture.

LAND AND PEOPLE

Once the tide of history moved south, large areas of northern Spain were left to themselves. As a result, today many parts of Galicia, Asturias and the Pyrenees feel distinctly remote, dotted with mountain farms and isolated villages whose buildings seem to have remained virtually unchanged since the 1600s. This remoteness has aided the survival of a rich vein of traditions. Both Galicians and Basques have their own extensive folklore and myths, and are known for witchcraft and magic.

These traditions are inseparable from the landscape. Abrupt mountainsides and narrow sea cliffs have imposed a special way of life. In Galicia the misty green countryside is a natural haunt for the many spirits of Celtic folklore, while to the Basques every inch of their beechwoods and valleys has some historical or mythological connection. The Cantabrian mountains, too, have ancient stories.

Besides the mountains, the life of the rugged north coast has been bound up with the sea. The Basques have historically been Spain's foremost seafarers, and furnished many of the skilled navigators who took Spanish explorers to the Americas. The Galicians have long relied on superb mussels and other inshore seafood as staples of their diet, and now outdo the Basques as deep-sea fishermen.

A woman in traditional Galician costume

The port of Malpica on the Galician coast

The peoples of the north also share some characteristics of all Spaniards – especially their Iberian gregariousness. They are just as devoted to socializing, whether on an evening *paseo* (stroll) or eating out in a convivial group. These are some of the friendliest parts of the country, less jaded by tourism than Mediterranean regions. Northern *fiestas* – great showcases of local traditions and foods – are among Spain's most exuberant, from Pamplona's San Fermín to the flower parades of Cantabrian harbours.

The Museo Guggenheim, Bilbao's prestigious new landmark

MODERN TIMES

In Spain's modern history the regions of the north have followed varying paths. Some joined the Industrial Revolution early in the 19th century, with shipbuilding, iron and steel in the Basque Country, coal mining and shipbuilding in Asturias. This also made them centres of progressive dynamism in the struggle to make Spain a modern state, while areas like Navarra and rural Galicia were known for an unchanging conservatism. The rise of Basque nationalism also undermined faith in the status quo. Asturias was the base for a socialist revolt in 1934, and when the Spanish Civil War erupted two years later both it and the Basques resisted General Franco's right-wing army. The victorious Franco regime regarded them with intense suspicion; their rebelliousness was met with harsh repression.

The northern regions have continued to fare differently in the new

The bull run *(encierro)* during Pamplona's San Fermín festival

Spain created since 1975, integrated into the European Union and with a system of regional self-government *(Autonomías)*. For Spanish-speaking regions like Asturias and La Rioja the "Autonomies" have become useful arms of local government. In Galicia, nationalism has always been quite mild, but has lately become more demanding. The Basque situation, however, has remained one of Spain's ongoing problems. The Basque government has greater powers than any other region in Europe, but a substantial proportion of Basques want total independence, and some sympathize with the militant nationalist group ETA. However, the declaration of a ceasefire by ETA in March 2006 has generated renewed optimism and raised hopes of a permanent solution.

The north's economic transformation has been almost as striking as the political one. The coal, steel and shipbuilding industries declined rapidly in the 1980s, causing severe hardship. Fishing, too, has come under pressure from EU quotas. Recently, though, tourism and Spain's industrial diversification have opened up new possibilities. Most dramatic of all has been the revitalization of a newly stylish Bilbao.

Architecture of Northern Spain

Northern Spain is remarkable for its exceptional architectural heritage. Preserved here are the foundations of Celtic homesteads and the ruins of Roman buildings, testifying to the region's ancient history. It is also here, especially along the pilgrimage route to Santiago de Compostela and in the Catalan Pyrenees, that beautiful Romanesque churches and lofty Gothic cathedrals are to be found. One of the area's most distinctive and visible features is the traditional architecture, unique to each region of Northern Spain, which reflects the terrain and traditional forms of livelihood – fishing, farming and agriculture.

Renaissance detail of the Hostal de San Marcos in León *(see p115)*

PRE-ROMANESQUE & ROMANESQUE (8TH–13TH C.)

Most notable among the pre-Romanesque buildings are the Asturian shrines. Romanesque churches built in the 10th–12th centuries in Catalonia, as well as along the pilgrimage route to Santiago de Compostela, feature massive walls, tall rounded arches, and few windows.

Santa Maria del Naranco (see pp92–3) *is a pre-Romanesque church with slender proportions. Barrel vaults and columns around arcaded galleries are typical of the style.*

Rounded arch — **Apses at the end of the aisles**

Romanesque San Climent in Taüll *(see p190)*

Four-arched window

Stone corbels

The Palacio de los Reyes de Navarra *in Estella (see p157), built at the end of the 12th century, is one of very few examples of secular Romanesque architecture.*

GOTHIC (12TH–16TH C.)

In most of Northern Spain, especially along the road to Santiago, where the French influence was strongest, the Gothic followed the French version of the Gothic style. It was based on verticality and the introduction of twin-towered façades and ribbed vaulting. Catalan Gothic had a heavier style of its own.

An ogival window

The Gothic retable *in Ourense cathedral (see p71) was carved by Cornelis de Holanda at the beginning of the 16th century. A scene of the Deposition appears in one of its richly decorated sections.*

The nave of León Cathedral (see pp116–17), *whose construction began in 1254, is covered in ribbed vaulting and lit by colourful stained-glass windows covering a staggering 1,800 sq m (19,375 sq ft).*

RENAISSANCE (16TH C.) & BAROQUE (17TH–18TH C.)

The Renaissance, with its predilection for Classical proportions and harmony, was raised to the extremely decorative style known as Plateresque, said to replicate the effects of silverware *(plata)* in stone, with heraldic motifs, arches with complicated curves, and stone openwork ornamentation. The Baroque style brought with it grand ornamentation, dramatic religiosity and splendour.

Detail of the cathedral at Santiago de Compostela

Universidad de Sancti Spiritus *in the Basque town of Oñati has a Plateresque façade adorned with figures of saints* (see p137).

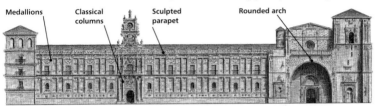

Medallions   Classical columns   Sculpted parapet   Rounded arch

The Hostal de San Marcos in León *(see p115)*, in the Plateresque style, with a long palatial façade

THE MODERN ERA

The sheer variety of forms and harmonious integration with the environment typify modern architecture in Northern Spain, where increasing numbers of foreign architects are working, from Canadian-born Frank Gehry to Portuguese Alvaro Siza. Innovative forms are evident in practical architecture, such as in Bilbao's metro (by Norman Foster) and airport.

Modernist 1950s church in Arantzazu *(see p137)*

Rare materials, *such as titanium, were used in the construction of the futuristic Museo Guggenheim in Bilbao* (see pp124–5) *by Frank Gehry.*

REGIONAL ARCHITECTURE

Because so much of the North is mountainous, many regions are dotted with big farmhouses where livestock were kept on the ground floor, and the family lived above. On the Galician coast fishermen's equipment was kept downstairs, and the family lived above. Galicia also has many *hórreos* (granaries), while *teitos* (shepherds' huts) are a symbol of Asturias.

Hórreos, *or granaries common in Galicia, are built on stone pillars to prevent rodents from eating the grain.*

Teitos *are traditional stone huts with thatched roofs, used by shepherds in Asturias.*

Stone houses *in Cantabria usually have wooden balconies, a broad entrance and projecting eaves to protect the walls from rain.*

The Road to Santiago

St James on horseback

According to legend the body of Christ's apostle James was brought to Galicia. In 813 the relics were supposedly discovered at Santiago de Compostela, where a cathedral was built in his honour *(see pp62–3)*. In the Middle Ages half a million pilgrims a year flocked here from all over Europe, crossing the Pyrenees at Roncesvalles *(see p150)* or via the Somport Pass in Aragón *(see p174)*. They often donned the traditional garb of cape, long staff and curling felt hat adorned with scallop shells, the symbol of the saint. The various routes, marked by the cathedrals, churches and hospitals built along them, are still used by travellers today.

19th-century painting of the Pórtico da Gloria in Santiago's cathedral

Astorga *(see p113), once a Roman city, was an important halt on the pilgrim route in the Middle Ages. The museum within its cathedral has a collection of gold and silver plate including a 13th-century gold filigree cross.*

A certificate *is given to pilgrims covering 100 km (62 miles) of the route on foot, or 200 km (125 miles) on horseback.*

O Cebreiro *(see p74)* has a 9th-century church and some of the ancient *pallozas* the pilgrims often used for shelter.

León *was one of the main pilgrim stops. Its cathedral* (see pp116–17) *contains one of Spain's finest collections of stained glass.*

Ribadeo

A Coruña

Oviedo

Maritime Route

SANTIAGO DE COMPOSTELA

Vilar de Donas

Ligonde

Villafranca del Bierzo

O Cebreiro

LEÓN

PORTO LISBOA

Silver Route

Ponferrada's huge Templar castle stands close to the town centre *(see p113).*

Ponferrada

Astorga

Hospital de Órbigo

Sahagún

Vigo

Scallop shells, staffs and gourds to carry water are symbols of the pilgrimage.

SALAMANCA

0 kilometres   50

0 miles   50

ROMANESQUE CHURCH ARCHITECTURE

The Romanesque style of architecture *(see p18)* was brought to Spain from France during the 10th and 11th centuries. As the pilgrimage to Santiago became more popular, many glorious religious buildings were constructed along its main routes. Massive walls, few windows, round heavy arches and barrel vaulting are typical features of Romanesque architecture.

Carved capital

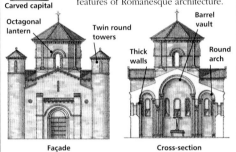

Octagonal lantern

Twin round towers

Barrel vault

Thick walls

Round arch

Façade

Cross-section

San Martín de Frómista (see p166), *built in the 11th century, is the only complete example of the "pilgrimage" style of Romanesque. The nave and aisles are almost the same height and there are three parallel apses.*

Parallel apses **Aisle** **Nave**

Floorplan

Pamplona's (see p153) *Gothic cathedral was one of the pilgrims' first stops after crossing the Pyrenees at Roncesvalles.*

Santo Domingo de la Calzada's *(see p163)* pilgrim hostel is now a parador.

Puente la Reina (see p157) *takes its name from the 11th-century humpbacked bridge (puente), built for pilgrims and still used by pedestrians.*

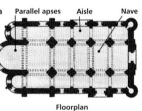

Frómista preserves one of the finest Romanesque churches on the French Route.

Santander

Donostia (San Sebastián)

PARIS

Northern Route

Bilbo (Bilbao)

LE PUY VEZELAY

Valcarlos

ARLES

Orreaga (Roncesvalles)

Iruña (Pamplona)

Lizarra (Estella)

Santo Domingo de la Calzada

San Juan de Ortega

Nájera

Logroño

French Route

Puente la Reina

Sangüesa

Jaca

San Juan de la Peña

Aragonese Route

BURGOS

ROUTES TO SANTIAGO

Several traditional pilgrimage roads converge on Santiago de Compostela. The main road from the Pyrenees is known as the French Route, with the Aragonese Route as a variation.

Burgos has a magnificent Gothic cathedral *(see pp168–9).*

Basque Culture

The Basques may be Europe's oldest race. Long isolated in their mountain valleys, they preserved their unique language, myths and art for millennia, absorbing outside influences while retaining their identity. Many families still live in isolated, chalet-style stone *caseríos*, or farmhouses, built by their forebears. Their music and high-bounding dances are unlike those of any other culture, and their cuisine is varied and imaginative. The ancient Basque laws were suppressed under General Franco, but since the arrival of democracy in 1975 the Basques have won great autonomy over their own affairs.

Basque folk dancer

La Ikurriña – *the Basque flag – symbolizes Christianity (white cross) and a battle won by St Andrew (green cross).*

Basque cuisine *is among the best in the world, and the region is known for its men's gastronomical societies that arrange cookery sessions and banquets. Traditional dishes are dominated by fish and seafood and exquisite* pintxos, *the distinctive Basque style of* tapas.

A tome of Basque laws

Basque fishermen with oars and nets

The Museo Arqueológico, Etnográfico e Histórico Vasco *in Bilbao presents examples of Basque art and folk crafts, as well as scenes from the everyday life of the Basques.*

Picasso's Guernica *was inspired by the tragic Nazi bombing (at Franco's request) of this Basque town in 1937, during the Spanish Civil War. The original painting is in the Museo Nacional in Madrid; the one in Gernika is a copy.*

TRADITIONAL LAW-MAKING

A ceiling in the historic parliament of Vizcaya *(Casa de Juntas)* in Gernika is covered by this 1985 stained-glass window. It depicts the great oak tree that was a symbol of Basque rights and liberties, around which representatives once gathered to engage in debate and to pass laws.

Traditional Basque instruments *include the* txalaparta, *a percussion instrument made up of two hollowed logs, that was used historically as a means of communication across mountain valleys. The four-hole flute known as the* txistu *is played with one hand.*

BASQUE LANGUAGE

The Basque language, *Euskera*, is the only surviving pre-Indo-European language in Europe. Unrelated to any other tongue, it is exceptionally difficult to learn, requiring years of practice to become fluent. There are a staggering 11 grammatical cases and a highly complicated conjugation. Articles, adjectives, prepositions and other parts of speech are added to the ends of words, while surnames often refer to features in the landscape of the countryside. In the

Dances at fiestas *are masterful displays of agility and rhythm, such as the various* espatadantza *or sword dances or the* aurresku *– a courtship dance performed by men. At fiestas you may also hear the* irrintzi, *a high-pitched shriek traditionally used to communicate across long distances.*

Basque Country, road signs, street names, and information boards are in Euskera and Spanish. Euskera is also spoken in northern Navarra, which is counted as part of the wider Basque Country.

Gernikako Arbola – the sacred oak tree of the Basque people.

A coat-of-arms with an image of the oak tree

Parades, *such as this one in Hondarribia, are a key element of every fiesta. Musicians dressed in colourful costumes march through the town playing flutes and drums.*

The stained glass is framed by images of the most famous buildings in the Basque Country.

Basque farmers in traditional berets

Pelota *is the world's fastest game. The ball, which can reach speeds of 300 km/h (186 mph), is hurled against a wall by hand, or with a bat or a special curved wicker basket.*

Wines of Northern Spain

Spain's most prestigious wine region, Rioja, is best known for its red wines, matured to a distinctive vanilla mellowness. Some of the most prestigious bodegas were founded by émigrés from Bordeaux, and Rioja reds are similar to claret. Rioja also produces good white and rosé wines. Navarra reds, whites and especially rosés have improved dramatically, helped by a government research programme. The Basque region produces a tiny amount of the prickly, tart *txacoli (chacolí)*. Larger quantities of a similar wine are made further west in Galicia, whose best wines are full-bodied whites.

Repairing barrels in Haro, Rioja

Ribeiro, *the popular everyday wine of Galicia, is usually fizzy. It is often served in white porcelain cups* (tazas).

KEY

	Rías Baixas
	Ribeiro
	Valdeorras
	Txacoli de Guetaria
	Rioja
	Navarra

Lagar de Cervera *is from Rías Baixas, where Spain's most fashionable whites are made from the Albariño grape.*

WINE REGIONS

The wine regions of Northern Spain are widely dispersed. Cradled between the Pyrenees and the Atlantic are the important regions of Rioja and Navarra. Rioja is divided into the sub-regions of Rioja Alavesa, Rioja Alta and Rioja Baja, separated by the Río Ebro. The river also cuts through the wine region of Navarra. To the north are some of the vineyards of the Basque Country: the minuscule Txacoli de Guetaria region. In the far west lie the four wine regions of wet, rugged Galicia: Rías Baixas, Ribeiro, Valdeorras, and Ribeira Sacra.

Wine village of El Villar de Álava in Rioja Alta

Gathering the grape harvest in the traditional way in Navarra

Remelluri, *one of the new single-estate "château" Riojas, from the vineyards of Rioja Alavesa, is soft and not too oaky.*

Chivite, *from a family bodega in Navarra, is made from Tempranillo grapes and aged in the barrel, resulting in a style similar to Rioja.*

Viña Ardanza *is blended, as are most red Riojas. The best, like this reserva, are aged for two or more years in American oak casks.*

KEY FACTS ABOUT THE WINES OF NORTHERN SPAIN

 Location and Climate
Rioja and Navarra are influenced by both Mediterranean and Atlantic weather systems. The hillier, northwestern parts receive some Atlantic rain while the hot Ebro plain has a Mediterranean climate. The Basque region and Galicia are both cool, Atlantic regions with high rainfall. Soils everywhere are stony and poor, except in the Ebro plain.

Grape Varieties
The great red grape of Rioja and Navarra is Tempranillo. In Rioja it is blended with smaller quantities of Garnacha, Graciano and Mazuelo, while in Navarra Cabernet Sauvignon is permitted and blends excitingly with Tempranillo. Garnacha, also important in Navarra, is used for the excellent *rosados* (rosés). Whites of Navarra and Rioja are made mainly from the Viura grape. Galicia has many local varieties, of which the most important are Albariño, Loureira and Treixadura, which is now taking over from the inferior Palomino.

 Good Producers
Rías Baixas: Fillaboa, Lagar de Fornelos, Martín Codax, Morgadío, Santiago Ruiz. **Ribeiro:** Cooperativa Vinícola del Ribeiro. **Rioja:** Bodegas Riojanas (Canchales, Monte Real), CVNE (Imperial, Viña Real Oro), Faustino, Marqués de Cáceres, Marqués de Murrieta, Martínez Bujanda, Paternina, Remelluri, Viña Ardanza. **Navarra:** Bodega de Sarría, Guelbenzu, Julián Chivite (Gran Feudo), Magaña, Ochoa, Príncipe de Viana.

Landscapes and Nature of Northern Spain

Purple emperor butterfly

A mountain wall extends right across Northern Spain, through the length of the Pyrenees, the Basque Country and along the north coast in the Cordillera Cantábrica, before spreading out and turning south into the hills of Galicia. The mountains contain the most spectacular scenery, and separate Northern Spain from central Spain, creating the green, Atlantic climate that gives the northern regions their distinctive feel. Many parts of the northern mountains remain remote, thinly populated and thickly wooded, and so provide a home for a fascinating range of wildlife.

Medieval stone bridge across a fast-flowing river, Picos de Europa

MOUNTAINS

The mountains reach their highest points in two great massifs, the High Pyrenees and the Picos de Europa, much of them above 2,000 m (6,560 ft), and with alpine landscapes of massive rockfaces, gorges and near-infinite views. They are dotted with alpine flowers and animals found only in high mountains such as snow voles and chamois. High above fly eagles, falcons and vultures. On the lower slopes, meadows explode into colour with flowers and butterflies each spring.

The Picos de Europa, *straddling Asturias and Cantabria, form Europe's largest national park. With an excellent network of paths and refuges, it's a fabulous area for walking and climbing, with beautifully contrasting scenery of peaks, meadows and valleys.*

Eagle owls *are recognizable by their large 'ears', or tufts above each eye. Living in the woods around mountain valleys, they hunt for small birds and animals at dusk and at night.*

Chamois *live amid the highest peaks, on mountain grasses and flowers found in rock gardens between the bare crags and scree. Astonishingly agile, they can leap remarkably quickly into the rocks whenever eagles or other predators appear.*

Blue, purple and yellow gentians *are characteristic flowers of the high mountain pastures and rocky plateaux of the Pyrenees and the Cantabrian mountains.*

Griffon vultures *are a frequent sight in the Picos de Europa and the Pyrenees. In their search for prey they circle on huge wings high above the slopes, riding the rising air currents.*

Rippling river in the Parque Nacional de Ordesa, the Pyrenees

FOREST

Thanks to their remoteness, steep terrain and rainfall, huge areas of the northern mountains are still clad in forest. Mainly of beech, chestnut, ash and Pyrenean oak, they are among Europe's oldest broad-leaf forests. They are also the refuge of Spain's rarest birds and wildlife – wildcats, wolves and bears.

Beech martens are shy and nocturnal, and so hard to see, but are still quite common in the lower forests. Asleep during the day, they emerge at night to feed on fruit, nuts and sometimes small mammals and birds.

The woods of Galicia, *dense and often shrouded in rain and Atlantic mists, are closely associated with local folklore, as the homes of witches and Celtic spirits and fairies.*

Gold and russet colours *spread across the broad-leaf forests each autumn. The colours are richest in the beech woods of the Basque Country, Navarra and Asturias.*

Spotted flycatchers *are plentiful from spring to autumn. Feeding on insects, they can be seen in the trees around meadows and other clearings in the woods.*

The brown bears *of Asturias – the last substantial bear population in western Europe – still number about 100, mostly in the Parque Natural de Somiedo.*

THE COAST

The mountains approach the sea in cliffs and giant headlands of granite and slate, separated by an enormously varied mix of deep, wooded inlets, rocky coves, rolling sand dunes and marshy wetlands. There are huge seabird colonies, especially on the tiny offshore islands. Sheltered estuaries provide feeding-grounds for many wading birds, and are visited by porpoises and dolphins.

View of the Rías Baixas from Mirador de La Curota, near Noia in Galicia

Around Praia das Catedrais beach, near Foz in the Rías Altas of northern Galicia, the schist and slate cliffs have been eroded by the sea into spectacular rock 'cathedrals'.

Sand dunes at Corrubedo in Galicia

The Atlantic Coast from Galicia to the Basque Country

Ruggedness and a green exuberance are characteristics of Spain's spectacular north coast. Majestic headlands, bizarre rock formations and massive granite cliffs loom up out of the ocean, but in between them there are soft-sand beaches in well sheltered bays, backed by tranquil woods and meadows. Fabulous views meet the eye at every turn, and the Atlantic air is invigorating. The coastal scenery is at its finest in Galicia, with its exquisite winding inlets, or *rías*, and wild capes, while the best beaches are in Cantabria and the Basque Country. The sea is also the source of many of Northern Spain's finest foods.

Cudillero *is one of the most picturesque villages of the Asturian coast, with a dramatic lighthouse and a tiny harbour crammed into a steep cove below the cliffs.*

Cabo de Peñas, *just northwest of Gijón, is dotted with small villages, windswept cliffs and sand dunes rising up behind fine beaches that are pounded by crashing surf.*

A Toxa island *is the most exclusive resort in Galicia's Rías Baixas. The tiny, pine-covered island has luxurious hotels and villas, a casino, secluded beaches and a famous church covered entirely in scallop shells.*

Cabo Fisterra, *"the end of the world" is the westernmost point of continental Spain. Travellers to Santiago traditionally finished their pilgrimage here, to gaze at the vast horizons and fabulous sunsets.*

Llanes *is a charming fishing port that is now a popular small resort, with delightful beaches reached by footpaths along the cliffs.*

Laredo *looks onto 5 km (3 miles) of beaches, the finest on the Cantabrian coast. A busy summer resort, it is famous for its fiestas, such as the Battle of Flowers, held each August.*

Hondarribia *has distinctive historic houses typical of the Basque fishing villages, with intricately carved and brightly painted woodwork, and balconies loaded with flowers.*

Santander
A8
Bilbao
(Bilbo)
San Sebastián
(Donostia)
A8
N621
N611
N623
N634
A68
N1
N1
Vitoria
(Gasteiz)
Logroño

THE ATLANTIC COAST

The rocky crags and islands, sand dunes and sheltered estuaries and wetlands of this coast provide varied habitats for an enormous range of birds, both residents and migratory visitors.

Kittiwakes are members of the gull family. Each summer they breed in clefts in sea-cliffs, and spend all winter far out at sea, cruising the oceans for fish. There are large colonies on the islands off Galicia.

Oyster-catchers are easily recognizable by their black and white plumage and bright red beak – strong enough for them to crack open shellfish. They are common around cockle and mussel beds.

Snipes are most common in the marshes near Santoña, in Cantabria. In spring male snipes perform a strange diving display to attract females, making a drumming sound with their feathers.

Ospreys are the only birds of prey that live solely on fish. They migrate between Northern Europe and West Africa, stopping over in Asturias and Cantabria each spring and autumn.

0 kilometres 50
0 miles 25

San Sebastián's *La Concha beach is one of the most beautiful on the north coast. Forming an elegant curve, it faces the green promontories at the mouth of the bay, and is lined by a gracious promenade.*

NORTHERN SPAIN THROUGH THE YEAR

ove of a fun-filled fiesta is a Spanish national trait. In Northern Spain every town or village has its patron saint whose day is celebrated with parades, *corridas*, singing and firework displays. Major religious festivals, such as *Semana Santa* (Holy Week), are occasions for spectacular celebrations. Some fiestas, such as the Sanfermines in Pamplona or St James' Day in Santiago de Compostela, attract crowds of tourists. Many farming or fishing towns also celebrate the harvest or their catch with fairs, colourful rituals and displays of local produce. There are plenty of music, theatre, dance and film festivals, many internationally renowned, like the San Sebastián Film Festival. Check the dates with local tourist offices, as some vary from year to year.

A Galician piper

Wild horses brought in from the countryside during the Rapa das Bestas

SPRING

The inhabitants of Northern Spain enjoy outdoor life in spring. People turn out on streets and meet in bars and cafés. Fields burst forth with wild flowers after the winter cold. Eastertime abounds in colourful processions.

MARCH

Festa da Arribada (*1st weekend Mar*), Baiona (Galicia). The re-enactment of the arrival of the *Pinta* – the 1493 caravel that brought news of the discovery of America – accompanied by a medieval fair.
Fiesta Santa Áurea (*11 Mar*), Villavelayo (La Rioja). The feast of the town's patron saint, with dancing to bagpipes and castanets.

Semana Santa (*Mar–Apr*). Holy Week is celebrated in grand style. Colourful processions are led by religious brotherhoods in brilliantly coloured robes and hoods. The biggest processions are those in Northern Castile and Navarra.

APRIL

Güevos Pintos (*1st Tue after Easter*), Langreo (Asturias). Easter festival of painted eggs.
Aberri Eguna (*20 Apr*), the Basque Country. Basque National Day.
La Folía (*1st Sun after Easter*), San Vicente de la Barquera (Cantabria). A statue of

the Virgin is carried aross the harbour in a procession of beautifully lit and decorated boats, to bless the sea.

MAY

White-water Rafting Day on the Esca River (*1–2 May*), Burgui (Navarra). Prominent figures from the world of science, sport or culture are presented with the Golden Raft Award.
La Victoria (*1st Fri in May*), Jaca (Pyrenees). Parades, banquets and medieval jousts celebrating a legendary 8th-century battle against the Moors.
Fiesta del Santo (*10–15 May*), Santo Domingo de la Calzada (La Rioja). The feast of the town's patron saint, who was believed to protect pilgrims travelling to Santiago, is celebrated with three days of colourful dances and processions. In the most famous, young girls carry baskets of fresh bread on their heads. Hearty feasts are centred on 'the Saint's Lunch' of lamb and chickpeas.
Día das Letras Gallegas (*17 May*), Galicia. Celebration of the Galician language, in literature and culture.
Bicycle Marathon (*late May*), Cangas de Onís (Asturias).

La Folía in San Vicente de la Barquera

AVERAGE DAILY HOURS OF SUNSHINE

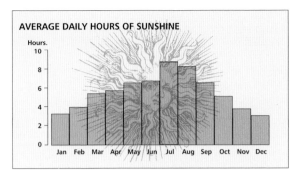

Hours.

Jan Feb Mar Apr May Jun Jul Aug Sep Oct Nov Dec

Average Hours of Sunshine

July and August are the sunniest months in Northern Spain, and also the peak tourist season. December and January are the cloudiest, especially in Galicia and in the mountain areas.

SUMMER

Late summer is harvest time, with many fiestas celebrating crop gathering. August is a holiday month, and Spaniards flock to the coastal towns and beaches, or the mountains.

JUNE

Corpus Christi *(Thu in May or Jun)*. Religious processions.
Festival of Flower Carpets *(weekend after Corpus Christi)*, Ponteareas & Gondomar (Galicia). Streets are laid with colourful carpets of flowers.
Wine Battle *(29 Jun)*, Haro (La Rioja). Manic fiesta in which thousands of people squirt wine at each other.

JULY

Semana Negra *(1st or 2nd week Jul)*, Gijon (Asturias). Contemporary cultural festival.
Coso Blanco *(1st weekend Jul)*, Castro Urdiales (Cantabria). Nighttime parade of carriages.
Rapa das Bestas *(1st weekend Jul)*, Pontevedra & Lugo (Galicia). Wild horses are rounded up for their manes and tails to be cut, the occasion for horse-centred events.
Los Sanfermines *(6–14 Jul)*, Pamplona (Navarra). Bull running, with festivities.
Festival de la Sidra *(2nd week Jul)*, Nava (Asturias). Cider festival with tastings.
International Jazz Festivals Getxo *(1st week)*, Vitoria *(mid-Jul)*; San Sebastián *(3rd week)*.
Danza de los Zancos *(21–24 Jul & last weekend Sep)*,

Pamplona's *corrida* during Los Sanfermines

Anguiano (La Rioja). Costumed dancers on stilts walk the steep streets trying to knock each other off.
Feast of St James *(25 Jul)*, Santiago de Compostela (Galicia). Fireworks on the eve of the saint's feast day.
Celtic Festival *(3rd weekend Jul)*, Ortigueira (Galicia). International festival with music

Cider being poured during the Festival de la Sidra in Nava

and piper parade.
Fiesta Patronales *(end Jul)*, Tudela (Navarra). Bull running, dancing and singing in honour of Santa Ana.

AUGUST

Festa María Pita *(Aug)*, A Coruña (Galicia). Month-long programme of concerts, *corridas*, medieval fairs and sea battles in honour of this war heroine.
Descent of the Río Sella *(1st Sat Aug)*, Asturias. Spectacular kayak and canoe race from Arriondas to Ribadasella.
Semana Grande *(2nd week Aug)*, Gijón (Asturias). Lavish festival with concerts, dances, parades and food displays.
Feast of the Assumption *(15 Aug)*. Festivities include a sardine feast at Sada (A Coruña) and El Rosario, a fishermen's festival in Luarca (Asturias).
Aste Nagusia *(3rd week)*, San Sebastián; *(last week)*, Bilbao. Week-long programmes of parades, music, dancing and Basque sports.
Romería de Naseiro *(26–9 Aug)*, Viveiro (Galicia). Huge celebration of Galician cuisine.
Festival Internacional de Santander *(Aug)*, Santander (Cantabria). Cultural festival for lovers of theatre, opera, classical dance and ballet.
Batalla de Flores *(last Fri Aug)*, Laredo (Cantabria). Parade of extravagant floats, made of flowers, ending in a flower-throwing 'battle'.

AVERAGE RAINFALL

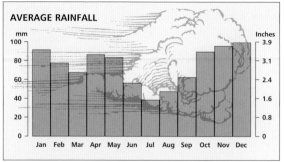

RAINFALL
Northern Spain receives much more rain than the rest of the country. Galicia is the rainiest and windiest region, followed by the Pyrenees. In winter, some mountain villages are cut off, due to heavy snowfall. High up in the mountains, snow cover can persist as late as June.

Visitors on a hike in the Picos de Europa

AUTUMN

Autumn marks the beginning of vine harvest festivities, and the first juice extracted from the grapes is blessed. The start of the mushroom picking season becomes evident in restaurants, and the hunting season also

The treading of grapes during the Fiesta San Mateo in Logroño

opens, continuing until February. In larger towns the music and theatre seasons begin, and San Sebastián hosts the famous film festival.

SEPTEMBER

Vuelta Ciclista a España *(late Aug–mid Sep)*. Round Spain cycle race.
Regatas de La Concha *(1st and 2nd Sun Sep)*, San Sebastián (Basque Country). Traditional Basque rowing races across La Concha bay.
Nuestra Señora de Covadonga *(8 Sep)*, Picos de Europa (Asturias). People pay homage to the patron of Asturias.
Fiesta San Mateo *(20–26 Sep)*, Logroño (Rioja). Rioja wine harvest is celebrated on St Matthew's day with food, drink, concerts and *corridas*.
Día de Campoo *(late Sep)*, Reinosa (Cantabria). Celebra-

A woman in traditional costume

tion of Cantabrian folk music, costumes and traditions, with a parade of bullock carts.
San Sebastián Film Festival *(last 2 weeks Sep)*, San Sebastián (Basque Country). One of the world's top film festivals, inaugurated in 1953.
San Antolín *(2–5 Sep)*, Lekeitio (Basque Country). Wild goose festival, including a contest in which people try to hang onto the greased neck of a dead goose above the harbour.

OCTOBER

San Froilán *(1st & 2nd week)*, Lugo (Galicia). Food tasting, parades, dancing and singing.
Seafood Festival *(2nd Sun)*, O Grove (Galicia). Tasting of seafood, enlivened with dancing in traditional costumes.
Virgen del Pilar *(12 Oct)*. National day of the patron saint of Spain.

NOVEMBER

All Saints' Day *(1 Nov)*. Traditional cakes are made the day before, and then people take flowers to cemeteries to remember deceased relatives.
Os Magostos *(11 Nov)* Galicia. Many towns and villages celebrate the sweet chestnut harvest.
Fiesta del Humo *(last Sun Nov)*, Arnedillo (La Rioja). Bonfires and feasts in honour of St Andrew.
Gijón Film Festival *(late Nov–early Dec)*, Gijón (Asturias), going for over 40 years.

AVERAGE TEMPERATURE

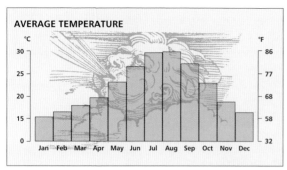

Temperature
The warmest months are July, August and September, although the heat is less ferocious on the northern coast than inland. In mountain areas it can be cold even in summer, and the weather can change very rapidly.

WINTER

Mountainous Northern Spain has fairly harsh winters. The mountain passes close to traffic, the skiing season starts, and Christmas brings family gatherings and religious reflections, before carnival starts.

DECEMBER

Santo Tomás *(21 Dec)*, Bilbao, San Sebastián and other Basque towns. Pre-Christmas fairs in celebration of St Thomas, with food and traditional products for Christmas.
El Gordo *(22 Dec)*. Televised draw of the top prize in the Spanish lottery, "the Fat One".
Noche Buena *(24 Dec)*. Christmas Eve is spent in Spain within the family circle.
Santos Inocentes *(28 Dec)*. Spanish April Fool's Day.
Noche Vieja *(31 Dec)*. New Year's Eve is an exuberant farewell to the passing year.

Women banging pots during a fiesta in honour of Santo Tomás

JANUARY

Fiesta del Aguinalso (Guirria) *(1 Jan)*, San Juan de Beleño (Asturias). This small town is visited by Guirria – a mysterious masked figure who, accompanied by 40 young horse riders, asks people for presents.
La Vijanera en Silió *(1st Sun)*, Cantabria. The *Zarramacos* dressed in furs and with blackened faces parade through the streets noisily with big bells to frighten away the evil spirits of the past year.
Epiphany – Tres Reyes *(6 Jan)*. Arrival of the 'Three Kings' (wise men) celebrated everywhere with parades, presents and children's events.
La Tamborrada *(19–20 Jan)*, San Sebastián (Basque Country). The feast of St Sebastian is celebrated with ear-splitting parades of pipe-and-drum bands and fireworks, commemorating the fire that swept the town during the Napoleonic Wars.

FEBRUARY

Carnival Procession *(late Jan or Feb)*, Lantz (Navarra). Parade of large figures made of hay, burned ceremoniously afterwards. Famous and popular carnival celebrations take place in many towns throughout Spain.

Os Peliqueiros Carnival in Laza

Os Peliqueiros Carnival *(last Sun of Carnival, Feb–Mar)*, Laza (Galicia). Os Peliqueiros wearing comical masks stroll along the town streets, beating passers-by with birch sticks.

PUBLIC HOLIDAYS

New Year's Day (1 Jan)
Epiphany (6 Jan)
Good Friday, Easter Sunday (Mar/Apr)
Labour Day (1 May)
Assumption (15 Aug)
Virgen del Pilar (12 Oct)
All Saints' Day (1 Nov)
Constitution Day (6 Dec)
Immaculate Conception (8 Dec)
Christmas Day (25 Dec)

THE HISTORY OF NORTHERN SPAIN

*I*nhabited from remote times, the varied regions of Northern Spain have played a significant role in the peninsula's history. It was from here that the Reconquest began, and from here that many of Spain's great navigators originated. The north was involved in the Carlist Wars, and was a Republican stronghold during the Spanish Civil War.

PREHISTORY

Remains of some of our earliest pre-human ancestors were discovered in caves at Atapuerca, in Burgos province, in 1976. They are estimated to be 800,000 years old. About 20,000 years ago, humans of Cro-Magnon type (very similar to modern humans) appeared on the Iberian Peninsula. Skilled artists, they decorated the walls of caves with engravings and polychrome paintings of animals. The finest of these caves is Altamira, in Cantabria, which was discovered in the 19th century.

At the end of the Ice Age, several thousand years ago, people began to abandon their nomadic lifestyle for a more settled existence. Instead of hunting animals they learnt to breed them, and to cultivate crops. They began to make increasingly sophisticated tools and to smelt metals.

The Mikeldi Idol, a sculpture of the Iron Age

CELTS, PHOENICIANS AND GREEKS

In about 1200 BC Celts began to migrate south, settling in the peninsula. Over the following centuries they mixed with Iberian tribes, laying the foundations of the Celtiberian culture. In Northern Spain, particularly in Galicia, the Celts built distinctive hilltop settlements – *castros* – with round stone houses. The best-known Celtiberian tribe are the Arevacos, who famously defended Numantia against the Romans in 133 BC.

The peninsula's north-eastern coast was colonized by Greeks, who established the colony of Emporion, near present-day Barcelona, in about 600 BC. The Phoenicians, who settled in the south, founded Cádiz, the oldest town in this part of Europe. They coined the name "Spain", meaning "Island of Rabbits", and they also introduced the grapevine, the olive tree and the donkey. Both the Greeks and the Phoenicians were interested in Spain's deposits of ore. Galicia, for example, yielded gold and tin, which was needed to make bronze. In time, the Phoenicians were displaced by the Carthaginians.

The origins of the mysterious Basques, who already inhabited the north, are not clear, but it's possible they are descended from the earliest inhabitants of Iberia (Cro-Magnon). The earliest written reference to them appears in Roman writings.

TIMELINE

800,000 BC	200,000 BC	1000 BC	600 BC	228 BC
c.800,000 BC Pre-human presence in Atapuerca caves, Burgos	**c.5000 BC** Beginning of the Neolithic Revolution	**c.1200 BC** Celts start to settle in the Iberian Peninsula		*The golden helmet of a Celtiberian warrior*
Painting of a bison at Altamira cave.		**c.18–12,000 BC** Cave paintings at Altamira. Cantabria	**c.600 BC** Greek colony of Emporion founded on the coast of Girona	**264–241 BC** First Punic War between Carthage and Rome

◁ The body of St James being brought to Galicia, after his martyrdom in Jerusalem

Fragment of a Roman mosaic of the 4th century BC, now in the Museu Arqueològic in Girona

ROMAN AND VISIGOTH SPAIN

The Romans entered Spain as part of their war with the Carthaginians (the Punic Wars), trying to control the whole of the Iberian peninsula. The tribes in the north, who occupied land rich in minerals, resisted the longest, but their lands were finally taken over.

The Romans also built an extensive network of roads, bridges and aqueducts. The towns of Astorga, in León, and Lugo, Galicia, still have their Roman walls, and Pamplona, founded in 74 BC by the Roman military commander Pompey, later became the capital of the kingdom of Navarra. Although Latin was widely spoken, the indigenous population continued to use local languages as late as the 2nd century (the Basques never stopped). Christianity began to spread, replacing the worship of local deities.

When the Roman Empire began to crumble, Germanic tribes invaded from the north. The Vandals and the Suevi occupied León and Galicia, but the Visigoths gained control, almost succeeding in creating the first unified state in Spain. However, the Visigoths failed to subjugate the Basques, who continued to expand their territory. In the final stages of the Visigothic state, Septimania (its northern part) attempted to break away. Civil wars fought under Wamba's reign hastened the kingdom's disintegration.

MOORISH SPAIN

In 711 the declining Visigothic kingdom was invaded and quickly conquered by the Moors. Most of the Iberian peninsula became part of a vast Islamic empire. Christians who did not accept Muslim rule retreated into the northern mountains, which remained unconquered due to their terrain, fierce resistance and an inhospitable climate. In 756 Abd al Rahman I proclaimed an independent emirate on the peninsula, and made Córdoba its capital. For 300 years the Caliphate of Córdoba was Europe's most opulent society. Periods of peace and trade were interspersed

Portrait of Wamba, the Visigothic king who ruled from 672 to 680

TIMELINE

219–201 BC Second Punic War. Expansion of Roman territory on the Iberian peninsula

61 BC Julius Caesar begins final conquest of Galicia and northern Lusitania

19 BC Agrippa conquers Cantabria and Asturias, completing the Roman conquest

Visigothic relief on a Christian theme, 7th century

200 BC	1 BC	AD 200	400

155 BC Lusitanian War

219 BC Hannibal captures Sagunt

Stone disk, 1st century BC

AD 74 Emperor Vespasian extends Roman law to the Spanish provinces

476 Fall of the Western Roman Empire

589 Reccared and the Visigothic nobility embrace Christianity; Toledo becomes capital of Visigothic Spain with continual wars with the northern Christian kingdoms, and with the Frankish empire of Charlemagne from across the Pyrenees. In the late 10th century the vizier of Córdoba, Al Mansur, led 100 raids into the Christian territories, plundering towns across the north, including Santiago de Compostela (the site where St James' relics were discovered), and halting further Christian advances for another century. Around 1013 the Caliphate disintegrated into bickering emirates.

A miniature from the *Cantigas de Santa María* by Alfonso X, the Wise

THE RECONQUEST

The collapse of the Caliphate favoured the expansion southwards of the Christian states that had taken shape in the north. Among them was the kingdom of Asturias, whose origins date from the perhaps-legendary Battle of Covadonga in 722, when a small band led by the Visigoth Pelayo are said to have halted the Muslim advance. After the battle, seen as the starting point of the long 'reconquest' of Spain from the Moors, Pelayo became king of Asturias. This kingdom won its greatest victories against the Moors during the reign of Alfonso II (791-842).

In the 9th century, after a short period of Moorish rule in the Basque territories at the foot of the Pyrenees, the kingdom of Navarra came into being. Previously the Basques had demonstrated their independence on all sides by defeating the rearguard of Charlemagne's

A 9th-century stone cross

army at the famous Battle of Roncesvalles (778). Another part of Christian Spain developed around 800, when Charlemagne's armies crossed into the eastern Pyrenees, making the area the 'Spanish March' of the Frankish empire – the origin of the future Catalonia. Around this time vast numbers of pilgrims from all over Europe were journeying on the Road to Santiago, which resulted in Northern Spain becoming culturally and economically connected to the rest of Europe.

Battles for the expansion of territory gradually took on the status of crusades against the Muslims. In 1085 Alfonso VI, king of Castile and León, captured Toledo from the Moors, and expelled the Muslim rulers. His kingdom became the dominant power in central Spain. In the 12th century Muslim Spain was again unified under the rule of two militant dynasties from north Africa – the Almoravids and their successors the Almohads – who halted the Reconquest. But in 1212, the combined forces of several northern kingdoms crushed the Almohad army at Las Navas de Tolosa, paving the way for the final victory of Christian power in the Iberian peninsula.

711 Moors defeat Visigoths at Battle of Guadalete

c.810 St James' tomb supposedly discovered at Santiago de Compostela

905 Sancho I founds the kingdom of Navarra

1085 Alfonso VI takes Toledo

1230 Ferdinand the Saint (El Santo) reunites Castile and León

800	1000	1200	1400

778 Battle of Roncesvalles

722 Battle of Covadonga. The kingdom of Asturias founded

1212 Combined Christian forces defeat the Moors at the Battle of Las Navas de Tolosa

Illuminated manuscript, 9th century

The Northern Kingdoms and the Reconquest

The regions of the north were the only parts of Iberia not conquered by the Moors, and their identities were all formed in the difficult, centuries-long struggle to retake lands further south from Muslim rule. Political disunity among the Christian strongholds, their remote mountain locations, and a severe climate all made the effort to retake the lands that much harder. The main Christian states that took shape were Asturias, León, Castile, Navarra, Aragón and Catalonia.

Ferdinand the Great
By uniting León and Castile in 1037, Ferdinand created the first Christian coalition of significant military strength.

Navarra's troops were commanded by Sancho III, the Strong.

Pelayo the Warrior
The Reconquest began after the Battle of Covadonga (722), where Pelayo, a Visigothic nobleman, defeated a Moorish army. He became king of Asturias.

Several Spanish kingdoms answered the Pope's call for a united campaign against the Moors. This war between Christians and Muslims assumed the character of a crusade.

The Almohad army was finally crushed by the Christian cavalry.

Santa María del Naranco
This imposing pre-Romanesque building near Oviedo was erected in the 9th century as the palace of Ramiros I, and was later converted into a church.

The Battle of Clavijo (844)
In this battle that probably only existed in legend, St James, known as the Moor-slayer, led Christian knights on to victory against the Muslims.

THE BATTLE OF LAS NAVAS DE TOLOSA (1212)

Fired with Christian zeal and the backing of Pope Innocent III, the combined forces of the kingdoms of Castile, Aragón and Navarra defeated the Almohads at Las Navas de Tolosa. This victory led to the collapse of Moorish power in Spain.

Cantigas de Santa María
This manuscript detail by Alfonso the Wise, king of Castile (1252–84), shows Christians confronting Moors. Alfonso encouraged cooperation between Christian, Arabic and Jewish scholars.

Cross of Angels (808)
This jewelled cross is an exquisite example of early Asturian art. Alfonso II, who bequeathed it to Oviedo Cathedral, had it inscribed:"Whosoever dares remove this cross from the place which my will destined for it shall be thunderstruck by God."

The combined armies of Castile, Aragón and Navarra numbered 70,000 knights.

The Church of San Miguel in Estella
In the Christian kingdoms, religious architecture flourished along the pilgrimage route, an example being the late Romanesque church in Estella.

The Cathedral in Huesca
The mudéjar style developed in regions that were influenced by the Moors. One example of this style is the richly decorated gallery above the portal of the cathedral in Huesca.

The body of a Moorish soldier

Shield with the coat of arms of Sancho VII of Navarra

The Tomb of King Alfonso VII
Alfonso VII of Castile led many military campaigns in southern Spain. In 1147 he captured Calatrava, opening the way to Andalusia. He also occupied Córdoba and Almería.

The *Santa Maria*, Christopher Columbus's caravel

DISCOVERY AND EXPLORATION

Through their marriage in 1469, the Catholic Monarchs – Fernando II of Aragón and Isabel I of Castile – united almost all the territories of the peninsula. The process was completed when Navarra was incorporated in 1512.

When Christopher Columbus discovered America in 1492, this marked the beginning of Spain's overseas expansion. Many of the ships and navigators came from the Basque Country and Cantabria. Among notable seamen were Juan Sebastián de Elcano – the first to circumnavigate the globe after Magellan died during his journey – and Juan Sebastián de la Cosa, who sailed with Columbus and mapped the new lands.

Juan Sebastián de Elcano

In 1517 Carlos I, of the Habsburg dynasty, inherited the thrones of Spain, Austria and Burgundy, giving him huge territories across Europe. Under him, Spain acquired vast lands in the Americas, becoming the first world-wide empire. His successor, Felipe II, made Madrid the capital.

THE GOLDEN AGE

The discovery voyages led to growth in trade, which encouraged the development of north coast towns. Growth was somewhat limited by the king's insistence that all large-scale trade with the American colonies go through Seville. The Spanish Empire also engaged in constant wars – in the colonies, against the French, Turks and Protestants. The Dutch wars started in the 1560s, and in 1588 part of the Spanish Armada set out from Vigo to attack England. In 1589, Francis Drake led attacks on Vigo and A Coruña, in response to the Armada.

The north provided a lot of Spain's soldiers. Related to this militarism was the founding of the Jesuits by the Basque Saint Ignatius, himself a soldier once. The constant wars exhausted the country, however, and by 1650 the process of inexorable imperial decline began, following defeats against the Dutch and French.

El Escorial, the palace designed by Juan de Herrera

TIMELINE

A 15th-century knight

1491 Birth of St Ignatius of Loyola, founder of the Jesuits

1502 Expulsion of unconverted Moors from Spain

1512 Annexation of Navarra completes the unification of Spain

1521 Basque seaman Juan Sebastián de Elcano completes circumnavigation of the globe

1618 Spain joins the Thirty Years' War against France

1400	1450	1500	1550	1600	1

1492 Columbus discovers America

1500 Juan de la Cosa creates the first map of the New World

1540 Founding of Basque university in Oñati

Isabel I, Queen of Castile (1474–1504)

1659 Peace of the Pyrenees signed with France

Fernando VII agreeing to accept the Constitution

BOURBON SPAIN

In 1701 Carlos I died without an heir. In the subsequent War of the Spanish Succession, Castile and most of the north supported Felipe V (of the French Bourbon dynasty). Catalonia, Aragón and Valencia supported the Archduke Charles of Austria, who promised to restore their traditional rights. Felipe V was victorious, and in 1715 made Spain into a unified state, abolishing the local rights of Catalonia, Aragón and other regions. In return for their loyalty, however, the Basque Country and Navarra were allowed to keep their local rights.

The 18th-century Bourbon kings and ministers sought to reform Spain's adminstration and halt the country's decline. Most important was Carlos III (1759–88), who in his efforts to encourage economic expansion ended Seville's monopoly on trade with Spanish America. This had an immediate effect in the north, which saw vigorous expansion in shipbuilding, trade and agriculture.

The French Revolution was the start of a traumatic period. Initially Spain joined European monarchies in attacking Republican France, with heavy losses. Later, unpopular PM Godoy allied Spain with Napoleon. In 1808 Napoleon kidnapped the Spanish royal family and declared his brother, Joseph, king of Spain, triggering the Peninsular War, with Spain aided by Britain. During the war, a *Cortes* or parliament met in Cádiz and approved Spain's first constitution in 1812.

At the end of these wars in 1814 Spain's institutions were severely weakened. The restless 19th century also saw the awakening of nationalist sentiments in the Basque Country. Galicia and Catalonia sought to rescue their languages and traditions from the dominance of the official Spanish-speaking culture.

CARLIST WARS

When Fernando VII died in 1833, a dispute arose over his successor – his brother Don Carlos or daughter Isabel – and civil conflict, the Carlist Wars, began. The Carlists had support in the northern provinces, particularly in the Basque Country, Navarra and north Catalonia, which opposed state centralization. The Carlists were defeated; the First Republic was proclaimed in 1873.

A battle between loyalists and Carlists during the Carlist Wars

1767 Jesuits expelled from Spain and its empire by Carlos III

1702–14 War of the Spanish Succession

1846–9 Second Carlist War

1833–9 First Carlist War

1898 Following the Spanish-American War, Spain loses the last of its major colonies

| 1700 | 1750 | 1800 | 1850 | 1900 |

Felipe V (1700–24), the first of the Bourbon kings

1808–1814 War of Independence with Napoleon

1812 Promulgation of liberal constitution in Cádiz leads to uprising

1875 Bourbon dynasty restored

1872–6 Third Carlist War

General Primo de Rivera, who ruled Spain from 1923 to 1930

proved ineffective, however, and the country was rocked by outbreaks of anticlericalism, and unemployment rose.

CIVIL WAR AND FRANCO

In 1936, when the general election was won by the left, the army rose in revolt, starting the Spanish Civil War. In much of southern Spain, Madrid, Catalonia, and part of the Basque Country, Cantabria and Asturias Republican forces defeated the initial revolt. The rest of the country was controlled by the Nationalists (the army and the right), led by General Francisco Franco. The war dragged on for three years, the Nationalists supported by Germany and Italy, and the Republicans, much less so, by the Soviet Union. The International Brigades fighting on the Republican side included volunteers from many other countries.

In the north, the Basque Country, Cantabria and Asturias were cut off from the rest of the Republican-controlled zone, and were gradually

UNREST & THE SECOND REPUBLIC

In the first 30 years of the 20th century, during the reign of Alfonso XIII, the country was plagued by strikes and political crises. Successive governments were incompetent, and disorder grew. During World War I Spain remained neutral, which boosted the economy but also encouraged demands for reform, with violent confrontations between the government and radical forces. In 1923 General Miguel Primo de Rivera suspended the constitution and declared himself Dictator, with the support of the king. He ruled with an iron hand, curtailing civil liberties and banning regional languages.

In 1930 Primo's dictatorship collapsed, and the following year local elections showed huge support for Republican candidates. The king was forced to leave the country, and in 1931 Spain's Second Republic was proclaimed, amid high hopes that it would deal with the country's problems. Reforms

The Basque town of Gernika (Guernica), after the bombing of 1937

TIMELINE

Second Republic election poster

1923–30 Dictatorship of General Primo de Rivera

1937 Battle for Madrid rages; on 27 April Nazi planes bomb Gernika

1939 National Army enters Madrid on 28 M Franco declares the war ended on 1 April

1900	1920	1940

1909 Semana Trágica (Tragic Week) in Barcelona

1934 Revolution in Asturias, suppressed by General Franco

1936 Start of the Spanish Civil War

Post-World War II ration card

overrun by Franco's forces during 1937. One of the most notorious episodes of the war was the Nazi bombing of the Basque town of Gernika.

The Nationalists ultimately triumphed. With the end of the war in 1939, Franco's dictatorship began. Devastated and impoverished, the country stood in international isolation until the 1950s. Republicans suffered repression and many were forced into exile. In the centralized state, regional diversity was repressed. The use of the Catalan and Basque languages was prohibited, there was moral censorship, and political parties were banned. The 1960s saw the emergence of the violent campaign of the Basque separatist group, ETA.

Mass demonstration against ETA, the Basque separatist group

MODERN SPAIN

Franco died in 1975, having named Juan Carlos I (grandson of Alfonso XIII) as his successor. The country's transition to democracy was relatively peaceful. Political parties were legalized, and in 1978 a new constitution declared Spain a parliamentary monarchy. The constitution granted autonomous status to Spain's regions, which enabled the Basque Country, Galicia, Asturias and Cantabria to set up local administrations from 1979 onwards. However, in the Basque Country this still did not satisfy ETA, and terrorism became one of Spain's constant problems.

King Juan Carlos I and Queen Sofia

In 1982 Spain elected its first Socialist government, led by Felipe González. In 1985 it joined NATO, and in 1986 became a member of the European Union. The Olympic Games were staged in Barcelona in 1992.

The 1996 general election was won by the centre-right People's Party, led by José María Aznar. Under his prime ministership Spain enjoyed further economic success. However, the government's handling of the environmental disaster caused by the sinking of the oil tanker *Prestige* off Galicia in 2002 was criticized, and Aznar's decision to send troops to Iraq in 2003 was unpopular.

In March 2004 Islamic extremists blew up four suburban trains in Madrid. Aznar's government initially blamed ETA, but as the truth emerged this only increased the popularity of the Socialists (PSOE), led by José Rodríguez Zapatero, who were voted into power. In spring 2006, ETA announced a ceasefire.

1979 Catalonia, Basque Country and Galicia granted autonomy

2004 On 11 March Islamic extremists carry out a terrorist attack in Madrid; on 14 March PSOE wins the general election

1986 Spain joins the EEC (now the European Union)

2006 In March ETA declares a permanent ceasefire

1980

2000

2020

1975 Death of Franco (20 Nov)

1997 Museo Guggenheim opens in Bilbao

2003 As an ally of the USA, Spain sends troops to Iraq

2002 Spain adopts the euro

General Franco

NORTHERN SPAIN REGION BY REGION

Castle of Olite.

Northern Spain at a Glance

Increasing numbers of visitors are drawn to Northern Spain, where the climate is milder than in the southern Iberian Peninsula, and the autonomous regions offer all the ingredients of a wonderful holiday. The Atlantic coast boasts attractive sandy beaches, while the mountain ranges are criss-crossed by numerous footpaths. Magnificent examples of Romanesque architecture mark the famous pilgrimage route to Santiago de Compostela, while in the region's cities fine modern buildings can be seen. Fiestas and festivals take place throughout the year in Northern Spain, many of them hailed as important international events.

Santillana del Mar (see pp106–107) *is one of the region's most picturesque towns, with beautifully preserved medieval houses. Inside the Convento de Regina Coeli is a museum with a rich collection of painted figures of saints. Near the town are the famous Cuevas de Altamira.*

ASTURIAS AND CANTABRIA *(see pp80–117)*

GALICIA *(see pp48–79)*

The Picos de Europa mountain range (see pp100–3) *dominates the landscape of Asturias and Cantabria. The towns, situated in beautiful valleys, boast a plethora of pre-Romanesque buildings, while hiking trails lead through the spectacular scenery of the national park.*

The Rías Baixas *form one of Northern Spain's prettiest coastlines. Around the towns and villages here are many quaint* hórreos – *wooden granaries raised on stone stilts* (see p19).

Santiago de Compostela (see pp60–65) *attracts thousands of visitors each year. In the Middle Ages, the cathedral in Santiago was one of the most important places of pilgrimage in Christendom.*

◁ The grape harvest in the Álava region of La Rioja

San Sebastián (see pp132–5), *the most elegant holiday resort in the Basque Country, is situated around a beautiful horseshoe bay. Visitors flock here for the fine food, street life, sandy beaches and the International Film Festival.*

The Monasterio de San Juan de la Peña (see pp176–7) *is built beneath a vast wall of rock; its two churches house a pantheon of the early kings of Aragón, as well as Romanesque cloisters with capitals bearing sculpted biblical scenes.*

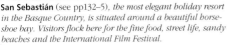

BASQUE
NTRY
*see
18–43)*

**NAVARRA
AND LA RIOJA**
(see pp144–69)

CENTRAL AND
EASTERN
PYRENEES
(see pp170–93)

0 kilometres   100

0 miles   50

Pamplona (see pp152–3), *the capital of Navarra, is best known for its annual fiesta,* Los Sanfermines, *immortalized by Ernest Hemingway. The highlight of each day of riotous celebration is the* Encierro, *in which bulls stampede through the streets.*

The Parque Nacional de Ordesa (see pp182–5) *in the Aragonese Pyrenees is a haven for walkers and hikers. The rocky massifs are enchanting, and in the mountain valleys many species of flora and fauna can be seen.*

GALICIA

R*emote in the northwest corner of the Iberian peninsula, Galicia is a green, rainswept region remarkable for the diversity of its landscape, where coastal cliffs alternate with lowlands and rías. The region is famous for its excellent cuisine, while pilgrims flock here to visit the city of Santiago de Compostela. The Galicians, whose origins are Celtic, are fiercely proud of their culture and language.*

Traditionally, Galicia was seen as a poor agricultural region, whose economy did not lend itself to modernization. It absorbed little Roman influence, was never conquered by the Moors, and in the Middle Ages fell under the control of the kingdom of Asturias. It was only very briefly an independent monarchy, in the 10th and 11th centuries.

Bordering Portugal to the south and enclosed by the waters of the Atlantic Ocean, Galicia could offer its inhabitants little in the way of new land for cultivation; overpopulation and unemployment forced many to emigrate. Yet, in the 20th century, Galicia began to develop, and today traditional lifestyles rub shoulders with modernity.

Galicia has always maintained strong links with the sea; the port cities of Vigo and A Coruña are centres of culture, commerce, and industry. Fishing is vital to the economy, and Galician seafood is the best in Spain. The coastline, cut with fjord-like *rías*, is dotted with fishing villages. Enormous efforts have been made to clean up damage caused by the 2002 sinking of the *Prestige* oil tanker, and most of the coast has now recovered.

Mainland Spain's most westerly point – the heather-clad Cabo Fisterra – is situated on this rugged stretch of coast. Even more magical is the pilgrimage centre of Santiago de Compostela, the region's capital. Romantic hillsides shrouded in mist conceal the remains of Celtic settlements; at road junctions and in the towns stand weathered stone crosses, while in the villages old granaries can be seen. The picture is completed by the sound of Galicians' favourite instrument – the bagpipes – and their language, *gallego*, which bears strong similarities to Portuguese.

The picturesque Galician coast in the vicinity of Ézaro, near the remote headland of Cabo Fisterra

◁ Detail of the Baroque reredos in the Convento de San Martiño Pinario, Santiago de Compostela

Exploring Galicia

Santiago de Compostela is Galicia's major tourist
attraction. This beautiful city is the centrepiece
of a region with many fine old towns, especially
Betanzos, Mondoñedo, Lugo and Pontevedra.
The resorts along the coastline of the wild Rías
Altas, with their backdrop of forest-covered hills,
offer good bathing. The Rías Baixas, the southern part of Galicia's west coast, have sheltered
coves and sandy beaches, and excellent seafood.
Travelling through the interior, where life seems
to have changed little in centuries, is an ideal
way to spend a peaceful, rural holiday.

SEE ALSO

• *Where to Stay* pp202–3.

• *Where to Eat* pp220–21.

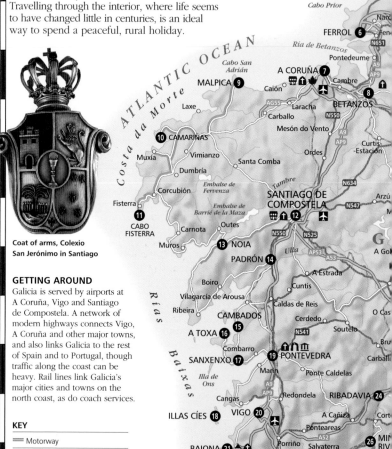

**Coat of arms, Colexio
San Jerónimo in Santiago**

GETTING AROUND

Galicia is served by airports at
A Coruña, Vigo and Santiago
de Compostela. A network of
modern highways connects Vigo,
A Coruña and other major towns,
and also links Galicia to the rest
of Spain and to Portugal, though
traffic along the coast can be
heavy. Rail lines link Galicia's
major cities and towns on the
north coast, as do coach services.

KEY

▬▬	Motorway
▬▬	Major road
▬▬	Minor road
▬▬	Scenic route
▬▬	Main railway line
▬▬	Railway line
▬▬	National border
▬▬	Regional border
✕	Bridge, tunnel

For key to symbols *see back flap*

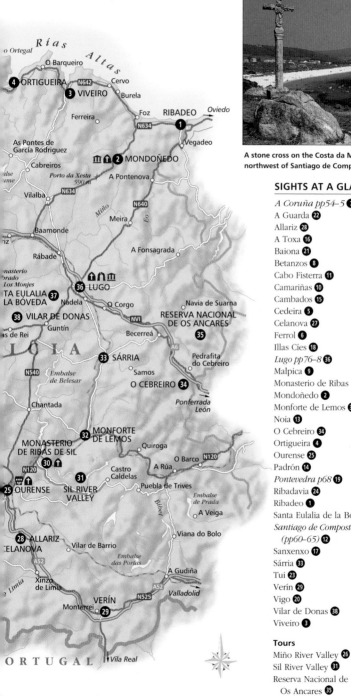

A stone cross on the Costa da Morte, northwest of Santiago de Compostela

SIGHTS AT A GLANCE

Amazing rock formations at the beach at As Catedrais, near Ribadeo

Ribadeo ❶

Lugo. ⚉ 9,000. ℹ Plaza de España;
982 12 86 89. 🖰 Wed. 🎊 San
Roque (16 Aug), Santa Maria del
Campo (8 Sep). www.ribadeo.org

Galicia's north coast, between
Ribadeo and Ferrol, is an area
of natural beauty known as
the **Rías Altas**, formed from
ría inlets and beautiful bays.
The characterful fishing town
of Ribadeo, with its attractive
harbour, occupies a pic-
turesque setting on the banks
of the Ría de Ribadeo. Among
the many observation points
here are the hill of Santa Cruz,
with its monument of a piper,
and **La Atalaya**, formerly a
bastion. The beach at **As
Catedrais** is known for its
rock formations that recall
Gothic buildings and arches.
The waters of the *ría* can be
explored by pleasure boat from
the nearby haven of Porcillán.
 The town itself is home to
the **Colegiata de Santa María
del Campo** (18th century),
with two Baroque altarpieces.
Inside are earlier elements –
Romanesque arches and
two Gothic portals with
plant ornamentation.
Another attraction is the
Modernist residence of the
brothers Moreno, which
recalls the work of Antoni
Gaudí. Iron and ceramic
tiles were used in its
construction.

Environs
North of Ribadeo lies the
18th-century **fort of San
Damián**, which once
defended the mouth of the
ría. It is now a museum.

About 10 km (6 miles) west
of Ribadeo is the fishing town
of **Foz**, which also has fine
beaches. Nearby is the vast
Romanesque **Iglesia de San
Martín de Mondoñedo**.

Mondoñedo ❷

Lugo. ⚉ 5,000. ℹ Plaza de la
Catedral 34; 982 50 71 77. 🖰 Thu
& Sun. 🎊 As Quendas (1 May), Rapa
das Bestas (Jun), Fiestas Patronales
(around 8 Sep), As San Lucas (18
Oct). www.mondonedo.com

Situated in a valley, this was
the provincial capital for nearly
four centuries, and as a result
has an unusual number of fine
buildings for such a small
town. Its oldest and most
important monument is the
13th-century Romanesque
Catedral de la Asunción,
which was remodelled during
the Gothic and Baroque

The portal of San Martín de Mondoñedo

periods. It features 14th-
century murals and a figure of
the Virgin brought here from
St Paul's Cathedral in London.
Its **Museo Diocesano** has
works by Zurbarán and El
Greco, and the 18th-century
Palacio Episcopal contains a
Neo-Gothic chapel. Nearby is
the **Fonte Vella**, a 16th-
century fountain decorated
with the coat of arms of
Charles V; beyond it extends
the old Jewish quarter.

🏛 **Museo Diocesano**
Plaza de la Catedral. **Tel.** 686 41 61
11. 🌙 Oct–May: 11am–1pm & 4–
6:30pm Tue–Sat (until 7:30pm Sun);
Jun–Sep 10:30am–1pm & 4–6:30pm
Tue–Sat (until 7:30pm Sun). 📷 ✔

Viveiro ❸

Lugo. ⚉ 15,500. ℹ Benito Galcerán;
982 56 08 79. 🖰 Thu; 1st day and
3rd Sun of the month. 🎊 Rapa das
Bestas (1st Sun in Jul), San Roque
and Nuestra Señora (week of 15
Aug). www.viveiro.es

Situated on the beautiful *ría*
of the same name, Viveiro is
the prettiest and most popular
town in the Rías Altas, with
good hotels and restaurants.
Fragments of its medieval walls
survive – their most beautiful
feature is the Plateresque Gate
of Charles V, by Maestro Pedro
Poderoso. It is decorated with
coats of arms, medallions and
an image of St Roch, the town's
patron saint. Facing the gate
is the 15th-century bridge,
Ponte de la Misericordia.
 Of note is the Romanesque
**Iglesia de Santa María del
Campo**, with a Baroque belfry
and a 19th-century clock
tower. The Romanesque-
Gothic **Iglesia de San
Francisco** has a beautiful
apse. On the Praza Maior,
where a cheese and
vegetable market is held
each Thursday, stands the
town hall, with a sundial
and 17th- and 19th-century
houses. Nearby rises the
Renaissance Casa de los
Leones, with lions on the
coat of arms.
 The district of Covas
borders a long white beach.
The hill of San Roque
overlooks the town and
offers fine views.

Houses in Ferrol with typical glass-enclosed balconies

Environs

The Ría de Viveiro constitutes the mouth of the Landro river and is part of the Rías Altas region. The area is character-ized by high waves, beaches with fine white sand, and an abundance of fish. During a storm in the 19th century, two ships – the *Magdalena* and the *Paloma* – sank here.

Ortigueira ❹

A Coruña. 🏠 *8,000.* 🚹 *Plaza de Isabel II; 981 40 00 00.* 🚌 *Thu.* 📅 *Santa Marta (28 Jul–1 Aug), International Celtic Festival (2nd w'end Jul).* **www**.concellodeortigueira.com

The main attractions here are the fantastic beaches and the diverse landscape of fertile valleys, hills and steep cliffs. The town's architecture dates mainly from the 19th and 20th centuries, but in the **Centro Arqueolóxico de la Fundación Ortegalia** an exhibition traces the region's prehistory, including the oldest Galician megaliths (4400 BC). North of town lie the ruins of **Punta dos Prados** – a settlement dating from the 4th to the 1st centuries BC.

Centro Arqueolóxico de la Fundación Ortegalia
Avenida Francisco Santiago 6.
Tel. *981 40 24 13.* 🕐 *11am–2pm & 5–8pm Tue-Fri, 11am–2pm Sat–Sun.* ● *public hols.* ♿

Cedeira ❺

A Coruña. 🏠 *8,500.* 🚹 *Ezequiel López 17; 981 48 21 87.* 🚌 *Sat & 2nd Sun of month.* 📅 *Rapa das Bestas (Curro de Capelada) (last Sun Jun), Fiestas Patronales and Nuestra Señora del Mar (around 15 Aug).* **www**.cedeira.org

One of the prettiest villages in the Rias Altas, Cedeira spans the river Condomiñas, and has excellent beaches, exquisite seafood, a tiny fishing harbour and good conditions for watersports. The surrounding area is ideal for fishing and hunting.

In the medieval old town, fragments of the town walls are preserved. The parish **Iglesia de Nuestra Señora del Mar de Cedeira** dates from the 15th century.

Some 12 km (8 miles) away, perched above the Atlantic atop sheer surf-battered cliffs in wild, windswept countryside is the 12th-century **Monasterio de San Andrés de Teixido**, a Galician shrine that once belonged to the Knights of Malta. The earliest preserved fragments in the monastery are the late-Gothic north portal, and the murals depicting the martyrdom of St Andrew. It is customary for pilgrims to throw breadcrumbs into the nearby spring, which flows from underneath the church's altar. Legend has it that if a crumb floats, your wish will be fulfilled.

A figure of St Andrew in San Andrés de Teixido

Ferrol ❻

A Coruña. 🏠 *80,000.* 🚹 *Puerta Nueva; 981 44 67 00.* 🚌 *Mon & Wed.* 📅 *San Julián (7 Jan), A Noche de las Pepitas (18 Mar), Fiestas Patronales (31 Aug).* **www**.ferrol-concello.es

Ferrol has strong links with the sea – some of the ships in the Spanish Armada set sail from its port. Yet it wasn't until the 18th century that the town became an important naval base, acquiring an arsenal, shipyards, and the castle of San Felipe, which defended the mouth of the local *ría*.

The intriguing Magdalena district was laid out in symmetrical Neoclassical style in the 18th century. It features many houses with glass balconies, as well as the 18th-century **Iglesia de San Xulián** with Mannerist elements, designed by Julián Sánchez Bort.

Environs

Lying 10 km (6 miles) south of Ferrol is **Pontedeume**, an attractive medieval town that boasts a tower with a huge coat of arms, built in the 14th century in honour of Count Andrade. There is also an equally old bridge, in the middle of which once stood a hostel for pilgrims and a hermitage. Andrade's castle is nearby, while hidden in the forest is the 12th-century monastery of Caaveiro.

Fishing boats in a bay near the picturesque village of Cedeira

A Coruña ❼

The oldest town in Galicia, A Coruña is mentioned in Irish myths about a Celtic hero by the name of Breogán, who came to the Iberian coast and built a tower here. The famous lighthouse – Torre de Hércules – dates from the Roman period. A Coruña is also the birthplace of María Pita, who became a Galician heroine by leading local resistance to a raid by Sir Francis Drake in 1589. The town has been an important commercial port for centuries.

Plaza María Pita, lined with arcaded houses

Exploring A Coruña

A Coruña boasts the longest sea promenade in Europe, with magnificent red-pillared lighthouses and old trams running along its length. The most important historic monuments, as well as the town centre, are laid out on an isthmus leading to a headland.

🏛 Museo de Bellas Artes

Calle Zalaeta. *Tel* 981 22 37 23.
⬤ 10am–8pm Tue–Fri, 10am–2pm & 4:30–8pm Sat, 10am–2pm Sun.
This modern building houses Spanish and European paintings from the 16th to the 20th centuries, as well as 19th- and 20th-century Galician art. There are also prints by Goya

and ceramics by the celebrated local factory of Sargadelos.

🚇 Avenida de la Marina

The harbourfront promenade known as the Avenida de la Marina is one of A Coruña's great landmarks. Houses with gleaming glass-enclosed balconies, or *galerías*, run along its length; these are best viewed from the Real Club Náutico. At one end of the promenade rises a memorial obelisk topped by a clock with four dials (1845) – a favourite meeting point.

🚇 Plaza María Pita

This sumptuous, harmoniously designed square bears the name of Galicia's national heroine, who defended the town against the English, led by the navigator and buccaneer Francis Drake. A popular spot for pavement cafés, it is surrounded by houses with arcades that offer protection against the sun and rain. Here, too, is the monumental neo-Renaissance town hall

(Palacio Municipal), with three huge domes. The building contains Spain's finest clock museum. Beside the town hall rises the 17th-century Baroque Iglesia de San Jorge.

🔒 Iglesia de Santiago

Calle del Parrote 1. ⬤ 8am–1pm & 5:30–7pm Mon–Fri, 10am–1pm & 4:30–7pm Sat–Sun.
Stone from the Torre de Hércules was used to build this Romanesque-Gothic hall church (12th–15th century) where, in the Middle Ages, the town council met. It is the

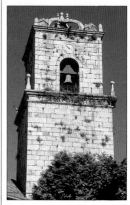

The Romanesque-Gothic tower of the Iglesia de Santiago

oldest church in A Coruña, featuring three apses. In the tympanum above the main entrance is a sculpted image of St James, reminding visitors that this is the start of one of the stages of the pilgrimage route to Santiago de Compostela.

🔒 Colegiata de Santa María del Campo

The saint to whom this 13th-century church is dedicated is particularly venerated by sailors, who pray for her protection before setting off on voyages. The church was originally situated beyond the town walls and, according to legend, was where the daughters of King Alfonso IX lived. The main portal's decoration recalls the Pórtico da Gloria on the cathedral in Santiago de Compostela *(see pp62–3).* On the square in front of the church is a 15th-century *cruceiro* (stone cross), one of the oldest in Galicia.

GLASS HOUSES IN A CORUÑA

Houses with large glass balconies, glistening in the sun, are common all over Galicia, but the most famous ones are found here in A Coruña. It was this particular architectural feature that led visiting sailors to dub A Coruña the "City of Glass". These extensive glass *galerías*, which have been

Houses with impressive glass balconies in the port area of A Coruña

used in thousands of advertising photographs, were designed to face the harbour, and so are located at the back of the buildings. The façades face the Calle de Riego de Agua and Calle Real, streets that once formed the main axis of the town.

♣ Jardines San Carlos

The Romantic-style San Carlos gardens, laid out on the site of a fortress whose walls have survived to this day, form one of the most charming corners of A Coruña. Buried at their centre is the Scottish General John Moore, killed by the French at the Battle of Elviña (1809). Among the many species of indigenous and exotic trees are some especially fine elms.

🏛 Museo Arqueológico

Paseo Parrote. **Tel** 981 18 98 50.
◯ Sep–Jun: 10am–7pm Tue–Sat, 10am–2:30pm Sun; Jul–Aug: 10am–9pm Tue–Sat, 10am–3pm Sun. 📷
This museum, housed in the Castillo de San Antón, an 18th-century fortress, traces the history of Galicia. On show are exhibits from the Palaeolithic period up to the time of the Roman conquest, more exhibits presenting the culture of the *castros* (fortified villages) and medieval sculptures and coats of arms used to illustrate the most important events in A Coruña's history.

The modern building of the Museo Domus

🏛 Domus

C/Santa Teresa 1. **Tel** 981 18 98 40.
◯ Sep–Jun: 10am–7pm daily; Jul–Aug: 11am–9pm daily. 📷 ♿ ⑪
Also known as the *Casa del Hombre* (Museum of Mankind), this is the world's first interactive museum devoted entirely to the human being. The futuristic building was designed by the Japanese architect Arata Isozaki.

🏛 Torre de Hércules

Avenida de Navarra. **Tel** 981 22 37 30. ◯ Oct–Mar: 10am–5:45pm daily; Apr–Jun & Sep: 10am–6:45pm daily; Jul–Aug: 10am–8:45pm Sun–Thu, 10am–11:45pm Fri–Sat. 📷
The Tower of Hércules is the world's oldest working lighthouse. Since the

VISITORS' CHECKLIST

A Coruña 🏘 244,000. ✈ 981 18 73 15. 🚆 C/Joaquín Planells. 🚌 C/Caballeros 21. **Tel** 981 18 43 35. 🚢 Avda. de la Marina 3. **Tel** 981 21 96 21. 🛈 Dársena de la Marina; 981 22 18 22. 🎉 Fiestas de María Pita (Aug). www.turismocoruna.com

2nd century its beam has warned sailors that they are approaching land. The lighthouse was built during the reign of the Emperor Trajan, but according to legend it was built by Hercules. Its current appearance is the result of renovation carried out in the 18th century. The 59.5 m (180 ft) shaft rests on a square base; you can climb the 234 steps to the top.

🏖 Playas (Beaches)

On the other side of the isthmus from the harbour, but within walking distance, is the town's most important beach, Riazor-Orzán. Near the Tower of Hercules are the smaller beaches of Das Lapas and San Amaro.

Torre de Hércules lighthouse

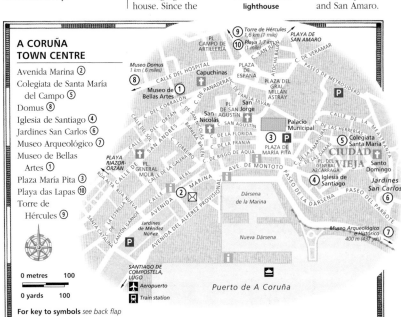

A CORUÑA TOWN CENTRE

0 metres 100
0 yards 100

For key to symbols see back flap

Townscape overlooking the fishing port in Malpica

Betanzos ⑧

A Coruña. 🕅 13,000. 🚊 🚌
🛈 Emilio Romai; 981 77 36 93.
🗓 Tue, Thu, Sat. 🎪 San Roque
(16 Aug). www.betanzos.es

At the centre of this fascinating
town of narrow lanes is the
Praza García Hermanos, an
elegant 18th-century square.
The steep streets, which arose
on the site of the former *castro*,
are lined with old houses and
Gothic churches. The tympanum of the 15th-century **Iglesia
de Santiago** is decorated with
an equestrian figure of St
James. Hidden inside
the aisleless 14th-
century **Iglesia de
San Francisco** are
beautiful tombs,
including that of
Count Fernán Pérez
de Andrade, support-
ed on figures of a
wild boar and bear.
The **Iglesia de Santa**   Iglesia de Santiago
María de Azogue,   portal, Betanzos
with a beautiful façade and
rose window, has a 15th-
century Flemish reredos.

Malpica ⑨

A Coruña. 🕅 6,800. 🛈 Avenida
Emilio Gonzáles 1; 981 72 00 01.
🎪 San Adrián (16 Jun), Nuestra
Señora del Mar (last Sun Aug).
www.concellomalpica.com

This small fishing town has
good beaches and enchanting
views of the nearby Sisargas
islands – an important nature
reserve especially rich in birds.
Of interest is the Romanesque
Iglesia de Santiago de Mens;

legend has it that the church
was linked with Mens castle
by an underground tunnel.
Near Malpica is the partially
destroyed **Cerqueda dolmen**.

Camariñas ⑩

A Coruña. 🕅 6,500. 🚊 🛈 Praza
da Insuela; 981 73 72 34. 🗓 Wed,
Sat. 🎪 San Bonifacio (5 Jun), Carmen
(17 Jul). www.camarinas.net

This pretty fishing town is
known for the bobbin lace
that is manufactured and sold
here. In the local 18th-
century **Iglesia de San
Jorge** is a valuable
reredos sculpted by
José Ferreiro bearing
images of saints.

Environs
Among the wild land-
scape of the **Cabo
Vilán** headland, 5 km
(3 miles) away, stands
a lighthouse with the
longest beam of all Galician
lighthouses. Here, too, are
wind turbines for electricity.

Cabo Fisterra ⑪

A Coruña. 🕅 5,050. 🚊 🚌 🛈 Rúa
Real 2, A Coruña; 981 74 07 81.
🚢 Tue, Fri. 🎪 Virgen del Carmen
(8–10 Sep), Fiesta del Cristo (Easter
week). www.concellofisterra.com

Known in English as Finisterre,
and translated as "World's
End", this cape with fabulous
views was long considered to
be Continental Europe's most
westerly point, though in fact
that distinction belongs to
Portugal. The lighthouse, on
the perilous Costa da Morte,
is a symbol of Galicia.
A village of the same name
lies 3 km (1.9 miles) from the
cape. Nearby is the Romanesque **Iglesia de Santa María
de las Arenas**, with a figure of
the Santo Cristo da Barba
Dourada (Christ of the Golden
Beard). Before it stands a 15th-
century *cruceiro* (stone cross).
This is the last part of the Road
to Santiago – here pilgrims
traditionally burn the clothes
they wore on the pilgrimage.

A lighthouse on the treacherous
Costa da Morte at Cabo Fisterra

COSTA DA MORTE

Between Cabo San Adrián, near
Malpica, and Fisterra headlands
extends the "Coast of Death",
whose grim name is due to the
many ships that have been smashed
against the rocky shoreline over
the centuries. The landscape here
is characterized by a wild beauty;
the steep cliffs, sea birds, stone
cruceiros and gigantic *hórreos* will
long remain in the memory. At great
risk, fishermen scour the coast for
barnacles for use in local cuisine.

**Stone *cruceiros* on the
Costa da Morte**

Regional Galician Architecture

Traditional buildings that reflect Galicia's own vernacular style give the region its unique charm. In A Coruña the glass *galerías (see p54)* are a common sight, but there are also distinctive, narrow, two-storey fishermen's cottages, which can be seen in Pontevedra. Visitors can experience the mansions known as *pazos*, some of which date back to the Middle Ages, as many have been converted into hotels or exclusive *paradores* (state-operated hotels). Beyond the larger towns, there are many reminders of times gone by. Grain is still stored in stone granaries *(hórreos)* used as far back as Roman times; ancient stone crosses stand by the roadsides; and many villages feature *pallozas* – oval stone buildings with thatched roofs that survive as the oldest type of Galician architecture.

This hórreo *(granary) in Carnota, dating from 1760 and extending 35 m (126 ft), is one of the largest in Galicia. Hórreos were built on stone legs to protect the grain from damp and pests. The cross is a decorative motif.*

Pallozas *are among the oldest structures built in Europe. Dating from Celtic times, these houses have thick walls and thatched roofs. The inhabitants used to divide the space into living quarters, animal stables and a food store.*

Pazos *are traditional stone mansions that form an attractive feature of this picturesque region. Nowadays many of them have been converted into hotels.*

The distinctive cruceiros *(stone crosses) can be found throughout Galicia, at places of worship, next to cemetery gates, by the Stations of the Cross (as in A Guarda), and on roadsides where accidents have occurred.*

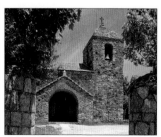

Many pilgrimage churches *were built in Galicia, as various strands of the Road to Santiago pass through the region. The churches give the region a special charm.*

These narrow two-storey houses *with glass-enclosed balconies are common in fishing villages. Their functional plan creates living space on the upper floor, with storage for fishing equipment on the ground floor.*

The remnants of Celtic *castros* near A Guarda ▷

Street-by-Street: Santiago de Compostela

In the Middle Ages Santiago de Compostela was Christendom's third most important place of pilgrimage, after Jerusalem and Rome. Around the Praza do Obradoiro is an ensemble of historic buildings that has few equals in Europe. The local granite gives a harmonious unity to the mixture of archi-tectural styles. With its narrow streets and old squares, the city centre is compact enough to explore on foot. Of its many monuments, two others are especially worth seeking out – the Convento de Santo Domingo de Bonaval, to the east of the centre, and the Colegiata Santa María la Real del Sar, a 12th-century Romanesque church located to the east of the city.

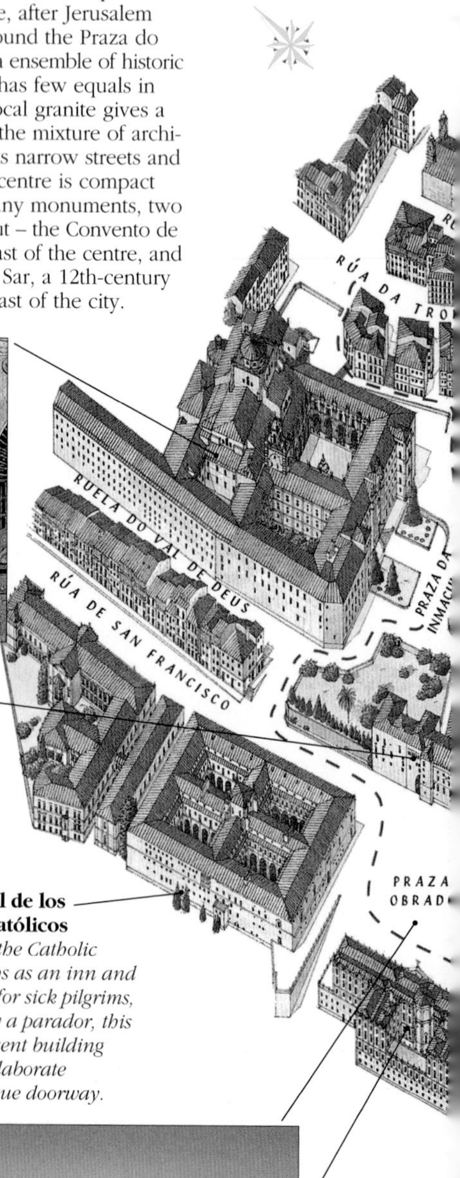

Vegetable stall in Santiago market

★ **Convento de San Martiño Pinario**
The Baroque church of this monastery has a huge double altar and an ornate façade in the Plateresque style, with carved figures of saints and bishops.

Pazo de Xelmírez (1120–49)

★ **Hostal de los Reyes Católicos**
Built by the Catholic Monarchs as an inn and hospital for sick pilgrims, and now a parador, this magnificent building has an elaborate Plateresque doorway.

Praza do Obradoiro
This majestic square is one of the world's finest and the focal point for pilgrims arriving in the city. The cathedral's Baroque façade dominates the square.

The Pazo de Raxo with its Neo-Class façade, was built 1772 and houses the town hall.

RÚA DA TRO

RÚELA DO VAL DE DEUS

RÚA DE SAN FRANCISCO

PRAZA DA INMAC

PRAZA OBRADO

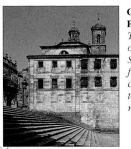

Convento de San Paio de Antealtares

This is one of the oldest monasteries in Santiago. It was founded in the 9th century to house the tomb of St James, now in the cathedral.

VISITORS' CHECKLIST

A Coruña. 👥 *94,000.* ✈ *Lava-colla.* 🚉 *Rúa do Hórreo 75a, 981 59 60 50.* 🚌 *Pl. de Camilo Díaz Baliño, 981 58 77 00* ℹ *Rúa do Vilar 63, 981 55 51 29.* 📅 *Thu, Sat.* 🎉 *Easter Week, Ascension (40 days after Easter), St James (24 Jul).* www.santiagoturismo.com

Praza da Quintana, in front of the cathedral clock tower, is one of the city's most elegant squares.

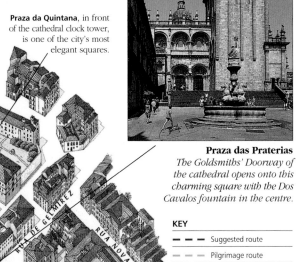

Praza das Praterias

The Goldsmiths' Doorway of the cathedral opens onto this charming square with the Dos Cavalos fountain in the centre.

KEY

– – – Suggested route

– – – Pilgrimage route

The Rúa Nova is a handsome arcaded old street leading from the cathedral to the newer part of the city.

→ To tourist information

0 metres 100

0 yards 100

Colegio de San Jerónimo

STAR SIGHTS

★ Cathedral

★ Convento de San Martiño Pinario

★ Hostal de los Reyes Católicos

★ Cathedral

This grand towering spectacle has welcomed pilgrims to Santiago for centuries. Though the exterior has been remodelled over the years, the core of the building has remained virtually unchanged since the 11th century.

Santiago Cathedral

The gigantic botafumeiro

With its twin Baroque towers soaring over the Praza do Obradoiro, this monument to St James is a majestic sight, as befits one of the great shrines of Christendom (*see pp20–21*). The core of the present building dates from the 11th–13th centuries and stands on the site of the 9th-century basilica built by Alfonso II. Behind the Baroque façade and through the original Pórtico da Gloria is the same interior that met pilgrims in medieval times.

"Passport" – proof of a pilgrim's journey

The twin towers are the cathedral's highest structures at 74 m (243 ft).

Statue of St James

Pazo de Xelmírez

★ West Front
This richly sculpted Baroque façade was added in the 18th century in front of Mateo's Pórtico da Gloria.

★ Pórtico da Gloria
The cathedral's most impressive element is the sculpted Doorway of Glory, with its statues of apostles and prophets. It dates from the 12th century.

The Santo Dos Croques is a statue of Maestro Mateo – touching the statue with the forehead is said to bring luck and to impart wisdom.

STAR SIGHTS
★ Porta das Praterias
★ Pórtico da Gloria
★ West Front

Tapestry Museum
A new addition to this collection of antique tapestries is an exhibition of Oriental medieval weavings dating back to the 13th century.

The botafumeiro, a giant censer, is swung high above the altar by eight men during important services.

The Mondragon Chapel (1521) contains fine wrought-iron grilles and vaulting.

Clock Tower

Cloisters

Chapterhouse

VISITORS' CHECKLIST

Praza do Obradoiro. ☐ 7am–9pm daily. **Tel.** 981 58 35 48. ✛ ♿ **Museum Tel.** 981 56 15 27. ☐ Oct–May: 10am–1:30pm & 4–6:30pm Mon–Sat; Jun–Sep: 10am–2pm & 4–8pm Mon–Sat. ◐ pm: Sun & public hols. ▨ ▧

High Altar
Visitors can pass behind the altar to embrace the silver mantle of the 13th-century statue of St James, and to access the crypt.

★ Porta das Praterias
Bas-relief sculptures of biblical scenes cover the 12th-century Goldsmiths' Doorway.

Crypt
The relics of St James and two disciples are said to lie in a tomb in the crypt, under the altar, in the original 9th-century foundations.

The two-level Praza Quintana behind the cathedral

Exploring Santiago de Compostela

The centre of Santiago is a pedestrianized zone. The most important monuments are found in the vicinity of the Praza do Obradoiro.

🏛 Praza do Obradoiro

This huge square is the focal point for arriving pilgrims. On the square's eastern side rises the cathedral's famous Baroque façade; to the west is the Pazo de Raxoi; to the north the Hostal de los Reyes Católicos (today an exclusive parador); and to the south the Colexio de San Jerónimo.

🏠 Convento de San Francisco

Rúa Campiño de San Francisco 3. *Tel* 981 58 16 00.

The founding of the monastery of San Francisco de Valdediós is traditionally ascribed to St Francis of Assisi, who came to Santiago in 1214. All that remains of the original structure are Gothic arches in the cloister and the tomb of the master mason Cotolay. The current buildings date from the 18th century. In the atrium is a *cruceiro* (stone cross) dedicated to St Francis. The monastery now houses a hotel.

🏛 Praza Quintana

Situated behind the cathedral, at the foot of a Baroque clock tower called the Berenguela, is this elegant square divided into two sections by steps. One side of the square is occupied by the monastery of San Paio de Antealtares, with its imposing façade sporting a row of windows with wrought-iron grilles. The Baroque Casa de la Parra, decorated with plant ornaments, is also here.

🏛 Cathedral Museum

Praza do Obradoiro. *Tel* 981 56 05 27. ☐ Jun–Sep: 10am–2pm & 4–8pm Mon–Sat, Sun 10am–2pm; Oct–May: 10am–1:30pm & 4–6:30pm Mon–Sat, 10am–1:30pm Sun. 🖼

The museum's rich collections cover religion as well as the cathedral itself. Preserved in the library are incunabula and manuscripts, as well as two examples of a giant censer known as the *botafumeiro*. You can also see the cathedral cloisters, medieval reliquaries and some old ornaments, which were taken down during construction of the new façade.

🏛 Pazo de Xelmírez

Praza do Obradoiro. ☐ Apr–Sep: 10am–1:30pm & 4–7:30pm Tue–Sun. 🖼

Dating from the 12th–13th centuries, this building is regarded as the most important work of secular Romanesque architecture in Galicia. It was built as the Archbishop's Palace, and continues to fill this role. The severe appearance of the building contrasts with its lavish interior. On the

Buildings of the Pazo de Xelmírez, housing the Archbishop's Palace

ground floor is the Weapons Chamber. From the small patio you can ascend via stairs to the cross-vaulted refectory, where magnificent reliefs depicting life in the Middle Ages are preserved.

⚜ Pazo de Raxoi

Praza do Obradoiro. ◉ to the public.

Initially, this 18th-century palace was a residence for students of the seminary and choirboys; since 1970 it has served as the town hall. The palace was built upon the former city walls, the master-mason being Charles Lemaur. A curiosity here is the extraordinary variation in the height of the land on which the building stands. The long arcaded façade is supported on Ionic columns. A figure of St James designed by J. Ferreira is visible on the roof. The interior of the building is noted for its Rococo staircase.

The late-Romanesque portal of the Colexio San Jerónimo

🏛 Colexio San Jerónimo

Throughout its history, the Colexio San Jerónimo has served many purposes: hospital, grammar school, art school, and later a hostel for poor students. Today, it accommodates the chancellor of the University of Santiago de Compostela. Preserved from the earlier, 15th-century building is a late Romanesque portal, richly decorated with figures of the Virgin and Child surrounded by saints. The structure you see today, dating from the 17th century, has an inner courtyard with a fountain.

🔒 Colegio de Fonseca

Rúa de Franco s/n

The Colegio arose in the 16th century as one of the university buildings. The Renaissance design is the work of the architects Juan de Alava and Alonso Covarrubias, and was completed by Rodrigo Gil de Hontañón. The façade is decorated with the coat of arms of the Fonseca family, figures of saints (the Virgin, St James the Lesser, St Peter, St Paul), and the Church Fathers of Spanish origin (St Isidore, St Leander). For a time, the Galician Parliament was housed here. Today the university library is located here, and numerous exhibitions are held in the elegant cloisters.

🏛 Museo de las Peregrinaciones

Rúa de San Miguel 4. *Tel* 981 58 15 58. ◻ 10am–8pm Tue–Fri, 10:30am–1:30pm & 5–8pm Sat, 10:30am–1:30pm Sun.

The Pilgrimage Museum, devoted to the cult of St James and the cultural impact of pilgrimages over the ages, is located inside the Casa Gótica (Gothic House). The eight rooms contain exhibits that describe the beginnings of the apostle's cult and the history of pilgrimages. They also display the iconography of St James (including several sculptures and *Santiago Peregrino* – the famous painting by Juan de Juanes) and even musical instruments reproduced from the cathedral's Pórtico da Gloria. The museum library has a rich collection of books, journals and photographs connected with St James.

🔒 Convento de San Martiño Pinario

Praza da Inmaculada 5. *Tel* 981 55 40 48. ◻ 10:30am–2pm & 4–8:30pm Tue–Sat. 🎥 compulsory.

The imposing Benedictine monastery complex of San Martiño Pinario occupies more space than the cathedral itself. Its construction began during the Renaissance period, but it was given its current Baroque appearance by Gabriel Casas and Fernando Casas y Novoa. The superb church dome and grand interior were designed in the 17th century by

Bartolomé Fernández Lechuga. The façade, which is supported on massive columns, is decorated with figures of saints, the evangelists, and the Church Fathers. There are two sets of cloisters within

The Baroque reredos at the Convento de San Martiño Pinario

the monastery complex – one centred on a Baroque fountain. The monastery building itself is modest and rather severe.

🏛 Museo do Pobo Galego

San Domingo de Bonaval. *Tel* 981 58 36 20. ◻ 10am–2pm & 4–8pm Tue–Sat, 11am–2pm Sun. 🎥

Housed inside the 17th-century Convento de Santo Domingo de Bonaval, this museum contains an interesting collection of pieces illustrating the social history of Galicia. The thematic layout covers subjects ranging from the sea to the countryside, traditional

occupations, costumes, music, architecture, painting and sculpture throughout Galicia. Inside the church is a pantheon of famous Galicians – among others, the local poet Rosalía de Castro is buried here.

🏛 Centro Gallego de Arte Contemporanea

Ramón María del Valle Inclán. *Tel* 981 54 66 19. ◻ 11am–8pm Tue–Sun. 🚻 🎥

Designed by Álvaro Siza, this interesting building houses a modern art centre, whose aim is to present trends in both Galician and international art since the 1960s. A variety of courses, concerts, workshops, conferences and film shows are offered. The centre also has a library, an audiovisual library and a film archive.

🔒 Colexiata Santa María a Real do Sar

◻ 10am–1pm & 4–7pm Mon–Sat.

Huge buttressed arches support the walls of this simple 17th-century collegiate church; they were added in the 17th–18th centuries when the walls and interior columns began to lean dangerously. Near the main entrance stands a 12th-century baptismal font. Through the sacristy you emerge onto the cloisters, one wing of which is the only Romanesque building of this kind that has survived in Galicia. Other elements of the building date from the 17th and 18th century. The sacristy and cloisters accommodate liturgical and archaeological museums.

THE LEGEND OF ST JAMES

According to legend, the apostle St James was responsible for bringing Christianity to Spain. Though martyred in Palestine around AD 45, centuries later it was said that before his death the saint had visited Spain to bring the Gospel to her people, and that after his death his body had been brought to Galicia on a ship led by angels. In 814 a hermit claimed to have been guided to rediscover the saint's tomb by a shower of stars – (*compostela* means "field of stars") – and the bishop declared the miracle genuine. The tomb rapidly became a centre of pilgrimage.

St James (Santiago), the patron saint of Spain

The palm-lined promenade in Noia

Noia ⓭

A Coruña. 🏘 *14,600.* ⓘ *C/Rosalía de Castro; 981 84 21 00.* 🚌 *Thu, 1st & 3rd Sun of month.* 🎉 *San Marcos (25 Apr), San Bartolomé (24 Aug).* **www**.dicoruna.es/municipios/noia

According to legend, this town was founded by the great-grandson of Noah; hence, Noia's coat of arms features a dove with an olive sprig in its beak. The town's golden age was in the 15th century, when it was one of Galicia's main ports. The medieval town plan and houses bearing coats of arms survive from that period.

Worth seeing is the late-Romanesque **Iglesia de San Martino**; its portal is richly decorated with saints and biblical figures. The Romanesque **Santa María a Nova**, dating from the 14th century, stands in the middle of the Quintana dos Muertos, an exceptionally interesting cemetery. In its northern part rises Cristo de Humilladoiro, a conical stone chapel that contains a 16th-century *cruceiro* (cross). The four columns supporting it have fine decoration depicting the phases of the moon and injured animals fleeing from hunters and hounds. In the southern part of the cemetery, which is overlooked by a second *cruceiro* from the 13th century, are some 200 gravestones; the most interesting are those that show the symbol of the guild to which the deceased belonged.

Near Noia is the Celtic **Castro de Baroña**, one of the best-preserved stone fortifications in Galicia.

Padrón ⓮

A Coruña. 🏘 *9,100.* 🚉 🚌 ⓘ *Avenida de Compostela.* 🚌 *Sun.* 🎉 *St Isidore (15 May); St James (25 Jul).*

According to legend, the name of this town derives from the stone *(padrón)* to which the ship carrying the body of St James was moored when it arrived in Galicia *(see p65)*. Numerous Baroque buildings remain standing, such as the town hall and Palace of Alonso Peña Montenegro. You can also visit the **Casa-Museo**

Room in Padrón's Casa-Museo Rosalía de Castro

Rosalía de Castro to learn more about this 19th-century poet. The **Fundación Camilo José Cela** is a cultural institution devoted to Padrón's other major writer.

Environs
The 17th- to 18th-century estate of **Pazo de Oca**, a fine example of Galician architecture, was built on the ruins of a fort. The complex comprises a palace, a Baroque church, and workers' houses. The estate gardens feature a pond divided by a stone footbridge.

🏛 **Casa-Museo Rosalía de Castro**
La Matanza (Retén). **Tel** 981 81 12 04. ⏰ 10am–1:30pm & 4-7pm Tue–Sat (until 8pm Mar–Sep), 10am–1:30pm Sun & hols. 🎫

🏛 **Fundación Camilo José Cela**
C/Santa María 22. **Tel** 981 81 03 48. ⏰ Nov–Jun: 10am–2pm & 4-7pm Mon–Thu, 10am–2pm Fri. 🎫 🎫

Cambados ⓯

Pontevedra. 🏘 *13,500.* ⓘ *Plaza del Ayuntamiento; 986 52 07 86.* 🎉 *San Benito (11 Jul), Santa Margarita (25 Jul), Fiesta del Vino Albariño (1st w'kend Aug).* **www**.cambados.com

In Cambados' historic centre is the **Pazo de Bazán**, a manor house built in the 17th century by the ancestors of renowned 19th-century writer Emilia Pardo Bazán. Today it is a parador *(see*

RÍAS BAIXAS (RÍAS BAJAS)

The southern part of Galicia's beautiful west coast consists of four large *rías,* or inlets, between pine-covered hills. The beaches are good, the scenery is lovely, the bathing safe and the climate much milder than on the wilder coast to the north. Though areas such as Vilagarcía de Arousa and Panxón have become popular holiday resorts, much of the Rías Baixas coastline is unspoiled, such as the quiet stretch from Muros to Noia. This part of the coastline provides some of Spain's most fertile fishing grounds, and also produces excellent wines.

An unspoiled stretch of Galicia's Rías Baixas shoreline

p202). A century older is the **Pazo de Fefináns**, decorated with Baroque coats of arms, in which one of the town's oldest bodegas has been established; the estate also comprises the late 16th-century **Iglesia de San Benito**. For a strange experience, visit the ruins of the roofless **Iglesia de Santa Mariña de Dozo**, which stands near the hill of A Pastora. Close by is the **Museo Etnográfico e do Vino**, where you can see exhibits connected with the region's history and culture and learn about wine production in the Rías Baixas.

In the Santo Tomé district, you can visit the ruins of the ancient medieval tower of San Sadurnino, dating from the 10th century.

🏛 **Museo Etnográfico e do Vino**
Avenida de Pastora 104. *Tel 986 52 61 19.* ⏲ 10am–2pm & 4:30–7:30pm Tue–Sun. 🖼 🖻 🅿 ♿

A Toxa ⑯

Pontevedra. 🚃 🛈 *Ayuntamiento, O Grove, Praza do Corgo; 986 73 14 15.* 🚌 *Fri.* 🎣 *Shellfish fiesta (weekend before 12 Oct).*

A tiny pine-covered island joined to the mainland by a bridge, A Toxa is one of the most stylish resorts in Galicia. The *belle époque* palace-hotel and luxury villas add to the island's elegant atmosphere. A Toxa's best-known landmark is the small church covered with scallop shells. Aross the bridge is **O Grove**, a thriving family resort and fishing port on a peninsula, with holiday hotels and flats alongside glorious beaches.

Sanxenxo ⑰

Pontevedra. 🚶 *16,300.* 🛈 *Puerto Deportivo Juan Carlos I; 986 72 02 85.* 🎣 *Tourist Day (25 Aug); Santa Rosalía (4 Sep); Feria de la Cebolla (4 Sep); Nosa Señora do Carmen (5 Sep).* **www**.sanxenxo.com

With its good restaurants, lively nightlife, big promenade and attractive beaches, Sanxenxo

The picturesque coast near Sanxenxo

is one of the most popular resorts in the Rías Baixas. **Silgar beach** has the most modern sports harbour in Galicia. Its Old Town features the 17th-century **Iglesia de San Xinés** as well as the 16th-18th-century **Pazo de los Patino**, with a tower, the coats of arms of its former inhabitants, and stone steps leading out onto a terrace.

The Sanxenxo area also enjoys a good reputation for its *albariño* white wine.

Environs

One of the best-known local beaches is **Praia a Lanzada** – a superb long beach that's a favourite with windsurfers. On Midsummer's Eve, near the Romanesque hermitage of Santa María, a colourful pilgrimage of women used to enter the sea to perform the ancient ritual of *bano das nove ondas*. Nine waves had to envelop the body of each woman, who during this time made a wish – single women wished for marriage, married women for children.

Illas Cíes ⑱

Pontevedra. ⛴

The three islands of the tiny archipelago of Cíes are uninhabited, if you don't count the lighthouse keeper and guards. You can get here from Vigo by one of the boats moored at the improvised port on the Illa Norte (or Monteagudo), or from Baiona in summer. The Illa Norte is joined to the Illa do Faro by a sandbar and an artificial embankment along which runs the road. There is a campsite on Faro, but no other accommodation. The third island is called Sur or San Martín.

The entire archipelago is a national park and a paradise for waterfowl. It boasts breathtaking landscapes, beaches (also for nudists), the ruins of a Celtic *castro*, and an ancient Suevi monastery that was plundered by the Vikings and later by English pirates. The islands have a first-aid post, telephone, café, police station and tourist information office.

ROSALÍA DE CASTRO AND CAMILO JOSÉ CELA

These two writers from Padrón left a profound mark on Galicia. Rosalía de Castro (1837–85), a Galician national icon, was the foremost figure of the 19th-century renaissance in the Galician language, with such works as *Cantares Gallegos*. Her poetry was written in Gallego, and coloured by her difficult life. Born an illegitimate child, she herself lost seven children, and died prematurely of cancer after a lifetime of illness. Camilo José Cela (1916-2002), winner of the Nobel Prize in 1989, wrote in Spanish and was renowned for his superb mastery of language and knowledge of the human character.

The 19th-century Galician poet, Rosalía de Castro

Pontevedra ⑲

Pontevedra. 🏛 *80,000.* 🚉 🚌
ℹ️ *Calle General Gutiérrez Mellado 1;
986 85 08 14.* 🚢 *1st, 8th, 15th &
23rd of month.* 🎭 *Fiestas de la
Peregrina (2nd week in Aug), Feira
Franca (1st Fri & Sat in Sep).*
www.concellopontevedra.es

Legend has it that Pontevedra
was founded by Teucro, one
of the heroes of the Trojan
War, but in reality it was the
Romans who constructed a
bridge across the Lérez river,
around which the town began
to emerge. The bridge – the
freshly restored A Ponte do
Burgo – remains to this day

one of the town's
landmarks. A tour of
Pontevedra, which is
also the provincial
capital, is best begun
on the Alameda boule-
vard – the green lungs
of the city. Along here
stand numerous 19th-
century buildings that
today house impor-
tant offices. At the
end of the boulevard
are the **Ruinas do
Santo Domingo**, ruins
of a Gothic church
that form part of the **Museo
de Pontevedra**, where you
can see Roman steles and
medieval coats of arms and

Façade detail from
the Basílica de Santa
María la Mayor

tombs. The main
buildings of the
museum – regarded
as one of the best in
Galicia – are situated
on the **Praza da
Leña**. The collections
include Celtic gold
bracelets and neck-
laces, and locally
found Bronze Age
treasures. Apart
from 15th-century
paintings, the art-
works on display
include canvases
by Zurbarán and Goya. There
are also several works by the
Galician painter and writer
Alfonso Castelao.

Near to the tiny Praza das
Cinco, sporting an 18th-century
cruceiro, is the huge, partially
treed **Praza da Ferrería**, with
a beautiful fountain. Worthy
of mention here are the
Renaissance **Casa das Caras**,
decorated with sculpted
faces, the 14th-century **Iglesia
de San Francisco**, and a
branch of the Ministry of the
Economy, which incorporates
the Santo Domingo gate from
the medieval town walls.

The greatest monument of
the Galician Renaissance style
is the 16th-century **Basílica de
Santa María la Mayor**, with a

The huge Praza da Peregrina in Pontevedra

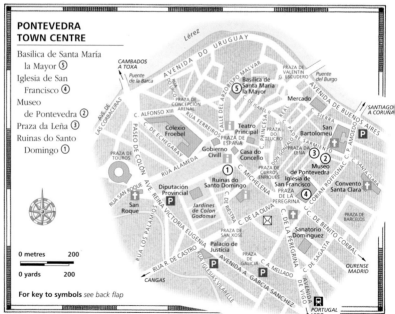

PONTEVEDRA TOWN CENTRE

Basílica de Santa María
la Mayor ⑤
Iglesia de San
Francisco ④
Museo
de Pontevedra ②
Praza da Leña ③
Ruinas do Santo
Domingo ①

0 metres   200
0 yards   200

For key to symbols see back flap

Plateresque west façade, funded by the sailors' guild; its richly sculpted portico resembles a reredos. Next to it is the Jewish Quarter and cemetery.

The church dedicated to Pontevedra's patron saint – the Virgen de la Peregrina – is built to a circular plan and features a bow-fronted façade.

🏛 Museo de Pontevedra
Pasantería 2–12. **Tel** 986 85 14 55.
◯ *Jun–Sep: 10am–2:15pm & 5–8:45pm Tue–Sat, 11am–2pm Sun and holidays; Oct–May: 10am–2pm & 4–7pm Tue–Sat, 11am–2pm Sun & hols.* ● *ruins closed Oct–May.*
Temporary exhibitions ◯ *6–9pm Tue–Sat, 11am–2pm Sun & hols.*
⬚ www.museodepontevedra.es

The ruins of the Gothic Iglesia de Santo Domingo in Pontevedra

Vigo ⓴

Pontevedra. 🏘 *292,000.* ✈ 🚆 🚌
🛈 *Calle Teófilo Llorente 5; 986 22 47 57.* 🖎 *Wed & Sun.* 🎭 *Cristo de los Afligidos (3rd Sun in Jul); Cristo de la Victoria (1st Sun in Aug).*
www.hoxe.vigo.org

Vigo is Galicia's largest city, with a vibrant fishing port and a busy industrial centre. Visitors are drawn to the **Barrio de Berbes**, an old quarter of cobbled alleyways and excellent *tapas* bars. On the **Praza de España**, you can admire the striking modern face of Vigo in the form of Juan José Oliveira's horses statue.

In the surrounding area there are up to 1700 *hórreos* and 30 *cruceiros*, as well as numerous dolmens and the remnants of Celtic settlements *(see p57).*

FISHING IN SPAIN
The Spanish eat more seafood than any other European nation except the Portuguese. Each year, some 61,000 fishermen and 16,000 boats land over a million tonnes of hake, tuna, lobster and other species popular in Spanish cuisine. Nearly half of the fish and shellfish caught in Spain is supplied by the modern Galician fishing fleet, one of the largest in the EU. In recent years, fish stocks in the seas around Europe have become depleted through overfishing, forcing deep-sea trawlers to look for new fishing grounds as far away as Canada or Iceland.

Fishing boats in the port at A Coruña

Baiona ㉑

Pontevedra. 🏘 *12,000.* 🚌 🛈 *Paseo da Ribeira; 986 68 70 67.* 🖎 *Mon.* 🎭 *Festa da Arribada (Mar), Santa Liberata (20 Jul), Virgen Anunciada (1st Sun in Aug).* www.baiona.org

The *Pinta*, one of the caravels from Columbus's fleet, arrived at this small port in 1493, bringing the first news of the discovery of the New World. This event is commemorated in the Festa da Arribada.

Today Baiona, which is sited on a broad bay, is a popular summer resort, its harbour filled with pleasure and fishing boats. There are wonderful beaches here, especially the long Praia America.

A royal fortress once stood on the Monterreal promontory, north of the town. Sections of its defensive walls remain, but the interior has been converted into a smart parador. There are superb views from here.

A Guarda ㉒

Pontevedra. 🏘 *11,300.* 🚌 🛈 *Praza do Reló 1; 986 61 45 46.* 🖎 *Sat.* 🎭 *San Amaro (15 Jan), Fiesta Homara (last weekend in Jun).*

Situated at the end of the Miño river, opposite Portugal, is this small fishing port. On the slopes of Monte de Santa Tecla (a steep climb) are the remains of one of the most complete Celtic *castros* (settlements) in Galicia, dating from the 1st century BC. Also here are the **Museo Arqueológico de Monte Santa Tecla**, a Christian sanctuary, and panoramic views.

🏛 Museo Arqueológico de Monte Santa Tecla
A Guarda. **Tel** 986 61 00 00. ◯
Mar–Dec: 10am–8pm Tue–Sun. ⬚

Environs
Some 13 km (8 miles) north, by the beach at Oia, stands the 12th-century Cistercian **Monasterio de Santa María**.

The Cistercian Monasterio de Santa María de Oia, near A Guarda

Tui ❷

Pontevedra. 🏘 16,300. 🚉 🚌
ℹ️ Edificio área panorámica, Calle
Colón; 986 60 17 89. 🛒 Thu.
🎭 San Telmo (week after Easter),
rafting along the Miño river (Aug).
www.concellotui.org

As the inhabitants of Tui like
to say, their small city is history
carved in stone. It lies on the
Miño river, on the border with
Portugal. The **old quarter**, with
its narrow streets and secret
passageways, has arcaded
houses with coats of arms,
churches and former manor
houses. Rising above this is
the fortress-like 12th-century
Catedral de Santa María.
    The town's defensive walls
and battlements lend it the
appearance of a fortress, and
indeed it performed this role
due to its border location. The
Torre Soutomaior affords a
magnificent view over Tui,
the river, and the Portuguese
town of Valença do Minho.

**A fountain in Tui along the border
between Spain and Portugal**

The banks of the Miño are
linked by the iron **Puente
Internacional** (1884), a bridge
by Gustave Eiffel, and by a
modern motorway bridge.

Environs
Not far from Tui is the hill of
Aloia – a national park with a
wide variety of flora and fauna.
Many archaeological finds
have been made here, including Roman walls. The hill has
good observation points.

Ribadavia ❷

Ourense. 🏘 6,000. 🚉 🚌 ℹ️
Praza Maior 7; 988 47 12 75. 🛒
10th and 25th of each month. 🎭
Feria del Vino del Ribeiro (4th week in
Apr or 1st week in May), Virgen del
Portal (8 Sep). **www**.ribadavia.com

Set in a fertile valley, Ribadavia
has for centuries produced
Ribeiro wines. It was also once
home to a Sephardic community, and a walk through the
Jewish quarter today is like
stepping back in time. The
modest houses, with perfectly
preserved façades, conceal
former *bodegas* within their
walls. The Jewish Information
Centre, housed above the
tourist information office, has
information and exhibitions.

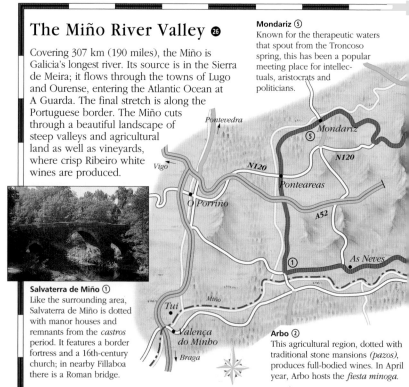

The Miño River Valley ❷

Covering 307 km (190 miles), the Miño is
Galicia's longest river. Its source is in the Sierra
de Meira; it flows through the towns of Lugo
and Ourense, entering the Atlantic Ocean at
A Guarda. The final stretch is along the
Portuguese border. The Miño cuts
through a beautiful landscape of
steep valleys and agricultural
land as well as vineyards,
where crisp Ribeiro white
wines are produced.

Mondariz ⑤
Known for the therapeutic waters
that spout from the Troncoso
spring, this has been a popular
meeting place for intellec-
tuals, aristocrats and
politicians.

Salvaterra de Miño ①
Like the surrounding area,
Salvaterra de Miño is dotted
with manor houses and
remnants from the *castros*
period. It features a border
fortress and a 16th-century
church; in nearby Fillaboa
there is a Roman bridge.

Arbo ②
This agricultural region, dotted with
traditional stone mansions *(pazos)*,
produces full-bodied wines. In April
year, Arbo hosts the *fiesta minoga*.

Pontevedra

Vigo

O Porriño

Ponteareas

N120

N120

A52

As Neves

Mondariz

Tui

Miño

Valença
do Minho

Braga

The Puente San Clodio in the area near Ribadavia

Located on **Praza Maior** are houses with characteristic arcades, a town hall with a wrought-iron belfry and 16th-century tower bearing a sundial, and the Baroque Pazo de los Condes de Ribadavia. Also preserved is the 15th-century **Sarmiento castle**. Important elements of the castle complex are the 9th-century rock-hewn tombs whose outlines reflect those of human figures, and

fragments of the old town walls. The Gothic Casa de Inquisición – an 11th-century House of Inquisition - bears on its façade as many as five coats of arms of families connected with the Holy Office.

By the road leading out of town stands the **Monasterio de Santo Domingo**. The 14th-century monastery church, the best example of local Gothic style, contains medieval tombs.

Ourense ㉕

Ourense. 👥 109,500. 🚆 🚌 ℹ️
Rúa As Burgas 12; 988 36 60 64.
📅 *7th, 17th & 27th of each month.*
🎭 *Os Maios (3 May), Corpus Cristi (Jun), Os Magostos (San Martín, 11 Nov).* www.ourense.es

The town was built around the thermal springs of As Burgas. In Roman times, Ourense also attracted visitors on account of the abundance of gold in the Miño river. The Romans built a 307-m (1007-ft) bridge here, which has been subsequently restored.

Built on the site of a ruined Suevi temple is the **Iglesia de Santa María Madre**, a Baroque church that incorporates 1st-century AD Suevi columns.

The trapezium-shaped **Praza Maior** is lined with 18th- and 19th-century buildings, including the town hall and the former bishop's palace.

The 12th- to 13th-century **Catedral de San Martín** has several entrances. The main one (the Pórtico del Paraíso) has partially preserved polychrome decoration. By the high altar is a huge 16th-century Gothic-Renaissance reredos by Cornelis de Holanda.

The 14th-century **Convento San Francisco** in the Parque San Lázaro houses the **Museo Arqueológico Provincial**.

🏛 **Museo Arqueológico Provincial**
Convento San Francisco. *Tel. 988 22 04 30.* ⏰ *9am–2pm & 4–9pm Tue–Sat, 9am–2pm Sun.*

Detail of the high altar at the Catedral de San Martín in Ourense

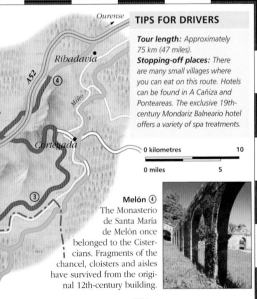

Ourense

TIPS FOR DRIVERS

Tour length: *Approximately 75 km (47 miles).*
Stopping-off places: *There are many small villages where you can eat on this route. Hotels can be found in A Cañiza and Ponteareas. The exclusive 19th-century Mondariz Balneario hotel offers a variety of spa treatments.*

Ribadavia

A52

Miño

Cortegada

0 kilometres   10

0 miles   5

Melón ④
The Monasterio de Santa María de Melón once belonged to the Cistercians. Fragments of the chancel, cloisters and aisles have survived from the original 12th-century building.

Crecente ③
Numerous Roman remains are found here, as well as medieval ones, such as the castle of Fornelos. Excellent observation points can be found in the surrounding area.

KEY

▬ Motorway
▬ Tour route
▬ Scenic route
═ Minor road

Horses on the road to Celanova

Celanova ㉗

Ourense. 🏛 6,000. 🚌 Praza Maior 1; 988 43 22 01. 📅 As Marzas (1–3 Mar), San Roque (16 Aug). **www**.celanova.es

This village of Celanova is known for its unusually large and grand **Praza Maior**. The Benedictine **Monasterio de San Salvador** was founded in the 10th century, though the current church dates from the 18th century. In the garden is the well-preserved 10th-century Mozarabic Capilla de San Miguel.

Environs
In Bande, 26 km (16 miles) south of the village, is the 7th-century **Iglesia de Santa Comba**, one of the few surviving Visigothic shrines in Europe. Built on the plan of a Greek cross, with thick walls, the barrel-vaulted church contains the tomb of St Torcuato.

Allariz ㉘

Ourense. 🏛 5,500. 🚌 🚉 🛈 Calle Alameda; 988 44 20 08. 📅 1st & 15th of each month. 📅 San Benito (11 Jul); A Empanada (Aug). **www**.allariz.com

The most attractive feature of Allariz is its location by the Arnoia river, crossed by a medieval stone bridge, next to which you can swim and hire rowing boats. The town is built on a medieval plan, with narrow streets and old houses decorated with coats of arms. In the **Monasterio de Santa Clara**, visitors can admire a Gothic ivory figure of the Virgin and a crystal cross dating from the same period. Also worth visiting is the **shrine of San Benito**, with a lofty 17th- to 19th-century tower, and the **Parque Etnográfico do Rio Arnoia**, in which there are museums of leather crafts, textiles and toys.

The portal and façade of the Iglesia de Santiago in Allariz

The Sil River Valley ㉛

This picturesque Sil river valley, replete with chestnut and oak trees, is part of the wine-producing region of Ribeira Sacra. Fresh white wines from the *godella* grape, and a few reds using the *mencía* grape, are produced here. The region owes its name to the local monasteries – for centuries, the monks were involved in the cultivation of vines. The Sil valley and its branches are often extraordinarily steep, with vineyards seeming to climb up near-sheer valley sides.

0 kilometres   10
0 miles   5

N120
Embalse de San Pedro ①
Santiago de Compostela
Luíntra   *Ribas de Sil*
N525   *N120*
Ourense
Verín   *C536*   *Esgos* ②
Lebo

The Sil Canyon ①
The Sil river flows through a deep gorge with walls rising 300 m (984 ft). According to legend, Juno disfigured the 'face' of Galicia with a gorge so that Jupiter would not find it appealing.

Monasterio San Pedro de Rocas ②
The ruins of this early Christian monastery include altars in the form of a table and eight anthropomorphic tombs.

Parque Etnográfico do Rio Arnoia

mid-Jul–mid-Sep: noon–2pm Tue–Sun & 7–9pm Thu–Sat; mid-Sep–mid-Jul: noon–2pm & 5–7pm Sat–Sun & hols.

Verín ❷⑨

Ourense. 9,400. Avenida San Lázaro 26–28; 988 41 16 14. 3rd, 11th and 23rd of the month. Lázaro (after Easter), Santa María la Mayor (15 Aug). **www**.verin.net

Verín is noted for its thermal springs, which have therapeutic powers. There are also many 17th-century arcaded houses with glass-encased balconies *(galerías)*, but the area's biggest attraction is **Castillo de Monterrei**, some 3 km (2 miles) to the west. It was built to defend the border during the wars with Portugal; within its three rings of walls is a 15th-century square keep, an arcaded courtyard, and a 13th-century church with an intricately carved portal.

The Monasterio de San Esteban de Ribas de Sil, set high above a gorge

Castillo de Monterrei

Oct–May: 10:30am–1:30pm & 4–7pm Wed–Sun; Jun–Sep: 10:30am–1:30pm & 5–8pm Wed–Sun.

Monasterio de Ribas de Sil ❸⓪

Ourense. San Esteban de Sil (15 km/ 9 miles away). from Ourense (then 15-minute drive); 988 01 01 01. daily.

Near its confluence with the Miño, the Sil river carves an exceptionally deep gorge in which dams form two reservoirs. A hairpin road winds to the top, where the Romanesque-Gothic **monastery of San Esteban de Ribas de Sil** is situated high above the gorge. Some elements of the monastery exhibit different architectural styles, such as the Renaissance cloisters and Baroque façade. The monastery was recently restored and modernized (with a glass wall in the cloisters); the building has now been converted into an exclusive parador.

Parada do Sil ⑤
The Monasterio de Santa Cristina de Ribas de Sil and the Balcones de Madrid observation point, with splendid views, are found here.

Castro Caldelas ④
The town has a 17th-century castle, from which three towers and a wall still survive.

Monasterio de Montederramo ③
The monastery buildings are in Plateresque and Baroque styles, while the church has a Castilian Baroque façade.

KEY

- Tour route
- Scenic route
- Minor road
- Viewpoint

TIPS FOR DRIVERS

Tour length : Approximately 70 km (43 miles).
Organized excursions: Tourist agencies offer guided tours (including a meal) and boat trips along the river; these are arranged by Viajes Pardo **www**.riosil.com and by Hemisferios Viajes **www**.hemisferios.es/ribsacra.htm

Monforte de Lemos **32**

Lugo. 🏘 *19,400.* 🚉 🚌 🛈 *Las Casitas de la Compañía; 982 40 47 15.* 🛒 *6th, 16th, 24th & 30th of each month.* 🎉 *Nuestra Señora de Montserrat (12 Aug), San Mateo (21 Sep).* **www**.concellodemonforte.com

On a hill overlooking the town are the remnants of a fortress – fragments of the massive walls, the palace of the Lemos family and the **Monasterio de San Vicente do Pino** are preserved here. The monastery's Renaissance façade conceals a Gothic interior. Of note is the 30-m (98-ft) tower, from the 13th century. Spanning the Cabe river is a bridge supported on semicircular arches. Originally Roman, the current structure dates from the 16th century.

The **Monasterio de Santa Clara**, dating from the 17th century, accommodates a museum of religious art with some fine Italian reliquaries.

In the suburbs of Monforte stands the **Colegio de Nuestra Señora de la Antigua**, a Piarist (originally Jesuit) college in the Herrera style, dating from the early 16th century. The small picture gallery within displays two paintings by El Greco and five works by the Mannerist painter Andrea del Sarto.

The **Colegio de Nuestra Señora de la Antigua** in Monforte de Lemos

Environs
The Cistercian **Monasterio de Santa María de Oseira**, one of many monasteries in the area, was founded in the 12th century. Its name derives from the word *oso* (bear), as bears once roamed the remote area where it was built. The complex includes a Gothic church, remodelled during the Baroque period, with two huge towers;

Imposing Monasterio de Santa María de Oseira, near Monforte de Lemos

its construction was based on the cathedral in Santiago de Compostela *(see pp62–3)*. The chapterhouse rooms have columns with twisted shafts and capitals resembling palm leaves. The monastery also features a well-preserved staircase in the Herrera style and three cloisters – the Knights', Medallions' and Pinnacles' cloisters, which date from the 16th century. Medicinal liqueurs are produced by the monks who live here.

Sárria **33**

Lugo. 🏘 *13,500.* 🚉 🚌 🛈 *Rúa Maior 14; 982 53 50 00.* 🛒 *6th, 20th, 27th of each month.* 🎉 *San Juan (Jun), Noite Meiga (last Sat in Aug).*

Sárria is a common starting point for pilgrimages to Santiago de Compostela, which lies 111 km (69 miles) away (100 km is the minimum distance required to receive the certificate of completion of the pilgrimage).

The town was established by Alfonso IX, who died en route to Santiago. Due to its location, Sárria had many hostels for pilgrims. The 13th-century hostel near the **church** and **monastery of La Magdalena** has been transformed into a youth hostel, as have many others. The monastery has a Renaissance façade and a late Gothic cloister. Another building that spans Romanesque and Gothic styles is the 13th-century **Iglesia de San Salvador**, beside the **fortress** of the same period, of which only the tower remains. The town also has four medieval bridges, and many Romanesque churches in the surrounding area.

O Cebreiro **34**

Lugo. 🏘 *16.* **Tel** *982 36 70 25.* 🎉 *Virgen de O Cebreiro (8–9 Sep).*

High up in wild, windswept mountain countryside, famous for its volatile weather and with wonderful mountain views, is tiny O Cebreiro. Here are several *pallozas* – Celtic thatched stone huts.

Many pilgrims begin the last stage of the Road to Santiago from here; the local church is one of the oldest monuments on the route. According to legend, the 9th-century pre-Romanesque **Iglesia de Santa María La Real** was the scene of a miracle involving the transformation of bread and wine into the flesh and blood of Christ. Inside the church is a 12th-century chalice, known as the Holy Grail, in which the transformation is said to have taken place. One of the *pallozas* contains the **Museo Etnográfico**, which presents the daily life of the settlement's former inhabitants.

🏛 **Museo Etnográfico**
O Cebreiro. ⬜ *11am–2pm & 3–6pm (7pm in summer) Wed–Sun.*

A typical stone *palloza* with a thatched roof in O Cebreiro

Reserva Nacional de Os Ancares 35

Os Ancares is a mountainous nature park lying on the border between Galicia and León. Thanks to its varied landscape, in which high, snow-covered mountains alternate with deep valleys and rivers and waterfalls, the region boasts an abundance of plants and wildlife, including such rare species as the capercaillie, deer and wild boar. The highest peaks reach an altitude of almost 2,000 m (6,562 ft).

TIPS FOR DRIVERS

Tour length: Approximately 55 km (34 miles).
Stopping-off places: Club Ancares Degrada (*Tel. 982 18 11 13*); Os Ancares Monteiro camp-site; & Campa La Brana mountain shelter (*Tel. 982 29 45 38*).

Navia ⑤
Aside from the picturesque single-span bridge, several *castros* and the castle of the Altamira family are to be found here.

Piornedo ④
Reachable only on foot, Piornedo contains the pre-Roman oval or rectangular thatched huts known as *pallozas*.

Degrada ③
The Degrada trail encompasses the tallest peaks of Os Ancares – Pena Rubia, Tres Obispos, and Mustallar, good for experienced climbers.

Castro de Cervantes ②
The district of Cervantes is home to important historic monuments, such as the castle of Doiras and the *castro* of San Román.

Becerreá ①
Nestled between steep hills and valleys, Becerreá is the starting point of most trails into the park. Here are also several bridges and the 17th-century Monasterio de Santa María.

KEY

▬	Motorway
▬	Tour route
▬	Scenic route
═	Minor road
–·–	Park boundary

Street-by-Street: Lugo ㊱

Lugo is the oldest of Galicia's provincial capitals. A settlement already existed here 2,000 ago, and its name is probably Celtic in origin (*Lugh* means "God of the Light"). The Romans built a wall here, which today encircles the Old Town. Apart from the fortifications in Ávila, it is the best-preserved old town wall in Spain; over the centuries, it enabled the city to be defended against the Suevi, the Moors and Norman pirates.

Virgin in the Cathedral

Nowadays, visitors can walk along the top of the wall, from where there are good views of the city.

Porta Nova

This was the main northern gate, through which people would enter and leave the town. The current gate dates from 1900; it replaced the original gate, which had become unstable.

★ Museo Provincial

Housed in the former monastery of San Francisco, this museum has exhibitions of Celtic and Roman finds and a collection of sundials.

Porta Miña

One of 10 gates in the town walls, the Porta Miña is closest to its original form; also known as Carmen, it gives access to the Miño river.

0 metres	100
0 yards	100

STAR SIGHTS

★ A Mosquera

★ Cathedral

★ Museo Provincial

★ Cathedral

The imposing Romanesque-Gothic cathedral, dating from the 12th century, was modelled on the cathedral in Santiago de Compostela. It has a neo-Classical façade and Baroque cloisters.

CARRIL SAN FROILAN

CARRIL DE AMOR MEILAN

RUA BOLAÑO RIBADENEIRA

QUIROGA

RAMONY Y CAJAL

RUA NOVA

RUA DO MIÑO

PRAZA PIO XII

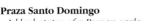

Praza Santo Domingo
*A black statue of a Roman eagle
dominates the Praza Santo
Domingo; it commemorates
Augustus's capture of
Lugo from the Celts in the
1st century BC.*

VISITORS' CHECKLIST

Lugo. 94,300.
Praza Maior 27 (galerías); 982
23 13 61. Tue & Fri.
Corpus Cristi (Jun), San Froilán
(4–12 Oct), Entroido (carnival).
www.concellodelugo.org

Town Hall
*This is one of the more
important buildings in
the secular Galician
Baroque style. Built in
1738, it acquired its
clock tower a few
decades later.*

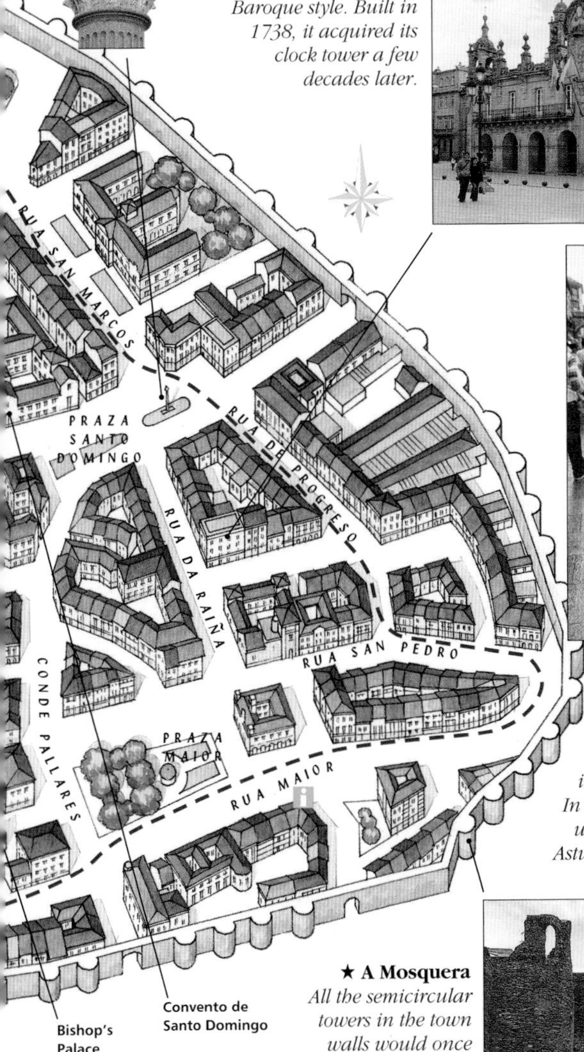

**Pilgrim on the
Road to Santiago**
*The northern route to
Santiago de Compostela
runs through Lugo, link-
ing various coastal towns.
In 829, this pilgrimage was
undertaken by the king of
Asturias, Alfonso the Chaste.*

RUA SAN MARCOS

PRAZA
SANTO
DOMINGO

RUA DE PROGRESO

RUA DA RAIÑA

RUA SAN PEDRO

CONDE PALLARES

PRAZA
MAIOR

RUA MAIOR

★ A Mosquera
*All the semicircular
towers in the town
walls would once
have been topped by
windows, a lone
example of which
can be seen here.*

Bishop's
Palace

Convento de
Santo Domingo

KEY

- - - Suggested route

Exploring Lugo

Lugo's main attraction is its town walls, but also well worth visiting is the maze of Old Town streets, including Rua da Raíña, opened in the 19th century by Isabel II, and the two squares – Praza Santo Domingo and Praza Maior (also known as Praza España), whose colonnades are home to cafés and restaurants. Be sure not to miss the charming Praza do Campo – the old Roman forum. On the Feast of St Vincent, the fountain here spouts wine, not water.

🏛 Town Walls

The 1st- to 2nd-century Roman fortifications are 2 km (1.2 miles) long, 4-7 m (13-22 ft) thick, and up to 12 m (39 ft) high. They are among the best-preserved town walls in Spain, with ten gates (five old and five new) as well as 71 towers. On A Mosquera tower, two broad windows have survived. The main building materials used in the construction of the walls were granite and slate. Visitors can walk along the walls, which form an unbroken circle around the Old Town.

🔒 Cathedral

Museo Diocesano ⬭ Sep–Jun: 11am–noon Mon–Sat; Jul–Aug: 11am–1pm Mon–Sat.
The Romanesque-Gothic cathedral dates from the 12th century and was modelled on the cathedral in Santiago de Compostela (see pp62–3). Over the centuries, it acquired elements of other styles, including a Neoclassical façade and a Baroque cloister.

Also Baroque is the freestanding chapel containing the alabaster statue of the Virgen de los Ojos Grandes, by architect Fernando Casas y Novoa. The cathedral has a Renaissance chancel and altars, and a **Museo Diocesano** set in the cloisters.

The 12th-century Romanesque-Gothic cathedral in Lugo

♟ Bishop's Palace

Rising opposite the cathedral on the beautiful Praza Santa María is the Baroque Bishop's Palace, dating from the 18th century. The palace resembles an aristocratic *pazo*, while the Galician granite used in its construction lends it a certain dignified austerity.

🏛 Town Hall & Praza Maior

The Town Hall in Lugo is one of the more important secular buildings in the Galician Baroque style. It was raised in 1738 by one of the most renowned master-masons of the day, Lucas Ferro Caaveiro. The building dates from the same period as the cathedral's chapel of the Virgen de los Ojos Grandes, and is similarly decorated with gargoyles, turrets, and semicircular arches. The clock tower was added in 1873.

The Town Hall is situated on Praza Maior, which, together with Praza Santo Domingo, forms the hub of Lugo's Old Town. In Roman times, there was probably an amphitheatre on Praza Maior; a market was later established here.

The square is popular with local people, who come to relax in the nearby cafés, or stroll along the tree-lined boulevard that is guarded by two lions that once decorated Praza Maior's now-vanished fountain.

🔒 Iglesia de Santo Domingo

The monastery church of Santo Domingo dates from the 13th century. It was built in a combination of Romanesque and Gothic styles (this can be seen in the three apses with tall windows). The façade is hidden behind the monastery wall, which has 18th-century arcades. The chapel and altars are all Baroque; one of them contains a painting by the 18th-century Galician artist Antonio García Bouzas. Of note are the tomb slabs that are embedded in the walls and are framed by richly decorated arches, in particular the tomb slab of Fernando Díaz Rivadeneyra, which features a figure of the knight.

🏛 Museo Provincial

Praza da Soidade. **Tel** 982 24 21 12. ⬭ Sep–Jun: 10:30am–2pm & 4:30–8:30pm Mon–Fri, 10:30am–2pm & 4:30–8pm Sat, 11am–2pm Sun; Jul–Aug: 11am–2pm & 5–8pm Mon–Fri, 10am–2pm Sat. 🔲 🔲 www.museolugo.org
The museum is housed in the former monastery of San Francisco, of which the cloister, kitchen and refectory have survived. The museum's main aim is to present Galician art, which it achieves well. The exhibits include Celtic and Roman finds (jewellery), coins, ceramics from Sargadelos, sundials and paintings.

Walkers on the Roman walls that encircle Lugo

A wall painting of birds in Santa Eulalia de la Bóveda

Santa Eulalia de la Bóveda ㉗

Lugo. **Tel** 609 23 77 79. ☐ 11am–2pm & 3:30–5pm (in summer 4:30–8:30pm) Tue–Sat, 11am–2pm Sun & public hols.

Situated 14 km (9 miles) from Lugo, this small temple was originally pagan, was later put into use by early Christians, and then forgotten until its rediscovery in 1962.

One of the great mysteries of Lugo province, the building probably dates from the 3rd or 4th century AD, and its purpose has been the subject of various interpretations. Some suggest it was a bathhouse, others say it was a temple to the Phrygian goddess Cybele (the Roman equivalent of the Greek goddess Rea, the mother of all the gods). It is possible that sacrificial bulls and rams were slaughtered here, their blood being collected in a special shallow basin. Centuries later, the temple was used as a church for christenings.

Originally, the church had two storeys, but only the lower one has survived – an almost perfectly preserved square crypt, whose vaulting was damaged during the demolition of the chapel that had been added to the upper floor. Three sides of the crypt are covered with earth; the fourth has two small windows providing the only source of light, apart from the entrance.

Inside the church you can see the atrium leading to the semicircular entrance, the basin, a few columns, various bas-reliefs, and, above all, the barrel vaults covered with murals of birds. The symbolism

of birds seemingly points to the cult of Cybele, but it also facilitated the Christianization of the temple, since St Eulalia is the patron saint of birds.

Vilar de Donas ㉘

Lugo. 🏠 130. 🚍 Carretera de Santiago 28; 982 38 00 01. **Church** ☐ 11am–2pm & 3–6pm Tue–Sun. 🎉 San Antonio (13 Jun), San Salvador (6 Aug).

In this hamlet on the road to Santiago stands the small, aisleless Romanesque **Iglesia de San Salvador**, dating from the early 13th century and built on the plan of a cross. Initially, it belonged to a

The portal of the church of Vilar de Donas

convent, inhabited first by nuns (hence the name – *Donas*) and later by the Knights of the Order of St James. The Knights' Chapter would meet here each year.

Tombs of the knights are preserved inside the church, as are 14th-century Gothic murals depicting biblical scenes and the figures of King Juan II and his wife with melancholy expressions. The external ornamentation comprises plant motifs, birds, figures that are half human and half bird, griffins and angels. The doors of the church bear the original Romanesque fittings – precise and elegant.

Notable, too, is the tower (a later addition) that is visible from afar, and the remnants of the portico, which stands in front of the main western entrance. The church was built of granite, which in places has now become covered with weeds.

Environs
West of Vilar de Donas, the village of **Palas de Rei** has an abundance of Romanesque churches and chapels; there are also several dolmens and *castros* here.

GALICIAN FIESTAS

Os Peliqueiros (Feb/Mar), Laza. Dressed in grinning masks and outlandish costumes, with cowbells, Os Peliqueiros take to the streets on the last Sunday of the carnival.

A Rapa das Bestas (May–Jul), various places. Semi-wild horses are rounded up by local farmers for their manes and tails to be cut.

Flower pavements (May/Jun), Ponteareas and Gondomar. The streets along the Corpus Christi procession are carpeted with designs in petals.

St James's Day (25 Jul), Santiago de Compostela. Firework display in Praza do Obradoiro on the night before.

A band of folk musicians performing at a fiesta in Lugo

ASTURIAS AND CANTABRIA

T*he spectacular Picos de Europa massif sits astride the border between Asturias and Cantabria. In this rural region cottage crafts are kept alive in villages in remote mountain valleys and forested foothills. There are many ancient towns and churches, and pretty fishing ports on the coasts. Cave paintings, such as those at Altamira, were made by people living here over 18,000 years ago.*

An ancient principality, Asturias is also known as the Costa Verde (Green Coast). The secluded mountain valleys and wooded hills have attracted settlers to the region since time immemorial. Asturias is proud that it resisted invasion by the Moors. The Reconquest of Spain is traditionally held to have begun in 718, when a Moorish force was defeated by Christians at Covadonga in the Picos de Europa.

The Christian kingdom of Asturias was founded in the 8th century, and in the brilliant, brief artistic period that followed many churches were built around the capital, Oviedo. Some of them still stand. In 1037 Asturias was absorbed into Castile.

Asturias was a strong player in the 19th-century industrial revolution in Spain, with coal mining from Gijón to Oviedo, and steelmaking and ship-building in Gijón. Though much of this industry has closed, its legacy is reflected in the Austurian character, which is rough-edged but friendly. Today Asturian towns have a lively cultural life.

Cantabria centres on Santander, its capital, a port and a lively resort. It is a mountainous province with a legacy of isolated Romanesque churches and well-preserved towns and villages such as Santillana del Mar, Carmona and Bárcena Mayor.

Mountains cover more than half of both provinces, so mountain sports are a major attraction. Expanses of deciduous forests remain, some sheltering Spain's dwindling population of wild bears. Equally beguiling is the beautiful coast, with pretty fishing ports and resorts, such as Castro Urdiales, Ribadesella and Comillas, and sandy coves for bathing.

A picturesque *ría* in the vicinity of San Vicente de la Barquera

◁ The 12th-century Colegiata de Santa Juliana in Santillana del Mar

Exploring Asturias and Cantabria

The biggest attraction in this area is the group of mountains that straddles the two provinces – the Picos de Europa. These jagged peaks offer excellent rock climbing and rough hiking. The coast offers sandy coves, spectacular cliffs and remote villages. Santander and Oviedo are lively university cities with a rich cultural life. There are innumerable unspoiled villages to explore, especially the ancient town of Santillana del Mar. Some of the earliest examples of art exist in Cantabria, most notably at Altamira, where the cave drawings and engravings are among the oldest to be found in Europe. It is also worth going slightly further afield to visit some interesting places that lie just outside the region, in Castilla-León, such as El Bierzo, with its medieval monasteries, the Roman town of Astorga, and León.

A flower-covered balcony in Bárcena Mayor, Valle de Cabuerniga

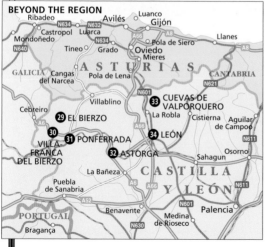

GETTING AROUND

The main road through the region is the N634. Most other major roads run north to south. Minor roads are generally good but can be slow and winding. The private FEVE railway, which follows the coast from Bilbao to Ferrol, in Galicia, is extremely scenic. A twice-weekly Brittany Ferries service links Santander with Plymouth. Asturias has a small international airport near Avilés. Be aware that as Spain is changing its road-numbering system some roads featured here may differ from new road signs.

| 0 kilometres | 25 |
| 0 miles | 25 |

SIGHTS AT A GLANCE

The Virgin and Child,
Convento de la Regina
in Santillana del Mar

SEE ALSO

• *Where to Stay* pp204–6.

• *Where to Eat* pp 221–3.

A view along the crowded beach of Playa del Camello, Santander

KEY

 Motorway

 Motorway under construction

 Major road

 Minor road

 Scenic route

 Main railway line

 Regional border

△ Summit

⤬ Bridge

Castropol **1**

Asturias. **i** *Plaza del Ajuntamiento; 98 536 50 01.* 🎭 *Corpus Cristi (May–Jun).*

This pretty fishing port, with its narrow streets and white-washed buildings, occupies the eastern bank of the Eo river, which marks the border between Asturias and Galicia. The town lies opposite Ribadeo in Galicia *(see p52)*. Its name derives from nine well-preserved *castros*, or ancient Celtic settlements with dwellings arranged in a circle.

For centuries, the town was an important commercial centre, where trade in grain, timber, iron, salt, wine and textiles flourished. The significance of the port was recognized by King Juan I of Castile, who in 1386 accorded it numerous privileges.

Castropol also played an important role as a town situated on the pilgrimage route to Santiago de Compostela. The parish **Iglesia de Santiago** dates from the 17th century, having been built on the site of an earlier church. Until the 19th century, it served as a shelter for weary pilgrims.

Also noteworthy is the **Capilla Santa María**, built in 1461, with a Gothic alabaster figure of the Virgin and Child inside. It was apparently the only building in the town to have escaped the devastating fire of 1587.

Of interest, too, are the palaces that once belonged to the port's richer inhabitants, such as the Palacio Vellador, the Palacio de los Marqueses de Santa Cruz, and the Palacio Villarosita, which bear family coats of arms on their façades.

The town's green space is the **Parque de Vicente Loriente**, opened in 1911; it is named after a Cuban émigré who undertook several initiatives to aid the town's development.

Taramundi **2**

Asturias. 🏘 *800.* **i** *Avenida Galicia; 985 64 68 77.* 🎭 *San José (19 Mar), Día del Turista (last Sun in Jul).* www.taramundi.net

Situated in the remote Los Oscos region, on the border with Galicia, is the small village of Taramundi. In the surrounding forests visitors can admire not only the beautiful natural environment but also acquaint themselves with the traditions of local craftsmanship at various forges. The tourist information office can provide information on five hiking routes through the area. Of particular interest is **Grandas de Salime** – 30 km (19 miles) to the southeast – where handicrafts are displayed in the local **Museo Etnográfico**. Yet Taramundi is celebrated above all for its tradition of wrought-iron craftsmanship. Iron ore was first mined in the area by the Romans, and today there are approximately 13 forges in and around the village, where craftsmen can be seen making traditional knives with decorated wooden handles. Here, the skill of artistic smithery is still passed down from father to son.

Taramundi is also justly renowned for the high-quality liqueurs produced here.

Detail of the monument to Fernando Villamil in Castropol

🏛 **Museo Etnográfico**
Calle del Ferreiro 17. **Tel.** *985 62 72 43.* ◯ *11:30am–2pm & 4–6:30pm (until 7:30pm Jul–Aug) Tue–Sat, 11:30am–2:30pm Sun.* 🎦

Castro de Coaña **3**

Asturias. 🚉 *5 km (3 miles) SW of Navia.* **Tel.** *985 97 84 01.* ◯ *Apr–Sep: 11am– 2:30pm & 4–7pm Tue–Sun; Oct–Mar: 11am–2:30pm Tue–Sun.* 🎦 ♿

This is one of the most important centres of Celtic-Iberian culture. *Castros* were the most common type of settlement at the end of the Bronze Age, consisting of chaotically arranged circular dwellings surrounded by moats and palisades. The Castro de Coaña, with its 80 dwellings spread over a hillside in the Navia valley, dates from the Iron Age; the first archaeological digs took place here in 1877. The on-site museum displays many of the finds that have been unearthed.

Environs
Nearby, in a picturesque location at the foot of the mountains, is **Navia**, a typical Asturian fishing village. On 15 August is its festival of the cult of the Virgin, who, according to legend, saved a group of fishermen from drowning in a stormy sea. The *fiesta* is a good time to sample the local delicacy – *Venera de Navia*, a beautifully decorated almond cake.

There are beautiful beaches just to the east at **Frexulfe**.

The remains of a Celtic settlement in Castro de Coaña

**The old harbourmaster's office
near the seafront in Luarca**

Luarca ❹

Asturias. 🏠 5,720. 🚉 🚌 🛈 Calle
Los Caleros 11; 985 64 00 83.
🎭 Noche Celta (last Sat in Jul), Rosario
(15 Aug), San Timoteo (22 Aug).

Luarca is nicknamed Villa
Blanca de la Costa Verde
(White Town on the Green
Coast) on account of its
houses with white façades.
This picturesque fishing port,
specializing in tuna, arose at
the mouth of the meandering
Rio Negro, across which
many bridges have been built.
On a cliff overlooking the
narrow beach are a chapel
and an impressive lighthouse.
    Luarca is considered to be
one of the most attractive
places on the northern coast.
Its traditional character is
reflected in the charmingly
old-fashioned *chigres*, or
tavernas, where one can
sample the excellent local
cider. The port is brimming
with bars and restaurants
offering inexpensive fresh fish,
which is sold every day in the
afternoon once the fishermen
have returned with their catch.
    The most beautiful building
in Luarca is undoubtedly the
town hall, which was commissioned in 1906 by an influential
family who had returned after
making a fortune in Spain's
colonies. Some of the rooms
have been converted into
exclusive tourist accommodation. Luarca's most important
fiesta is San Timoteo, which
begins in the evening of 21
August with a fireworks
display on the seafront.

Cudillero ❺

Asturias. 🏠 500. 🛈 Puerto del Oeste;
985 59 13 77. 🗓 Fri. 🎭 San Pedro
(29 Jun). www.cudillero.org

With its streets winding down
an impossibly steep cliffside
to end at a picture-perfect
harbour, this fishing village
attracts large numbers of
visitors, thanks to its outdoor
cafés and excellent seafood
restaurants. The houses, with
their red roofs, seem to merge
imperceptibly with the hillsides that cascade down
towards the sea.
    Its name derives from the
word *codillo* (elbow), referring
to the shape of the village.
The place looks most seductive
in the evenings, when
attractively lit – a pleasant
walk can be made to the port
and observation point, from
where there is a panoramic
view of the surrounding area.
The view certainly inspired
director José Luis Garci, who
shot here some of the scenes
of *Volver a Empezar* – the first
Spanish film to win an Oscar.
    The port boasts fine architec-
ture. The oldest buildings are
a 13th-century Romanesque
chapel – the **Capilla de
Humilladero** – and the Gothic
Iglesia de San Pedro, dating
from the 16th century. On 29
June, when a *fiesta* in honour
of St Peter is held, locals meet
on the plaza to describe to
each other, in a humorous and
ironic way, the events of the
previous year in local dialect.

A verdant square in Pravia, near Cudillero

Environs
Some 10 km (6 miles) south of
Cudillero is **Pravia**, with its
charming 12th-century Capilla
de la Virgen de Valle.

**The façade of the 16th-century
Iglesia de Santa María in Salas**

Salas and
Valle del Narcea ❻

Asturias. 🏠 7,000. 🚌 🛈 Plaza de
la Campa (Salas); 985 83 09 88.
🎭 Fiesta del Bollo (3rd week in Aug).

Salas is the birthplace of the
Marquis de Valdés-Salas, the
founder of the university in
Oviedo and one of the main
instigators of the Inquisition.
The main highlight is the
beautiful Old Town, built
around the imposing **castle**,
which once served as the
residence of the archbishop.
    The **Iglesia de San Martín**
was consecrated in
896 and later rebuilt
in the 10th century.
Also noteworthy
is the collegiate
**Iglesia de Santa
María**, which dates
from 1549 and is
situated on the
main square.
    South of Salas
extends a beautiful,
wild valley known
as the **Valle del
Narcea**. Green and
secluded, it is an
excellent place for
walking, hiking and
fishing. The villages
here are known for
fine ham and
traditional crafts.

The 12th-century Iglesia de San Nicolás de Bari in Avilés

Avilés ❼

Asturias. 🏛 83,000. 🛈 Calle Ruiz Gómez 21; 985 54 43 25. 🕒 Mon. 🎉 San Agustín (28 Aug).

Ringed by large factories, Avilés is an industrial town once known for steel production; it is also an important transport hub, with services to many destinations. Visitors should head straight for the Plaza de España in the Old Town, which is surrounded by 14th- and 15th-century buildings. Here, too, are the majority of shops, bars and hotels, as well as the vast **Parque de Ferrera**, covering an area of 80,000 sq m (20 acres), which is maintained in the style of an English garden. Well worth visiting is the 12th-century Romanesque **Iglesia de San Nicolás de Bari**, occupying the site of an earlier pre-Romanesque shrine, which was built as part of a Franciscan monastery. The church contains a beautiful 14th-century chapel as well as the fine Spanish-Flemish tomb of the first Governor of the American state of Florida.

The town boasts four well-preserved palaces: the 14th-century **Palacio de Valdecarzana**, the oldest secular building in Avilés; the **Palacio del Marqués de Camposagrado**, completed in 1663 but Renaissance in appearance; the **Palacio de Ferrera**, from the start of the 18th century, frequented by visiting royalty; and the early 20th-century **Palacio de Balsera**, which accommodates a music conservatory.

Gijón ❽

Asturias. 🏛 274,000. 🚉 🚌 🛈 Calle Rodríguez San Pedro; 985 34 17 71. 🕒 Sun. 🎉 San Pedro (29 Jun), La Virgen de Begoña (15 Aug). **www.**gijon.info

Gijón is Asturias' largest city, with a metal- and chemical-producing industry, but still an enjoyable place to visit. There are interesting museums, nice beaches and a lively nightlife. A good place to start a tour is the **Parque del Cerro de Santa Catalina**, which features the 1990 sculpture *Elogio del Horizonte* – the symbol of the city – by the Basque artist Eduardo Chillida.

Near the park is Gijón's most interesting building – the Baroque **Palacio de Revillagigedo**. Built between 1704 and 1721 at the initiative of Carlos Miguel Ramírez de Jove, the first Marquis of Esteban del Mar, it accommodates a Centre for Modern Art, opened in 1991. Opposite the palace stands a statue of Pelayo, the Visigothic ruler who began the Reconquest *(see p37)*. Nearby is the **Torre del Reloj**, a modern tower erected on the site of a 16th-century building; there are beautiful views of the city and its attractive surroundings from the top of the tower.

This part of Gijón, stretching out along a headland, is called **Cimadevilla**. Fishermen began to settle here in Roman times. Today, the district has preserved its maritime character, offering visitors one of the

most breathtaking views of the Cantabrian Sea. Narrow streets cluster around the Plaza Mayor, with its 19th-century town hall, near to which stands the **Museo Casa Natal de Jovellanos**. This 16th-century house is the birthplace of Gaspar Melchor de Jovellanos, an eminent 18th-century author, reformer and diplomat. The house, which dates from the end of the 16th century, abuts the walls of the medieval citadel. To the right of the Plaza Mayor are the **Baños Romanos**, or Roman baths, built in the 1st century BC.

The seafront leads to the long sandy beach, **Playa San Lorenzo**, which is popular with surfers.

The **Museo del Pueblo de Asturias**, opened in 1968, has a wealth of documentation as well as an archive and library. You can learn about the history

The balcony of a house on Calle del Marqués de San Esteban, Gijón

---

ASTURIAN BAGPIPES

In Spain, the Celtic legacy is also evident in bagpipe music, which combines elements of Celtic and Iberian culture. There are six types of bagpipes, the best-known being the Galician *(gaita)* and the slightly larger Asturian. Although similar in appearance to Scottish bagpipes, they differ in terms of the number of bourdon pipes as well as range and fingering. Air from the leather bellows is squeezed into the two pipes, which produce the characteristic rich sound. Men dressed in traditional Asturian costume can often be seen on the streets of Asturias playing old folk melodies.

Musician playing the bagpipes

The port in Gijón, with the Palacio de Revillagigedo in the background

of Asturias, see the interior of a traditional Asturian cottage, or visit one of the numerous exhibitions on local history that are held here. Occupying an area of 35,000 sq m (376,700 sq ft) are two granaries, a period house from 1759 (Casa de los Valdés) and a typical homestead from the central part of the Asturian region, among other exhibits. In 1993, the pavilion that had showcased Asturias at '92 Expo in Seville was transferred to the museum premises. Today, it houses a permanent exhibition

entitled "Asturians in the Kitchen. Everyday Life in Asturias, 1800–1965". Part of the museum, in a house dating from 1757, is the **Museo de la Gaita** (Bagpipe Museum), which contains a collection of instruments from Europe and North Africa.

Art enthusiasts will be drawn to the **Museo de**

The Museo de la Gaita in Gijón

Evaristo Valle, devoted to the Asturian painter Evaristo Valle (1873–1951), which is hidden away among the gardens of the La Redonda estate. The museum has more than 200 works by the artist, including his well-known *Dusk* (1903), *Emigrants* (1904) and *Pierrot* (1909).

Cabo de Peñas, the small peninsula between Avilés and Gijón, has good beaches, impressive dunes, and little resorts at **Luanco** and **Candás**.

🏛 Museo Casa Natal de Jovellanos

Plazoleta Jovellanos. *Tel* 985 18 51 52. ☐ Jul–Aug: 11am–1:30pm & 5–9pm, Tue–Sat, 11am–2pm & 5–7pm Sun & hols; Sep–Jun: 10am–1pm & 5–8pm Tue–Sat, 11am–2pm & 5–8pm Sun & hols.

🏛 Museo del Pueblo de Asturias

Paseo del Doctor Fleming 877. *Tel* 985 18 29 60 ☐ Jul–Aug: 11am–1:30pm & 5–9pm Tue–Sat, 11am–2pm & 5–8pm Sun & hols; Sep–Jun: 10am–1pm & 5–8pm Tue–Sat, 11am–2pm & 5–7pm Sun & hols. 🈚 (free Sun).

🏛 Museo de Evaristo Valle

Camino de Cabueñas 261 (Somió). *Tel* 985 33 40 00. ☐ May–Oct: 5–8pm Tue–Sat, noon–2pm Sun & hols; Nov–Apr: 4–6pm Tue–Sat, noon–2pm Sun & hols. 🈚 🈯

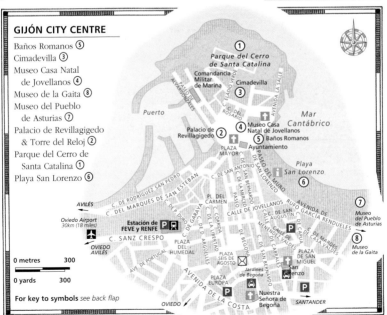

GIJÓN CITY CENTRE

0 metres 300
0 yards 300

For key to symbols *see back flap*

Street-by-Street: Oviedo ❾

Oviedo, considered to be one of the most beautiful cities in northern Spain, is also the country's oldest Christian city. Founded in the 8th century at the initiative of the Asturian ruler Fruela, son of Alfonso I, it soon became the cultural and commercial capital of the region. To this day, Oviedo boasts one of the best universities in Spain. The delightful Old Town, with its narrow winding streets, invites visitors to contemplate the rich artistic legacy of the capital of Asturias.

Palacio de Valdecarzana
The façade of this 18th- to 19th-century palace is adorned with a huge coat of arms of the Heredia family, the former owners of the residence.

Palacio de Camposagrado
This magnificent 18th-century building is today the seat of the regional court.

The Plaza de Porlier is home to *El Viajero*, a sculpture by Eduardo Úrculo.

Palacio de la Rúa
This small palace, dating from the 15th century, is the oldest secular building in Oviedo.

STAR SIGHTS

★ Catedral de San Salvador

★ Iglesia de San Tirso

★ Museo de Bellas Artes

Ayuntamiento
Built in the 16th and 17th centuries, this imposing town hall was destroyed during the Civil War; it was meticulously rebuilt in 1939–40.

★ Catedral de San Salvador

Built from the late 14th to the early 16th centuries, the cathedral's flamboyant Gothic interior houses many works of Asturian art, including two gold crosses – the Cross of Angels and the Cross of Victory.

VISITORS' CHECKLIST

Asturias. 209,000. Marqués de Santa Cruz (Oviedo); 985 22 75 86. Calle Uria (Asturias); 985 21 33 85; Thu & Sun. San Mateo (21Sep).

Monasterio San Pelayo
Inside this 12th-century monastery is an imposing sculpture of Pelayo – the ruler of the Visigoths and a national hero.

PLAZA ALFONSO II EL CASTO"

SANTA ANA

★ Iglesia de San Tirso
This 9th-century church has been rebuilt several times. Apart from the triforium in the eastern wall, it has lost its original pre-Romanesque appearance.

PLAZA MAYOR

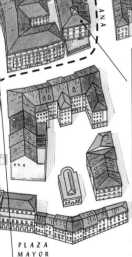

The medieval Plaza de Alfonso II is the historic centre of Oviedo; the city's most important buildings are concentrated in its vicinity.

★ Museo de Bellas Artes
Opened in 1980, this museum houses rich collections of Spanish art from the 15th to the 20th centuries, as well as Asturian, Italian and Flemish works.

| 0 metres | | 50 |
| 0 yards | | 50 |

KEY

‑ ‑ ‑ Suggested route

Exploring Oviedo

Although many of Oviedo's historic monuments were destroyed during the Civil War, the city centre still has several medieval churches and squares as well as 19th-century tenements. Most of the buildings are located around the Plaza de Alfonso II, making it easy to explore the city on foot.

South of the Plaza Mayor is one of the oldest parts of Oviedo, with charming narrow streets that converge on the **Plaza del Fontán**, home to a lively food market and surrounded by striking old traditional buildings above colonnaded porticos, which have been restored and now house an attractive range of restaurants and cafés.

🔒 Catedral de San Salvador

⬜ *Mar–May: 10am–1pm & 4–7pm Mon–Sat; Jul–Sep: 1–8pm Mon–Sat; Jun & Oct–Feb: 10am–1pm & 4–6pm Mon–Sat.* 📷

Dating from the 16th century, Oviedo's cathedral is the best example in Asturias of the style known as flamboyant Gothic. In the 9th century, Alfonso II ordered the construction of the Cámara Santa. Part of this chapel, which was meant to house reliquaries recovered from Toledo after the Moorish invasion, does indeed date from Alfonso's reign; the other, Romanesque part is the result of remodelling carried out in 1109. Alfonso II's tomb

The medieval Plaza de Alfonso II "El Casto"

is found inside the cathedral, as is a gilded altar of 1525 – one of the largest in Spain – by Giralte of Brussels.

🔒 Iglesia de San Tirso

Also on the Plaza Alfonso II, "El Casto", to the left of the cathedral, stands the Iglesia de San Tirso, commissioned by King Alfonso II at the end of the 8th century. This aisled structure, on a basilican plan, was restored several times. It has consequently lost its original appearance, except for the triforium in the eastern wall, whose columns are adorned with plant motifs. Of note, too, is the Gothic chapel of St Anne, which was destroyed during a fire and later rebuilt by Juan Caeredo in the second half of the 16th century.

🏛 Plaza Alfonso II, "El Casto" & Palacio de la Rúa

🔘 *closed to the public.*

The nucleus of the medieval city is this stately square, also known as Plaza de la Catedral, though officially named in honour of the founder of the capital of Asturias, King Alfonso II. After defeating the Moors, Alfonso transferred the Asturian court to Oviedo in 792 and turned the town into an important pilgrimage centre.

The flamboyant Gothic Catedral de San Salvador

On the square stands the fortress-like Palacio de la Rúa, built by Alonso González, the treasurer to the Catholic Monarchs, Fernando and Isabel. This elegant and beautiful small 15th-century palace is thought to be the oldest secular building in Oviedo.

🏛 Palacio de Camposagrado

Praza Porlier. 🔘 *closed to the public.*

Commissioned by José Bernaldo de Quirós in the first half of the 18th century, the massive four-storey Palacio de Campo-sagrado was designed by two renowned architects: Francisco de la Riba Ladrón de Guevara and, after 1746, his pupil Pedro Antonio Menéndez de Ambás. The Baroque palace sports a Rococo façade embellished with masks, shields, cornices and fanciful recesses.

🏛 Palacio Toreno

Plaza del Portlier 5.

The palace was designed in 1663 for the Malleza Doriga family by the architect Gregorio de la Roza. Featuring an asymmetrical Baroque façade, the building accommodates the head-quarters of RIDEA (Real Instituto de los Estudios Asturianos), or the Royal Institute for Asturian Studies, which was established in 1946 with the purpose of encouraging research on Asturian culture. Inside the building is a patio with Tuscan columns.

🏛 The University

Oviedo's international university was founded in 1608 by the Inquisitor and Archbishop of Seville, Valdés-Salas; it was officially opened on 21 September 1608. The present rectorate building was designed by Bracamonte and Juan de Rivero. Especially impressive is the library, designed by Rodrigo Gil de Hontañón. In the 19th century, Oviedo University was one of ten universities in Spain; today, it is the only public institution of higher education in Asturias.

🏛 Museo de Bellas Artes

Calle Santa Ana 1. **Tel** 985 21 30 61. ☐ Jul–Aug: 11am–4:30pm & 5–9pm Tue–Sat, 11am–2:30pm Sun & hols; Sep–Jun: 10:30am–2pm & 4:30–8:30pm Tue–Fri, 11:30am–2pm & 5–8pm Sat, 11:30am–2:30pm Sun & hols. ♿ www.bbaa.com

In the city's old quarter, just next to the cathedral, Oviedo's Museum of Fine Art occupies three buildings: the Palacio de Velarde (1767); the Baroque Casa Oviedo-Portal (1660) by the Cantabrian architect Melchior de Velasco; and a building from the 1940s. The museum, opened in 1980, boasts the most exciting collections in the

The spacious interior of the Museo de Bellas Artes

region. The permanent exhibition comprises Spanish painting from the 15th to the 20th centuries, Asturian art, Italian and Flemish works from the 14th to the 18th centuries, as well as Spanish and Asturian sculpture from the 15th to the 20th centuries. In total, the museum's inventory numbers 8,000 items, including works by Goya, Murillo, Zurbarán, Picasso, Dalí and Miró.

🏛 Plaza Mayor and Iglesia San Isidoro

On this square, also known as Plaza Constitución (Constitution Square), stands the town hall, which dates from the 16th–17th century.

THE FIRST KINGS OF ASTURIAS

By the time Asturias was annexed by the kingdom of León in 910, 13 rulers had sat on the Asturian throne. The first of these was the legendary Pelayo (718–35). Another outstanding ruler was Alfonso I (739–51), who undertook several armed raids in the Duero river basin. The new state grew powerful during the reign of Alfonso II (791–842), whose contemporary was Charlemagne, with whom he maintained close contact. Alfonso's successor, Ramiro I (842–50), was another colourful figure: an avid art enthusiast, he began the construction of several pre-Romanesque churches in the vicinity of Oviedo that still exist to this day.

A statue of Alfonso II, known as "El Casto" (the Chaste) (791–842)

Almost completely destroyed during the Civil War, the town hall was rebuilt in 1939-40. Looming over the square is the tower of the Jesuit Iglesia de San Isidoro, which adjoins a college that was run by the Jesuits until 1767, when Carlos III banished them from the city. The church, featuring a neo-Classical façade and Baroque ornamentation within, was consecrated in 1681. The building has only one tower; a second, identical tower was planned but was never completed.

🏛 Museo Arqueológico Provincial

Calle San Vicente 5. **Tel** 985 21 54 05. ● closed for restoration.

Since 1952, the Archaeological and Ethno-graphical

A sculpture depicting traders at the market in Oviedo

Museum has been housed in the old Benedictine monastery of San Vicente, founded in 761. On display are Palaeolithic tools, Roman finds – including a beautiful mosaic from Vega del Ciego – pre-Romanesque treasures, such as an altar from the Iglesia de Santa María del Naranco, as well as Romanesque and Gothic exhibits. The permanent exhibitions are arranged thematically.

🏛 Monasterio de San Pelayo

Calle de San Pelayo 5. ● closed to public.

San Pelayo is a functioning Benedictine monastery with a strict monastic rule, and is therefore closed to visitors. Its construction was begun in the 10th century under the patronage of Teresa Ansúrez, the widow of Sancho de León, dubbed El Gordo (The Fat One). Initially, the church was to be dedicated to St John the Baptist, but this was changed in 987 when the reliquary of the martyr San Pelayo was brought to Oviedo. Imprisoned by the Moors, Pelayo refused to relinquish his faith, for which he was brutally tortured: his hands and his feet were cut off, and he was beheaded on 26 June 925. Pelayo's remains were recovered from the river into which they had been cast, and they were taken to León, from where they were trans-ferred to Oviedo (see p37).

Romanesque Churches of Oviedo

Established in the 10th century, the Kingdom of Asturias cultivated Visigothic traditions, creating a local, highly original style of art known as Asturian. Long before the appearance of Romanesque, the Asturian style was characterized by barrel vaults covering entire buildings, the use of buttressing and elongated arches, as well as sculptural decoration in low relief, inspired by Visigothic art. Preserved around Oviedo are several superb examples of this style, such as Santa María del Naranco, San Miguel de Lillo and San Julián de los Prados, which are considered to be the most interesting historic monuments in Asturias.

Santa María del Naranco
The interior of this aisleless church is illuminated by sunlight entering through the arcaded galleries (solaria) – a novel solution in European architecture of the time.

Arcaded galleries create a light church interior

Triple-arched Windows
The arches of the arcades are slightly elongated rather than semicircular, which lends the building a certain slenderness.

Byzantine Medallion
The interior of Santa María del Naranco features, among other things, a Byzantine medallion. There are also medallions above the columns supporting the arcades.

The column shafts are carved with a rope motif.

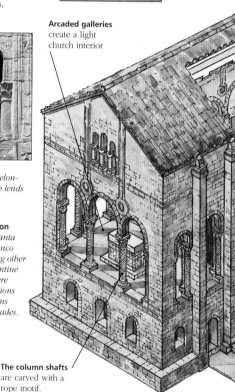

Church Interior
The grand and austere interior of the church is built on a rectangular plan, 20 m (66 ft) long and 60m (197ft) wide. The use of barrel vaults with a 6-m (20-ft) span was a major technical achievement.

SANTA MARÍA DEL NARANCO

The church, built in 848, was used as a royal chamber known as the *aula regia*, where royal councils of the court of King Ramiro I would be held. It was a two-storey building, with its lower part divided into three sections.

San Julián de los Prados

Also known as Santullano, this is the oldest pre-Romanesque shrine in Asturias. It was built by Alfonso II in 812-42.

Murals

The Iglesia de San Julián de los Prados boasts lavish murals with plant and geometrical motifs. The colours are still vibrant today.

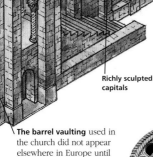

Richly sculpted capitals

The barrel vaulting used in the church did not appear elsewhere in Europe until the 11th century.

San Miguel de Lillo

The Church of the Archangel Michael was built in the 9th century by Ramiro I as a royal chapel. Following 18th-century remodelling, it now resembles a Byzantine building. It was made a UNESCO World Heritage Site in 1985.

Columns

The richly carved stone columns feature the spiral rope motif (soqueado) – a decorative element typical of the Romanesque style. The capitals are embellished with plant motifs.

Decorative Elements

The Iglesia de San Miguel de Lillo is famous for its decorative motifs, based on geometric and animal themes.

The 12th-century Iglesia de San Pedro in Teverga

Valle de Teverga ⑩

Asturias. 🛈 *Plaza del Ayuntamiento;*
985 76 42 93. 🎎 *Nuestra Señora*
del Cébrano (15 Aug).
www.infoteverga.com

This area, almost half of which
is covered in forest, lies to the
south of Oviedo. Its main
attractions are wild scenery,
three meandering rivers
(Valdesanitbanez, Valde-
sanpedro and Valdecarzana)
and foaming waterfalls. Wild
animals, such as foxes, deer
and chamois, can be spotted
here. No less interesting,
however are the caves – Cueva
Huerta, Cueva de Vistulaz and
Vegalonga – with their fascinating prehistoric wall paintings.

The regional capital is **La
Plaza**, whose **Iglesia de San
Pedro**, built in 1069-76, is
picturesquely set among hills.
The church features a small
but interesting exhibition of
18th-century Asturian
painting. Just to the west of
La Plaza is **Villanueva**, with its
equally beautiful Romanesque
Iglesia de Santa María.

The local culinary delicacies
of Teverga are roast mutton
and *masera* cheese – a must
for visiting gourmets.

Barzana and
Bermiego ⑪

🛈 *Ayuntamiento, Quirós; 985 76
81 60.*

Among the most beautiful
mountain villages in Asturias,
it was here that the Visigothic
aristocracy hid during the
Moorish invasion.

Both Barzana and Bermiego
are primarily known for their

excellent bread and colourful
fiestas. Bermiego, which is
surrounded by the Gamonitero
and Gamonal hills, features
traditional red-roofed houses
and characteristic *bórreos* –
wooden structures built on
stone pillars to prevent rodents
from eating the grain stored
inside. It's an easy hike to the
summit of Gamonitero, from
which there are beautiful
panoramic views. Next to the

A typical red-roofed wooden
hórreo (granary) in Barzana

THE BROWN BEAR

The brown bear – Europe's
largest land predator – is found
in the mountain regions of
Asturias and in nature reserves
such as Somiedo. It is adept at
navigating the steep hillsides in
search of forest fruits, frogs,
birds and eggs. In the Middle
Ages, the brown bear enjoyed
respect, as evidenced by the fact
that images of the animal often
appeared in coats of arms.
Today, however, hunting and
the destruction of the natural
forest habitat have caused a
rapid decline in numbers.

church of Santa María stands
a locally famous yew tree of
impressive dimensions: 140 m
(460 ft) high, and with a trunk
some 13 m (43 ft) in diameter.

Barzana is another attractive
village. Of greatest interest to
the visitor is undoubtedly the
Museo Etnográfico de Quirós,
which opened in 1998 on the
site of a former marketplace.
The aim of the museum is to
present life in the Asturian
countryside in times past. On
the first floor are a series of
reconstructed farm buildings
and cattle pens; on the second,
a display of tools and craft
products. The museum also
puts on temporary exhibitions.

🏛 **Museo Etnográfico
de Quirós**
Barzana. **Tel** *985 76 80 96.*
🕐 *May–Sep: 11:30am–2pm &
5–7:30pm Wed–Sun; Oct–Apr:
11:30am–1:30pm & 4–6pm
Wed–Sun.* 🎎 🎫 *(call in advance).*

Parque Natural
de Somiedo ⑫

🛈 *Centro de Recepción, Pola de
Somiedo; 958 76 37 58.*
www.somiedorural.com

One of the wildest pieces of
wilderness left in western
Europe, this large park
straddles the Cantabrian
mountains, covering an area
of 300 sq km (116 sq miles).
Somiedo is one of the most
representative mountain
ecosystems on the Iberian
Peninsula, its beech and oak
forests providing a sanctuary

Brown bear in the Parque
Natural de Somiedo

for wolves, brown bears and capercaillies (a large European grouse). The post-glacial Saliencia lakes are remarkable for their breathtaking settings and diverse geology. The largest of them, Lago del Valle, is also the largest lake in Asturias, and is situated at an altitude of 1,550 m (5,085 ft) above sea level. The park is home to several species of wild flowers, which temper the harsh landscape.

Traditional thatched stone cabins, or *teitos*, are the park's most distinguishing feature. Herdsman live in these cabins in spring and summer while their animals graze on the mountain pastures.

Geologically, the landscape of the park is made up of slate, sandstone, quartzite and limestone.

Stone cabins with thatched roofs in the Parque Natural de Somiedo

Valdediós ⑬

Asturias. 🏘 150. ℹ️ Monastery; 985 89 23 24.

The hamlet of Valdediós in the Boides valley is worth visiting on account of its interesting pre-Romanesque **Iglesia de San Salvador**. Founded by Alfonso III in 893, the church is built on a basilica plan, meaning that the nave is taller than the aisles. The church's interior painted decoration is surprisingly well preserved, assuming in places geometric, Moresque forms. The frescoes found on the ceiling are particularly vivid.

Nearby stands a **Cistercian monastery** dating from 1200, with beautiful cloisters from 1522. Since the early 20th century, the monastery has housed a seminary.

The pre-Romanesque Iglesia de San Salvador in Valdediós

Environs

Approximately 5 km (3 miles) southeast of Valdediós is **Nava**, well known for its July cider festival, with cider pourings and tastings. The local **Museo de la Sidra** (Museum of Cider) is devoted to this beverage, and the four rooms house an interesting exhibition on the cider-making process.

🏛 **Museo de la Sidra**
Plaza Príncipe de Asturias, Nava.
⭕ *mid-Jun–mid-Sep: noon–2pm & 4–8pm Tue, 11am–2pm & 4–8pm Wed–Sat; mid-Sep–mid-Jun: 11am–2pm & 4-7pm Tue-Fri, 11am-3pm & 4:30-8pm Sat, 11am–2pm Sun.*

Villaviciosa ⑭

Asturias. 🏘 14, 200.

The Ría de Villaviciosa, which cuts inland for 8 km (5 miles), is rich in plants and animal life. You can take a fishing boat or kayak trip along the *ría*, which

is lined by nice beaches. At the end of the *ría* lies Villaviciosa, a graceful little resort town that attracts visitors, thanks to its well-preserved Romanesque buildings. The most famous of these is the **Iglesia de Santa María de Oliva**, built in the late 13th century. The stonemasons introduced elements of early Gothic style. The side entrances and most of the decorative elements are still Romanesque, but the pointed arches in the main portal and the use of rose windows attest to an interest in new architectural trends.

This mixing of styles and the gradual transition from one style to the next is very much in evidence in **Amandi**, a small but picturesque district of the town. The **Iglesia de San Juan** of 1134, initially designed as a monastery church, is an example of the late Romanesque style. The chancel was entirely dismantled in the 18th century due to subsidence, and was later rebuilt. The highlight of the interior is the sculptural decoration – the religious scenes are infused with plant motifs (fruits, leaves, rosettes), geometric motifs, zigzags and chequered patterns, as well as animal motifs (birds and reptiles).

Villaviciosa is also known as the cider capital of Asturias, and is surrounded by apple orchards, with many traditional *sidrerías* (cider bars) in town.

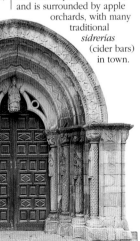

Romanesque portal of the Iglesia de Santa María de Oliva in Villaviciosa

A Romanesque bridge in Cangas de Onís, in the Picos de Europa ▷

The richly decorated altar at the church of San Salvador in Llanes

Ribadesella ⓯

Asturias. **6,500.** 🚉 *Paseo Princesa Letizia; 985 86 00 38.* 🛒 *Tue.* 🎉 *Descent of the Río Sella (1st Sat in Aug).*

The old port straddling the mouth of the Sella river dates from the reign of Alfonso X of Castile, who founded this enchanting seaside town. For many years, Ribadesella had to defend itself against pirates, who were well aware of the port's strategic importance for the surrounding area.

Today, on one side of the river is the lively seaport full of *tapas* bars serving fresh fish, while on the other is the more modern part; its beautiful broad beach is the reason why Ribadesella has become a popular holiday resort. A multicoloured flotilla of kayaks arrives here on the first Saturday in August, in an international regatta that is held every year.

On the edge of the town is the **Cueva de Tito Bustillo**, a series of interconnected caves with beautiful prehistoric paintings. Discovered in 1968, the drawings date from the Palaeolithic era – from 25,000 to 12,000 BC – and include superb black and red images of stags' and horses' heads. To protect the paintings, only 300 visitors are allowed in per day. Be sure to take warm clothing when entering the cave, as the temperature is surprisingly cool. Also it's important to wear sturdy,

comfortable walking boots and watch your step, as the surfaces of the cave floors are uneven.

🏛 **Cueva de Tito Bustillo**
Ribadesella. **Tel** *985 86 11 20.* ⬜ *Apr–mid-Sep: 10am–1pm & 3:30–5:15pm daily.* ⬛ *Apr–Jun & Sep: Mon; Jun–Aug: Sun.* 🎫 *(free Wed, but it's necessary to reserve in advance by calling the number above). Children over 7 only.*

Environs

Beyond Ribadesella is the charming town of **Llanes**, ever popular on account of its well-preserved medieval quarter, its busy fishing port with plenty of good seafood, and its 30 beautiful sandy beaches – considered the best in Asturias, if not on the whole of the north coast. The town has several historic monuments, among them the 18th-century **Palacio de los Duques de Estada** and the 12th- to 13th-century **Iglelsia de San Salvador**, which exhibits a style typical of the Asturias region.

Picos de Europa ⓰

See pp100–3.

San Vicente de la Barquera ⓱

Asturias. 🚉 *942 71 07 97.* 🎉 *La Folía (1st Sun after Easter).*

This first mention of this beautiful maritime town dates from Roman times, when a

major port already existed here. Alfonso I of Asturias populated the expanding town under his colonization policy, while Alfonso VIII of Castile granted it numerous privileges in 1210, which further accelerated economic development and allowed San Vicente de la Barquera to flourish.

For centuries, the town was an important stopover for pilgrims travelling to Santiago de Compostela *(see pp20–21)*. Today, San Vicente boasts a rich artistic legacy, which includes the **Iglesia de Santa María de los Angeles**, built between the 13th and 16th centuries on the site of an earlier church. The interior features the beautiful tomb of the Inquisitor Antonio del Corro, who is shown in a reclining pose immersed in the pages of a book.

Of the other interesting buildings in the town, worth mentioning is the monastery of **El Santuario de la Barquera** and **El Convento de San Luis**. Constructed in the 15th century under the patronage of the de Guevara family, the walls, apse, vaults and Gothic arches are survivors from the original building. Carlos I was a guest here when he arrived in Spain for his coronation in 1517. Now a private property, the monastery is open to the public between April and July, and in mid- to late September.

In the vicinity of San Vicente are broad picturesque beaches – Meron, Tostadero and Oyambre.

The picturesque port in San Vicente de la Barquera

Asturian Specialities

Asturian food is hearty, based on flavourful meat (especially bacon and sausage), fresh fish, and very strong cheeses. Trout from mountain streams, as well as salmon and cod caught in the sea, often feature on menus, and the Gijón region is famous for its delicious sardines. Also popular are shellfish, particularly gooseneck barnacles, lobster and shrimps. Fish and shellfish are among the ingredients of *la*

Cabrales – strong, soft sheep's cheese

caldereta (fish stew). Flavour is further enhanced by the delicious local vegetables, such as peppers, artichokes, lettuce and, above all, beans, which are used to make the traditional Asturian *fabada*. High-quality milk enables the large-scale production of excellent cheeses, of which there are over 40 varieties. But, above all, Asturias is famous for its cider *(sidra)* – a mildly alcoholic drink that is used in many dishes, too.

Cider *is stored in wooden casks at the optimum temperature of 9–10ºC (48–50ºF). Too low a temperature will hinder the fermentation process; too high a temperature will overly accelerate it; ideally, the maturation process should take five to six months.*

The original labels *on the bottles of cider are a guarantee of high quality and traditional production methods; the labels are usually very colourful and bear attractive images of fruit.*

During Nava's July Cider Festival, *you can sample this drink while enjoying traditional dancing and Asturian folk songs. The cider is poured into a glass from a bottle held high above the head to give it a fizzy head.*

Fabada, *a tasty, satisfying dish, is made from Asturian beans* (fabes) *and various meats, including local sausage* (chorizo), *bacon* (tocino) *and ham, which infuse the beans with flavour.*

The Asturian village of Llanos de Somerón *is famous for its delicious mixed-blossom honey, produced from the nectar of heather and chestnut flowers.*

Asturian cheese (queso asturiano), *made from cow's, sheep's and goat's milk, has a slightly strong, pungent flavour and smell. The best-known are* cabrales *and* taramundi.

Parque Nacional de los Picos de Europa ⓖ

Lefebvre's Ringlet

These beautiful mountains were reputedly christened the 'Peaks of Europe' by returning sailors for whom this was often the first sight of their homeland. The range straddles three regions – Asturias, Cantabria and Castilla y León – and has diverse terrain. In some parts, deep winding gorges cut through craggy rocks while elsewhere verdant valleys support orchards and dairy farming. The celebrated creamy blue cheese, *cabrales*, is made here. The Picos offer rock climbing and upland hiking as well as a profusion of flora and fauna. Tourism in the park is well organized.

Covadonga
The Neo-Romanesque basilica, built between 1886 and 1901, stands on the site of Pelayo's historic victory.

Lago de la Ercina
Together with the nearby Lago Enol, this lake lies on a wild limestone plateau above Covadonga and below the peak of Peña Santa.

RIBADESELLA Cangas de Onís

Covadonga

Sames

LAGO ENOL   LAGO DE LA ERCINA

Oseja de Sajambre   Puerto de Panderruedas   Posada de Valdeón

Puerto de Pontón   RIAÑO

Desfiladero de los Beyos
This deep, narrow gorge with its high limestone cliffs winds spectacularly for 10 km (6 miles) through the mountains. Tracing the course of the Río Sella below, it carries the main road from Cangas de Onís to Riaño.

KEY

═══	Major road
══	Minor road
– –	Footpath
───	National park boundary
🚡	Cable car
ℹ	Tourist information
🅿	Parador
☀	Viewpoint

Desfiladero del Río Cares
The Río Cares forms a deep gorge in the heart of the Picos. A dramatic footpath follows the gorge, passing through tunnels and across high bridges up to 1,000 m (3,280 ft) above the river.

ramatic view of the mountains of the Picos de Europa

nes, one of the remotest villages in Spain, enjoys
e views of Naranjo de Bulnes and can be accessed
foot, and now also by funicular railway up through
unnel from Puente Poncebos.

VISITORS' CHECKLIST

 Cangas de Onis; 985 84 86
14. Posada de Valdeón; 987
74 05 49. Potes; 942 72 05
55. From Oviedo to Cangas
de Onis. **Fuente Dé cable car
Tel.** 942 73 66 10. Jul–Sep:
9am–8pm daily; Oct–Jun: 10am–
6pm daily. 6 Jan–1 Mar.
www.mma.es/oapm

THE BEST TRAILS
The best walking expeditions
in the Picos de Europa can
be started from Turieno,
Cosgaya and Sotres, where
several well-marked trails
begin. Free guided expeditions are organized
every day in summer
from June to
September, leaving
from the boundary
of the park.
Hikers who wish
to explore the
higher areas
of the
mountains
should
remember to
take the
appropriate
equipment,
boots and warm
clothing, as the
weather is prone
to sudden and
dramatic
change.

**Statue of a
hiker, near Potes**

Naranjo de Bulnes, with its
tooth-like crest, is in the heart of
the massif. At 2,519 m (8,264 ft)
it is one of the highest summits
in the Picos de Europa.

Fuente Dé Cable Car
*The 900-m (2950-ft) ascent
from Fuente Dé takes visitors
up to a wild rocky plateau
pitted with craters. From
here there is a spectacular
panorama of the Picos'
peaks and valleys.*

The 18th-century Ermita de Santa Cruz, in Cangas de Onís

Exploring the Picos de Europa

Aside from exploring the mountain trails, it is well worth spending time discovering the towns and villages located within the national park, where many important historic monuments can be found.

🏛 Cangas de Onís

Asturias. 🔼 3,500. 🚉 Plaza Camila Beceña; 985 84 80 05. 🚌 Sun. 🎭 Fiesta de San Antonio (13 Jun), Fiesta del Pastor (25 Jul). **www**.cangasdeonis.com

The first capital of the kingdom of Asturias, Cangas de Onís is one of the gateways to the Picos de Europa National Park. Preserved here is the **Ermita de Santa Cruz**, which was built in 733 on the site of an earlier shrine, with a fascinating Bronze Age dolmen by the entrance. The ivy-clad bridge, with its tall arches, dates from the reign of Alfonso XI of Castile (1312–50).

Watersports enthusiasts might wish to attempt the three-hour canoe trip along the Río Sella.

🏛 Covadonga

Asturias.

Set in the northern range of the Picos de Europa, Covadonga is a place of importance for Asturias, and for the whole of Spain. It was here, in 722, that Pelayo, a leader of the Visigothic nobles, won a battle to stop the further advance of the Moors in this part of Asturias. According to

Cave containing Pelayo's tomb in Covadonga

Christian tradition, Pelayo's men, encouraged by the appearance on the battlefield of the Virgin Mary, destroyed the Moorish army. The town remains an important shrine, and crowds of pilgrims come to visit the cave where Pelayo is said to have lived, which is picturesquely set on a hillside. Inside the cave is a chapel containing the warrior's tomb. In 1886–1901, a neo-Romanesque basilica was built on the spot where Pelayo scored his historic victory. The name of the town derives from *cova longa* (*cueva larga* in Spanish) – the long cave where the warriors prayed to the Virgin before the battle.

🏛 Arenas de Cabrales

Asturias. 🔼 923 🚉 Carretera General; 985 84 64 84. 🎭 San Juan (24 Jun), San Pedro (28 Jun), Fiesta del queso (last Sun in Aug).

This village, situated 25 km (16 miles) east of Cangas de Onís, is famous as the place where *cabrales*, a pungent blue goats' cheese, is made. On the last Sunday in August, an Asturian cheese festival takes place here, during which the place comes alive with music and dancing.

The village features many beautiful 17th- and 18th-century homesteads, of which the most arresting is the **Casa Palacio de los Mestas**. On the right bank of the Ribelas river rises the small Gothic **Iglesia de Santa María de Llas**, affording fine views of the surrounding area. In the vicinity of Arena de Cabrales are three caves: **Cueva El Bosque**, **Cueva de los Canes** and **Cueva de la Covaciella**. Though quite difficult to get to, the caves are well worth visiting on account of the superb Palaeolithic cave art to be seen inside.

🏛 Fuente Dé

Asturias. **www**.cantur.com

The cable car in Fuente Dé takes visitors up to an altitude of 1,900 m (6,234 ft) above sea level. As it ascends 750 m (2,461 ft) up the steep

---

PELAYO, RULER OF THE VISIGOTHS

Leader of a group of Visigothic nobles, Pelayo encouraged the Asturian villages not to pay dues to the Moors and even to resist them by force of arms. The Moors, in turn, sent troops to the region to quell the rebellion. At the Battle of Covadonga in 722 the scales turned in favour of the Christians, and as the legend of the battle grew, Pelayo became a national hero. It is worth noting, however, that the Asturians did not – as tradition would have it – fight at Covadonga in defence of their faith, but rather in defence of their freedom, just as the barbarian tribes had fought the Romans. It was not until the 11th century that the war against the Moors took on the character of a crusade.

A statue of Pelayo in Covadonga

mountain, panoramic views of the beautiful, if harsh, surrounding landscape are gradually revealed. From the Mirador del Cable, the observation point at the summit, ambitious walkers can carry on to the peaks of **Pico Tesorero** (2,570 m/ 8,432 ft) and **Peña Vieja**. Despite the high altitude, the trails are not difficult and your efforts will be rewarded by unforgettable views of the Picos' central massif.

Potes

Cantabria. *1,600.* Plaza de la Serna; 942 73 81 26. Mon. Nuestra Señora de Valmayor (15 Aug), Santísima Cruz (14 Sep).

This small town on the Deva river, picturesquely set amid snowcapped peaks, is the main centre of the eastern Picos de Europa. The narrow winding streets lined with medieval stone houses are full of small shops, and on Mondays a colourful flea market takes place here.

The town's most characteristic monument is a 15th-century defensive tower, the

15th-century Torre del Infantado in Potes, currently the town hall

Torre del Infantado. Also worth seeing is the late Gothic 14th-century **Iglesia de San Vicente**, with a beautiful façade and interesting Baroque altars brought here from the Dominican Convento de San Raimundo.

A good way to spend an afternoon in Potes is to hire a bicycle and ride for 9 km (5 miles) to the **Iglesia de Santa María Piasta**. This ideally

proportioned building – pure Romanesque in style – boasts beautiful exterior sculptures.

Valle de Valdeón

Castilla y León.

The Posada de Valdeón lies on the main tourist trail that runs through the Picos de Europa national park. Huge outcrops of rock dominate the valley, leaving a lasting impression on those who stay in the village of Valdeón.

There is an astonishing variety of flora and fauna, and the valley's meadows provide grazing ground for cattle. Hiking trails to the picturesque ravine of **Garganta del Cares** begin in Valdeón, but shorter walks in the surrounding area are also worthwhile, for every corner of the valley has beautiful views.

Every year on 8 September a festival in honour of the Virgen de Corona (Virgin of the Crown) takes place in the villages of the Valle de Valdeón. Local inhabitants believe that the warrior king Pelayo was crowned here.

FLORA AND FAUNA OF PICOS DE EUROPA

Foxes, otters and wolves inhabit the lush vegetation in the beech and mixed forests. Eagles, vultures and kestrels circle above the soaring peaks. The flowers that appear in the meadows include Alpine violets, foxgloves and colourful perennials. Visitors are invariably impressed by the richness of the flora and fauna, which include many endemic species.

The steep hillsides, *soaring peaks and peaceful valleys and ravines of the Picos form the park's picturesque backdrop.*

The pyramidal orchid, *with an 8-cm (3-inch) long inflorescence and pink or purple flowers, grows in the park's open meadows.*

The chamois *is one of the larger species to inhabit the park. Herds of these agile animals graze in the mountain meadows.*

Thistles, *reaching 1.5 m (5 ft) in height, with blue cone-shaped flowers and broad thorny leaves, are one of many species of plants.*

The owl, *with a flat head, short tail, and large bright yellow eyes, is active both during the day and at night; its characteristic soft hoot can often be heard in the park.*

The spring gentian, *which flowers between March and August, has short stems with single leaves and often grows on the limestone base of screes.*

Comillas ⑱

Cantabria. 🏘 2,500. 🚹 Calle la Aldea 6; 942 72 07 68. 🚌 Fri. 📅 San Pedro (29 Jun), El Cristo & Virgen del Carmen (16 Jul).

This pretty resort is known for its unusual buildings designed by Catalan Modernista architects. Antonio López y López, the first Marquis of Comillas, invited King Alfonso XII here for a holiday; in the early 20th century the town became a haunt of the Spanish aristocracy. López y López hired Joan Martorell to design the **Palacio Sobrellano** (1881), a huge Neo-Gothic edifice. Comillas' best-known monument is Gaudí's **El Capricho** (now a restaurant). It was built in 1883–5 for a wealthy relative of López y López and is a part-Mudéjar-inspired fantasy with a minaret-like tower covered in green and yellow tiles. Another of the town's Modernista buildings is the **Universidad Pontificia**, which was designed by Joan Martorell to plans by Domènech i Montaner.

♣ Palacio de Sobrellano
Comillas. **Tel** 942 72 03 39. ◯ May–Sep: 10am–9pm Wed–Sun; Oct–Apr: 10:30am–2pm & 4–7:30pm Wed–Sun. 🎫

One of the villages picturesquely set in the Valle de Cabuérniga

the salt trade. Of note are the magnificent residences, especially the 18th-century **Palacio de la Bodega** with the coat of arms of the de los Cevallos family inlaid in its façade, and the Baroque **Iglesia de San Martín**, dating from the beginning of the 17th century. The best time to visit Cabezón de la Sal is on the second Sunday in August – Regional Cantabria Day – when you can gain an insight into the colourful local traditions.

Valle de Cabuérniga ⑲

Cantabria. 🚹 Ayuntamiento, Ruente; 942 70 91 04. **www**.ruente.com

This picturesque valley is home to many interesting *pueblos*. A good place to start is **Bárcena Mayor**, which is notable for its typical

Cantabrian rural architecture. The inhabitants of the village cultivate old craft traditions – in particular carpentry.

Lamiña features a 10th-century hermitage (Ermita de San Fructoso) while **Ucieda** has a beautiful nature reserve with beech and oak forests.

Alto Campoo ⑳

Cantabria. 🏘 1,900. 🚹 Estación de Montaña; 942 77 92 23.

Sited high in the Cantabrian mountains, this small but excellent ski resort lies below the three alpine peaks of El Cuchillón, El Chivo and Pico de Tres Mares (2,175 m/7,136 ft). The last of these, whose name translates as "Peak of the Three Seas", is so called because the rivers rising near it flow into the Mediterranean, the Atlantic and the Bay of

The huge, neo-Gothic Palacio Sobrellano in Comillas

Environs
Some 11 km (6.6 miles) from Comillas is the tiny **Cabezón de la Sal**, known already in Roman times as a centre of

---

GAUDÍ IN CANTABRIA

Antoni Gaudí's El Capricho palace is one of his very few designs to be seen outside Barcelona. This fantasy building owes its name to the minaret-like tower. Typifying his eclectic style, it combines various materials including ceramics, and displays the characteristic freedom of composition, resulting in the stylized 'fairytale' appearance.

Gaudí came to work in Comillas through Antonio López y López, who married into the Güell family of industrialists – patrons of the great architect and artist.

Exterior of Gaudí's fairytale-like El Capricho palace in Comillas

Biscay. A chairlift reaches the summit of Pico de Tres Mares, from where there is a breathtaking panorama of the Picos de Europa and other mountain chains. The resort has downhill runs totalling 17 km (11 miles) in length and 20 pistes.

Puente Viesgo ㉑

Cantabria. 🏠 2,500. 🚌 Calle Manuel Perez Mazo 2; 942 59 81 05. 🎉 San Miguel (28–29 Sep).

Charmingly situated amid verdant landscape, this village is best known for its two nearby caves with prehistoric paintings that are open to the public. The **Cueva "El Castillo"**, discovered in 1903, has walls that are covered in drawings of horses and bison, but the highlight is the series of hand prints. Experts regard these as the earliest examples of cave art in the Franco-Cantabrian zone, preceding all other geometric and figural images. The prints were made by blowing mineral dyes – probably through a bone pipe – onto the hand while it was pressed against the wall. The colours used to create the images were extracted from minerals within the cave.

The **Cueva "Las Monedas"** contains beautiful stalactites and stalagmites, with unusual coloration due to the mixture of minerals and calcium. The paintings in this cave were made

with coal and thus are black; they represent horses, reindeer, goats, bears, bison and some signs. They date back 13,000 years.

Other caves here are "El Pendo", "Covalanas", "Chufín", and "Hornos de la Peña", but these are closed to the public.

⛰ **Cueva "El Castillo" & Cueva "Las Monedas"**
Puente Viesgo. **Tel** 942 59 84 25. ⏰ May–Sep: 9:30am–7:30pm daily; Oct–Apr: 9:30am–5pm Wed–Sun. www.turismodecantabria.com

Valle de Besaya ㉒

As early as Roman times, a north–south road linking the Cantabrian coast with the Meseta ran through this long valley. Romanesque buildings are also to be found here, including small churches, which would have been covered initially with wooden roofs, to which vaults and

FIESTAS IN ASTURIAS AND CANTABRIA

La Folía (Apr) San Vicente de la Barquera. Procession of decorated and lit boats.
Fiesta del Pastor (1st Fri in Jul) Castro Urdiales. Shepherds' Festival.
Virgen del Carmen (16 Jul) Comillas. Homage to the Virgin.
Coso Blanco (25 Jul) Cangas de Onís. Night-time parade of carriages.
Battle of the Flowers (last Fri in Aug) Laredo. Flower parade and festivities.
Nuestra Señora de Covadonga (8 Sep) Picos de Europa. Homage to the patron saint of Asturias.

Girls in traditional dress participating in a regional fiesta

Gothic chancels were later added. Of special interest is the severe-looking **Iglesia de Barcena de Pie de Concha**, with beautiful sculptures on its exterior, and the **Iglesia de Santa María de Yermo**, with an interesting portico comprising five archivolts; below it is a tympanum containing a sculpture of a knight fighting a dragon.

Torrelavega, the capital of the Valle de Besaya, boasts several historic monuments, such as the Convento de las Adres, the Iglesia de la Virgen Grande, and the Iglesia de Nuestra Señora de Asunción.

Environs

Nearby are two places worth visiting: **Retortillo**, which is famous for its excellent therapeutic spa, and **Julióbriga**, the remains of a town built by the Romans against the wild tribes of Cantabria.

The colourful park in Puente Viesgo planted with flowers and palm trees

Street-by-Street: Santillana del Mar ㉓

In his novel *Nausea*, Jean-Paul Sartre called Santillana del Mar ("Santillana of the Sea") the most beautiful town in Spain. Despite its name, it is actually 3 km (nearly 2 miles) away from the sea. The ensemble of opulent 15th- to 18th-century buildings, attesting to the town's aristocratic legacy, grew up around the collegiate church of Santa Juliana. The church houses the tomb of the martyr Juliana, who is said to have captured the devil – an event depicted in the murals on the walls of the church. The town was laid out along a north–south axis, delineated by its only major street – Calle de Santo Domingo.

Calle Carrera
This cobblestoned street has several houses built by local noblemen, including the 18th-century Casa de Los Bustamante with its characteristic balconies. One of the oldest houses is the Torre de la Villa, which in the 15th century belonged to the Velarde family.

Casa del Águila y la Parra
These two historic houses, dating from the 16th and 17th centuries, accommodate a collection of Cantabrian art.

Houses
The main streets of the town are lined with golden stone houses, lending it an unforgettable character.

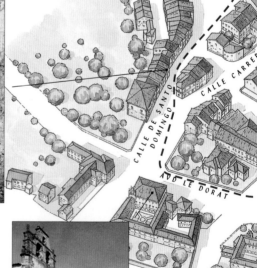

PLAZA MAYOR

CALLE DE SANTO DOMINGO

CALLE CARRERA

AV. DE LE DORAT

STAR SIGHTS

★ Colegiata de S Juliana

★ Museo Diocesano

★ Torre de Don Borja

★ Museo Diocesano
Housed in the Convento de Regina Coeli (1592), the museum boasts a rich collection of painted figures of saints.

Church Cloisters
The cloister arcades are supported on Romanesque columns with capitals bearing images of animals and hunting scenes.

VISITORS' CHECKLIST

Cantabria. 4,000.
C/Jesús Otero; 942 81 82 51. Santa Juliana (28 Jun), San Roque (16 Aug).
www.turismocantabria.com
Museo Diocesano
Tel 942 84 03 17.
Jul–Aug: 10am–2pm & 4–8pm daily; Sep–Jun: 10am–2pm & 4–7pm Tue–Sun.
www.santillanamuseo diocesano.com

★ **Colegiata de Santa Juliana**
An important Cantabrian pilgrimage centre and the most beautiful monument in Santillana, this Romanesque jewel attracts believers and art-lovers alike.

★ **Torre de Don Borja**
This late 14th- to early 15th-century Gothic defensive tower, with its beautiful patio, is now the headquarters of the Fundación Santillana, where exhibitions and conferences are held.

APARCA-MIENTO

A car park enables visitors to leave their car before embarking on a tour of the pedestrianized town centre.

0 metres	50
0 yards	50

KEY

– – – Suggested route

GOLDEN AGE OF THE NOBILITY

The nobility often placed extravagant mottoes and coats of arms on the façades of their residences. The most beautiful example is the Casa de los Hombrones, which has a family cartouche encircled by two bearded figures; the most unusual is the Casa de Bustamante, which is adorned with the surprising yet eloquent inscription, "The Bustamante daughters are given as wives to kings". On Calle Carrera stands the 18th-century house of the Valdevieso family, whose coat of arms is visible.

A coat of arms on an aristocratic residence in Santillana del Mar

Cuevas de Altamira ㉔

In 1985, the Altamira Caves near Santander were added to UNESCO's World Heritage list. The magnificent paintings, the earliest of which date back to 16,000 BC, depict herds of bison, horses, deer and anthropomorphic figures in black contours. The animals are painted with remarkable accuracy that was evidently based on close observation. To protect the works, public entry to the caves is no longer permitted, but the on-site museum contains replicas of the caves and the paintings, with additional exhibitions.

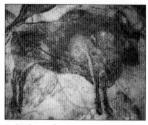

Painting of a Bison
On the ceiling of the cave is a herd of bison painted with amazing realism and expressiveness; some of the bison are standing still, others are running or kneeling, still others have fallen to the ground.

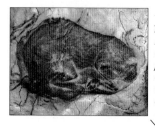

★ **Horse's Tail**
In the final section of the new cave, a replica of part of the original cave, one can admire the lesser-known but still beautiful paintings.

★ **Cave with Paintings**
Most of the depictions of animals were painted on the ceiling of a chamber in the main section of the caves, which measure 100 sq m (1,076 sq ft).

Bears made a lair of the caves once they were abandoned by humans. The skeleton of a bear that perished in the winter can be seen in a shallow oval cavity on the floor of the new cave.

Entrance to the new cave

KEY

- ☐ New cave
- ☐ Cave with paintings
- ☐ Palaeolithic campsite
- ☐ Archaeological dig
- ☐ Painter's workshop
- ☐ Horse's tail
- ☐ Permanent exhibitions
- ☐ Auditorium
- ☐ Terrace
- ☐ Children's workshops

STAR SIGHTS

★ Cave with Paintings

★ Daily Life

★ Horse's Tail

Archaeological Dig
In the new cave, fragments of tools used by Palaeolithic hunters can be seen near the dig.

Discovery of the Caves
In 1868 a hunter discovered the entrance to the caves. Marcelino Sanz de Sautuola began to investigate them in 1875, but it was his daughter María who found the paintings in 1879.

VISITING THE MUSEUM
Apart from the 20-minute tour, visitors can also take part in workshops entitled "hunting" and "fire", which are designed for both adults and children. The new cave is an impressive replica of part of the original cave, and helps to put the paintings into context for visitors.

★ Daily Life
The museum rooms present the daily life of people in the Palaeolithic era. This exhibit demonstrates fishing and hunting techniques, and the methods by which hides were tanned.

Main entrance

Children's Workshop
Through museum lectures and workshops, children become acquainted with the earliest human history and embark on an exciting journey into the Palaeolithic era.

MAP OF THE CUEVAS DE ALTAMIRA
The highlight of the caves is the chamber known as the Sistine Chapel, situated close to the entrance, which has the greatest number of animals painted on its ceiling. Most impressive is the huge deer, measuring 2.25 m (7 ft) in length. The paintings in this section (marked in green on the diagram) are reproduced in the museum in the new cave.

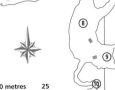

Entrance

KEY
Cave with paintings ①
Signs and lines ②
Horses ③
Deer ④
Bison and deer ⑤
Deer and goat ⑥
Signs and lines ⑦
Signs and lines ⑧
Black quadruped ⑨
Human figures ⑩

0 metres   25

0 yards   25

Santander ㉕

Cantabria. 🏛 200,000. ✈ 🚆 🚌
🚢 🛈 *Jardines de Pereda; 942 20
30 00.* 🅿 *daily.* 🎭 *Semana Grande
(Santiago) (25 Jul), San Emeterio &
San Celedonio (31 Aug), Baños de
Ola (2nd half of Jul).*

Cantabria's capital enjoys a
splendid location near the
mouth of a deep bay, with the
port on one side and mountains on the other. A good
place to begin a tour of this
lively resort is the **Museo de
Bellas Artes**. Apart from works
by Cantabrian landscape artists,
the museum has a fine portrait
of Fernando VII by Goya,
interesting canvases by
Miró, and paintings by
the 17th-century
Portuguese artist
Josefa de Obidos. The
Museo de Bellas Artes
was founded in 1907.
Since 1924 it has occupied
a building designed by
Cantabrian architect
Leonardo Rucabado, located
near the main square;
on the latter stands
the Iglesia de San
Francisco. Just east
of the museum is Santander's
market, with a wide selection
of produce, fish and meats.

**Exhibit in the Museo
de Prehistoria**

Cloisters at Santander Cathedral

Santander has an array of interesting 19th- to 20th-century
architecture. Of note is the
Iglesia de Santa Lucia (1868)
by Antonio de Zabaleta, an
artist who introduced Romantic
architecture to Spain. A good
example of neo-
Gothic architecture
is the Jesuit **Iglesia
del Sagrado Corazón**.
The much-remodelled
cathedral, whose
Romanesque-Gothic crypt
(c.1200) was built on the
remains of an earlier
Roman building, was
rebuilt after a fire in 1945.
The aisled interior, measuring 31 m (102 ft)
long and 18 m (59 ft)
wide, is a combina-
tion of Romanesque
and Gothic. Found here are
the reliquaries of two martyrs –
San Emeterio and San

Celedonio – who were
Roman legionnaires
born in León. When the
Romans began to
persecute Christians, the
courageous brothers
made a public declara-
tion of their faith, for
which they were
sentenced to death by
beheading; their severed
heads were brought by
fishing boat to Santander.
The city is named after the
first of these two martyrs
(Portus Sancti Emeterii –
Sant'Emter – Santander).

After leaving the cathedral,
it is worth paying a visit to
the **Museo de Prehistoria**,
with its interesting collection
of finds from numerous
Cantabrian caves that were
inhabited in prehistoric times.

There's no better place to
relax than on Santander's
beautiful beaches. The 2-km
(1.2-mile) long **Playa el
Sardinero**, which shares its
name with the city's northern
suburbs, is one of the eight
most unpolluted beaches in
the world. It became popular
in the mid-19th century, when
the Madrid aristocracy began
to visit. Bordering the beach
are gardens and good cafés,
luxury hotels, including the

**SANTANDER
CITY CENTRE**

Cathedral ③
Market ②
Museo de Bellas Artes ①
Museo de Prehistoria ④
Palacio de la Magdalena ⑥
Playa el Sardinero ⑤

0 metres   500
0 yards   500

For key to symbols *see back flap*

imposing Hotel Real, as well as casinos. Here, too, stands the **Palacio de la Magdalena**, a summer residence of Alfonso XIII. Built in 1911, the palace was designed by two Cantabrian architects – Javier González Riancho and Gonzálo Bringas – and is furnished in the belle époque style. In July and August, El Sardinero plays host to a theatre and music festival.

🏛 **Museo de Bellas Artes**
C/Rubio 6. **Tel.** 942 20 31 20.
🕐 mid-Jun–mid-Sep:
11:15am–1pm & 5:30–9pm
Mon–Fri, 10:30am–1pm Sat; mid-Sep–mid-Jun: 10:15am– 1pm &
5:30–9pm Mon–Fri, 10am–1pm Sat.

🏛 **Museo de Prehistoria**
C/Casimiro Sainz 4. **Tel.** 942 20 71
09. 🕐 Summer: 10am–1pm &
4–7pm Tue–Sat, 11am–2pm Sun
and hols; Autumn, Winter & Spring:
9am–1pm & 4–7pm Tue–Sat,
11am–2pm Sun and hols. Prior
booking for groups essential. 📷
call in advance.

Exhibits at the Convento de San Francisco museum in Laredo

Laredo 26

Cantabria. 🏘 14,000. 🛈 C/ Lopez
Sena; 942 61 10 96. 🎉 Batalla de
Flores (last Fri in Aug), Carlos V's last
landing (w'kend closest to 15 Sep).

Laredo is a historic port and Cantabria's biggest beach resort. Its beautiful old town contains the remains of medieval walls and gates. The narrow streets lead up to the 13th-century Gothic **Iglesia de Santa María de la Asunción**, which contains a 15th-century Flemish reredos of the Virgin Mary of Bethlehem. Worth visiting, too, is the 16th-century **Convento de San Francisco** and its museum, designed in the Herrera style with a Renaissance cloister.

The picturesque Soba valley, location of Soba and Ramales de la Victoria

Environs
On the opposite side of the bay lies the resort of **Santoña**, the birthplace of Juan de la Cosa, Columbus' mapmaker. This small fishing port has great views from the hilltop **Castillo Fuerte de San Carlos**. To the west is a huge area of dunes and sea marshes that are home to wetland birds.

Soba and Ramales de la Victoria 27

🛈 942 64 65 04. www.citason.com

These two villages are set in the mountain valley of Asón, once used as a route linking the port of Laredo with the Meseta. Soba offers excellent sightseeing trails with panoramic views of the mountains. Ramales de la Victoria owes the second part of its name to the victorious battle fought here by the liberals during the first Carlist War (see p41). While in Ramales, be sure to visit the mid-17th century **Iglesia de San Pedro** and the **Iglesia Gibaja**, which was begun in the mid-16th

century. Also worthy of mention is the 17th-century **Palacio de Revillagigedo**, though it is closed to the public. Prehistoric caves can be seen near the village.

Castro Urdiales 28

Cantabria. 🏘 28,000. 🛈 Avenida
de la Constitución 1; 942 87 13 37.
🗓 Thu. 🎉 Coso Blanco (1st Fri Jul),
San Andrés (30 Nov).

Visitors flock to this popular holiday resort for the beautiful beaches: **Playa del Brazomar** and **Playa Ostende**, which can be reached along an attractive trail that skirts the cliffs. There is also a pretty harbourside paseo. Rising on a promontory above the town is the imposing **Iglesia de Santa María**, a fascinating example of Cantabrian Gothic. It was built in the 13th century, after which numerous Gothic elements were added. Inside is a tall Gothic sculpture of the seated Mary with the infant Jesus in her lap, and a moving canvas of The Dying Christ attributed to Francisco de Zurbarán.

The massive Gothic Iglesia de Santa María in Castro Urdiales

The picturesque Las Médulas hills in El Bierzo

El Bierzo ㉙

León. ℹ *Ponferrada; 987 42 42 36.*
www.turismobierzo.com

This northwestern region of León, cut off from the outside world by beautiful mountains, has breathtaking landscapes, pretty villages and picturesque lakes. This is an area with its own identity – the inhabitants speak a dialect of Gallego, and have a unique tradition of folklore and very hearty food.

Since Roman times, the area has also been mined for coal, iron and gold. The ore was extracted from millions of tonnes of alluvium washed from the hills of Las Médulas by a system of canals and sluice gates. It is estimated that the Romans extracted more than 500 tonnes of precious metal from the hills between the 1st and 4th centuries AD.

The impressive landscape, colonized by gnarled chestnut trees, is best appreciated from the viewpoint at Orrelán. Also

worth seeing is the **Sierra de Ancares**, a wild region of slate mountains, part of which is a nature reserve – the eastern part of the Reserva Nacional de Os Ancares *(see p75)*. The heathland, dotted with oak and birch copses, is home to wolves and capercaillies.

The area around El Bierzo has much to offer architecture enthusiasts. In the eastern part, along the old road to Santiago de Compostela, are typical pilgrim churches. Several isolated hill villages, such as **Campo del Agua**, contain pre-Roman *pallozas (see p57)*.

Villafranca del Bierzo ㉚

León. 🏘 *3,000.* ℹ *C/ Díez Ovelar 10; 987 54 00 28.* 🛒 *Tue & Fri.* 🎉 *Fiesta del Cristo (14 Sep).*

The tiled-roof houses, hilly surroundings and crystal-clear Burbia river lend this town a

special charm. It was here, in the Romanesque **Iglesia de Santiago** (1186), that pilgrims who were too weak to make the final gruelling hike across the hills of Galicia to Santiago de Compostela could obtain dispensation at the Puerta del Perdón (Door of Mercy).

Another interesting building is the collegiate **Iglesia de Santa María**, housed since 1544 in a former Cluniac monastery. Noteworthy, too, is the **Iglesia de San Francisco** on the Plaza Mayor, which, according to legend, was founded by St Francis of Assisi during his pilgrimage to Santiago. The interior features a beautiful Mudéjar ceiling made of wood.

Visitors to the town can also sample the local speciality, cherries marinated in *aguardiente*, a strong spirit.

Stained-glass window, Iglesia de Santiago, Villafranca del Bierzo

Ponferrada ㉛

León. 🏘 *70,000.* ℹ *Calle Gil y Carrasco 4; 987 42 42 36.* 🛒 *Wed, Sat.* 🎉 *Virgen de la Encina (8 Sep).* **www.**ponferrada.org

Set among hills, this town owes its name to a medieval bridge reinforced with iron *(pons ferrata)*. Rising above a deep valley is its most interesting building – the majestic **Castillo**

SAUSAGE FROM LEÓN

León is famous for its *chorizo* sausage made from pork and bacon flavoured with paprika, salt, garlic and oregano. There are many variations of it. The traditional method of making *chorizo* goes back to ancient times. After the ritual slaughter of animals during fiestas, any uneaten meat would be preserved. El Bierzo is also known for *botillo* – a heavy, coarse sausage unique to this region. Today, the places best known for delicious *chorizo* are El Bierzo, Astorga and La Baneza.

A selection of León's famous sausages

de los Templarios (Castle of the Knights Templar), built from 1218 to 1380. This imposing fortress, equipped with towers and battlements, was built to protect pilgrims travelling to Santiago.

Clustered around the foot of the castle is the **old quarter**, whose narrow streets with delightful arcades accommodate most of Ponferrada's monuments. These include the 17th-century Baroque **town hall** on the Plaza Mayor, entered through the Puerta del Reloj (Clock Tower gate), and the 10th-century **Iglesia de Santo Tomás de las Ollas**, a mix of Visigothic and Mozarabic architecture with later Romanesque and Baroque elements. The most impressive feature in the church is its oval chancel, with blind arcades and Moorish arches.

Astorga ❷

Gaudí's Palacio Episcopal in Astorga

León. 🏔 *13,500.* 🚉 🚍 🚻 *Glorieta Eduardo de Castro 5; 987 61 82 22.* 🛒 *Tue.* 🎭 *Santa Marta (last week in Aug).* **www**.astorga.com/turismo

The Roman town of Asturica Augusta was a strategic halt on the Vía de la Plata (Silver Road) linking Andalusia and Galicia. Destroyed by the Moors in the 11th century, the town soon recovered its status as an important stage on the pilgrimage route to Santiago de Compostela.

Its character is influenced by the Maragatos, a people probably descended from Carthaginian and Punic slaves brought here by the Romans to work the mines. Astorga was an important trading centre for them from the 8th century onwards, and until the building of railways in the 19th century, they were the main transporters of goods between Galician ports and Madrid. Among the goods they brought were chocolate and sugar, which is why this inland town is known for producing chocolates and *mantecados* (sweet biscuits).

Aside from the beautiful Gothic **cathedral**, begun in 1471, Astorga's most interesting monument is the fairy-tale

Palacio Episcopal (1889-93) by Catalan architect Antoni Gaudí. The turreted grey granite block ringed by a moat, with a spacious interior decked out in ceramic tiles – so horrified the diocese that no bishops ever lived in it. Inside is the **Museo de los Caminos**, which is devoted to the pilgrimage to Santiago.

Cuevas de Valporquero ❸

León. *Tel. 987 57 64 82.* ⬜ *Mar–mid-May & Oct–mid-Dec: 10am–5pm Fri–Sun & hols; mid-May–Sep: 10am–2pm & 3:30–7pm daily.* ⬛ *mid-Dec–Feb.* 🎥 **www**.cuevadevalporquero.org

Beneath the village of Valporquero extends a complex of limestone caves. Iron and sulphur oxides have tinted the beautiful stalactites and stalagmites with subtle shades of red, grey and black. Skilful lighting picks out the beautiful limestone concretions, creating a memorable effect.

Guided tours take parties through the impressive series of galleries and chambers. They begin with the Pequeñas Maravillas (Small Wonders), which feature fantastic rock formations with imaginative names, such as Las Gemelas (Twins), La Torre de Pisa (Tower of Pisa) and Virgen con Niño (Virgin and Child).

The massive Gran Rotonda, covering an area of 5,600 sq m (60,200 sq ft) and reaching a height of 20 m (66 ft), is the most stunning cave in the Cuevas de Valporquero complex. As the interior is cold and the surfaces uneven, it is advisable to wear warm clothes and sturdy shoes.

Impressive stalactites in one of the Cuevas de Valporquero

León ③④

León was founded in AD 68 as a camp for the Romans' Seventh Legion. In 914, King Ordoño II transferred the Christian capital here from Oviedo. After repeatedly uniting with, then separating from Castile, the two finally united in the 13th century though Castile, with its capital in Burgos, began to overshadow León as the pre-eminent regional power. León remained strong, however, and the town's most stunning monuments date from this period.

Exploring León
Most of the old quarter *(casco viejo)* is encircled by walls and pedestrianized. The magnificent cathedral is a good pace to begin a tour of the historic monuments that have survived from the Golden Age of this former regional capital. The city's most important buildings are found in the charming streets around the cathedral.

Arcaded period houses lining the Plaza Mayor

🔒 Cathedral
See pp116–17.

⛩ Plaza Mayor
The square, in the picturesque old quarter, is surrounded by old houses with delightful arcades. The Plaza Mayor is home to León's administrative offices. A good time to visit is on the feast days of St John, in the last week of June, when the square comes alive with fireworks on the riverside, fairs and medieval festivities as well as modern forms of entertainment. More religious in tone are the *Semana Santa* (Easter Week) celebrations, when the square plays host to processions of monks dressed in special costumes and cone-shaped hats with openings only for

the nose and eyes. The monks carry richly decorated *pasos* – platforms bearing figures of saints and scenes from the Passion of Christ.

⛩ Palacio de los Guzmanes
One of the most beautiful Renaissance residences in León, built in 1559–66, stands just next to the Plaza de Santo Domingo. This three-storey building, currently the seat of the provincial authorities, is centred on an attractive arcaded patio, with gargoyles on the roof, corner towers, and numerous coats of arms on the façade. There are offices on the ground floor, but the upper sections of the building are closed to visitors.

⛩ Casa de Botines
This magnificent building, which resembles a Gothic castle, was designed by Antoni Gaudí in 1892. It was erected in record time – a mere 11 months. Gaudí agreed to take on the task as he was working simultaneously on the Palacio Episcopal in nearby Astorga *(see p113)*, and could oversee both projects at once. The façade sports a figure of St George fighting the dragon, a replica of which later appeared

Part of the Renaissance façade of the Palacio de los Guzmanes

in Gaudí's Sagrada Familia in Barcelona. The building is currently used by a bank.

🔒 Basílica de San Isidoro
Plaza San Isidoro 4. ◯ 7am–11pm daily. **Museum** ◯ Jul–Aug: 9am–8pm Mon–Sat, 9am–2pm Sun & hols; Sep–Jun: 10am–1pm & 4–6:30pm Mon–Sat, 10am–1:30pm Sun & hols. 🔲
Adjoining the city walls, the basilica was built on the remains of an earlier church destroyed in 998 to house the relics of San Isidoro of Seville. Its construction spanned the 10th to mid-18th centuries. The walls of the royal mausoleum – the final resting place of 23 monarchs, 12 princes and 19 counts – are decorated with beautiful 12th-century Romanesque murals depicting biblical scenes. Among them is a cycle devoted to the life of Christ, including a powerful *Last Supper*, and one surviving sign of the zodiac. There is also a museum that contains paintings and frescoes from the royal mausoleum.

The castle-like Casa de Botines, designed by Antoni Gaudí

🏛 City Walls

The entire old quarter is encircled by imposing walls, which have served a defensive purpose since ancient times. Indeed, the history of this Roman town is a stormy one; it had to repel attacks by the Moors, in which it was not always successful. In 996, for instance, León was plundered by the ruler of the Cordoban Caliphate, Al-Mansur. Subsequently, however, the walls were strengthened and performed their function well; the remnants that are visible today are a reminder of the city's ancient past.

🏛 Museo de León

Plaza de San Marcos. **Tel.** 987 24 50 61. ◯ 10am–2pm & 4–8pm Tue–Sat (until 8:30pm May–Sep); 10am–2pm Sun and holidays. 🏷 (free Sat–Sun).

This small museum near the Convento de San Marcos has in its collections a famous ivory crucifix, the *Cristo de Carrizo*, dating from the 11th century. The piece originates from the Cistercian Monasterio de Carrizo, which was founded

Cristo de Carrizo, Museo de León

in 1176. Also displayed here are another striking crucifix – the *Cruz de Penalba*, which is encrusted with precious gems – and an altar from the Iglesia de San Marcelo.

🏛 Hostal de San Marcos

Plaza de San Marcos 7. **Tel.** 987 23 73 00. **www**.parador.es

This exclusive parador is one of the real jewels in this state-owned hotel chain. It was built in the 16th century by King Ferdinand as the headquarters of the Knights of Santiago. The order was headed by the monarch himself until the end of the Reconquest (*see pp37–9*). The richly decorated façade is designed in the characteristic Spanish style of the late Renaissance – known as Plateresque. This name refers to the method of preparing and decorating the stone surfaces, which are meticulously polished all over and bring to mind the techniques of goldsmiths (*plateros* in Spanish). All the characteristic features of this exuberant style are evident in the

VISITORS' CHECKLIST

León. 🚶 150,000. 🚉 🚌 ℹ️
Plaza de la Regla 4; 987 23 70 82. 🛒 Wed, Sat. 🎉 San Juan (24–29 Jun), San Froilán (5 Oct). **www**.castillayleon.com

hotel's façade – the arches with varied and complicated curves, panelling, openwork balustrades, turrets, bay windows, and sets of armorial cartouches and medallions bearing images of famous people and various monarchs.

A section of the façade of the Hostal de San Marcos

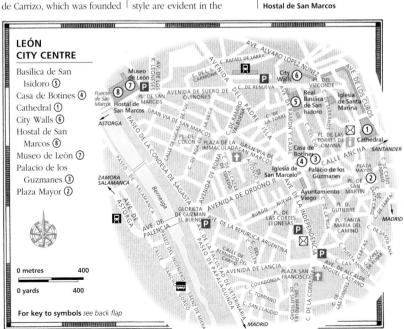

LEÓN CITY CENTRE

Basílica de San Isidoro ⑤
Casa de Botines ④
Cathedral ①
City Walls ⑥
Hostal de San Marcos ⑧
Museo de León ⑦
Palacio de los Guzmanes ③
Plaza Mayor ②

0 metres　　　400
0 yards　　　400

For key to symbols see back flap

Catedral de León

Detail of carving in the choir

The master-builders of this Spanish Gothic cathedral par excellence were inspired by French techniques of vaulting and buttressing. The present structure of golden sandstone, built on the site of King Ordoño II's 10th-century palace, was begun in the mid-13th century and completed less than 100 years later. It combines a slender but very tall nave with huge panels of stained glass that are the cathedral's most magnificent feature. Although it has survived for 700 years, there is concern now about air pollution attacking the soft stone.

West Rose Window
This largely 14th-century window depicts the Virgin and Child, surrounded by 12 trumpet-blowing angels.

The 13th- to 14th-century cloister galleries are decorated with Gothic frescoes by Nicolás Francés.

Cathedral Museum
Pedro de Campaña's panel, The Adoration of the Magi, *is one of the many magnificent treasures displayed in the museum.*

Entrance

★ **West Front**
The three portals are decorated with 13th-century carvings. Those above the Portada del Juicio *depict a scene from the Last Judgment, where the Blessed pass into paradise.*

Inside the Cathedral
The plan of the building is a Latin cross. The tall nave is slender but long, measuring 90 m (295 ft) by 40 m (130 ft) at its widest. To appreciate the dazzling colours of the stained glass, it is best to visit on a sunny day.

VISITORS' CHECKLIST

Plaza de la Regla. *Tel. 987 87 57 70.* ☐ 8:30am–1:30pm & 4–7pm Mon–Sat, 8:30am–2:30pm & 5–7pm Sun. ☐ 9am, noon, 1pm & 6pm daily (plus 11am & 2pm Sun). ☑ ☐ **Museum** 9:30am–1:30pm & 4–7pm Mon–Fri, 9:30am– 1:30pm Sat (plus 4–7pm Jun–Sep). ☐ www.catedraldeleon.org

The altarpiece includes five original panels created by Gothic master Nicolás Francés.

Virgen Blanca
This is a Gothic sculpture of a smiling Virgin. The original is kept in this chapel. A copy stands by the west door.

The choir has two tiers of 15th-century stalls. Behind it is the carved and gilded retrochoir, in the shape of a triumphal arch.

★ Stained Glass
The windows, covering an area of 1,800 sq m (19,350 sq ft), are the outstanding feature of the cathedral.

CATEDRAL DE LEÓN'S STAINED GLASS

This cathedral's great glory is its magnificent glasswork. The 125 large windows, 57 smaller, circular ones and three rose windows date from the 13th to the 20th centuries. They cover an enormous range of subjects, from fantastical beasts to plants. Many depict saints and characters from biblical stories. Some of the windows reveal fascinating details of medieval life: *La Cacería*, in the north wall, depicts a hunting scene, while the rose window in the Capilla del Nacimiento shows pilgrims at the tomb of St James in Santiago de Compostela in Galicia (*see pp62–3*).

Window with plant motif

A large window in the south wall

STAR FEATURES

★ Stained Glass

★ West Front

THE BASQUE COUNTRY

Situated on the Bay of Biscay, and bordering France to the east, the Basque Country is a region where green hills meet Atlantic beaches. Visitors can enjoy the varied coastline, historic inland towns, avant-garde art and architecture, excellent cuisine and the unique culture of the Basque people. Basque customs and traditions – very much alive today – add a richness and colour to the region.

The Basque Country is divided into three provinces – Vizcaya, Álava and Guipúzcoa – with the capital in Vitoria. Little is known about the origins of the Basque people, except that they are the oldest pre-Indo-European ethnic group on the Iberian peninsula.

Secure in their mountain homeland, the Basques lived in isolation from the rest of Spain for centuries, and so retained their distinct traditional language (Euskera) and laws *(fueros)*. When, in the 19th century, Spain started to become more centralized, the Basques felt threatened and began to fight to maintain their privileges. With the onset of industrialization and the influx of thousands of people in search of work, nationalist sentiment took hold. At the end of the century, during the Second Republic, the Basque Country was granted autonomy, though this was later repealed by the Franco regime. In the 1960s, the ETA organization began an armed struggle against Franco's repression, demanding complete Basque independence. When democracy returned to Spain in the 1970s, the Basque Country was again granted autonomy, which was accepted by most moderate Basque nationalists.

As a holiday destination, the Atlantic coast offers a tempting variety of sandy beaches, *rías* and cliffs. In the larger cities, museums give visitors the chance not only to learn about the history of the Basque lands, but also, in Bilbao for instance, to admire fantastic modern art. Those wishing for a more low-key experience can head inland to the region's historic towns, such as the former university town of Oñati.

A typical Basque farmhouse in the countryside near Gernika-Lumo

◁ The extraordinary, gleaming Museo Guggenheim in Bilbao

Exploring the Basque Country

The cliffs of the Basque Country are broken by rocky coves, *rías* and wide bays with beaches of fine yellow sand, interspersed with fishing villages. Inland, minor roads wind through wooded hills, valleys and gorges past lonely castles and isolated homesteads. Apart from its beautiful landscapes and numerous historic monuments, the region is known for its world-famous cuisine based on fish and seafood, the vibrant street and bar life, and the distinctive cultural life of the Basques, reflected both in cultural festivals and their spectacular fiestas.

SEE ALSO

- ***Where to Stay*** pp206–8
- ***Where to Eat*** pp223–5.

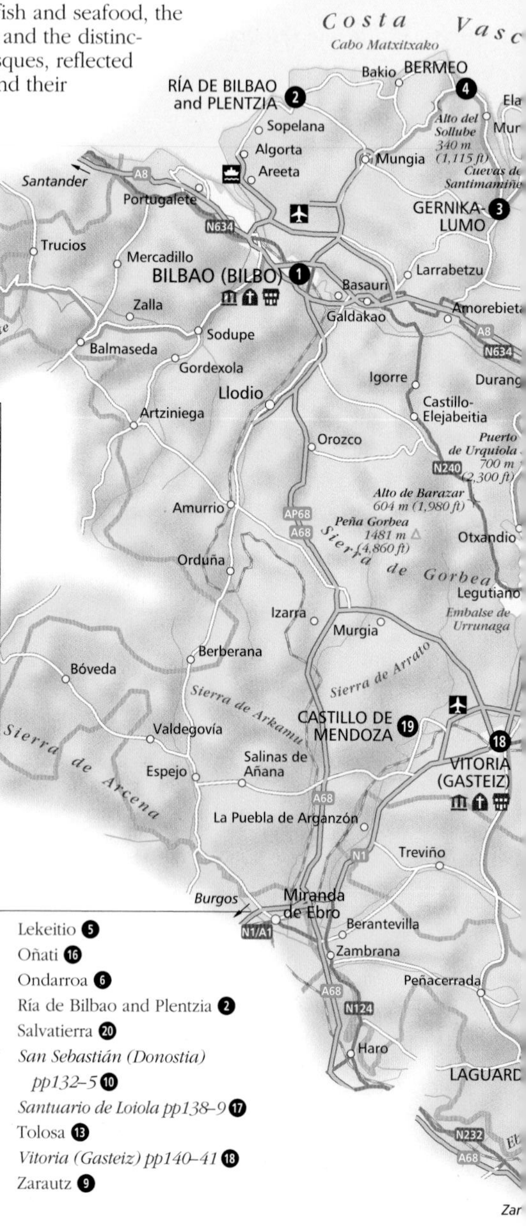

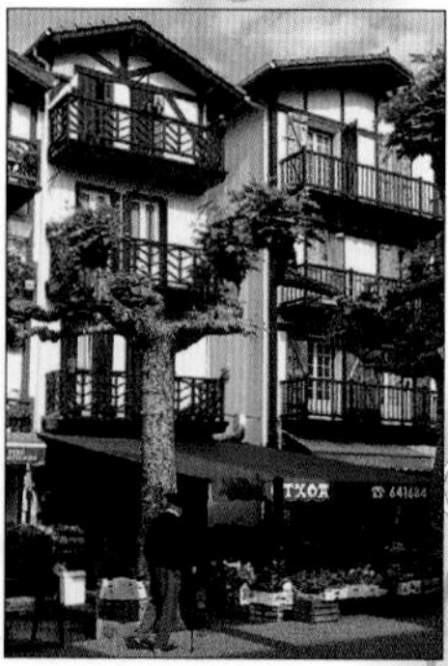

Colourful houses in the port town of Hondarribia

0 kilometres 10

0 miles 5

SIGHTS AT A GLANCE

Azpeitia 14
Bergara 15
Bilbao (Bilbo) pp122–7 1
Bermeo 4
Castillo de Mendoza 19
Deba 7
Gaceo and Alaiza 21
Gernika-Lumo 3
Getaria 8
Hernani 12
Hondarribia (Fuenterrabia) 11
Laguardia 22
Lekeitio 5
Oñati 16
Ondarroa 6
Ría de Bilbao and Plentzia 2
Salvatierra 20
San Sebastián (Donostia) pp132–5 10
Santuario de Loiola pp138–9 17
Tolosa 13
Vitoria (Gasteiz) pp140–41 18
Zarautz 9

GETTING AROUND

The A8 (E70) road runs behind the Basque coast and through Bilbao, which also has an international airport. Most towns are linked by national and local bus services. The local rail network is comfortable and has the added advantage of following some unforgettable routes. However, several of the more remote places worth visiting can only be reached by car.

Bilbao's Museo Guggenheim, one of several modern attractions

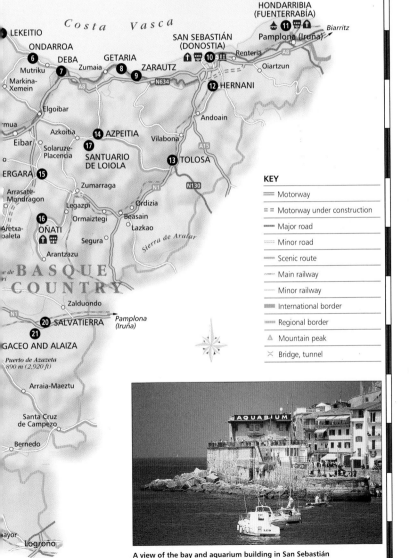

KEY

═══	Motorway
═ ═	Motorway under construction
▬▬	Major road
▬▬	Minor road
▬▬	Scenic route
┈┈	Main railway
----	Minor railway
▰▰▰	International border
▰▰▰	Regional border
△	Mountain peak
⤬	Bridge, tunnel

A view of the bay and aquarium building in San Sebastián

Street-by-Street: Bilbao (Bilbo) ❶

Bilbao's *casco viejo* – the Old Town – emerged in the 14th century along the banks of the river. Here, amid lively streets, are the Gothic Catedral de Santiago (St James) and other churches and museums. The famous Siete Calles (Seven Streets), from Barrenkale Barrena to Somera, are the focal point, busy with street life, lined with tapas bars serving delicious food, and full of crowds of boisterous locals every weekend. The splendid 19th-century Plaza Nueva is another hub of the Old Town.

Iglesia de San Nicolás de Bari
Built on an octagonal plan, this Baroque church is dedicated to the patron saint of sailors. The interior features a beautiful reredos.

Coat of arms
Visible on the façades of the ancient, often richly decorated, Old Town houses are the imaginative coats of arms of their former owners.

★ **Teatro Arriaga**
Rich in ornamentation, this early 20th-century building is a symbol of the Plaza de Arriaga (known as El Arenal).

ATHLETIC BILBAO FOOTBALL CLUB

Athletic Bilbao is the oldest football (soccer) club in the Basque Country, having been established in 1898. It is almost unique in top-flight European football in that only native Basques can play for the team. Athletic Bilbao has always been in Spain's top league – it has won the title eight times, the King's Cup 24 times and the Super Cup once. The team, also known as the *rojiblancos* on account of their red and white strips, play at the San Mamés stadium. Supporters queue for hours for tickets.

The badge of Athletic Bilbao football club

0 metres   50

0 yards   50

KEY

‐ ‐ ‐   Suggested route

★ Plaza Nueva
This Neoclassical arcaded square
is lined with attractive pavement
cafés. It is also the venue for the
Sunday plant, animal and
antiques markets.

VISITORS' CHECKLIST

Vizcaya. 354,000. Loiu.
Estación de Abando, Plaza
Circular 2. Termibus, Gurtubay
1; 944 39 52 05. in Santurce;
944 87 12 00. Plaza
Ensanche 11; 944 79 57 60.
Sun. Semana Grande
(mid-Aug), St. James (25 Jul),
San Ignacio de Loiola (31 Jul).
www.bilbao.net/bilbaoturismo

★ Catedral de Santiago
This 14th-century Gothic
cathedral, with a small
cloister, acquired a Neo-
Classical façade and tower in
the 19th century. A square
with an elegant fountain
extends in front of the church.

Museo Vasco
This museum's best-known treasure is
the Mikeldi Idol, a wild boar carved
from stone, dating from the Iron Age.
There are also displays of tools, model
ships and Basque gravestones.

STAR SIGHTS

★ Catedral de Santiago

★ Plaza Nueva

★ Teatro Arriaga

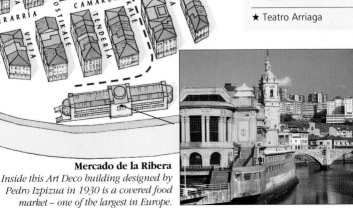

Mercado de la Ribera
Inside this Art Deco building designed by
Pedro Izpizua in 1930 is a covered food
market – one of the largest in Europe.

Bilbao: Museo Guggenheim

The Museo Guggenheim is the jewel in Bilbao's cultural crown. The building itself is a star attraction: a mind-boggling array of silvery curves by the American architect Frank Gehry, which are alleged to resemble a ship or a flower. The Guggenheim's collection represents an intriguingly broad spectrum of modern and contemporary art, and includes works by Abstract Expressionists such as Willem de Kooning and Mark Rothko. Most of the art shown here is displayed as part of an ongoing series of temporary exhibitions and major retrospectives. Some of these are also staged at the Guggenheim museums in New York, Venice and Berlin.

Roofscape
The Guggenheim's prow-like points and metallic material make it comparable to a ship.

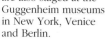

The tower, on the far side of the bridge, was designed to resemble a sail. It is not an exhibition space.

The Puente de la Salve was incorporated into the design of the building, which extends underneath it.

★ Titanium Façade
Rarely employed in buildings, titanium is more usually made into parts for aircraft In total, 60 tonnes were used here, but the layer is only 3 mm (0.1 in) thick.

The Snake, by Richard Serra, was created in hot-rolled steel. It is over 30 m (100 ft) long.

★ Fish Gallery
Dominated by Richard Serra's Snake, *this gallery is the museum's largest. The fish motif, seen in the flowing shape, is one of architect Frank Gehry's favourites.*

★ **Atrium**
The space in which visitors to the museum first find themselves is the extraordinary 60-m (165-ft) high atrium. It serves as an orientation point and its height makes it a dramatic setting for large pieces.

Puppy, by American artist Jeff Koons, has a coat of flowers irrigated by an internal system. Originally a temporary feature, the sculpture's popularity with Bilbao's residents earned it a permanent spot.

Second-floor balcony

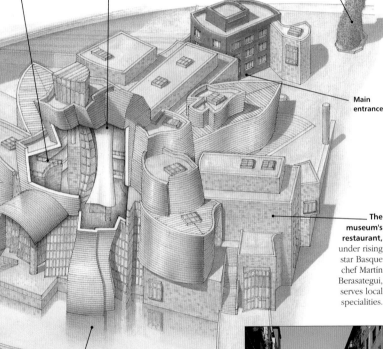

Main entrance

The museum's restaurant, under rising star Basque chef Martín Berasategui, serves local specialities.

Water garden beside the Río Nervión

View from the City
Approaching along the Calle de Iparraguirre, the "Guggen", as the museum has been nicknamed by locals, stands out amid traditional buildings.

Exploring Bilbao

Visitors flock to Bilbao to see its museums. By the river is the city's medieval heart, the *casco viejo* (Old Town), built in the 14th century. This area, which can be explored on foot, is home to most of the main sights.

🏠 Cathedral de Santiago

Plazuela Santiago 1. *Tel.* 944 15 36 27.
☐ 10am–1pm & 5–7:30pm
Mon–Sat, 10am–1pm Sun & hols.
Dating from the 14th century, the Gothic cathedral has a slender tower rising proudly above the rooftops of the Old Town. The building is dedicated to St James, the patron saint of Bilbao since 1643. The neo-Gothic façade – the work of Severino de Achúcarro – dates from the 19th century. There is also a Tuscan-style portico and a small cloister.

🏠 Iglesia San Nicolás de Bari

Plazuela de San Nicolás 1.
Tel. 944 16 34 24.
☐ 10:30am–1pm &
5:30–7:30pm Mon–Sat .
This 18th-century Baroque church is dedicated to

Belfry of the Iglesia San Nicolás de Bari

St Nicholas – San Nicolás de Bari – the patron saint of sailors. Designed on an octagonal plan, the church boasts valuable retables and sculptures by Juan de Mena. The broad façade is adorned with two identical towers and the coat of arms of Bilbao.

🏠 Basilica de Begoña

Calle Virgen de Begoña 38. *Tel.* 944 12 70 91 (sacristy). ☐ 9:30am–1:30pm & 5:30–8:30pm.
Long revered by the inhabitants of Bilbao, the Madonna of Begoña's shrine is the city's most important church. It was built on a hilltop at the very spot where the Madonna is said to have appeared in the 16th century. The style of the basilica is Basque Gothic. The interior has a Neo-Classical reredos with a niche containing a 13th-century sculpture of the Madonna and Child. The portico with the huge triumphal arch dates from the Renaissance while the belfry is a 20th-century addition.

Detail of the high altar in the Basilica de Begoña

🏛 Museo Arqueológico, Etnógrafico e Histórico Vasco

Plaza Miguel de Unamuno 4.
Tel. 944 15 54 23. ☐ 11am–5pm Tue–Sat, 11am–2pm Sun. & 🖼 (free Thu). 🗝 by prior arrangement.
The Museum of Archaeology and Local History, also known as the Museo Vasco de Bilbao, occupies the Baroque building of the Jesuit Colegio de San Andrés. The exhibits focus on the history of the Basques. In addition to archaeological finds, there are sections on traditional Basque

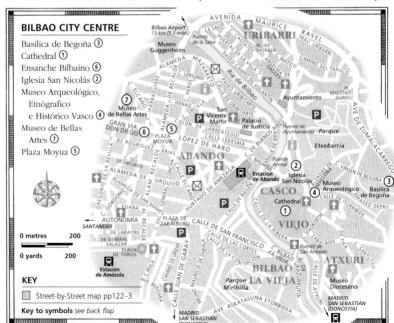

BILBAO CITY CENTRE

Basilica de Begoña ③
Cathedral ①
Ensanche Bilbaíno ⑥
Iglesia San Nicolás ②
Museo Arqueológico,
   Etnógrafico
   e Histórico Vasco ④
Museo de Bellas
   Artes ⑦
Plaza Moyua ⑤

0 metres   200
0 yards   200

KEY

▨ Street-by-Street map pp122–3

Key to symbols see back flap

sports, the Basque maritime legacy, heraldry and weapons. On the top floor is a model of Vizcaya province, while the ground floor features one of the oldest archaeological finds – the Mikeldi Idol, a sculpture in the shape of the boar from the Iron Age.

Plaza Moyua

This oval plaza is laid out with formal gardens, with a fountain at the centre. Ernest Hemingway *(see p155)* stayed at the Carlton Hotel nearby.

Ensanche Bilbaíno

The newer part of Bilbao stretches along the Gran Vía de Don Diego López de Haro. Of note here are the Abando and Santander railway stations, the stock exchange building, several churches and the Estadio de San Mamés – home of Athletic Bilbao Football club *(see p122)*. Also worth visiting is the Parque Doña Casilda de Iturrizar.

A sculpture by Eduardo Chillida in front of the Museo de Bellas Artes

Museo de Bellas Artes

Plaza del Museo 2. ***Tel.*** *944 39 60 60.* 10am–8pm Tue–Sat, 10am–2pm Sun. (free Wed).
Set in the Parque Doña Casilda de Iturrizar, in the newer part of town, the large Museum of Fine Art has more than 6,000 exhibits from the 12th century to the present day. Apart from works by artists of international fame, such as Velázquez, Ribera, El Greco and Zurbarán, there are paintings by leading modern Basque artists, including Regoyos, Zuloaga and Echevarría, as well as drawings and sculptures. In the contemporary art section are works by Chillida and Tàpies, among others.

The Ría de Bilbao cut by the Nervión river

Ría de Bilbao and Plentzia ❷

The Ría de Bilbao, created by the Nervión river, is known as the "main street of Vizcaya". It stretches 14 km (9 miles) northwest of Bilbao before entering the sea off the working-class town of **Portugalete**, known for its "hanging bridge" (Puente Colgante) across the Nervión. Along the less industrial east bank of the *ría* is the attractive suburb of **Getxo**, with its beaches, marina and waterfront lined with 19th-century villas. At the *ría's* northern end is **Algorta**, a former fishing port that has a beach, pretty old harbour and streets winding up a steep cliff. Beyond there, the *ría* runs up to **Plentzia** – a small but busy port town with an attractive old quarter.

All these places can be reached by metro from Bilbao.

Gernika-Lumo ❸

Vizcaya. 15,500. Artekalea 8; 946 25 58 92. Mon. Anniversary of bombing of Gernika (26 Mar). www.gernika-lumo.net

This little town is of great symbolic significance to the Basques as an ancient seat of lawmaking and as the target of the world's first saturation bombing raid, carried out by Nazi aircraft at Franco's request in 1937 *(see p43)*.

The most important place in the town is the Neo-Classical Casa de Juntas, which houses the parliament of the province of Vizcaya.

In the Parque de los Pueblos de Europa are sculptures by Henry Moore and Eduardo Chillida. Also of note are the Gothic Iglesia de Santa María, the Museo de la Paz (Museum of Peace) and Museo Euskal Herria (Museum of the Basque Country).

THE TREE OF GERNIKA

For centuries, Basque leaders met in democratic assembly under an oak on a hillside in Gernika-Lumo. In the garden of the Casa de Juntas, inside a pavilion and closely guarded, is the petrified trunk of the *Gernikako Arbola* – the oldest of the oak trees preserved here – symbolizing the ancient roots of the Basque people. It was already over 300 years old when it caught fire in 1860. Subsequent oaks at the site have all been grown from acorns taken or descended from the original oak, most recently in February 2005.

The petrified trunk of the *Gernikako Arbola*

The jagged rocks of the inaccessible Matxitxako headland west of Bermeo

Bermeo ❹

Vizcaya. 🏠 18,000. 🚉 *Lamera s/n; 946 17 91 54.* 📷 *Andra Mari Jaiak (7–16 Sep).* **www**.bermeo.org

Bermeo is the best-known small port on the Basque coast, with a busy fishing harbour and excellent seafood restaurants. The town's oldest church is Santa Eufemia (13th–15th century), an aisleless Gothic structure that incorporates Byzantine elements. The Gothic Torre Ercilla accommodates the **Museo del Pescador**, which has an exhibition on the Basques' long heritage of fishing and whaling across the Atlantic.

Several hermitages are located in Bermeo and the surrounding area. The most famous of these is the **Ermita San Juan de Gaztelugatxe**, situated on a rocky island a few kilometres from the town and reached by climbing a flight of 231 steps.

🏛 **Museo del Pescador**
Torre Ercilla. **Tel** 946 88 11 71.
⭕ *10am–2pm & 4-7:30 pm Tue–Sat, 10am–12:30pm Sun.* ♿ 🎧

Environs
Cabo Matxitxako is a remote headland with two lighthouses. The best beaches are to be found in **Mundaka**, which also has the best surfing in northern Spain. **Elantxobe**, in turn, is a picturesque fishing village that spreads up the precipitous slopes of the highest cliff on the Basque coastline – Monte Ogoño (280 m/918 ft above sea level).

Lekeitio ❺

Vizcaya. 🏠 7,300. 🚌 🚉 *Independentzia Enparantza; 946 84 40 17.* 📷 *San Pedro (29 Jun), San Antolín (1–8 Sep).* **www**.lekeitio.com

Lekeitio is one of many fishing villages on the Basque coast and its architecture is maritime in style. It also has several historic buildings, including the Gothic **Basilica de la Asunción de Santa María**. Inside is a 16th-century altar. Visible from the town's beautiful beach is the island of **San Nicolás**, which can be reached on foot at low tide.

For years, Lekeitio rivalled San Sebastián as the Basque Country's summer capital, with elegant 19th-century villas lining its pretty seafront. The surrounding area has good terrain for off-road biking and horse-riding.

The town is famous for one of the most raucous of Basque fiestas – the 'goose games' of San Antolín *(see p32).*

Boats in the port of Ondarroa

Ondarroa ❻

Vizcaya. 🏠 9,600. 🚌 🚉 *C/ Erribera 9; 946 83 19 51 or 946 16 90 69.* 📷 *Andra Mari Jaiak (14–17 Aug).* **www**.ondarroa.net

The road between Lekeitio and Ondarroa is pleasantly planted with pines. Ondarroa is a small but charming old port on the border with Guipúzcoa province, with an animated harbour and a colourful fishing fleet. It has preserved its medieval town plan, with the names of the streets referring to geographical locations or to traditional Basque sports.

Spanning the Artibai river is the **Puente Viejo**, a Roman bridge that was reconstructed in the 20th century.

Other buildings typical of the area include the 15th-century Gothic **Iglesia de Santa María**, built on a clifftop, and the **Torre de Likona**, a border watchtower from the same period. It was here that the mother of St Ignatius Loyola, founder of the Jesuit order, was born.

The **old town hall** has a façade with Tuscan columns. On a nearby hilltop rises the **Iglesia de Nuestra Señora de la Antigua**, dating from the 12th century but rebuilt in the 17th century. It affords breathtaking views of the surrounding area.

Deba ❼

Guipúzcoa. 🏠 *5,250.* 🚌 🚆 **ℹ**
Farkalia 4; 943 19 24 52. 🎭 *San
Roque (14–20 Aug).* **www**.deba.net

Deba was a fashionable resort
in the 1900s, and so has a line
of grand old villas beside its
long, wide beach. With crashing
surf, it still attracts scores of
visitors on summer weekends.

In the town are a few palaces
from its 16th-century Golden
Age. An important monument
is the massive Gothic **Iglesia de
Santa María**, with a beautiful
cloister and colourfully
decorated entrance – one of
the province's landmarks.

Another well-known site is
the shrine in Itziar dedicated
to the Virgin Mary. Its interior
has a Romanesque sculpture
of Mary, patron saint of sailors,
and a Plateresque altar. Outside
is the bronze sculpture, *La
Maternidad* by Jorge Oteiza.

Environs

A clifftop footpath with magnificent coastal views leads through
green fields and past huge old
farms to **Zumaia**. This popular
resort has broad, sandy beaches,
including the Playa Santiago. A
pleasant afternoon can be spent
strolling in the old quarter and
visiting the attractive marina.

In the **Museo de Ignacio
Zuloaga**, home of a celebrated
early 20th-century Basque
painter, are displayed Zuloaga's
colourful studies of Basque
rural and maritime life.

🏛 **Museo de Ignacio Zuloaga**
Casa Santiago, Etxea 4. **Tel** *943 86
23 41.* ◯ *Apr–Sep: 4–8pm Wed–
Sun.* 🖥 *www*.ignaciozuloaga.com

NAVIGATORS OF THE BASQUE COAST

Juan Sebastián Elcano, born in Getaria, led the first expedition
to circumnavigate the globe. Following the death of Magellan,
Elcano assumed command on the famous round-the-world
voyage. On 6 September 1522, after a voyage
lasting three years of 78,000 km
(48,500 miles), Elcano returned to
Seville on his ship, the *Victoria*.

Another Basque, Andrés de Urdaneta,
led the second Spanish round-the-world
voyage in the 1530s. In the 1560s Miguel
López de Legazpi conquered the
Philippines for Spain. Basque sailors
later took part in the exploration
of Mexico. In the 1600s navigator
Sebastián Vizcaíno explored and
mapped the coast of California.

**Portrait of the navigator
Juan Sebastián Elcano**

Getaria ❽

Guipúzcoa. 🏠 *2500.* 🚌 **ℹ** *Parque
Aldamar 2; 943 14 09 57.* 🎭 *San
Antón (17 Jan), San Salvador (6–8
Aug).* **www**.getaria.net

Getaria is a charming trawler
port with lively cafés. It is also
the centre of Txakolí wine production and known for good
food. Just off the coast lies the
tiny island of **Monte San Antón**,
which is artificially joined to the
mainland. It is known as *El
Ratón de Getaria* – the Mouse
of Getaria – on account of its
weird shape. Several archaeological finds have been made
near the 14th-century **Iglesia
de San Salvador**.

Getaria also features the
Museo Cristobal Balenciaga, a
showpiece for the fashion
designer who lived here.

🏛 **Museo Cristobal
Balenciaga**
Parque Aldamar 6. **Tel** *943 00 47
77.* ◯ *10am–2pm & 4–7pm
Tue–Sat, 10:30am–2pm Sun–Mon.*

**The octagonal tower of the Iglesia
de San Salvador in Getaria**

Zarautz ❾

Guipúzcoa. 🏠 *22,000.* 🚆 🚌
ℹ *Nafarroa 3; 943 83 09 90.*
🎭 *San Pelaio (25–27 Jun), Virgen
(14–17 Aug), Fiesta Vasca (9 Sep).*

Like many old towns in the
region, Zarautz was traditionally associated with whaling.
Nowadays, the mainstay of
the local economy is tourism.
The town boasts the
province's longest beach and
promenade. The sea here
offers excellent conditions for
surfing, while the nearby
vine-clad hillsides produce
the region's famous Txakolí
wines. In the old quarter are
houses with coats of arms,
the Gothic **Torre Luzea**, the
medieval **Iglesia de Santa
María La Real**, and the
Renaissance **Palacio de
Narros**. The local cuisine is
considered to be among the
best in the Basque Country.

The building of the Museo de Ignacio Zuloaga in Zumaia, near Deba

Eduardo Chillida's *The Comb of the Winds* on the beach at San Sebastián ▷

Street-by-Street: San Sebastián (Donostia) ❿

San Sebastián was the most fashionable summer resort
in Spain at the beginning of the 20th century, and has
an elegant traditional promenade all along its curving
beach. Today it is delicately old-fashioned.
The superb curving bay is closed
off by the green hills of Monte
Urgull and Monte Igeldo. In
the mouth of the bay lies
the tortoise-shaped island
of Santa Clara. The city
is renowned for its
summer arts festivals,
street life centred in the
old town, and unrivalled
pintxos (local version
of tapas).

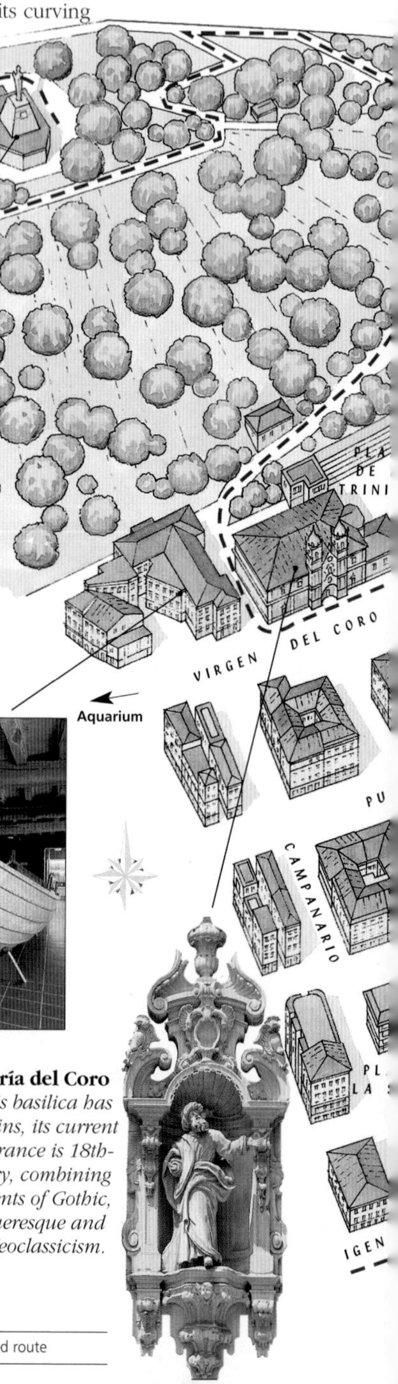

★ Monte Urgull
*Rising above the
Old Town, Monte
Urgull is home to the
ruined 16th-century
fortress of Santa
Cruz de la Mota. On
the summit stands a
statue of Christ – the
Sagrado Corazón.*

Aquarium

Museo Naval
*Set in an 18th-century build-
ing, the Maritime Museum
offers a comprehensive view
of the Basques and their
connections with the sea.*

Santa María del Coro
*Although this basilica has
earlier origins, its current
appearance is 18th-
century, combining
elements of Gothic,
Churrigueresque and
Neoclassicism.*

STAR SIGHTS

★ Monte Urgull

★ Museo San Telmo

★ Pl de la Constitución

KEY

– – – Suggested route

★ **Museo San Telmo**
This neo-Renaissance building at the foot of Monte Urgull was once a Dominican monastery (1531–51) and then the headquarters of the artillery.

VISITORS' CHECKLIST

Guipúzcoa. 182,600. 22 km (14 miles) from San Sebastián, Fuenterrabia; 943 61 70 40.
Estación del Norte, Paseo de Francia, 943 28 30 89, 943 28 35 99; Euskotren – Estación de Amara, Pl. Easo 9, 943 45 01 31.
Estación de Autobuses, Plaza Pío XII; 902 10 12 10. Reina Regeate 3; 943 48 11 66.
Sun. San Sebastián (20 Jan), Jazz Festival (end of Jul) Semana Grande (week of 15 Aug), Film Festival (2nd half Sep). www.donostia.org
www.sansebastianturismo.com

Iglesia de San Vicente
This 16th-century Gothic church is the oldest in San Sebastián, and has suffered several fires over time.

SANTA CORDA

31 DE AGOSTO

JUAN DE BILBAO

IÑIGO

PLAZA DE LA CONSTITU CIÓN

PESCADERÍA

S. JERONIMO

F. CALBETÓN

EMBALTRÁN

0 metres 50

0 yards 50

★ **Plaza de la Constitución**
The houses here have numbered balconies, dating from when the square was used as a bullring and the balconies were seating for the public.

ALAMEDA DEL BOULEVARD

NTXO

Town Hall
Erected in the 19th century as a casino, this building later became the town hall when gambling was banned in the city.

The tortoise-shaped island of Santa Clara with the city in the background

Exploring San Sebastián

The most interesting parts of the city are the Old Town and Monte Urgull, the spectacular bay and seafront promenade with its hugely popular beaches of La Concha and Ondarreta, and Monte Igeldo, on top of which stands a lighthouse. All of these sites can be visited on foot. The summits of the two hills are well worth the climb.

🏞 Bahía de la Concha

Between Monte Urgull and Monte Igeldo, along the Paseo de la Concha promenade, extend two beaches – the smaller and more fashionable Playa Ondarreta, and the larger Playa de la Concha. The beaches are divided by a curious rock formation, on which rises the Palacio de Miramar, a palace with carefully maintained gardens. There are excellent views of the bay and the island of Santa Clara from here.

Nearby is Eduardo Chillida's series of sculptures *The Comb of the Winds*. The huge russet-coloured claws complement the grey rock and emerald sea *(see pp130–31)*.

🏛 Old Town

Following a fire in 1813, the Old Town was reconstructed in a Neo-Classical style while preserving the medieval street plan. The Parte Vieja is the veritable heart of the old city. Its inhabitants are divided into the *Joshemaritarras* – those born in the vicinity of the Gothic church of San Vicente – and the *Koxkeros* – those born in the vicinity of the church of Santa María. In

the latter church is a sculpture of the city's patron – the Black Madonna and Child, known as the Virgen del Coro.

The main axis of the Old Town is the Calle Mayor. At one end of it stands the church of Santa María, and at the other the cathedral of Buen Pastor.

Another important site is the Plaza de la Constitución, a handsome arcaded square also known as the Consti. Bullfights used to occur here, and today fiestas are held. The Old Town is packed with bars serving delicious *pintxos*.

A street in the Parte Vieja leading to Santa María del Coro

🌳 Monte Urgull

Criss-crossed by numerous parkland paths, Monte Urgull is an ideal place for an afternoon stroll. Within its perimeter is the Cementerio de los Ingleses, a cemetery dedicated to the English who perished while trying to capture the city from the French in 1813; today, it is one of the most serene and

pleasant spots on the hill. The summit is occupied by the ruined 16th-century fortress of Santa Cruz de la Mota. Some old cannons can still be seen. The remnants of the building accommodate three chapels, including one dedicated to the Cristo de la Mota. Above this chapel rises a huge statue of Christ – the Sagrado Corazón.

🏛 Museo Naval & Aquarium

Museum Paseo del Muelle 24. **Tel** 943 43 00 51. ⬚ 10am–1:30pm & 4–7:30pm Tue–Sat, 11am–2pm Sun. 🎟 (free Thu).
Aquarium Plaza Carlos Blasco de Imaz. **Tel** 943 44 00 99. ⬚ Apr–Jun & Sep: 10am–8pm Mon–Fri, 10am–9pm Sat–Sun & hols; Oct–Mar: 10am–7pm Mon–Fri, 10am–8pm Sat–Sun & hols. Jul–Aug: 10am–9pm daily. 🎟
The Maritime Museum, housed in an 18th-century port building, is entirely devoted to the seafaring life of the Basque people. The display illustrates shipbuilding, the evolution of ports and the development of commerce, and includes a collection of navigational instruments.

In the nearby aquarium visitors can walk through an underwater tunnel while viewing sea creatures in their natural environment.

🏠 Iglesia de Santa María del Coro

Dedicated to the city's patron saint, this church contains a figure of the Black Madonna. According to legend, a certain monk – exhausted by having to climb into the choir to worship the figure – attempted to take it home with him. He hid the figure under his habit and tried to leave, but discovered he was unable to cross the threshold of the church. Only when he returned the figure to its rightful place was he able to leave.

The current church dates from the 18th century. Designed by the architects Lizardi and Ibero, it combines elements of Gothic, Churriguresque and Neo-Classicism. The Baroque façade, with two towers, a clock and a figure of St Sebastian, faces Calle Mayor. Inside is an alabaster cross by Eduardo Chillida.

The neo-Gothic Catedral del Buen Pastor

🏛 Museo San Telmo

Plaza Zuloaga 1. **Tel.** 943 42 49 70.
◻ 10am–1:30pm & 4–8pm Tue–Sat,
10:30am–2pm Sun & hols.

Inside this Neo-Renaissance building at the foot of Monte Urgull is a fascinating display on Basque culture, mythology and folk traditions. Its exhibits include ancient discoidal tombstones, magic charms, a reconstruction of a traditional cottage, musical instruments, tools and sports equipment. The ground floor comprises a church, a beautiful cloister accommodating the archaeological section, and rooms for temporary exhibitions.

There is also a picture gallery with paintings from the Gothic era to the 20th century, with works by El Greco, Alonso Cano, Rubens, Ribera, Depièce and Zuloaga, while contemporary Basque art is displayed on the second floor.

🔒 Cathedral

Plaza del Buen Pastor. **Tel.** 943 46 45 16. ◻ 8:30am–12:30pm & 5–8pm Mon–Fri, during services Sat–Sun.

The neo-Gothic cathedral was designed by Manuel de Echave, while the 75-m (246-ft) high tower is the work of Ramón Cortázar. It features rich ornamentation, including stained-glass windows by Juan Bautista Lázara, gargoyles and pinnacles.

🏛 New Town

Right up until the 19th century, San Sebastián was encircled by walls. When these became defunct, a new solution was needed – especially after 1854, when the city became the provincial capital. The architect Antonio Cortázar put forward a project for the redevelopment of the city: a new district arose with a grid of broad, airy boulevards leading down to the Paseo de la Concha, the beach-side promenade. Key elements of this redevelopment included the cathedral of Buen Pastor, the Palacio Miramar, and the tree-lined Plaza de Guipúzcoa. The most impressive building remains Goiko's Palacio de la Diputación, its façade decorated with the busts of famous Basques.

🎭 Kursaal

Avda. de Zurriola 1. **Tel.** 943 00 30 00. www.kursaal.org

This spectacular, avant-garde convention centre was designed by architect Rafael Moneo, and opened in 1999.

Located next to Gros beach, to the east of the old town, it has helped to revive this once under-used beach. The glass-walled structure now hosts the Film Festival, concerts and other big cultural events.

♣ Monte Igeldo

Monte Igeldo, which closes the western end of the bay, looks as if it has toppled over – the layers of rock at the foot of the hill lie vertically. The hill itself, with a funfair and a 19th-century lighthouse, is an ideal spot for rest and recreation. A **funicular railway** takes visitors to the summit.

🚡 Funicular Railway

Tel. 943 21 05 64 or 943 21 02 11.
◻ Spring & autumn: 11am–8pm Mon–Wed, 10am–9pm Thu–Sun & hols; summer: 11am–10pm; winter: 11am–6pm Mon–Tue & Thu–Fri, 11am–8pm Sat & hols. 🎫

The tower on Monte Igeldo – a good observation point

FESTIVALS IN SAN SEBASTIÁN

The International Film Festival, founded in 1953, is one of five leading European annual film festivals. It is held in September and draws more than 100,000 spectators. The special Donostia Prize is awarded as a tribute to the career of an actor or director; recent winners include the actor Jessica Lange and film director and screen writer Woody Allen. Prizes also go to new films. In addition, the city hosts one of Europe's oldest jazz festivals (July), an international theatre festival, and a classical music festival (August).

Jessica Lange at the Film Festival

Boats at the port in Hondarribia, with the town in the background

Hondarribia (Fuenterrabia) ⓫

Guipúzcoa. 🏘 *16,000.* 🚉 🚌 🚍
🛈 *Calle Javier Ugarte 6; 943 64 54 58.* 🎪 *La Kutxa Entrega (25 Jul).*
www.bidasoaturismo.com

The historic quarter of this port-town at the mouth of the Río Bidasoa (opposite France) is encircled by 15th-century walls with two gates – the **Puerta de Santa María** and the **Puerta San Nicolás.** Within the quarter are old houses with carved eaves, balconies and coats of arms. The narrow cobbled streets cluster around the church of **Santa María de la Asunción**, a Gothic structure dating from the early 15th century, which incorporates Renaissance and Baroque elements. Aside from the cross-vaulting, the highlight is a remarkable three-faced image of the Holy Trinity, found underneath the choir. In the 16th century, the

Church condemned such images, and this is one·of very few to have survived in Spain. Also of interest are the Churrigueresque-style retables.

Hondarribia is one of the prettiest of all Basque towns. The lively fishermen's quarter of **La Marina** is famous for its tall, brightly painted houses all crowded together.

Environs

In the historic port-town of **Pasai-Donibane** is the house where the writer Victor Hugo once lived. Regattas are held in the local bay here.

Hernani ⓬

Guipúzcoa. 🏘 *18,800.* 🚌 🚍 🎪
San Juan (24 Jun). **www**.hernani.net

The principal attraction of Hernani is the **Museo Chillida-Leku**, dedicated to the life and work of Eduardo Chillida. It presents the evolution of the artist's work over a period of

50 years. The larger sculptures are displayed in the 12-hectare (30-acre) garden, the smaller ones in the Zabalaga *caserío.* The sculptures are made of alabaster, steel and granite.

The other interesting buildings are the 19th-century, two-storey town hall, supported on seven arches, and the Portalondo house, an example of medieval defensive architecture, whose walls are lined with stone facing.

🏛 **Museo Chillida-Leku**
Jáuregui 66. **Tel** *943 33 60 06.*
⏰ *Jul–Aug: 10:30am–8pm Mon & Wed–Sat 10:30am–3pm Sun & hols; Sep–Jun: 10:30am–3pm Wed–Sun.* 🎫 ♿

One of the charming streets in the small town of Hernani

Tolosa ⓭

Guipúzcoa. 🏘 *19,000.* 🚌 🚍
🛈 *Plaza Santa Maria 1; 943 69 74 13.* 🛍 *Sat.* 🎪 *San Juan (24 Jun).*

For centuries Tolosa was an important cultural, commercial and industrial centre. In the

CASERÍOS

The *caserío* (or *baserrí* in Basque), an often huge stone house with a sloping roof, is a typical feature of the Basque landscape. *Caseríos* stand alone in the countryside and are not part of villages; they were originally independent

A typical Basque *caserío*

farms, where many generations of a single family would live, with their animals on the ground floor below. Each *caserío* had its own name, from which the surname of the family dwelling there would derive.

19th century, it was occupied by the French and was the capital of Guipúzcoa province during the Carlist Wars *(see p41)*. Its renowned carnival was held even during the Franco era, and its November choral music festival is one of the best in the country. Tolosa is also famous for *alubias de Tolosa* – a red bean grown around the town and featured in hearty dishes.

Colourful houses along the river in Tolosa

In the Old Town's numerous narrow streets and squares, there are examples of Basque Gothic and Baroque; one such building is the imposing 17th-century Gothic aisled church of Santa María. The church boasts cross-vaulting and a Baroque façade designed by Martín de Carrera. Underneath the choir is a late-Romanesque portico.

Azpeitia ⑭

Guipúzcoa. 🚶 13,800. 🚌 ℹ️
Santuario de Loiola; 943 85 08 43.
🎭 San Sebastián (19–20 Jan), San Ignacio (30 Jul), Santo Tomás (21 Dec). www.azpeitia.net

As many as 360 *caseríos* are preserved in the vicinity of Azpeitia. The town itself features many beautiful buildings, some in the Mudéjar style; these include, for instance, the Casa Altuna, the magnificent Casa Anchieta – which once belonged to a musician employed by the Catholic Monarchs – and the 14th-century Magdalena hermitage. Also well represented is the Plateresque style, which is evident on the windows of the Casa Plateresca and on the portico of the church of San Sebastián de Soreasu, a Gothic structure whose tower was built by the Knights Templar.

One of the town's oldest buildings is the huge medieval Casa Torre de Enparan, now housing the municipal library. However, Azpeitia is most famous for its shrine to St Ignatius Loyola and other sites associated with the founder of the Jesuit order *(see p138)*.

Bergara ⑮

Guipúzcoa. 🚶 14,900. 🚉 🚌 ℹ️
Plaza San Martín de Aguirre. **Tel** 943 77 91 28. 🎭 San Martín de Aguirre (16 Sep). www.bergara.net

Bergara is one of the most characterful of Basque country towns, with an old centre full of distinguished colleges, churches and mansions built for aristocrats during the town's Golden Age in the 16th and 17th centuries. The first Carlist War ended here in 1839 *(see p41)* – the treaty was signed in the 17th-century **Casa Iritzar**, which features wrought-iron balconies and a coat of arms at the corner of the building.

There are other fine buildings, such as the 16th-century **Casa Arostegi**, which holds exhibitions, and the **Casa Jauregi** (c.1500), which has reliefs depicting plant motifs and figures of royal couples.

Basque Gothic is represented by the aisled church of **Santa Marina de Oxirondo**, built on a square plan. Its tower is Baroque, as is the impressive reredos by Miguel de Irazusta and Luis Salvador Carmona. Also Baroque is the **Iglesia de San Pedro de Ariznoa**, with its squat tower; inside is a canvas with shepherds paying homage to the Infant Jesus.

Oñati ⑯

Guipúzcoa. 🚶 10,700. 🚌 ℹ️ San Juan 14; 943 78 34 53. 🎭 San Miguel (29 Sep–4 Oct). www.oinati.org

A walk through old Oñati is a real treat for architecture enthusiasts. The Universidad de Sancti Spiritus – designed by Picart and Gibaja – was the first Basque university, funded by Bishop Zuazola; it operated between 1551 and 1901. The Plateresque façade is adorned with four pilasters and several figures referring to both mythological and religious tradition. A superb courtyard can be found within.

The Monasterio de Bidaurreta, in turn, is a mix of Gothic, Renaissance and Mudéjar. The interior contains aristocratic family tombs and two altars – one Baroque, the other Plateresque in style.

The Plaza de Santa Marina is surrounded by Baroque palaces.

🏛 **Universidad de Sancti Spiritus**
Calle Universitate Etorbidea 8.
Tel 943 78 34 53. ⏱ visits by appointment only; phone ahead to arrange. 🎥 📷 ♿

Environs

From Oñati, a mountain road ascends for 9 km (6 miles) to the **Santuario de Arantzazu**, which lies in the valley at the foot of Alona Hill. In 1469 it is believed a shepherd saw a vision of the Virgin here. This modernist church, built to replace an earlier one, was designed in the 1950s by Javier Sáiz Oiza and Luis Laorga. It has a tall belfry, huge wooden altar, and doors designed by the sculptor Eduardo Chillida. The Virgin of Arantzazu is the province's patron.

The Universidad de Sancti Spiritus in Oñati

Santuario de Loiola ⑰

Iñigo de Loiola, or St Ignatius (1491–1556), founder of the Jesuit order, was born in the stone manor known as Santa Casa (Holy House). The manor was incorporated in 1681–1738 into a shrine designed by Carlo Fontana, and the rooms where the Loyola family had lived were converted into chapels. The most important of these is the Chapel of the Conversion, the room where Ignatius, as a young soldier, had a profound religious experience while recovering from a battle injury. The Baroque basilica, with a circular nave and a Churrigueresque dome, is the shrine's highlight.

★ **Interior of the Basilica**
The richly decorated and gilded Churrigueresque interior is covered in grey and pink marble.

Figures by the Santa Casa
The bronze figures, by Juan Flotats, show the return of Ignatius, who had been injured while defending the castle in Pamplona.

★ **Santa Casa**
In the Holy House – the original home of the Loyola family, around which the Sanctuary was built – is the Chapel of the Conversion, with a beautiful sculpture of Ignatius Loyola.

THE FOUNDING OF THE JESUIT ORDER

The Jesuit order was founded in Rome in 1539 by St Ignatius, a former soldier, and a group of priests who were dedicated to purifying the Church and resisting Protestantism. Pope Paul III soon approved the order's establishment, with Ignatius as Superior General. The order, which grew wealthy, vowed military obedience to the Pope and became his most powerful weapon against the Reformation. Today, there are nearly 20,000 Jesuits working, mainly in education, in 127 countries.

St Ignatius of Loyola

★ **Museum of Religious Art**
The two rooms of the museum contain rare and valuable exhibits, such as a mahogany reredos, reliquaries, and copies of St Ignatius' Spiritual Exercises *in many languages.*

VISITORS' CHECKLIST

Loiola (Guipúzcoa)
Sanctuary *Tel.* *943 02 50 00.*
Santa Casa ☐ *7:30am–1pm & 3–7pm daily. Mass at 9am in the Chapel of the Conversion.*
🔲 *10am–1pm & 3–7pm daily.*
www.*santuariodeloyola.com*

Coats of Arms
The interior of the dome, 33 m (108 ft) in diameter, is covered in carved royal coats of arms set against a background of pink marble – the work of Gaetano Pace.

Entrance to the Library
The library has 150,000 volumes, of which as many as 30,000 date from the 15th to the 19th centuries. There is also a music archive.

Doors of the Basilica
The doors are made of cedar of Lebanon and mahogany imported from Cuba; in the niche above them is a figure of St Ignatius by Ignacio de Ibero.

STAR SIGHTS

★ Interior of the Basilica

★ Museum of Religious Art

★ Santa Casa

Vitoria (Gasteiz) ⑱

The inland city of Vitoria is the capital of the Basque Country and the seat of the Basque government. It was founded on a hill – the highest point in the province of Álava and the site of the ancient Basque town of Gasteiz. The city grew rich on the iron and wool trades, and today it is brimming with life. Visitors come to see Vitoria's beautiful architecture and extensive parkland, and to enjoy its excellent restaurants and tapas bars.

Exploring Santiago

The more impressive historic monuments are concentrated within the relatively small confines of the Old Town; several Renaissance palaces and the most important churches are located here. A good way to end the day is to embark on a *poteo* – a whistle-stop tour of several tapas bars to sample the delicious local cuisine.

🏛 Plaza de la Virgen Blanca

On this large square, named after the White Madonna, patron saint of Vitoria, stands a monument to a battle fought in 1813, when the

Plaza de la Virgen Blanca in the city centre

Duke of Wellington defeated the French during the Peninsular War *(see p41)*. Beethoven wrote a special concerto, *Wellington's Victory*, to commemorate this event. The monument, crowned with the figure of an angel, is the work of Gabriel Borrás. Old houses with glazed balconies surround the vibrant square, but the most important building is the Iglesia de San Miguel.

🏛 Iglesia de San Miguel

This late Gothic aisled church, with Renaissance elements, was built between the 14th and 16th centuries. The high altar, by Gregorio Fernández, is Baroque (1624–32). The church is devoted to the cult of the White Madonna, and a 14th-century statue of her can be found in an outside niche.

🏛 Plaza del Machete

On the wall of the Iglesia de San Miguel facing the Plaza del Machete is a recess

that once held an axe on which the city's rulers swore to uphold the laws or be slain. The square – one of Vitoria's oldest – was also known as the Plazoleta del Juicio (court square), because in former times public executions would take place here.

A figure of the White Madonna in the Iglesia de San Miguel

♣ Palacio de Escoríaza-Esquivel

Fray Zacarías Martínez 7. ◯ *closed to the public.*
Stone was used in the construction of this 16th-century palace. The façade is Plateresque in style, with chain-like ornamentation running under the roof.

🏛 Catedral de Santa María

Plaza Burulleria. 📞 *945 25 51 35.*
◯ *11am-2pm, 5pm-8pm.* 🎟 *compulsory. Reserve by phone or online.*
📷 🚫 www.catedralvitoria.com
The 13th-century Gothic Catedral de Santa María de Suso was once part of the city's fortifications. Preserved on the second buttress arch from the northern end is a stone decorated with a rose-like ornament, dating from Visigothic times. The interior has been undergoing restoration since 2000.

A stained-glass window in the Catedral de Santa María

THE AUTONOMOUS BASQUE GOVERNMENT

Since 1979, the Basque Country has enjoyed broad autonomy on the basis of the so-called Statute of Gernika. It has its own parliament and government, while the region's official languages are both Basque (Euskera) and

The prime ministers of Spain and the Basque Country

Spanish. For several years, the government has been headed by Prime Minister (*lehendakarí* in Basque) Juan José Ibarretxe of the Basque National Party (PNV). The Basque prime minister's official seat is the Palacio Ajuria-Enea. In recent years, Basque politicians have been working on a new statute that would ensure significantly greater independence from Spain's central government.

The façade of the 15th-century El Portalón

🏘 El Portalón

Correría 151. **Tel.** 945 14 42 01 (restaurant).

The famous El Portalón is a rare example of medieval secular architecture of the late 15th century. Originally a merchant's house, with a shop on the ground floor and an apartment above, in the 19th century it became an inn, and today it accommodates an excellent Basque restaurant (see p225).

The name derives from the huge gateway through which carriages would enter.

🏛 Catedral Nueva

Cadena y Eleta s/n.

When a new diocese was established in the 19th century, encompassing all three of the Basque Country's provinces, it was agreed that Vitoria needed a new cathedral. The construction of this huge neo-Gothic shrine lasted several decades. The cathedral has a nave and four aisles, and accommodates 15,000 people. Noteworthy are the tall stained-glass windows, the apse, and the stunning gargoyles.

🏛 Museo de Bellas Artes

Paseo Fray Francisco 8. **Tel.** 945 15 52 26. ◯ 10am–2pm & 4–6:30pm Tue–Fri, 10am–2pm & 5–8pm Sat, 11am–2pm. 🅿 By prior arrangement.

The Museum of Fine Art is housed in the eclectic Palacio Augusti, designed by Julián Apraiz and Javier de Luque. The collection of paintings and sculptures includes classical art and Basque art from 1850 to 1950.

Palace housing the Museo de Bellas Artes

🏛 Museo de la Armería de Alava

Paseo Fray Francisco 3. **Tel.** 945 18 19 25. ◯ 10am–2pm & 4–6:30pm Tue–Fri, 10am–2pm Sat, 11am–2pm Sun. 🅿 By prior arrangement.

The weapons displayed here range from prehistoric axes, through Oriental and Arabic weaponry, to 20th-century pistols. There are also military uniforms and other exhibits connected with war. Of particular interest is a section devoted to the Battle of Vitoria in 1813.

🏛 Artium

C/ Francia 24. **Tel.** 945 20 90 00. ◯ 11am–8pm Tue–Fri, 10:30am–8pm Sat, Sun & hols. 🅿 **www**.artium.org

Opened in 2002, this futuristic contemporary art museum showcases modern Spanish and Basque artists.

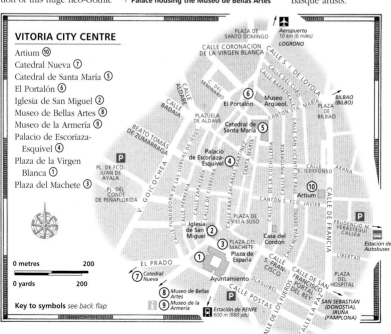

VITORIA CITY CENTRE

0 metres   200

0 yards   200

Key to symbols see back flap

Castillo de Mendoza ⓳

Mendoza (Álava). **Museo Heráldico**
Tel 945 18 16 17. ⭘ May–Sep:
11am–2pm & 4–8pm Tue–Fri,
11am–3pm Sat, 10am–2pm Sun &
hols; Oct–Apr: 11am–3pm Tue–Sat,
10am–2pm Sun & hols.

In the village of Mendoza,
10 km (6 miles) west of
Vitoria, stands a small, square,
much-restored fortress dating
from the 13th century. There
are marvellous views from the
tops of the four corner
towers, between which rises
the highest, five-storey tower
with a mansard roof.

The castle, once a ducal
residence of the Mendoza
family, now houses the **Museo
Heráldico**. On display at this
heraldry museum are the
coats of arms of noble
Alavese families as well
as graphical illustrations
of issues connected with
heraldry and the
interpretation of
family names.

Basque surnames
usually derive from
geographical terms
– often connected
with where a family
lived – or from
terms relating to the
natural environment,
which makes them
possible to translate.
For instance, one
common surname,
Mendizábal means
"broad mountain ridge", while
Bolivar means "mill valley",
and Velasco translates as
"young crow".

**Exhibit in the
Museo Heráldico**

Salvatierra ⓴

Álava. 🏔 4,100. 🚉 🚌 🛈 Mayor
8; 945 30 29 31. 🎊 San Juan
Bautista (24 Jun), Nuestra Señora
del Rosario (1st Sun in Oct).
www.agurain.biz

Set among green hills and
beech woods is the small
town of Salvatierra. Rising
above the surrounding area is
the walled Old Town. Also
worth seeing are the former
hospital of San Lázaro y la
Magdalena and the Gothic
church of Santa María.

The Romanesque Iglesia de San Martin de Tours in Gaceo

Gaceo and Alaiza ㉑

Tel 945 30 29 31. 🏛 by prior
arrangement. **www**.agurain.biz

Not far from Vitoria, the two
villages of Gaceo and Alaiza
conceal hidden treasure:
medieval murals. In the
**Iglesia de San Martin de
Tours**, in Gaceo, the
14th-century murals
adorn the crypt
and the chancel,
presenting the text
of the catechism
for the benefit of
non-Latin-speaking
believers. The
murals also depict
the *Holy Trinity*, the
Last Judgement,
scenes from the
life of Christ and
the *Way of the
Cross*, as well as
redeemed souls.
In Alaiza is the **Iglesia de
Santa María de la Asunción**,
featuring murals from the same
period but cruder than those at
Gaceo. The depiction is more
schematic and the figures less
complex. The subject-matter
relates to conflict, bringing to
mind stark and rather uncom-
promising war reportage.

Laguardia ㉒

Álava. 🏔 1,550. 🚌 🛈 Plaza de San
Juan; 945 60 08 45. 🎊 San Juan
and San Pedro (24–29 Jun).
www.laguardia-alava.com

Laguardia is a fascinating old
town encircled by 13th-century
walls, which is closed to traffic.
Underground, at a depth of

6 m (20 ft), are numerous wine
cellars – *bodegas* or *cuevas*,
which can be visited. Laguardia
is the most important town in
La Rioja Alavesa, a district that
has, for centuries, produced
excellent Rioja wines. The
land is extremely fertile, and
almost the entire local
population is involved in
vine cultivation. The town is
also celebrated for its food.

Laguardia is entered
through one of five fortified
gateways incorporated in the
ring of walls. At the centre of
Laguardia is the **Plaza Mayor**,
on which stand two town
halls – the old one, with the
coat of arms of Charles V, and
the current one, which bears
the town's crest. The Gothic
**Iglesia de Santa María de los
Reyes**, of 12th-century origin,
features a richly sculpted,
polychrome interior portal
(14th century), with a delicate
statue of the Virgin and Child
dating from the same period.

**One of the fortified gateways
leading to Laguardia**

Basque Fiestas and Sports

The Basques are devoted to sports, excelling at conventional games, and inventing many of their own. In football, Basque clubs have always played near the top of their leagues, despite many sticking to a rule of fielding only local, Basque-born players. First among indigenous Basque sports is *pelota*, played between two or four players with bare hands, bats or a long basket. Enormously popular, it's a fast-moving game that's spectacular to watch. The Basques also have a whole range of often outlandish traditional country sports – wagon lifting, sheep fights and tugs-of-war – many of which originated as tests of strength and skill between villages, fishermen and mountain farmers. They can be seen at the annual town and village fiestas, together with performances of the equally distinctive Basque poetry, music, dance and folklore.

A dancing Basque

Bertsolaris *are bards who improvise witty songs, whose verses relate current events or legends. They sing, unaccompanied, to gatherings in public places, often in competition.*

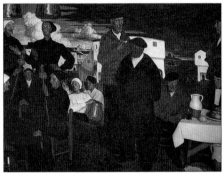

Estropadak *are colourful traditional rowing races held each summer in San Sebastián and all the smaller Basque ports. The long, narrow boats were once used for whale-hunting.*

The Tamborrada *is a cacophonous festival unique to San Sebastián, in which uniformed drum bands parade around the city during the night of 19 January, giving way to children's drum parades during the next day. Succulent food completes the fiesta.*

Harri-jasotzailea *(stone lifting), practised by massive-limbed mountain farmers, is one of the best-known Basque sports. Basque lifters regularly exceed the records set by standard, Olympic weightlifters, and legendary champion Iñaki Perureña was long considered the world's strongest man.*

Aizkolari *competitors have to cut through a row of beech logs in the fastest possible time while standing on top of them, jumping on to the next log as soon as the first one is cut.*

NAVARRA AND LA RIOJA

*N*avarra, the cradle of the Basques, and La Rioja, famous for its wines, witnessed key events in the Middle Ages, such as the Battle of Roncesvalles against Charlemagne's forces. Both regions were also important stages on the pilgrimage route to Santiago de Compostela. This is evidenced by the many monasteries, churches and bridges that survive, including the 11th-century bridge in Puente la Reina.

Navarra had its Golden Age in the 10th century, when it was a powerful independent kingdom. Its ruler, Sancho III, managed for a brief period to unite nearly all the Christian lands of the Iberian peninsula.

Nowadays, Navarra enjoys a degree of autonomy, with its own parliament and government. It is a small, sparsely populated region, but one that is geographically diverse and with an abundance of flora and fauna. More than 60 per cent of its territory is forested, providing an excellent habitat for the capercaillie and other animal species.

Navarra is divided into three subregions: the mountainous Montana, the Zona Media, and Ribera, which enjoys a Mediterranean climate. The region is known not only for captivating landscapes, but also for the magnificent towns of Olite and Pamplona, which were founded during Roman times.

Northwest Navarra is very strongly Basque, with Euskera an official language. Areas south of Pamplona have far less Basque influence. Medieval Estella and Sangüesa are also historic stopovers on the pilgrimage route of St James.

The first inhabitants of La Rioja – one of the smallest Spanish provinces – were dinosaurs, traces of which can be seen around the mountain village of Enciso. Today La Rioja is famous for its excellent wines, produced from grapes that mature slowly on the sunny hillsides. Visitors come here not only to attend the wine festival of *Batalla del Vino* (Wine Battle) in Haro. La Rioja, which in the Middle Ages was an important stage on the road to Santiago de Compostela, also boasts superb architecture, such as in Santo Domingo de la Calzada or at the monastery of San Millán de Yuso.

A prehistoric stone hut along the eastern edge of Navarra

◁ One of the figures in the Iglesia de Santa María del Palacio in Logroño

Exploring Navarra and La Rioja

These green, mountainous regions have diverse attractions. The Navarrese Pyrenees offer skiing in winter and climbing, caving and canoeing the rest of the year. Minor roads wind through wooded hills, valleys and gorges, passing castles – such as in Olite – Roman towns, and villages. Many of these places, including Roncesvalles, have been immortalized in the region's history. In La Rioja, to the south, the roads cross vineyards, passing towns and villages clustered around ancient churches and monasteries. While in the region, it is well worth venturing slightly further south, into Castilla y León, to visit Burgos, famous for its Gothic cathedral, Frómista with its Romanesque church of San Martín, and the fortified town of Briviesca.

Window in Roncesvalles depicting the Battle of Las Navas de Tolosa

SEE ALSO

- *Where to Stay* pp208–10.
- *Where to Eat* pp225–6.

0 kilometres   20

0 miles   10

BEYOND THE REGION

GETTING AROUND

Motorways and minor roads fan out from Pamplona in the direction of Huesca, Zaragoza, Logroño, San Sebastián, Vitoria, and the border with France. Both Navarra and La Rioja have good rail and coach connections with the rest of Spain and further afield. The regions can also be reached by plane. There are airports in Noáin, near Pamplona, and in the vicinity of Logroño.

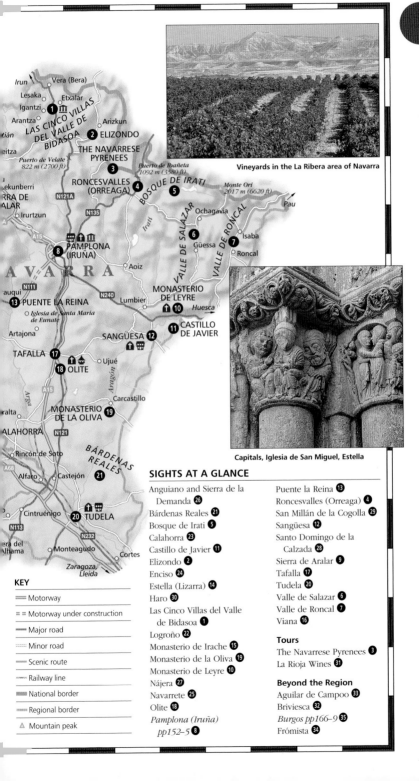

Vineyards in the La Ribera area of Navarra

Capitals, Iglesia de San Miguel, Estella

KEY

━━━ Motorway

= = Motorway under construction

━━━ Major road

━━━ Minor road

━━━ Scenic route

━━━ Railway line

━━━ National border

━━━ Regional border

△ Mountain peak

SIGHTS AT A GLANCE

Typical Basque house in the picturesque village of Etxalar

Las Cinco Villas del Valle de Bidasoa ❶

Navarra. 🚌 ℹ️ *Bera; 948 63 12 22.*
www.navarra.es

In the Bidasoa river valley are five attractive towns that owe their unique character not only to the beautiful forest scenery, but also to the proximity of the border with France and the iron industry that thrived here.

The most northerly is **Bera** (Vera), the largest of the five towns, which has a mix of agriculture and industry. Trade with France has played an important role in this town's history. The celebrated Basque writer Pío Baroja lived here. The highest point in the town is Larun hill, from where there are magnificent views of the forested surroundings.

Heading south to **Lesaka**, the houses here have wooden balconies under deep eaves. The road south continues to pass hills dotted with white farmsteads to reach **Igantzi** (Yanci), the smallest of the towns in the area; the nearby hills conceal several old *caseríos* (Basque farmhouses) as well as a spring with therapeutic powers.

Arantza is the most secluded and remote of the towns. Since the 12th century, pigeons have been caught in huge nets strung across a pass above **Etxalar** (Echalar). From the summit of La Rhune, on the French border above the valley, there are great views of the Pyrenees.

Elizondo ❷

Navarra. 🏠 *3,200.* 🚌 ℹ️ *Palacio de Arizcunenea; 948 58 12 79.* 🛒 *Sat (every two weeks).* 🎉 *Santiago (25 Jul).*

In the middle of a beautiful valley, straddling the banks of the Baztán river, lies the district capital of Elizondo. In Basque, the name of the town means 'beside the church'. Traditionally, the inhabitants of Elizondo farmed livestock, but today, despite the infertile soil, agriculture is the mainstay of the economy.

The local architecture features Gothic houses and nobles' residences decorated with coats of arms, testifying to Elizondo's long and splendid past. Reddish stone was used in the construction of most of these buildings.

The town's best-known buildings are the **Palacio de Arizcunenea**, an 18th-century Baroque palace with a façade characteristically set back from the street, and the arcaded **town hall**.

The eclectic **Iglesia de Santiago**, dedicated to the patron saint of Elizondo, was built at the beginning of the 20th century. The towers of the church are imitation Baroque; inside is a neo-Gothic organ. Two hermitages can be visited in the vicinity of Elizondo – **San Pedro** and **Santa Engracia**.

One of the many houses built for the nobility in Elizondo

Environs
On the northern border of Navarra lies **Zugarramurdi**, a town infused with the fragrance of herbs; surrounding it are pastures with grazing cows and hills dotted with large *caseríos* (country houses). Amid the scenery, in striking shades of green, stand ancient houses with coats of arms and the 18th-century **Iglesia de la Asunción**, partially destroyed during the Napoleonic Wars *(see p41)*. More famous, however, are the **Cuevas de Zugarramurdi**, just outside town. The caves are said to have been a meeting place for witches at the end of the 16th century.

🦇 **Cuevas de Zugarramurdi**
Tel. *948 59 93 05.* 🕐 *summer: 9am–8pm daily; rest of year: 9am–dusk.* 🅿️

THE WITCHES OF ZUGARRAMURDI

In 1609, the Inquisition initiated a trial of 40 women from Zugarramurdi, accusing them of witchcraft; 12 of the women were burnt at the stake. Since that time, the area has been associated with the Cuevas de Zugarramurdi, where witches' sabbaths *(akelarres)* are said to have taken place. *Akelarre* is a Basque word meaning "goat meadow" – it was believed that at these sabbaths the witches would meet with a demon in the form of a goat. A stream known as the Infernal River *(Infernuko Erreka)* flows through the 100-m (32-ft) long caves. Traditionally the witches' legend was commemorated by a summer festival at which roast lamb was eaten.

Cuevas de Zugarramurdi, where witches' sabbaths were supposedly held

The Navarrese Pyrenees ❸

The Navarrese Pyrenees are remarkable for the diversity of their landscape – from idyllic valleys to forbidding mountain peaks. They are a great place for active pursuits, including biking, rafting and paragliding, but also offer a good environment for pleasant walks, rest and relaxation. The towns and villages, whose inhabitants speak Basque, are full of culture and tradition. The megaliths dotted around the region testify to its long history. Wild animals find shelter in the national parks, and sheep graze in the meadows.

TIPS FOR DRIVERS

Tour route: *Approximately 140 km (87 miles).*
Stopping-off places: *Accommodation in hotels and casas rurales is easy to find in the main towns; there are also many places to eat.*
Equipment: *When hiking in the mountains take warm clothing, as the weather can change suddenly.*

0 kilometres   10

0 miles   5

Valle de Baztán ⑥
One of the most densely wooded Navarrese valleys, this offers excellent terrain for hiking and climbing.

Lesaka ⑤
This important industrial centre and charming town has *caseríos* and fortified manors (*casas-torre*). Dolmens and other ancient tombs have been discovered nearby.

Oieregi ④
Most of the village houses here display the valley's emblem – a mermaid with long hair, holding a comb and a mirror.

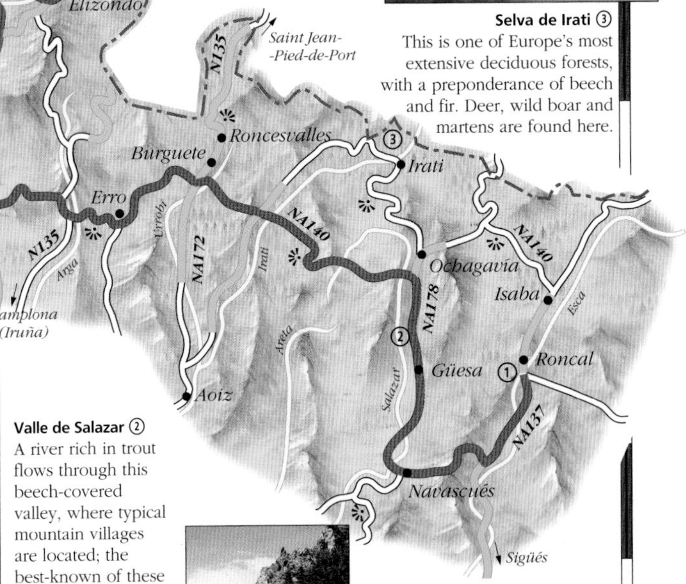

Selva de Irati ③
This is one of Europe's most extensive deciduous forests, with a preponderance of beech and fir. Deer, wild boar and martens are found here.

Valle de Salazar ②
A river rich in trout flows through this beech-covered valley, where typical mountain villages are located; the best-known of these is Ochagavía, with its six stone bridges.

Valle de Roncal ①
The most mountainous region of the Navarrese Pyrenees, this alpine area includes the highest peak – Mesa de los Tres Reyes (2,444 m/8,018 ft).

KEY

▬▬▬	Tour route
▭▭▭	Scenic route
═══	Minor road
✲	Viewpoint

Map labels: rtzun, Irun, Cambo-les-Bains, Zugarramurdi, antzi, NI21A, NI21B, Arizkun, Elizondo, Santesteban, Saint Jean-Pied-de-Port, N135, Roncesvalles, Irati, Burguete, Erro, NA140, NA172, Iraty, Ochagavía, Isaba, N135, Arga, Aritz, Arga, NA178, Güesa, Roncal, Pamplona (Iruña), Aoiz, Salazar, Navascués, NA137, Sigüés, Esca

The densely forested countryside around Roncesvalles

Roncesvalles ④

Navarra. 🏘 30. 🛈 *Antiguo Molino (Old Mill); 948 76 03 01.* 🎪 *Virgen de Roncesvalles (8 Sep).* **www**.roncesvalles.es

High on a pass through the Pyrenees – one of the oldest crossings in the mountains – is the village of Roncesvalles (Orreaga in Basque). This old settlement was built to serve travellers and pilgrims heading to Santiago de Compostela *(see pp62–3)*. Its most important building is the **Colegiata Real**, founded by Sancho VII, the Strong, who chose it as his burial place. Inside the church is Sancho's white tomb, lit by a stained-glass window depicting his great victory at the Battle of Las Navas de Tolosa in 1212 *(see p38)*. Below a high canopy is a silver-plated Virgin and Child (Virgen de Roncesvalles). The church dates from the 13th century and is one of the best examples of Navarrese Gothic, although in the 17th century it was given a more Baroque appearance.

The 18th-century **hospital** – the only one to have survived to the present day – now accommodates a youth hostel.

In a slightly out-of-the-way location is the 12th-century **Capilla del Espiritu Santo**, considered to be the oldest building in the village. According to legend, it was here, after the battle of 778, that Charlemagne ordered Roland and the other fallen knights to be buried *(see p37)*. A monument to the battle is nearby.

One of the village's more modern buildings is the **presbytery**, with an annexe containing a library and a museum displaying sculpture, painting, incunabula and precious jewellery.

Bosque de Irati ⑤

Navarra.

In the dampest part of Navarra, spread across the Salazar and Aezkoa valleys, is this large forest, covering an area of 17,000 ha (42,000 acres). The forest is composed chiefly of beech – often surprisingly tall and thick – and fir, and is inhabited by many species of wild animals, including red deer, fallow deer, wild boar and capercaillie.

Hidden deep in the forest is **Lago Irabia**; there are also refreshing natural springs and the fast-flowing Irati river.

At the confluence of the Urbeltza and Urtxuria rivers stands the **Ermita de la Virgen de las Nieves** (Madonna of the Snows), while between the villages of Lumbier, Sangüesa and Liédena lie the ruins of a Roman settlement. Rising high above the treetops are the imposing peaks of Ortha mountain.

In the district of **Aezkoa** are the ruins of a small 18th-century weapons factory – one of the best examples of Spanish industrial architecture of the period.

A figure of the Virgin in Roncesvalles

The Bosque de Irati leaves an unforgettable impression on visitors, especially in autumn, when the beech leaves turn beautiful colours.

Valle de Salazar ⑥

Navarra.

In the eastern part of the Navarrese Pyrenees extends the Salazar river valley. Thanks to its proximity to the sea, it is damper than other valleys in the region and is covered in beech woods.

Perched along the banks of the river are typical mountain villages featuring stone and timber houses with thatched roofs. The prettiest and most characteristic of these is **Ochagavía**. Preserved here are six stone bridges as well as the shrine of Santa María de Muskilda, where a lively fiesta in honour of the Virgin takes place in September.

The inhabitants of the Valle de Salazar earn their living principally from sheep farming and forestry. Aside from taking relaxing walks

---

ROLAND IN RONCESVALLES

The 12th-century French epic poem, *The Song of Roland*, describes how the rearguard of Charlemagne's army – in which Roland led the Frankish knights – was slaughtered by the Moors. The truth is somewhat different, however: the victors were not Moors but warlike Basque highlanders from Navarra, who wanted to manifest their independence. Preserved in Roncesvalles is the stone upon which Roland tried to break his sword. A boulder marks the spot where Charlemagne is said to have found the fallen knight who, according to legend, was buried in the Capilla del Espiritu Santo.

Monument bearing an image of Roland

The mountainous landscape of the Valle de Salazar

through the idyllic countryside, there is good terrain here for many active sports, including skiing and mountain biking.

Valle de Roncal ❼

Navarra. 🚌 from Pamplona.
🅸 Paseo Julian Gayarre, s/n, Roncal; 948 47 52 56.

Situated on the northeastern border of Navarra, the Valle de Roncal is the highest and most mountainous part of the province. Navarra's loftiest peak – Mesa de los Tres Reyes, or Table of the Three Kings – is situated here. Winters in the Roncal Valley are long and snowy; summers are mild.

The village of **Burgui** to the south affords a panoramic views of the valley, its contours carved by the Esca river. A medieval bridge can be seen here. **Roncal** (Erronkari), a village with cobbled streets and stone houses, is the geographical heart of the valley.

There are ski runs in the small, post-glacial **Valle de Belagoa**. The district can be toured in a variety of ways: on horseback, by bike, in a four-wheel drive, or on foot.

Environs
Isaba (Izaba), the largest town in the valley, is a ski resort and a popular base for skiers and mountaineers. Situated at the confluence of three rivers, Isaba features fine houses with steep roofs and coats of arms on their façades. The 16th-century church of San Cipriano contains a painted Plateresque reredos and a Baroque organ.

SPECIALITIES OF THE NAVARRESE PYRENEES

The rivers of the Navarrese Pyrenees are flowing with an abundance of trout, which can be caught in the spring and summer. Organized fishing trips are very popular among visitors to the area. Navarra-style trout, or *trucha a la Navarra*, is trout stuffed with *jamón serrano* (thinly sliced cured ham) and cheese, and then braised in olive oil and white wine. Lamb is the most popular meat and *cordero al chilindrón* (lamb stew) features on almost every menu. The Valle de Roncal is known primarily for its local cheese – *queso de Roncal*; it is made between December and July from local sheep's milk and has a distinctive, slightly piquant flavour.

Sheep's cheese from the Valle de Roncal

Pamplona ❽

See pp152–5.

Sierra de Aralar ❾

Navarra. 🅸 Alsasua, Plaza Fueros; 948 46 48 67 or Lekunberri, Edificio Concejo; 948 50 72 04.

The Aralar mountain chain runs along the border between Navarra and the Basque province of Guipúzcoa. This ancient massif, covered in beech, oak and bracken, is crisscrossed by rivers; its highest peak is **Irumugarrieta** at 1,427 m (4,682 ft) above sea level. Some of the mountainsides are so steep that, in order to cut the grass, farmers have to tie themselves to ropes attached to trees. This area is Basque-speaking.

Several megaliths still stand in the area, including the **Albi dolmen**, and a short distance away are circular shepherds' huts known as *arkuek*.

High in the mountains is the Romanesque **shrine of San Miguel**, with three aisles and apses. The Archangel Michael was traditionally venerated in the area; it was believed he shared some traits with Hermes and was a messenger between heaven and earth. Inside the shrine is a silver-coated figure of him with a crucifix on his head. There is also a superb 12th-century enamelled reredos in the Romanesque-Byzantine style; its centrepiece is an image of the Virgin and Child surrounded by 18 medallions depicting mythological and religious scenes.

Environs
Lekumberri (Lekunberri) is a base for excursions into the valley and mountains. Here are some excellent *caseríos* (Basque farmhouses) bearing coats of arms as well as the aisleless Gothic church of San Juan Bautista, dating from the 13th century. Local crafts can be purchased in the town.

Stone houses with characteristic white chimneys in the Valle de Roncal

Pamplona (Iruña) ❽

In 75 BC, the Roman general Pompey founded the town of Pompaelo on the site of the old Basque settlement of Iruña. Strategically located on the river at the foot of the Pyrenees, Pamplona played the role of a fortified border town. Today, it is the financial, commercial and academic centre of Navarra, offering visitors fine cuisine and pleasant walks along the riverside or through the Old Town. Each July, the world-famous San Fermín festival, with its bull running, totally transforms the city.

Exploring Pamplona

To fully appreciate its charms, the city is best explored on foot. From the old city walls – situated to the north in a loop of the Arga river – you can get a good overview. Going south, the Old Town ends at a massive citadel.

The walls of the city's 16th-century citadel, among parks and gardens

♣ Ciudadela

Felipe II ordered the construction of Pamplona's citadel in 1571. From the outside, the building looks rather decrepit – grass is yellowed by the sun, and its moats have long been

– but once you pass through the main entrance, the impression is very different. Encircling the well-kept lawn are the citadel's former buildings, now converted into exhibition rooms. The oldest structure is the powder magazine (Polvorín), dating from 1694. You can climb up the embankment onto one of the surviving bastions for a view of the area.

⚅ Praza de Navarra

Avenida Carlos III 2; 848 42 71 27.
⬜ Visits by prior arrangement only from 3:30–4:30pm Mon–Fri. ♿
This neo-Classical palace, designed in 1840 by Juan de Nagusia, is the seat of the provincial government. Set in the tympanum is the Navarra coat of arms flanked by two men – a highlander and an inhabitant of the river basin. Inside is a portrait of Fernando VII by Goya, as well as many other paintings – mostly portraits – from the 19th and 20th centuries. In front of the palace stands a column topped by a symbolic statue of a woman upholding the historic laws (*fueros*) of Navarra.

⚅ Plaza del Castillo

The square owes its name to a castle raised here in the 14th century. Initially used as a marketplace and place for fiestas, it later became a venue for bullfights, when the balconies of the surrounding houses were used as seating areas. Until the 19th century, the square was enclosed. In 1931, a theatre along one of its sides was destroyed to make way for Avenida Carlos III, an avenue linking the square with the city's new districts.

The colourful façade of one of the city's tenements

🔒 Iglesia San Saturnino

Also known as Iglesia de San Cernín, this Romanesque church (13th century) was built on the site where St Saturninus is said to have baptized some 40,000 pagan townspeople. One of its massive towers is a clock tower, topped by a cockerel – the Gallico de San Cernín, a symbol of the city. In the 18th century, the church's cloister was replaced by the Baroque Capilla della Virgen del Camino. Its beautiful reredos contains a 12th-century wooden robed figure of the Virgin, covered in silver tiles.

🏛 Museo de Navarra

C/Santo Domingo 47; 848 42 64 92.
⬜ 9:30am–2pm & 5–7pm Tue–Sat, 11am–2pm Sun and holidays. 📷 (free Sat pm & Sun).
🎫 by prior arrangement. ♿
The Museum of Navarra is located inside the former Hospital de Nuestra Señora de la Misericordia. Its highlights

---

THE KINGDOM OF NAVARRA

Navarra emerged as an independent Christian kingdom in the 9th century, after Sancho I Garcés became king of Pamplona. Sancho III the Great expanded the kingdom, and at his death, in 1035, Navarra stretched from Ribagorza (in Aragón) to Valladolid, but his heirs failed to hold the kingdom together. Sancho VI the Wise (1150–94), recognized the independent rights (*fueros*) of many towns. In 1234, Navarra passed by marriage to French rulers. In 1512, Fernando II of Castile annexed it as part of a united Spain.

Carlos de Viana, one of the last leaders of independent Navarra

include Roman mosaics, Gothic and Baroque murals, Romanesque capitals from the cathedral cloister, and an ivory casket that draws inspiration from Islamic decorative motifs.

Richly decorated stalls in the Catedral de Santa María la Real

🏛 Cathedral

C/Dormitalería 1; 948 22 56 79.
⏱ mid-Jul–mid-Sep: 10am–7pm Mon–Fri, 10am–1:45pm Sat; mid-Sep–mid-Jul: 10am–1:45pm & 4–7pm Mon–Fri, 10am–1:45pm Sat. 🎫
The cathedral of Santa María la Real was built during the 13th–16th centuries, and later remodelled several times. This aisled Gothic shrine has a Rococo sacristy, chapels from various periods, and a neo-Classical façade designed by Ventura Rodríguez. One of the two towers holds the 12-tonne María bell.

Inside, some of the painted decoration on the walls and pillars has been restored. The cloister, with its beautifully carved 14th-century gateways (Puerta Preciosa and Puerta de Amparo) is a masterpiece of European Gothic style.

The Museo Docesano houses a collection of religious art from all over Navarra, including a set of medieval statues of the Virgin.

🎪 Plaza de Toros

Pamplona's bullring, known as the Monumental, holds around 19,500 spectators and is surpassed in size only by the arenas in Madrid and Mexico City. Designed by Francisco

VISITORS' CHECKLIST

Navarra. 🏙 200,000. ✈ 948 10 87 00. 🚇 Avenida San Jorge; 948 13 02 02. 🚌 Calle Tudela; 848 42 04 20. 🛈 Calle Eslava 1; 948 20 65 40. 🎉 San Fermín (6–14 Jul), San Saturnino (29 Nov), San Francisco Javier (3 Dec). www.pamplona.net

Urcola, the Monumental was officially opened in 1922. Several improvements were made in 2005, including the addition of a lift and vehicles for disabled people, making it one of the most modern bullrings in Spain. The famous July bull run – the encierro – ends here.

A square with fountains in the city centre

PAMPLONA CITY CENTRE

Cathedral ⑥
Ciudadela ①
Iglesia San Saturnino ④
Museo de Navarra ⑤
Palacio de Navarra ②
Plaza de Toros ⑦
Plaza del Castillo ③

0 metres   200
0 yards   200

KEY

▨ Bull-running route

For key to symbols see back flap

San Fermín

This fiesta in honour of Navarra's patron, St Fermín (the first bishop of Pamplona), is famous for the *encierro* – a bull run through the Old Town of Pamplona. Starting at the Plaza de Santo Domingo and ending at the bullring, the 840-m (half-mile) bull run occurs daily from 7 to 14 July. However, San Fermín is not just about bulls – this hugely popular fiesta includes parades with orchestras, official state and religious ceremonies, and street dancing and singing. There is also a lot of drinking and good, spontaneous fun.

A statue of St Fermín, *Navarra's patron saint, is carried from the town hall to the cathedral in ceremonial procession on 7 July.*

Fighting bulls are bred at special ranches and must weigh 460–500 kg (1,014–1,102 lbs) before entering the *corrida*.

The encierro, *which lasts around four minutes, ends at the Plaza de Toros, where* corridas *are held in the evenings. Although running in front of enraged bulls is dangerous, this does not deter the local young men, keen to display their courage.*

Streets and squares *filled with colourful, joyous crowds epitomize the fiesta in Pamplona. The various events, especially the hair-raising bull runs, are attended by thousands of onlookers.*

The sand in the bullring must be clean and even so that nothing on its surface distracts the bull.

Encierro participants *must be physically fit, with good reflexes. Most are dressed in a white shirt and trousers (some wear jeans instead), with a red belt and scarf, and a matching beret.*

BULLFIGHTS (CORRIDAS)

The *corrida* begins with a parade set to the spirited music of the *pasodoble*. In the first stage of the bullfight, the mounted *picadores* goad the bull with their steel-pointed lances; in the second, the *banderilleros* provoke the wounded bull by sticking pairs of darts in its back; in the third stage, the matador is left to fight the bull alone.

The procession of St Fermín *includes clergy, town officials and crowds of local people. Dressed in traditional costumes, the men carry pennants displaying the coat of arms of Pamplona and the emblem of Navarra.*

Gigantes – huge figures dressed in vivid and often elaborate costumes, participate in the procession in honour of St Fermín. They add colour to the celebrations and are especially popular with children.

The scarlet and yellow cape is used in the second stage of the bullfight. The bull is attracted by the movement of the cape, not by its colour!

The matador wears a *traje de luces* (suit of lights) – a colourful silk outfit embroidered with gold sequins.

The bull's horns are deadly. Only true masters of the art of bullfighting dare to get this close to an angry bull.

The traditional orchestras *that take part in the processions and parades are composed of musicians playing* txistu *flutes, clarinets, bagpipes and drums. The parades often have orchestras made up of young boys, who take their role much more seriously than their older counterparts.*

ERNEST HEMINGWAY

It is thanks to Hemingway and his novel *The Sun Also Rises* that the previously obscure festival of Los Sanfermines was transformed into a riotous international event. In the 1920s and 1950s, Hemingway visited Pamplona on several occasions, not only to witness the fiesta but also to participate in it. Several of the places he frequented still exist: the Txoko bar, the La Perla hotel, the Iruña café. In 1968, a monument in honour of the Nobel prize-winning author was erected near the arena.

Hemingway – an admirer of the *corrida*

Fun and dancing *are an integral part of the fiesta. The* jota *is danced in honour of St Fermín, and people sing for blessing before the bull run.*

A church with three apses near the Monasterio de Leyre

Monasterio de Leyre ⑩

Yesa (Navarra). 🚌 to Yesa, 4km (2 miles) away. **Tel** 948 88 41 50. ⬜ daily. 📷 Group tours.

The monastery of San Salvador de Leyre is situated high above a reservoir, alone amid breathtaking scenery, backed by limestone cliffs.

The abbey is mentioned in documents dating from the 9th century; in the 10th and 11th centuries, the kings of Navarra found refuge here from the Moors. The abbey experienced its Golden Age in the 11th century, when it was reconstructed by Sancho III the Great, having suffered damage at the hands of the Muslim general Al-Mansur.

In keeping with Cistercian rule, the church is austere in appearance. Of note are the three semicircular apses of equal height. The tower, built on a square base, has triforia (galleries) in each of its walls. Nearby is the entrance to the unusual crypt – underneath its arches rises a forest of squat, completely unadorned columns. The kings of Navarra are buried here.

The façade of the church is decorated with carvings of strange beasts, birds and human figures intertwined with plant motifs. The monks' Gregorian chant during services is wonderful to hear. Part of the monastery now accommodates a hotel.

Castillo de Javier ⑪

Javier (Navarra). 🚌 from Pamplona. **Tel** 948 88 40 24. ⬜ 9am–1pm & 4–8pm daily.

In the 10th and 11th centuries, prior to the construction of the castle, a watchtower stood here, to which new buildings were gradually added. In the 16th century, Cardinal Cisneros ordered the castle to be redesigned as a fortress, but in recent times the complex has been restored, including its towers and drawbridge. It now contains a Jesuit college.

St Francis Xavier, a missionary and co-founder of the Jesuit order (as well as the patron saint of Navarra sportsmen and *pelota* players), was born in the castle in 1506. Preserved here are the saint's bedroom and a chapel

A crucifix in the Castillo de Javier

containing a Gothic walnut crucifix. According to legend, at difficult moments in the saint's life, and on the anniversary of his death, droplets of blood appeared on the crucifix.

The walls of the chapel are decorated with a macabre mural of grinning skeletons, a fine depiction of The Dance of Death. Every year from 4–12 March, the inhabitants of Navarra make a penitent pilgrimage to the castle chapel.

Sangüesa ⑫

Navarra. 🏠 5,000. 🚌 🚊 Calle Mayor 2; 948 87 14 11. 🚗 Fri. 🎉 San Sebastián (11–17 Sep).

Set on the pilgrimage route of St James, this town was one of the main trading centres in the region. The **Iglesia de Santa María la Real**, whose construction began in the 12th century, has a splendid Romanesque portal. Preserved in the sacristy is a 15th-century processional monstrance, measuring 1.35 m (4.4 ft) in height. The Romanesque-Gothic **Iglesia de Santiago el Mayor** has a battlemented tower. Inside, it is decorated with motifs of the pilgrimage route – scallop shells *(vieiras)*, walking sticks and gourds. A polychrome stone figure of St James was discovered under the church.

The richly decorated Romanesque portal of the Iglesia de Santa María la Real in Sangüesa

The 11th-century bridge in Puente la Reina

Puente la Reina ⓭

Navarra. 🏘 2,600. 🚌 🛈 Calle Mayor 105; 948 34 13 01 or 948 34 00 07. 🗓 Sat. 🎭 Santiago (24–30 Jul).

Puente la Reina takes its name from the seven-span, humpbacked bridge built here for pilgrims in the 11th century. On the central section that no longer exists stood a figure of the Virgen del Txori, which was transferred to the church of San Pedro in the 19th century.

On the opposite side of town rises the Romanesque-Gothic **Iglesia del Crucifijo** (13th-century), a church ostensibly built by the Knights Templar. A walkway above the beautifully sculpted entrance connects the church with the pilgrims' hostel. Inside the church is a 14th-century Y-shaped crucifix that was carved from a single tree trunk.

Environs
Isolated in fields about 5 km (3 miles) east of Puente la Reina is the tiny Romanesque **Ermita de Santa María de Eunate**, built in the 12th century. The hermitage's irregular octagonal plan is clearly visible on the Mozarabic-inspired vaulting. Around the church runs a remarkable cloister with many arches; some claim the hermitage is named after the cloister – in Basque *ehun atea* means "one hundred doors".

Estella (Lizarra) ⓮

Navarra. 🏘 14,000. 🚌 🛈 C/San Nicolás 1; 948 55 63 01. 🗓 Thu. 🎭 San Andrés (last week Nov/ 1st week Dec), Medieval Week (Jul).

King Sancho Ramírez, who founded Estella in the 11th century, ensured that the pilgrimage route to Santiago passed through the town. Today, Estella is renowned for its historic churches, palaces and monasteries, for which it has been dubbed the Toledo of the North.

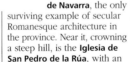

Coat of arms on a house in Estella

Close to the Ega river stands the **Palacio de los Reyes de Navarra**, the only surviving example of secular Romanesque architecture in the province. Near it, crowning a steep hill, is the **Iglesia de San Pedro de la Rúa**, with an original 13th-century portal and 12th-century cloister. The north portal of the Iglesia de San Miguel (12th- to 14th-century) is adorned with a bas-relief depicting St Michael slaying a dragon. Preserved on Calle Mayor are several houses with coats of arms, including a 17th-century Baroque palace.

Monasterio de Irache ⓯

Ayegui (Navarra). 🏛 **Monastery Tel** 948 55 44 64. ⏰ 9am–1:30pm Tue, 9am–1:30pm & 5–7pm Wed– Fri, 9am–1:30pm & 4–7pm Sat–Sun. **Museo del Vino Tel** 948 55 19 32. ⏰ 10am–2pm & 4–8pm Sat–Sun.

The word *iratze* means "fern" in Basque, and there were probably many ferns growing in the vicinity when the Benedictine monks began construction of their monastery in the 11th century. The pilgrims' hostel here was the first to be built in the region. Since the monastery has always been inhabited, the entire complex has been preserved in excellent condition. It comprises a 12th-century church, a cloister in the Plateresque style, a tower, and a Spanish Baroque building that served as a university from 1569 to 1824. The aisleless church, designed on the plan of a cross, features three semicircular apses. A bodega next to the monastery provides thirsty pilgrims with water and wine from two outdoor taps.

The Romanesque Palacio de los Reyes de Navarra in Estella

Viana

Navarra. 🏠 *3,700*. 🚌 *948 44 63 02*. 🚆 *Fri.* 🎉 *Santa María Magdalena (21–25 Jul)*. **www**.viana.es

In the Middle Ages, Viana was an important strategic town, fortified to defend Navarra from Castilian invasions, and a stop on the pilgrimage route of St James. Its massive **town walls** with four gates date from that period, as do the **castle** and churches of Santa María and San Pedro. Viana thrived between the 16th and 18th centuries, when aristocrats built Renaissance and Baroque palaces, decorated with coats of arms, wrought-iron balconies and wooden eaves.

Preserved to this day is the Gothic **Iglesia de Santa María**, with a 16th-century Plateresque façade. Its small windows testify to the building's original defensive purpose. Fine 18th-century paintings by Luis Paret y Alcázar hang in the chapel of San Juan del Ramo.

Near Viana, above the Embalse de las Canas reservoir, is a bird sanctuary.

Detail of a bas-relief on the Iglesia de Santa María in Viana

Tafalla ⑰

Navarra. 🏠 *10,900*. 🚌 🚆 *948 70 18 11*. 🎉 *San Sebastián (20 Jan), Virgen de la Asunción (14–20 Aug)*. **www**.tafalla.es

Legend has it that Tafalla was founded by Tubal, Noah's grandson. What is known for sure is that it performed an

The monumental Gothic palace in Olite

important defensive role by guarding the Pamplona road. It was first mentioned in a 10th-century Arabic chronicle.

The old quarter, with its cobbled streets, retains a medieval feel. The originally Gothic **Iglesia de Santa María**, rebuilt in the 16th to 18th centuries, is a monumental structure of rather spartan appearance. The **Iglesia de San Pedro** – originally Romanesque – was also remodelled; its Baroque tower is crowned by an octagonal lantern.

Environs
Artajona, situated 11 km (7 miles) northwest of Tafalla, is the only place in Navarra to feature completely preserved medieval walls (13th-century). The main element of the fortifications is the massive Gothic Iglesia de San Saturnino, which has loopholes in its walls and a tower that served as a prison, a belfry and an observation point.

Olite ⑱

Navarra. 🏠 *3,360*. 🚌 🚆 *Plaza Teobaldos 4; 948 74 17 03*. 🎉 *Virgen del Cólera (26 Aug), Fiestas Medievales (2nd half of Aug)*. **www**.olite.es

Olite, once a royal residence of the kings of Navarra, still has fragments of Roman and medieval walls. In the 15th century, Carlos III set about constructing here a monumental eclectic **Palacio Real**, regarded as a gem of Navarrese Gothic style. The palace was meticulously rebuilt in the 19th century after a devastating fire. Next to the complex is a network of medieval underground passageways – remnants of Carlos III's plan to link his residence with the palace in Tafalla. The Gothic **Iglesia de Santa María La Real** features a richly carved portal and a superb Renaissance reredos. The highlights of the 12th-century **Iglesia de San**

CESARE BORGIA (1475–1507) IN VIANA

The son of the corrupt Pope Alexander VI, Cesare Borgia was showered with a series of high church offices, becoming Bishop of Pamplona at 17 and a cardinal at 22, but he left the Church to become his father's chief henchman, and married the sister of Juan III of Navarra. Brutal and single-minded, he was an effective politician and soldier in Renaissance Italy, leading the papal armies in many campaigns. The sudden death of his father in 1503 ended his influence at the papal court. He fled from Italy to Aragón, only to be imprisoned, but escaped to Navarra, where Juan III was fighting against Castilian and French nobles. Cesare died in a 1507 siege in Viana.

A monument to Cesare Borgia in Viana

Pedro Apóstol are the Romanesque cloister and the squat Gothic tower topped by a huge spire.

🏛 **Palacio Real de Olite**
Tel 948 74 00 35. ◯ *Oct–Mar: 10am–6pm daily; Apr–Sep: 10am–7pm Mon–Fri, 10am–8pm Sat, Sun & hols.* ● *1 & 6 Jan.* 🖋

Environs
To the east of Olite is **Ujué**, one of the better-preserved villages in the lower Pyrenees. It has the medieval atmosphere of a stronghold concentrated around the imposing mass of the fortified church of Santa María (11th- to 14th-century). It has columns with capitals depicting human and animal figures. The heart of Carlos II is found inside the church.

Monasterio de la Oliva ⑲

Carcastillo (Navarra). 🚌 🚉 *from Tafalla.* **Tel** *948 72 50 06.* ◯ *9:30– 11:30am & 3:30–6pm daily.*

Window, Monasterio de la Oliva

Visitors are greeted with a serene atmosphere at this Cistercian monastery, whose design is characterized by asceticism and simplicity. The monastery was founded in 1143 by the king of Navarra, García Ramírez. Its aisled church has

five chapels, the largest closed by a semicircular apse. Nearby is the complex's oldest building – the Capilla de San Jesucristo.

Storks' nests on top of the Colegiata de Santa María in Tudela

Tudela ⑳

Navarra. 🏘 *31,660.* 🚌 🚉 ℹ *C/Juicio 4; 948 84 80 58.* 📅 *Sat.* 🎉 *Santa Ana (24–30 Jul).* **www**.tudela.es

In medieval times, Tudela was subject to both Christian and Moorish influence, as is aptly demonstrated by the Romanesque-Gothic **Colegiata de Santa María**. The church was built on the ruins of a mosque, and one of its Mudéjar chapels – dating from the 16th century – may have been a synagogue originally. Decorative elements from the former mosque are found in the Romanesque cloister. Next to the cathedral rises the 16th-century **Palacio Decanal**, with a Plateresque façade and arcaded gallery. Bullfights once took place on the busy **Plaza de los Fueros**, the city's main square. The **Judería Vétula** is the old Jewish quarter, with tall, narrow brick houses with broad eaves.

Bárdenas Reales ㉑

Navarra. **www**.bardenasreales.es

Between the Ebro and Aragón rivers extends a breathtaking landscape of weathered cliffs and crags. Bárdenas Reales is an uninhabited area almost devoid of vegetation. To the north rises a plateau known as El Plano de Bárdenas; in the middle is the Bárdena Blanca, so called on account of the white gypsum cliffs; and to the south is the Bárdena Negra, composed of reddish clay and limestone. Centuries of erosion have given rise to plateaus, plains, rock-needles and several ravines cut by rivers.

On the borders of the region, in Valtierra, the local caves have been converted into a guest house. This is a good place to stop before setting off on one of the trails through the geological formations.

Colourful rocks worn into fantastic shapes, the remarkable Bárdenas Reales

Logroño ⊘

La Rioja. 🏘 143,000. ✈ 🚉 ⓘ
C/ Portales 39; 941 27 33 53. ⌂
Sun. ⌖ San Bernabé (11 Jun), San
Mateo (21 Sep). **www**.logro-o.org

Logroño lies on the banks of
the Ebro river, spanned by
the **Puente de Piedra**, a 19th-
century stone bridge designed
by Fermín Manso de Zúniga. It
grew over the centuries, thanks
to its location on the Ebro as
well as along the pilgrimage
route of St James. Today, the
city's showpiece is the

The stone Puente de Piedra, spanning the Ebro river in Logroño

Baroque high altar in the cathedral
of Santa María de la Redonda

**Catedral de Santa María de
la Redonda**, with its massive
twin towers and rich Baroque
ornamentation. Of note inside
are the Capilla de Nuestra
Señora de la Paz, containing
a Plateresque reredos, and
the tomb of the cathedral's
founder, Diego Ponce de León.
   Near the cathedral stands
the 13th-century **Iglesia de
San Bartolomé**, which might
have formed part of the city's
fortifications. Its impressive
Gothic portal is adorned with
sculpted figures of Christ, the
Virgin, the apostles and saints.
The 16th-century tower
shows Mudéjar influence.
   Only a small section of the
Murallas de Revellín – 12th-
century city walls – survive,

encompassing the Puerta
Revellín, adorned with the
coat of arms of Carlos V. The
monumental 16th-century
Iglesia de Santiago el Real
once housed the archives of
the city council.
   The **Iglesia de Santa María
del Palacio** has taken on an
irregular form over the
centuries, and it is difficult
to imagine its original
appearance. The most
beautiful element is the
13th-century octagonal tower,
resembling a massive
pyramid, which locals have
dubbed the *aguja* (needle).
The Neoclassical main portal
is adorned with a figure of
the Virgin and of angels
playing instruments.

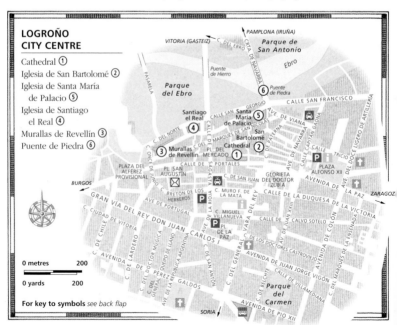

**LOGROÑO
CITY CENTRE**

Cathedral ①
Iglesia de San Bartolomé ②
Iglesia de Santa María
   de Palacio ⑤
Iglesia de Santiago
   el Real ④
Murallas de Revellín ③
Puente de Piedra ⑥

0 metres   200
0 yards   200

For key to symbols *see back flap*

Calahorra ㉓

La Rioja. ⚑ 22,450. 🚌 🚉 ⓘ *Calle Ángel Oliván 8; 941 14 63 98.* 📅 *Santos Emeterio y Celedonio (3 Mar, 25–31 Aug).* **www**.ayto-calahorra.es

Calahorra's history stretches back almost 2,000 years. Originally known by its Roman name of Calagurris, it was one of the Iberian peninsula's most important cities. On the banks of the Cidacos river, at the spot where its patron saints, the legionnaires Emeterio and Celedonio, are thought to have been martyred, rises a 15th-century **cathedral** with a neo-Classical façade by the Raón brothers. In the cathedral's chapel of San Pedro is a Plateresque reredos.

A figure from the church in Calahorra

The **Iglesia de San Andrés**, whose construction began in the 16th century, features a remarkable tympanum; a crucifix, with arms of unequal length. On the door at the main entrance is a carving that symbolizes the victory of Christianity over paganism, the latter represented by the sun, the moon and a synagogue. The austere tower is built of stone and brick. Inside the church is a magnificent Rococo altar by Manuel Adán.

The **Monasterio de San José** was built in the 16th century. At the high altar are murals depicting scenes from the life of St Theresa. To the side of the altar is a *Flagellation of Christ*, by Gregorio Hernández.

Enciso ㉔

La Rioja. ⚑ 160. 🚌 📅 *San Pedro (29 Jun), San Roque y Virgen de la Estrella (15–16 Aug).*

This tiny village of white houses with red roofs was once a centre of sheep farming and textiles, but its best days have long since passed. Nowadays only one factory produces the woollen rugs for which the village was once renowned. Enciso and the other villages in the area are now largely depopulated.

Two important churches survive here: the 16th-century **Santa María de la Estrella**, with a square tower and a beautiful 15th-century figure of the Virgin; and the aisleless **San Pedro**, featuring a 12th-century battlemented tower. A few hermitages and the ruins of a castle are also in the area.

Each year the region attracts a plethora of tourists to see the *huellas de dinosaurios* (dinosaur footprints), dating from the Mesozoic period and spread across several sites. The **Centro Paleontológico** conducts research on these ancient creatures, and provides an overview of the sites to visitors.

🏛 **Centro Paleontológico**
Calle Portillo 3. **Tel** *941 39 60 93.* 📅 *Jun–mid-Sep: 11am–2pm & 5–8pm daily; mid-Sep–May: 11am–2pm & 3–6pm Mon–Sat, 11am–2pm Sun & hols.* 🈂 🈯

Navarrete ㉕

La Rioja. ⚑ 2,610. 🚌 ⓘ *Cuesta El Cano; 941 44 00 05.* 📅 *Wed* 📅 *La Virgen y San Roque (15–16 Aug).*

The fortified town of Navarrete, situated on what was once the border between Navarra

The high altar at Iglesia de la Asunción in Navarrete

and Castile, had many different owners over the centuries. In recent times, its buildings have undergone renovation, and today the ancient houses with stone coats of arms (of which there are more than 50) have recovered some of their former splendour. Fine examples can be seen on **Calle Mayor**. Running behind the street is **Cal Nueva**, the former approach road to the underground bodegas.

The aisled **Iglesia de la Asunción**, with a Renaissance façade and two porticoes, was begun in the 16th century; inside is a Baroque reredos.

Not far from Navarrete is a **cemetery** whose entrance gate is the portico of a former pilgrims' hostel. This Romanesque structure, with elements of early Gothic, is composed of five arches, including pointed ones, decorated with scenes from the life of pilgrims and of St George fighting the dragon.

DINOSAURS FROM LA RIOJA

Approximately 100 million years ago, during the Mesozoic period, La Rioja was a vast river delta – a marshy landscape covered in rich vegetation. Among the numerous animals living here were dinosaurs, both carnivorous and herbivorous, who left their footprints in the mud. Over the millennia, due to geological changes, the mud turned into rock, and many of the footprints have been preserved; they can be seen by the marked trails that lead through the area.

Reconstructed dinosaurs in Valdecevillo

Anguiano and Sierra de la Demanda 26

La Rioja. 550. Ayuntamiento; 941 37 70 21. Santa María Magdalena (21–24 Jul).

With its stone bridge (Puente de la Madre de Dios) that spans the 30 m- (98 ft-) wide valley of the Najerilla river, Anguiano is famous for the *Danza de los Zancos* that occurs here during the feast of St Mary Magdalene (and on the last weekend in September). The dancers, balanced on stilts, have to negotiate the steep, cobbled street of Cuesta de los Danzadores in time to the music. The dance commemorates a rite of passage that young men had to undergo in the past.

The Sierra de la Demanda is an ancient mountain range that also extends into the province of Burgos. The forested hillsides (inhabited by wild animals) contain many post-glacial formations – moraines, cirques and lagoons; San Lorenzo (2,272 m/7,454 ft above sea level) is the highest peak. The mountain chain also conceals archaeological treasures such as medieval hermitages and necropolises. In **Cuyacabras**, there are 166 anthropomorphic tombs and the remnants of a church. **Mansilla de la Sierra** has a 16th-century stone bridge and is located next to the Embalse

Monasterio de Santa María la Real in Nájera

de Mansilla, a reservoir that is popular for watersports. The Sierra has examples of Romanesque architecture, such as in **Jaramillo de la Fuente**.

Nájera 27

La Rioja. 7,560. Plaza de San Miguel 10; 941 36 00 41. Thu. San Prudencio (28 Apr), San Juan and San Pedro (24–29 Jun), San Juan Mártir and Santa María La Real (16–19 Sep). www.aytonajera.es

At the beginning of the 11th century, when Sancho III of Navarra managed for a short period to unite the lands of the Iberian Peninsula, Nájera was capital of this vast empire. A pre-Roman town, Nájera had earlier played host to diverse cultures and communities, from ancient Basque

tribes to the Moors. Cut by the Najerilla river, the town has many historic monuments. The most important is the **Monasterio de Santa María la Real**, established in the 11th century on the spot where, according to legend, a statue of the Virgin was found in a cave. The present buildings date from 1422–53, with later elements added until the 16th century. The Gothic aisled church, incorporating other styles, is fortress-like in appearance. At the high altar is a Romanesque sculpture of the Virgin and Child. The beautiful late-Gothic choir is one of the finest examples of this style in Spain. At the back of this is a Renaissance royal pantheon holding the tombs of 12 former rulers of the kingdom of Nájera-Pamplona. Worth seeing, too, is the Knights' Cloister (Claustro de los Caballeros), which combines several different architectural styles, including ornate filigree Gothic and Plateresque elements.

The Tapa del Sepulcro de Blanca de Navarra, a 12th-century Romanesque tomb lid, is a treasure worth seeing.

Monasterio de Santa María la Real
Tel 941 36 36 50. 10am–1pm & 4–7pm Tue–Sat, 10am–12:30pm & 4–6 pm Sun & hols.

Typical scenery in the Sierra de la Demanda

MOUNTAIN VILLAGES IN THE SIERRA DE LA DEMANDA

Preserved in the Sierra de la Demanda are villages with typical highland homesteads, as well as important historic monuments. Romanesque churches can be seen in Vizcaínos and Jaramillos de la Frontera. The beautiful village of Canales de la Sierra is entirely made up of unchanged, centuries-old stone houses, including grand 16th-century buildings and the 12th-century Santa Catalina hermitage. At the Gothic church in the Valvanera monastery, people worship the patron saint of La Rioja – the Virgen de la Valvanera.

Virgen de la Valvanera, patron saint of La Rioja

Santo Domingo de la Calzada 28

La Rioja. 🏠 6,300. ▦ 🚌 Calle Mayor 70; 941 34 12 30. 🚍 Sat. 🎪 Fiestas Patronales (10–15 May).
www.santodomingodelacalzada.org

In the Middle Ages, a hermit named Domingo established a hospital and built a bridge over the Oja river to aid pilgrims on their journey to Santiago. In time, a town formed here.

St Dominic's remains are kept in the 12th-century **cathedral**. Ornamentation depicting the Tree of Jesse can be seen on the pilasters by the entrance to the chancel. The former high altar, currently placed in one of the aisles, is the Renaissance work of Damià Forment. The choir, decorated with figures of saints and inscriptions on the stalls, is a masterpiece of the Plateresque style.

The most bizarre element is a cage set in a wall in which a live cockerel and hen are kept. The animals commemorate a miracle attributed to St Dominic. It is said he resurrected a German pilgrim who had

St Dominic, patron saint of Santo Domingo de la Calzada

been unjustly hanged. When the poor wretch's parents found their son still alive on the gallows, they rushed to tell the judge, who exclaimed, "Nonsense, he's no more alive than this roast chicken on my plate!" Whereupon the chicken stood up on the plate and crowed.

San Millán de la Cogolla 29

La Rioja. 🏠 300. 🚌 🚍 Monasterio de Yuso; 941 37 32 59. 🎪 Traslación de las Reliquias (26 Sep), San Millán i Santa Gertrudis (12 & 17 Nov).

This village grew up around two monasteries. On a hillside above the village is the **Monasterio de San Millán de Suso** ("Suso" meaning upper). It was built in the 10th

Monasterio de San Millán de Yuso, in San Millán de la Cogolla

century on the site of a community of monks who lived in caves, founded by St Emilian (San Millán), a shepherd hermit, in 547. The church, hollowed out of pink sandstone, has Romanesque and Mozarabic features. It contains the tomb of St Emilian and the graves of seven infants of Lara who, according to legend, were kidnapped and beheaded by the Moors.

The **Monasterio de San Millán de Yuso** ("Yuso" meaning lower) is below it, in the Cárdenas Valley. It was built between the 16th and 18th centuries on the site of an earlier monastery from the 11th century. The part-Renaissance church has Baroque golden doors and a Rococo sacristy, where 17th-

century paintings are hung. The treasury has a collection of ivory plaques, once part of two 11th-century jewelled reliquaries, then plundered by French troops in 1813.

Medieval manuscripts are also displayed in the treasury. Among them is a facsimile of one of the earliest known texts in Basque and early Castilian. It is a commentary by a 10th-century Suso monk on a work by San Cesáreo de Arles, the *Glosas Emilianenses.*

Haro 30

La Rioja. 🏠 11,300. 🚉 🚌 🚍 🚌 941 30 33 66. 🚍 Tue, Sat. 🎪 La Batalla del Vino (29 Jun), Virgen de la Vega (8 Sep). **www**.haro.org

Set among extensive vineyards on the Ebro river, Haro is the capital of the Rioja Alta region. The town's main monument is a Baroque **basilica** devoted to the patron saint of Haro – Nuestra Señora de la Vega – a Gothic figure of whom is on the high altar. Of note, too, is the **Iglesia de Santo Tomás**, which features star vaulting and a Baroque tower. The portal was designed as an altar and depicts scenes from the Way of the Cross.

Several bodegas in Haro offer tours and wine tastings, and at the end of June the town's fiesta finishes with a wine-throwing orgy.

The town's **Aquapark** is good for a refreshing swim.

🏊 **Aquapark**
Ingenieros del M.O.P.U. s/n.
⏱ mid-Jun–mid-Sep. 🚿

The Aquapark in Haro, set among the hills

La Rioja Wines ㉛

The Rioja wine region, which extends into Navarra and Alava, has been producing wine since the Middle Ages. Vines have taken root extremely well on the sunny hillsides, the soil irrigated by the Ebro river and its tributaries. Atlantic winds blow across the western part, while the eastern part is subject to Mediterranean winds. There are three sub-regions: Rioja Alta, Rioja Baja and Rioja Alavesa. There are 450 wineries in the region. Typical grape varieties used are *tempranillo* and *garnacha*.

Haro ②
Haro is the capital of the Rioja Alta sub-region. Its limestone-clay soils produce dark, full-bodied wines that are typical of La Rioja. Among the local wineries is the Bodega Cooperativa, one of the largest in Europe.

Briñas ①
In this tiny village rises a proud 18th-century palace, which has been transformed into the wonderful Hospedería del Señorío de Briñas. The hotel puts on special events that introduce guests to the world of wine.

Bilbao (Bilbo)

San Vicente de la Sonsierra

Navarrete ⑧
The vineyards around this fortified town *(see p161)* can be seen by bicycle or on horseback. A local speciality is the *bollo de San Blas*, a sweet roll stuffed with *chorizo*.

| 0 kilometres | 5 |
| 0 miles | 5 |

HOW TO READ LABELS

The most important information on a label is the name of the producer or *bodega*. Next is the vintage, or *añada*, followed by the type of wine. All wines are classified according to four quality categories: *joven* or *cosecha* (young wine, one or two years old); *crianza* (matured in barrels for at least a year); and *reserva* and *gran reserva* (the best wines that have matured the longest). Each label displays the alcohol content and quality mark.

The producer's name or *bodega* is the first thing connoisseurs seek. Many labels also list the grape varieties.

Label decoration can be elegant, with illustrations by top graphic designers or painters.

Confirmation of source, or *denominación de origen*, is shortened to DO.

Designation of quality category and vintage

Briones ④
This fortified town is home to the headquarters of Finca Allende, a winery producing celebrated modern wines. The town's Museo de la Cultura del Vino has displays on the local wine culture.

TIPS FOR DRIVERS

Tour length: Approximately 90 km (56 miles).
Stopping-off places: Accommodation in hotels and casas rurales is easy to find in all the larger places on this route. Many of the bodegas – found in almost every town – offer tours combined with wine tastings.

Ollauri ③
Ollauri produces well-respected red wines. At the beginning of autumn, wine fairs are held here. These involve tastings, visits to the bodegas, and the preparation of wine-based meals.

San Asensio ⑤
This town is known for its high-quality wine. On 25 July it hosts a "wine battle" – the *Batalla del Clarete*, named after the local wine made from grapes cultivated on the light, sandy soils.

Cenicero ⑥
Vines grow on riverside terraces here, where numerous *casas-bodegas* (houses with wine cellars) are turned into meeting places for wine-lovers during fiestas.

Fuenmayor ⑦
Fuenmayor combines the features of Rioja Alta, Rioja Baja and Rioja Alavesa, which produce different types of wine. Here are major and local producers.

Logroño ⑨
In September, the San Mateo fiesta signals the start of the grape harvest. Events include the treading of grapes and offering of new wines to the Virgen de Valvanera.

KEY

▦	Motorway
▦	Tour route
▦	Scenic route
=	Minor road

Laguardia (Biasteri) ⑩
Under Laguardia's Old Town are numerous bodegas, and the Villa Lucía houses a winery museum. Located in Alava, this is the main town of the Rioja Alavesa.

The eclectic Colegiata de San Miguel in Aguilar de Campoo

Briviesca ②

Burgos (Castilla y León). ⌂ 7,000. 🚉 🚌 ⓘ Duque de Frias 9. 🎪 Nuestra Señora and San Roque (15–16 Aug). www.ayto-briviesca.com

Briviesca was originally located in the nearby hills, but in the 14th century it was moved lower down to its present site.

The town's best-known historic monument is the 16th-century **Convento de Santa Clara**, with a Renaissance walnut reredos carved with scenes depicting the Tree of Jesse and the Way of the Cross. On the Plaza Mayor stands the **Iglesia de San Martín**, with a 16th-century Plateresque façade. Nearby is a 17th-century **Ayuntamiento** (town hall) with a clock tower and three coats of arms. There are also coats of arms on many of the other houses from Briviesca's Golden Age.

Aguilar de Campoo ③

Palencia (Castilla y León). ⌂ 7,550. 🚉 🚌 ⓘ Plaza de España 30; 979 12 36 41. 🚌 Tue. 🎪 San Juan and San Pedro (24–29 Jun).

Aguilar de Campoo is a well-preserved medieval town. Rising above it is an 11th- to 12th-century castle, built on the ruins of a Celtic *castro*.

The houses and palaces in the town, including the **Palacio de Manrique**, are decorated with coats of arms; identical ones can be seen on the massive tower of the **Colegiata de San Miguel**. This eclectic church is mainly Gothic, but with a preserved Romanesque portal and a Spanish Baroque tower. Also worth seeing is the Romanesque **Iglesia de Santa Cecilia**, with its beautiful leaning tower. Its interior has column capitals bearing plant motifs and scenes of the *Slaughter of the Innocents*. A few medieval bridges also survive in Aguilar.

Frómista ④

Palencia (Castilla y León). ⌂ 1,000. ⓘ Paseo Central; 979 81 01 80. 🚌 Fri. 🎪 Fiestas Patronales (week after Easter), La Virgen del Otero (8 Sep). www.fromista.com

Tiny Frómista features traditional houses built in adobe – sun-dried brick made from clay and straw – but the village is chiefly famous for its Romanesque **Iglesia de San Martín**, with harmonious proportions and sculptural decoration. Restored to its original appearance, it has three apses, the central one being taller than the others; likewise, the nave is taller than the aisles. An octagonal tower rises above the transept, with two cylindrical towers crowning the façade. The portals are decorated with human and animal figures as well as plant motifs. Similar decoration can be seen on the capitals of the columns inside the church – note how the fable of the Raven and the Fox is presented.

Burgos ③⑤

Burgos (Castilla y León). ⌂ 169,690. 🚉 🚌 ⓘ Paseo del Espolón; 947 28 88 74. 🚌 Fri, Sat, Sun. 🎪 San Pedro and San Pablo (29 Jun). www.aytoburgos.es

Burgos was established in 884 for military reasons. Over the centuries, the city transformed into an important commercial and religious centre, as well as becoming the seat of Spanish monarchs and magnates. Burgos experienced its Golden Age in the 16th century when it enjoyed a monopoly on the Castilian wool trade.

Several gateways, including the **Arco de San Esteban**, have survived from the original fortifications. The grandest gateway is the **Arco de Santa María**, built in 1553 in the style of a triumphal arch in honour of Carlos I; its façade, designed by Juan de Vallejo, is carved with statues of dignitaries and contains a figure of the Virgin.

The city's showpiece is the **cathedral** (see pp168–9). The spires crowning its towers – by Juan de Colonia – are visible all from all over Burgos.

Arco de Santa María in Burgos

EL CID (1043–99)

Rodrigo Díaz de Vivar was born of a noble family in Vivar del Cid, north of Burgos. He served Fernando I, but was banished from Castile after becoming embroiled in the fratricidal squabbles of the king's sons, Sancho II and Alfonso VI. He switched allegiance to fight for the Moors, then switched again, capturing Valencia for the Christians in 1094, ruling the city until his death. For his heroism he was named El Cid, from the Arabic *Al-Sidi* (Lord). He was a charismatic man of courage, but it was the poem *El Cantar del Mío Cid* (1180) that immortalized him as a Christian hero.

Statue of El Cid, hero of the Reconquest

Inside the Gothic **Iglesia de San Nicolás** is a stone reredos by Simon of Cologne, depicting the life and miracles of St Nicholas. The **Iglesia de San Esteban** (13th- to 14th-century) accommodates Spain's only museum of altarpieces. Further east stands the **Iglesia de San Lorenzo**, which has superb Baroque vaulting. The **Iglesia de Santa Águeda** is the place where El Cid made Alfonso VI swear that he had nothing to do with the death of his brother, Sancho II.

A coat of arms in Burgos Cathedral

A magnificent example of 15th-century civic architecture is the **Casa del Cordón** (now a bank), so called on account of the ornamentation in the form of a Franciscan cord motif that surrounds two coats of arms on the façade. The 16th-century palace of the Casa de Miranda houses the **Museo de Burgos**, with exhibits on the archaeology, history and art of the region. Of special interest are the finds from the Roman city of Clunia, the tomb of Juan de Padilla, and an 11th-century Moorish casket.

On the outskirts of town stands the **Monasterio de Santa María la Real de las Huelgas**, a Cistercian convent founded by Alfonso VIII in 1187. The style of the building is Gothic, with added elements of Romanesque, Mudéjar and Renaissance. South of the Gothic church – the resting place of the convent's founder – is the **Claustro de San Fernando**, cloisters decorated with Moorish designs: geometric patterns, inscriptions, and figures of peacocks and griffins.

To the east of the city is the **Monasterio de la Cartuja de Miraflores**, a Carthusian monastery founded in 1441. This aisleless church has a polygonal apse covered in star vaulting. In front of the high altar, gilded with the first consignment of gold brought back to Spain from the New World, is a star-shaped tomb holding the remains of Juan II and Isabel of Portugal, the parents of Isabel the Catholic Monarch. Both the tomb and the altar are attributed to Gil de Siloé. The hill above the city, on which stands a 9th-century **castle**, offer spectacular views over the city.

🏛 **Museo de Burgos**
C/Calera 25. **Tel.** 947 26 58 75. ⬤ 10am–2pm daily, plus 4–7pm Tue–Sat (Oct–Jun) and 5–8pm Tue–Sat (Jul–Sep). 📷 (free Sun & hols). ♿

� **Monasterio de Santa María la Real de las Huelgas**
C/Compases de Huelga. **Tel.** 947 20 16 30. ⬤ 10am–1pm & 3:45–5:30pm Tue–Sat, 10:30am–2pm Sun. 📷 📷

� **Monasterio de la Cartuja de Miraflores**
Carretera de la Cartuja. **Tel.** 947 25 25 86. ⬤ 10:30am–3pm & 4–6pm Mon–Sat, 11am–3pm & 4–6pm Sun.

The richly decorated high altar in the Iglesia de San Nicolás

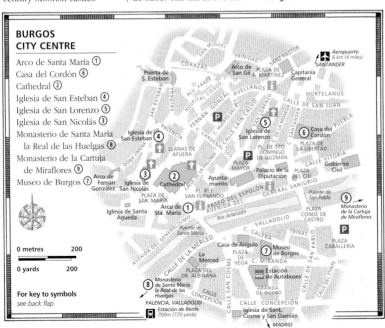

BURGOS CITY CENTRE

Arco de Santa María ①
Casa del Cordón ⑥
Cathedral ②
Iglesia de San Esteban ④
Iglesia de San Lorenzo ⑤
Iglesia de San Nicolás ③
Monasterio de Santa María la Real de las Huelgas ⑧
Monasterio de la Cartuja de Miraflores ⑨
Museo de Burgos ⑦

0 metres 200
0 yards 200

For key to symbols see back flap

Catedral de Burgos

Spain's third-largest cathedral was founded in 1221 by Bishop Don Mauricio under Fernando III. The ground plan – a Latin cross – measures 84 m (92 yds) by 59 m (65 yds). Its construction was carried out in stages over three centuries and involved many of the greatest artists and architects in Europe. The style is almost entirely Gothic, and shows influences from Germany, France, and the Low Countries. First to be built were the nave and cloisters, while the intricate, crocketed spires and the richly decorated side chapels are mostly later work. The architects cleverly adapted the cathedral to its sloping site, incorporating stairways inside and out.

Flagellation of Christ, by Diego de Siloé

West Front
The lacy, steel-grey spires soar above a sculpted balustrade depicting Castile's early kings.

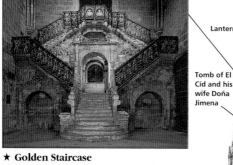

Lantern

Tomb of El Cid and his wife Doña Jimena

★ Golden Staircase
This elegant Renaissance staircase by Diego de Siloé (1522) links the nave with the street-level Coronería – a tall Gothic gate also known as one of the Apostles.

STAR FEATURES

★ Constable's Chapel

★ Crossing

★ Golden Staircase

Capilla de Santa Tecla

Puerta de Santa María (main entrance)

Capilla de Santa Ana
The altarpiece (1490) in this chapel is by the sculptor Gil de Siloé. The central panel shows St Anne with St Joachim.

Capilla de la Presentación (1519–24) is a funerary chapel with a star-shaped, traceried vault.

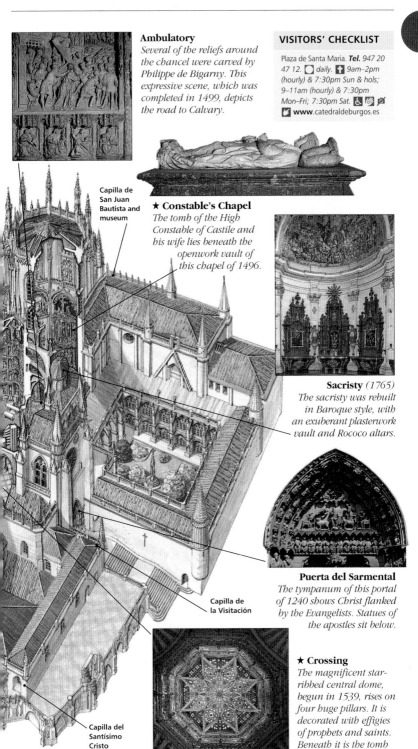

Ambulatory
Several of the reliefs around the chancel were carved by Philippe de Bigarny. This expressive scene, which was completed in 1499, depicts the road to Calvary.

VISITORS' CHECKLIST

Plaza de Santa María. *Tel. 947 20 47 12.* ◯ daily. ✚ 9am–2pm (hourly) & 7:30pm Sun & hols; 9–11am (hourly) & 7:30pm Mon–Fri; 7:30pm Sat. ♿ 🈦 📷
🖥 www.catedraldeburgos.es

Capilla de San Juan Bautista and museum

★ Constable's Chapel
The tomb of the High Constable of Castile and his wife lies beneath the openwork vault of this chapel of 1496.

Sacristy *(1765)*
The sacristy was rebuilt in Baroque style, with an exuberant plasterwork vault and Rococo altars.

Capilla de la Visitación

Puerta del Sarmental
The tympanum of this portal of 1240 shows Christ flanked by the Evangelists. Statues of the apostles sit below.

Capilla del Santísimo Cristo

★ Crossing
The magnificent star-ribbed central dome, begun in 1539, rises on four huge pillars. It is decorated with effigies of prophets and saints. Beneath it is the tomb of El Cid and his wife.

CENTRAL AND EASTERN PYRENEES

The Spanish Pyrenees encompass parts of two regions: Aragón, with the highest, wildest terrain, and Catalonia, where the peaks are more accessible and better developed for tourism. In the mountain villages life proceeds at a slower pace, old traditions are nurtured, and in places such as Broto or Bielsa colourful carnivals are staged.

Stretching 440 km (273 miles) from the Bay of Biscay on the Atlantic Coast to the Cap de Creus on the Mediterranean, the Pyrenean mountain chain forms a natural border between France and Spain. In the 8th century, these inaccessible lands provided excellent refuge from the Moorish invaders, and the Pyrenean valleys were the birthplaces of some of Spain's first Christian kingdoms. Later, after their rulers had moved south, the peoples who remained lived for centuries in isolation from the rest of Spain.

The foothills of the mountains, whose highest peak is Aneto (3,404 m/ 11,166 ft above sea level), are crossed by the Aragonese variation of the pilgrimage route to Santiago de Compostela, where some of the most interesting Romanesque sites are located. Among them is the Monasterio de San Juan de la Peña, an architectural gem. Huesca and Jaca, whose history goes back nearly 2,000 years, are the area's main towns.

Well-marked trails run through the mountain valleys, frequented by nature-lovers, who can get a close-up view of the deep ravines, the peaks and the many indigenous species of plants and animals.

The Pyrenees are a paradise for winter-sports enthusiasts. Popular places for winter activities include Formigal, which offers a variety of ski runs, and La Molina – the oldest ski resort in the Eastern Pyrenees.

The principality of Andorra, a tax-free paradise for shoppers, occupies land in the Pyrenees between France and Spain. Its rural charm matches that of the rest of the Pyrenees, and it is also excellent for walkers.

The town of Laspuña near Aínsa, surrounded by imposing massifs

◁ The 12th-century church in Durro, a village in the Parc Nacional d'Aigüestortes

Exploring the Central and Eastern Pyrenees

The two gateways to the Aragonese high Pyrenees are Huesca and Jaca. This region's most popular sights include the Monasterio de San Juan de la Peña, half-concealed beneath a rock overhang, and the impressively sited Castillo de Loarre. No itinerary would be complete without taking in the beautiful valleys of Ansó, Hecho and Tena, where fiestas are held. In the Catalonian Pyrenees, the main centres are Ripoll, on the route from Barcelona, Puigcerdà, La Seu d'Urgell, the forested Vall d'Aran with its flowery meadows, and the mountain principality of Andorra.

An ornate Romanesque capital in the Iglesia de Santiago in Agüero

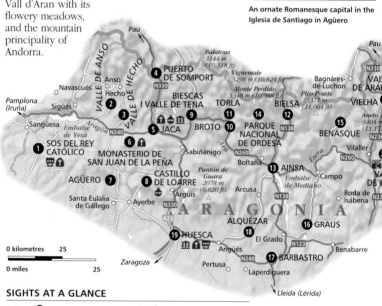

0 kilometres 25

0 miles 25

SIGHTS AT A GLANCE

A crystal-clear stream in the Parc Nacional d'Aigüestortes

GETTING AROUND

The best way of getting around the Central and Eastern Pyrenees is by car, but take special care on the mountain roads looking out for cattle herds and during winter snowdrifts. The more remote mountain locations are accessible only on foot.

There are train services from Zaragoza and Valencia to Huesca. Jaca can be reached by coach from Huesca and Zaragoza. Minor roads connect Jaca with Pamplona and Aínsa. Buses from Jaca will take you to the entrances to the valleys. The Parque Nacional de Ordesa can be reached from Sabiñánigo.

A Romanesque stone church in the Vall de Boí

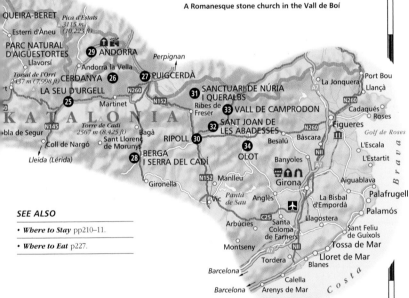

e Mauberm

QUEIRA-BERET · Pica d'Estats *3115 m (10,223 ft)*

· Esterri d'Àneu

PARC NATURAL D'AIGÜESTORTES

· Llavorsí

Tossal de l'Orrí *2437 m (7,998 ft)*

CERDANYA **26**

29 ANDORRA
· Andorra la Vella

Perpignan

27 PUIGCERDÀ

LA SEU D'URGELL

25

Martinet

N260

N152

31 SANCTUARI DE NÚRIA I QUERALBS

Ribes de Freser

33 VALL DE CAMPRODON

Port Bou

La Jonquera

Llançà

N260

Cadaqués

Roses

K A T A L O N I A

N145

bla de Segur

· Coll de Nargó

Lleida (Lérida)

Torre de Cadí *2567 m (8,425 ft)*

Bagà

Sant Llorenç de Morunys

RIPOLL **30**

28 BERGA I SERRA DEL CADÍ

· Gironella

Besalú

32 SANT JOAN DE LES ABADESSES

34

OLOT

Banyoles

Figueres

Golf de Roses

L'Escala

L'Estartit

Bàscara

NII

A7

Girona

Aiguablava

Palafrugell

C o s t a   B r a v a

N152

Manlleu

Panta de Sau

Vic

Anglès

La Bisbal d'Empordà

Palamós

SEE ALSO

- *Where to Stay* pp210–11.

- *Where to Eat* p227.

Arbúcies

Santa Coloma de Farners

Montseny

A7

Llagostera

Sant Feliu de Guíxols

Tossa de Mar

NII

Lloret de Mar

Blanes

Barcelona

Tordera

Calella

Barcelona · Arenys de Mar

C o s t a

KEY

═══	Motorway
▬▬	Dual carriageway
━━	Major road
┅┅	Minor road
──	Scenic route
┄┄	Main railway line
▬▬	National border
▬▬	Regional border
△	Mountain peak

25 km

A field of sunflowers in the Barbastro area

Road through the verdant Valle de Ansó, lined with craggy peaks

Sos del Rey Católico ❶

Zaragoza. 🏠 *900.* ❶ *Plaza de la Villa 1; 948 88 80 65.* 🚗 *Fri.* 📅 *San Esteban (3rd Wed in Aug).*

Sos del Rey Católico is one of the Cinco Villas – a group of five picturesque towns granted privileges by Philip V for their loyalty during the War of the Spanish Succession at the beginning of the 18th century, which ended in victory for the Bourbons *(see p41)*.

Coat-of-arms, Sos del Rey Católico town hall

The town owes its name to King Fernando de Aragón, the "Catholic King", who was born here in 1452 *(see p40)*. The **Palacio de Sada**, his reputed birthplace, was built on the ruins of an old castle and features an 18th-century chapel. Also worth visiting are the 15th-century Gothic **town hall** and, at the top of the town, the 11th-century **Iglesia de San Esteban**, with beautiful carved capitals, a Romanesque font, and 13th-century frescoes in two of the crypt apses.

Valle de Ansó ❷

Reached via the A176 motorway from Puente la Reina. ❶ *974 37 02 25.* **www**.losvalles.com

Covered in beach, fir and pine, the Valle de Ansó rivals the Valle de Hecho as the most beautiful valley in the Pyrenees. Formed by the Veral river, it features an amazing diversity of flora and fauna. Walking between the vertical crags, you might encounter capercaillie, fallow deer and squirrels. When exploring the valley on foot, it is worth stopping at the village of **Ansó**, situated 860 m (2,821 ft) above sea level. Until recently, it was almost completely cut off from the outside world. Thanks to its isolation, the villagers have retained their traditional customs and crafts. On the last Sunday in August, a huge fiesta takes place here, and local people wear traditional costumes resembling medieval attire.

Valle de Hecho ❸

Huesca. 🏠 *1,005.* ❶ *974 37 50 02 (Hecho).* **www**.losvalles.com

The stone villages in the green Hecho valley are characterized by red-roofed stone houses, typical of the Pyrenees. The people here speak the local dialect called *cheso*, virtually unchanged since early medieval times.

Stone houses in the village of Hecho

The valley offers good views of the peak of **Castillo de Macher**. Walking trips can be made to **Selva de Oza**, with its striking array of Atlantic flora, as well as to other places amid the mountain landscape.

The largest village in the valley is **Hecho**, which has a sculpture garden left from an open-air festival. Some 2 km (1.2 miles) north of Hecho lies the bucolic village of **Siresa**. It is home to an interesting Romanesque-Gothic church – San Pedro (1082) – which was once part of a monastery founded in the 9th century by Count Aznar Galíndez. The shrine soon became the region's spiritual capital, and in 922 the monastery was made the see of Aragón.

Puerto de Somport ❹

Huesca. ❶ *Plaza Ayuntamiento 1 (Canfranc); 974 37 31 41.* **www**.canfranc.com

On the French border, at the head of a long valley (Valle de Canfranc) that runs down to Jaca, the Puerto de Somport (Somport Pass) is one of the most historic crossing points in the Pyrenees. The pass was used by the Romans and medieval pilgrims, and takes its name from the Latin *Summu Portu*.

The pass marks the start of the Aragonese pilgrimage route to Santiago de Compostela, which is older than the more famous route through Navarra. The Aragonese route leads through Canfranc, Villanúa, Jaca, San Juan de la Peña and Santa Cruz de Serós, joining the Navarrese route in Yesa. The pass, on which stands a small chapel with a figure of St James, was a crossing point for the Romans and Moors. Nowadays, the austere scenery is speckled with holiday apartments built for skiing. **Astún** is the best-organized and most modern resort, while **Candanchú** in the Valle de Canfranc is one of Spain's major winter sports centres.

Jaca ❺

Huesca. 🏛 *Plaza de la Catedral; 974 36 00 98.* 🚌 *Fri.* 🎉 *La Victoria (1st Fri in May), Santa Orosia y San Pedro (25–29 Jun).* **www**.jaca.es

This picturesque town, situated in the heart of the Pyrenees, is Roman in origin (2nd century AD). In 795, at the Battle of Las Tiendas, the town repulsed the Moors, mainly due to the bravery of local women. In 1054, Jaca became the first capital of the kingdom of Aragón. This event precipitated the construction of the first Romanesque **cathedral** in Spain, which imitated French designs. Over time, the cathedral itself became a model for churches built on this side of the Pyrenees, and in the 20th century it was declared a World Heritage Site. Built on a basilican plan, the cathedral has a nave, aisles and a transept. While the exterior is predominantly Romanesque, inside one can trace the history of church architecture, from Gothic in the

star vaulting of the aisles, through Renaissance in the chapel of St Michael, to Baroque in the transept pilasters and some of the altars. The central apse has paintings by Manuel de Bayeu, the brother-in-law of Francisco de Goya.

In the cloisters, the **Museo Diocesano** has a fine collection of Romanesque and Gothic frescoes from local churches, including the Iglesia de los Santos Julián y Basilisa. The frescoes from the apse of the Ermita de San Juan Bautista in Ruesta date from the first half of the 12th century – a striking image of the head of Christ Pantocrator was uncovered beneath a layer of paint.

South of the cathedral, on Plaza la Cadena, stands the **Monumento Ramiro I** by Ramón Casadevall Callostro. It commemorates a king who had his court in Jaca and who founded a new

Romanesque capital in the portal of Jaca Cathedral

One of the gates of the citadel in Jaca

dynasty. Also worth seeing is the famous **Torre del Reloj**, a 15th-century Gothic clock tower that was built on the site of a former royal palace.

In 1591, Philip II built in Jaca the **Ciudadela** decorated with corner turrets. This is one of only two surviving pentagonal citadels in Europe.

Just west of the town centre lies the **Puente de San Miguel**, a famous medieval bridge on the pilgrimage route.

🏛 **Museo Diocesano**
Tel. *974 35 63 78.* 🔵 *closed for restoration.*

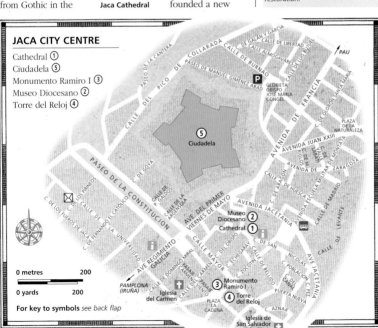

JACA CITY CENTRE

Cathedral ①
Ciudadela ⑤
Monumento Ramiro I ③
Museo Diocesano ②
Torre del Reloj ④

0 metres 200
0 yards 200

For key to symbols *see back flap*

Monasterio de San Juan de la Peña ❻

The history of this imposing monastery dates from the Moorish invasion, when hermit-monks, fleeing the Moors, settled here. According to legend it was an early guardian of the Holy Grail – the chalice from the Last Supper. In the 11th century the primitive monastery joined the Benedictine order, and it was the first monastery to use the Latin Mass in Spain. The church of the old monastery is on two floors. The lower one is a primitive crypt built in the early 10th century. The upper floor contains an 11th-century church. After a fire in the 17th century, the building was abandoned in favour of a newer one further up the hillside. This was later sacked by Napoleon's troops, although the Baroque façade survives.

View of the Monastery
This magnificent Romanesque monastery is half-concealed under a bulging rock overhang (peña).

★ Old Monastery
The oldest part of the complex is the lower Mozarabic church, built in 920 on the site of an earlier rock-hewn shrine dedicated to St John the Baptist.

Museum

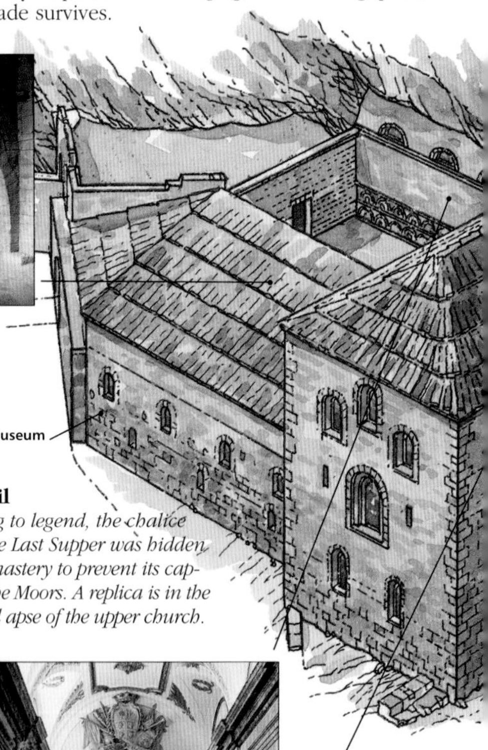

Holy Grail
According to legend, the chalice used at the Last Supper was hidden in the monastery to prevent its capture by the Moors. A replica is in the central apse of the upper church.

Romanesque church

Royal Pantheon
The 18th-century Neoclassical Pantheon whose walls are decorated with historical stucco reliefs, contains the stacked tombs of the early Aragonese kings: Ramiro I, Sancho Ramírez and Pedro I.

STAR FEATURES

★ Capilla de San Victorián

★ Cloister

★ Old Monastery

Lower Mozarabic Church
This church was built by Mozarabs – Christians who lived under Muslim rule, whose architecture and culture were strongly influenced by Islamic styles.

The Lower Church
features 12th-century Romanesque murals. Some of the abbots are also buried here.

VISITORS' CHECKLIST

🛈 974 35 51 19. ⏲ mid Oct–mid Mar: 11am–2pm & 4–5:30pm Tue–Sun; mid-Mar–May & Sep–mid-Oct: 10am–2pm & 4–7pm daily; Jun–Aug: 10am–2:30pm & 3:30–8pm daily.
www.monasteriosanjuan.co

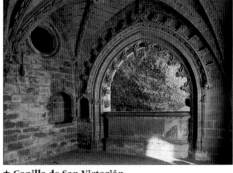

★ **Capilla de San Victorián**
The resting place of the abbots, this Gothic chapel is entered through a beautiful Mozarabic portal.

17th-century Capilla de San Voto y San Félix

CAPITALS

On the 20 Romanesque capitals dating from the 12th century are scenes from the Old and New Testaments in chronological order. They were created by an anonymous artist, referred to as the Master of San Juan de la Peña. The capitals constitute a pictorial Bible, beginning with the Creation and finishing with the Ascension of Christ. The Romanesque style treated sculpture as subordinate to architecture, which is why some of the figures seem out of proportion with each other and placed uncomfortably.

A Romanesque capital in the monastery cloister

★ **Cloister**
The cloistered courtyard was meant to symbolize the New Jerusalem. The capitals of its columns display wonderful carved biblical scenes.

The imposing fortress of the Castillo de Loarre, closely moulded around the contours of the rocky hillside

Agüero ➐

Huesca. 🚹 San Jaime 1; 974 38 04
89. 🎉 San Roque (15–19 Aug).
www.aytoaguero.es

The picturesque setting of this
attractive village, clustered
against a dramatic crag of
eroded stone, amply rewards a
brief detour from the Huesca–
Pamplona road. Rising above
the village is the Iglesia de
Santiago, whose construction
began c.1200. The capitals of
the columns in this aisled
building are carved with fantastic beasts, as well as scenes
from the life of Jesus and Mary.
The most beautiful carvings
are on the portal, depicting
scenes of the Epiphany and
Salome dancing. They appear
to be made by the Master of
San Juan de la Peña (see p177).

Castillo de Loarre ➑

Huesca. 🚹 974 38 26 27. ⏱ mid-
Mar–mid-Oct: 10:30am–1:30pm &
4–7pm; mid-Oct–mid-Mar: 10:30am–
1:30pm & 4–6pm. ⬤ Mon (except
Jul–Aug).

The ramparts of this sturdy
fortress rise majestically above
the road approaching from
Ayerbe. On a clear day, the
hilltop setting is stupendous,
with views of the surrounding
orchards and reservoirs of the
Ebro plain. Inside the curtain

walls lies a complex founded
in the 11th century on the site
of a Roman castle. It was later
remodelled under Sancho I
(Sancho Ramírez) of Aragón,
who established a religious
community here, placing the
complex under the rule of the
Order of Augustine.
    Within the castle walls is a
Romanesque church containing
the remains of St Demetrius.

Biescas and Valle de Tena ➒

Huesca. 🏘 1,100. 🚹 Plaza del
Ayuntamiento; 974 49 56 33. 🎉
Fiesta Popular (13 Jun), San Roque
(14 Aug), Fiesta de la Virgen (18 Aug).

The picturesque Valle de Tena
is ideal for walkers and hikers;
several well-marked trails lead
from here to the surrounding
peaks, some of which are
over 3,000 m (9,842 ft) above
sea level and also accessible
by cable car. The places most
often visited include the **Casita
de las Brujas** (Witches' Hut),
the **Ermita de Santa Elena**,
and the **Parque de Arratiecho**.
    Near the entrance to the
valley – famous for traditional
cheese-making techniques
and regional delicacies, such
as breadcrumbs with grapes –
is the small town of **Biescas**,
which spans the Gállego river.
The river divides the town into

its two districts of El Salvador
and San Pedro, to whom the
local churches are dedicated.
    The Gállego is one of the
most spectacular of the fast-
flowing Pyrenean rivers, and
Sallent de Gállego is a centre
for whitewater rafting, kayak-
ing, rock climbing, fishing
and other adventure sports.
For winter-sports enthusiasts,
the beautiful Panticosa gorge
is home to the ski resorts of
El Formigal and **Panticosa**.

Broto ➓

Huesca. 🏘 522. 🚌 from Sabiñánigo
or Aínsa. 🚹 Avenida Ordesa 1; 974
48 64 13. 🎉 San Blas (3 Mar), La
Vírgen del Rosario (7 Oct).

Situated in the Ordesa valley,
Broto is a good base for excursions to the western side of

**A roe deer taking a rest in a village
near Broto**

the Parque Nacional de Ordesa *(see pp 182–3)*. The medieval town once played an important strategic role. Its name derives from a Basque word meaning "place covered in blackberry bushes". Broto's inhabitants earn their living from cattle

Abandoned stone house near Broto

farming and tourism, and they maintain local traditions. On occasion they can be seen performing their dances: the *rapatan*, a shepherds' dance, and *os palateaos*, a war dance.

Rising above the small town is the 16th-century **Iglesia de San Pedro el Apóstol**, from which there are breathtaking views of the valley.

A short walk from Broto leads to two other equally fine views: the 50-m (164-ft) **Sorrosal waterfall** and the **Ermita de Nuestra Señora de Murillo**, some 1,470 m (4,823 ft) above sea level.

Torla ⓫

Huesca. ⌂ 344. ⓘ Calle Fatas 7; 974 48 61 52 *(Jul–Sep only)*.

This village, at the gateway to the Parque Nacional de Ordesa *(see pp182–3)* and huddled beneath the forbidding slopes of Mondarruego, is the main tourist centre in this part of the Pyrenees. Local guides can be hired to take experienced walkers up to the surrounding 3,000-m (9,842-ft) peaks; the most popular of these peaks is **Monte Perdido**, the "Lost Mountain" (3,355 m/11,007 ft above sea level).

Torla is a picturesque town with slate-roofed houses and a church dating from the beginning of the 16th century. Each year in February a carnival is held here, during which all the evil of the past year – personified by a man dressed up as a black beast – is destroyed by a brave hunter. In order to humiliate and overpower it, the beast is dragged through the streets of the town in a colourful procession accompanied by a lively singing crowd.

Bielsa ⓬

Huesca. ⌂ 472. ⓘ Carretera Parzán; 974 50 10 00.

Just 12 km (7.5 miles) from the border with France, the village of Bielsa is a popular base for hikers and mountaineers. It is the main gateway to the eastern side of the Parque Nacional de Ordesa, and especially the Valle de Pineta, one of the park's most beautiful parts. Information about area trails is provided at the local tourist office.

Bielsa was completely destroyed during the Spanish Civil War, so the architecture of the mountain village is relatively new. The principal attraction here is the **Museo Etnológico de Bielsa**, where one can learn about the history of the region and the local carnival. The latter is based on a ritual that was performed in pagan times, in which the participants would say a symbolic farewell to winter and greet the arrival of spring. The extraordinary participants of this fiesta, known as *Trangas*, have huge rams' horns on their heads,

Façade detail, Museo Etnológico de Bielsa

blackened faces and teeth made of potatoes. They are said to represent fertility.

> 🏛 **Museo Etnológico de Bielsa**
> Plaza Mayor. ◷ summer: 5–9pm Tue–Sun; mornings & rest of year: by prior arrangment only. ✉
> **www**.bielsa.com/museo

Aínsa ⓭

Huesca. ⌂ 1,600. ⓘ Avda. Pirenaico 1; 974 50 07 67. ✉ Tue. ✦ San Sebastián (20 Jan), Fiestas Mayores (14 Sep).

The history of Aínsa began in 742, when people fleeing the Moors took refuge in the Pyrenees. Having established a small settlement, they decided to repel the Moorish invaders by force. During one such clash, a shining cross reputedly appeared on the battlefield, to which the victory was attributed. The victory is commemorated every other September during the Fiesta de la Morisma.

In the years 1035–38, Aínsa was the short-lived capital of the kingdom of Sobrarbe. The 12th-century **Plaza Mayor**, a broad cobbled square, is surrounded by arcaded houses of brown stone. Also on the plaza stands the belfry of the Romanesque **Iglesia de Santa María**, which was consecrated in 1181. Behind the church, steep narrow streets lead up to the restored **castle** with a preserved citadel, dating from the times of the Reconquest.

Stone houses with arcades on the Plaza Mayor in Aínsa

Medieval Aínsa with the snow-capped peaks of the Pyrenees in the background ▷

Parque Nacional de Ordesa ⑭

Signpost in the national park

Within its borders, the Parque Nacional de Ordesa y Monte Perdido combines all the most dramatic elements of Spain's Pyrenean scenery. At the heart of the park are four glacial canyons – the Ordesa, Añisclo, Pineta and Escuaín valleys – which carve the great upland limestone massifs into spectacular cliffs and chasms. Most of the park is accessible only on foot: even then, snow during autumn and winter makes it inaccessible to all except those with specialist climbing equipment. In high summer, however, the crowds testify to the park's well-earned reputation as a paradise for walkers and nature-lovers alike.

Valle de Ordesa
The Río Arazas cuts through forested limestone escarpments, providing some of Ordesa's most popular walks

Torla
This village, at the gateway to the park, huddles beneath the forbidding slopes of Mondarruego. With its core of cobbled streets and slate-roofed houses around the church, Torla is a popular base for visitors to Ordesa.

Broto
Spanning a valley on the banks of the Río Ara, this village has traditional period houses. The extensive valley forms a fantastic backdrop for the fine regional architecture.

| 0 metres | 200 |
| 0 yards | 200 |

KEY

═══ Major road

══ Minor road

– – Mountain trail

▬▬ Spanish–French border

──── National park boundary

ℹ Tourist information

🅿 Parador

☆ Viewpoint

View from the Parador de Bielsa
The parador at the foot of Monte Perdido looks out at stunning sheer rock faces streaked by waterfalls.

VISITORS' CHECKLIST

Avenida Ordesa 19 (Torla); 974 48 64 72.
& Sabiñánigo.
www.ordesa.net

Cola de Caballo
The 70-m (230-ft) "Horse's Tail" waterfall is a scenic stopping point near the northern end of the long hike around the Circo Soaso. It provides a taste of the spectacular scenery found along the route.

Hikers in the national park

TIPS FOR WALKERS

Several well-marked trails follow the valleys and can be easily tackled by anyone who is reasonably fit, though walking boots are a must. The mountain routes may require climbing gear so check first with the visitors' centre (in Torla) and get a detailed map. Mountain weather changes fast, with snow early or late in the season. High altitude overnight camping is allowed, but only for one night.

Cañon or Garganta de Añisclo
A wide path leads along this beautiful, steep-sided gorge, following the wooded course of the turbulent Río Vellos through dramatic limestone scenery.

Flora and Fauna of Parque Nacional de Ordesa

With some of the most dramatic mountain scenery in Spain, the Parque Nacional de Ordesa makes excellent walking country. The most popular trails through the park are the Camiño del Soaso, Senda de los Cazadores and Faja de las Flores. Some of the animal species encountered here are in danger of becoming extinct but the park offers natural protection for the mountain eagle, capercaillie, chamois, deer, wild boar, marmot and vulture. As well as an abundance of gentians, orchids and belladonna, there are also lush pine and fir forests and many birch, beech and wild cherry trees.

Esparceta (sainfoin), *an important honey-yielding and fodder plant, is commonly found in the alpine meadows of the park. This long-lived perennial, reaching a height of 60 cm (24 in), produces clusters of pretty pink or carmine flowers.*

The rocky massifs border gentle hills covered in dwarf mountain pines.

The viper *is a poisonous snake that lives in cold places, avoiding direct sunlight. It hunts for mice, birds and frogs.*

The horses grazing in the alpine meadows have vivid colouring.

The meadows are home to many species of flora and fauna.

BIRDS OF THE PARQUE NACIONAL DE ORDESA

Dunnock
This small bird, also called the hedge sparrow, lives a secretive life among low vegetation. It is found in forests from the lowlands to the Pyrenean dwarf-pine belt, where its rapid flute-like trill can be heard.

Owl
There are several species of owl in the Pyrenees. In the park you'll find the low-flying barn owl, the eagle owl, the brown owl, which eats small rodents, as well as the charming long-eared owl.

Jay
The jay's sharp, screeching call can often be heard in the park. It flies ponderously, due to its slow-flapping wings, which are beautifully coloured and easily recognizable to ornithologists and amateurs alike.

Blue Tit
This graceful bird is also bold, making it easy to spot. It inhabits sparse woodland, making its nest in low hollows. It feeds on berries and seeds, as well as small insects, spiders and snails.

A VIEW OF THE PARK

The stunning mountain peaks and rare species of flora and fauna make Ordesa one of the most frequently visited parks in the Pyrenees. The park can only be visited fully after the snow melts in spring, and even then much of it has to be explored on foot.

The marten *is very shy, emerging only at night. A graceful and very agile creature, it is an excellent climber. It feeds on small mammals, birds, insects and berries.*

Edelweiss, *a symbol of the mountains, is a small flowering plant that grows in grassy alpine areas, usually on inaccessible rocky ledges. It prefers altitudes of 2,000–2,900 m (6,560–9,515 ft) above sea level.*

The breathtakingly steep rock faces are in places cut by waterfalls.

The alpine forest belt (up to 2,400 m/ 7,874 ft above sea level) is composed of fir and beech, or pines.

The mountain ash, *with its bright berries, is a member of the olive family and is found up to 1,000 m (3,280 ft) above sea level.*

Lush vegetation at lower elevations

The weasel *leads a solitary existence, becoming active during daytime and at dusk. It is a good runner and climber, feeding on fledglings, eggs and mice.*

The Valle de Bujaruelo *was once an important route, with a Romanesque bridge still over the Aro river. There are several treks across the valley.*

The walls of the Palacio de los Condes de Ribagorza in Benasque

Benasque ⓯

Huesca. 🏠 1,500. ℹ Calle San Sebastián 5; 974 55 12 89. 🚌 Tue. 🎉 San Marcial (30 Jun– 6 Jul). www.benasque.com

This village, tucked away in the northeastern corner of Aragón, lies at the head of the Esera valley. Its history stretches back to Roman times; from the 11th century, it belonged to the dukedom of Ribagorza. Its most interesting monuments are the 13th-century **Iglesia de Santa María Mayor** and the Renaissance **Palacio de los Condes de Ribagorza**.

Above the village rises the wild **Maladeta massif** ('Cursed Mountains'), offering ski runs and mountaineering routes, and behind it the two tallest Pyrenean peaks: Aneto (3,404 m/11,168 ft above sea level) and Posets (3,371 m/11,060 ft).

The neighbouring resort of **Cerler** has become a popular base for skiing and other winter sports. At **Castejón de Sos**, 15 km (9 miles) south of Benasque, the road passes through **Congosto de Venta- millo**, a scenic rocky gorge.

Graus ⓰

Huesca. 🏠 3,300. ℹ C/ Fermín Murg Mur 25; 974 54 61 63. 🚌 Mon. 🎉 Santo Cristo y San Vicente Ferrer (12–15 Sep). www.turismograus.com

The famous El Cid (see p166) took part in the Battle of Graus (1063), during which the king of Aragón, Ramiro I, was killed. Concealed in the heart of the

Old Town lies the unusual **Plaza de España**, surrounded by brick arcades and brightly frescoed half-timbered houses; one of these was home to the infamous Tomás de Torque- mada, who in 1483 became Spain's first Inquisitor General.

Also noteworthy is the **Basilica de la Virgen de la Peña**, dating from 1538, with a beautiful Renaissance portal.

Environs

About 20 km (12 miles) to the northeast, at the head of a picturesque valley, lies the hill village of **Roda de Isábena**, site of the smallest cathedral in Spain, built in 1056–67.

The high altar in the Gothic cathedral in Barbastro

Barbastro ⓱

Huesca. 🏠 16,000. ℹ Avenida de la Merced 64; 974 30 83 50. 🚌 Sat. 🎉 San Ramón (21 Jun), Natividad de Nuestra Señora (4–8 Sep).

This small town has strikingly beautiful architecture, including the 16th-century Gothic

cathedral and two smaller churches – **San Francisco** and **San Julian**, from the same period. Clearly visible on a hilltop is the **shrine of Santa María del Pueyo**. Originally a Moorish fortress stood here, which was later captured by Pedro II. The Virgin Mary is said to have appeared between the branches of an almond tree, and the site has been a place of pilgrimage ever since.

Barbastro is also the centre of the up and coming Somontano wine region.

Alquézar ⓲

Huesca. 🏠 300. ℹ C/ de la Iglesia; 974 31 89 40. 🎉 San Sebastián (21 Jan). www.alquezar.org

Some 48 km (30 miles) north- east of Huesca in a spectacular setting, the village of Alquézar was established by the Moors; its name derives from the Arabic al-qasr, meaning "the fortress". Indeed, a **castle** was built here by Jalaf ibn-Rasid in the 9th century.

In 1067, the valiant Sancho Ramírez captured the fortress and turned it into a Christian stronghold, the ruins of which can be seen above the village, testifying to the region's tem- pestuous past. Slightly later, in 1085, the king founded the **Iglesia de Santa María la Mayor** on the rocks above the Vero river canyon. From this church have survived Romanesque cloisters with carved capitals depicting biblical scenes as well as the free-standing **Capilla del Santo Cristo**. The current, stately collegiate church was built in 1525–32.

The ruins of Alquézar's castle, rising above the Moorish village

Patio of Huesca's Renaissance town hall

Huesca ⑲

Huesca. 🏛 50,000. ℹ️ Pl. López
Allue; 974 29 21 70. 🚌 Tue, Thu &
Sat. 🎉 San Vicente (22 Jan), San
Lorenzo (9–15 Aug).
www.huescaturismo.com

Founded under the Roman
empire in the 1st century BC,
the independent city of Osca
had one of the first colleges
in Spain. Captured from the
Moors in 1096 by Pedro I,
Huesca became the
capital of Aragón until
1118, when the title
passed to Zaragoza.
Today, it is the second-
largest city in the region.

Be sure to visit the
Palacio Real and the
Romanesque **Iglesia de
San Pedro el Viejo**,
which was built as a
Benedictine monastery;
it also served as a royal

pantheon, where
Alfonso I, Ramiro II,
and other Aragonese
rulers are buried.

North of the church,
in the heart of the city,
stands the beautiful
Gothic **cathedral** (1274–
1515), which was raised
on the ruins of a former
mosque. Its west front
is surmounted by an unusual
Mudéjar-style wooden gallery,
while the slender-ribbed star
vaulting in the nave is studded
with golden bosses. The
alabaster reredos (1520–33) is
considered to be the finest
work of the Valencian
sculptor Damià Forment; its
series of Passion scenes is
highlighted by illumination.

Opposite the cathedral is the
Renaissance **town hall** (1577
and 1610); inside it hangs

Detail of the reredos in Huesca's cathedral

La Campana de Huesca, a
gory 19th-century painting by
José Casado del Alisal that
depicts the beheading of a
group of troublesome nobles
in the 12th century by order of
King Ramiro II. The massacre
occurred in the Sala de la
Campana, later
belonging to the
17th-century
university, and
now part of the
**Museo Arqueo-
lógico Provincial**.
This museum has
excellent
archaeological
finds and an art
collection
featuring Gothic
frescoes and early Aragonese
painting. Among the exhibits
is a 15th-century wooden
relief from the former Hospital
de Nuestra Señora de la
Esperanza; the spot where the
hospital once stood is now
occupied by the **Colegio
Universitario** – a university
building erected in the 1980s.

**Relief, Museo
Arqueológico
Provincial, Huesca**

🏛 **Museo Arqueológico
Provincial**
Plaza de la Universidad 1; *974 22
05 86.* ⏰ *10am–2pm & 5–8pm
Tue–Sat, 10am–2pm Sun and hols.*
⏺ *1 & 6 Jan; 24, 25 & 31 Dec.*

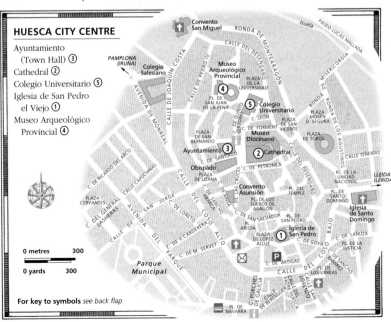

HUESCA CITY CENTRE

Ayuntamiento
(Town Hall) ③
Cathedral ②
Colegio Universitario ⑤
Iglesia de San Pedro
el Viejo ①
Museo Arqueológico
Provincial ④

0 metres   300
0 yards   300

For key to symbols *see back flap*

The lush scenery of the Vall d'Aran

Vall d'Aran ⑳

Lleida. *From Pallas on the C28; from France via the Pont de Rei on the N618.* 🏠 *7,130.* www.aran.org

This Valley of Valleys – *aran* means valley – is a beautiful 600-sq km (230-sq mile) haven of forests and flower-filled meadows on the north side of the Pyrenees, separated from the rest of Spain by towering peaks. The valley was formed by the Riu Garona, which rises in the area and flows out to France as the Garonne. With only two access routes

from Spain – the Vielha tunnel or the road from Esterri d'Aneu over the spectacular Port de la Bonaigua pass – the valley has a more natural connection with France, and locals speak *Aranés*, a variant of Gascon Provençal.

The fact that the Vall d'Aran faces north means that it has a climate similar to that found on the Atlantic coast. Rare wild flowers and butterflies flourish in the perfect conditions created by the damp breezes and shady slopes.

Tiny villages have grown up beside the Riu Garona, often around Romanesque churches, notably at **Bossòst**, **Salardú**, **Escunhau** and **Artíes**.

The valley is ideal for outdoor activities such as skiing and walking. Well-marked trails lead up to the surrounding peaks and glaciers.

Vielha ㉑

Lleida. 🏠 *3,692.* 🚌 *C/ Sarriulera 10; 973 64 01 10.* 🚉 *Thu.* 🎉 *Fiesta del Valle (17 Jun), Fiesta de Vielha (8 Sep), Feria de Vielha (8 Oct).*

Surrounded by alpine peaks, Vielha has experienced some dramatic moments in history. Napoleon's forces entered it in 1810, occupying the entire Vall d'Aran, which was returned to the Spanish crown five years later.

Today, Vielha is the capital of the valley and a modern ski resort that attracts visitors due to its picturesque setting and Romanesque **Església de Sant Miguel**. Inside the church is a superb wooden 12th-century crucifix – the *Mig Aran Christ*. It once formed part of

Santa María de Mig Aran, in Vielha

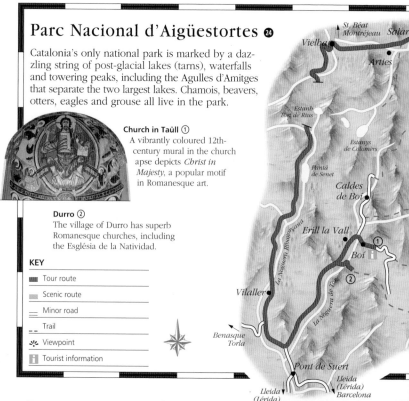

Parc Nacional d'Aigüestortes ㉔

Catalonia's only national park is marked by a dazzling string of post-glacial lakes (tarns), waterfalls and towering peaks, including the Agulles d'Amitges that separate the two largest lakes. Chamois, beavers, otters, eagles and grouse all live in the park.

Church in Taüll ①
A vibrantly coloured 12th-century mural in the church apse depicts *Christ in Majesty*, a popular motif in Romanesque art.

Durro ②
The village of Durro has superb Romanesque churches, including the Església de la Natividad.

KEY

▬▬	Tour route
▬▬	Scenic route
══	Minor road
--	Trail
🔆	Viewpoint
🅷	Tourist information

St. Béat
Montréjeau *Salar*
Vielha
Artíes
Estanh Tort de Rius
Estanys de Colomèrs
Pantà de Senet
Caldes de Boí
La Noguera Ribagorçana
Erill la Vall
Boí ①
②
Vilaller
La Noguera de Tor
Benasque Torla
Pont de Suert
Lleida (Lérida)
Lleida▼ (Lérida)
Lleida (Lérida) Barcelona

The ski resort of Baqueira-Beret, popular with Spanish skiers

a larger carving, since lost, which represented the *Descent from the Cross*. Also worth visiting is the **Museo Etnológico de Vielha**, in an imposing 17th-century building with a tower. The museum is devoted to Aranese history and folklore.

🏛 Museo Etnológico
Carrer Major 26; 973 64 18 15.
◯ 10am–1pm & 5–8pm Tue–Sat,
11am–2pm Sun & hols. ● 1 Jan,
17 Jun, 8 Sep, 25 Dec. ◱ ♿

Baqueira–Beret ㉒

Lleida. ⛷ 100. ⓘ 973 63 90 10. ◱
Romería de Nuestra Señora de
Montgarri (2 Jul). **www**.baqueira.es

This extensive ski resort, one of the best in Spain, is popular with both the public and the Spanish royal family. Baqueira and Beret were separate mountain villages before skiing became popular, but now form a single resort. There

is reliable winter snow cover, and over 50 km (30 miles) of pistes, serviced by 40 ski-lifts.

Vall de Boí ㉓

Lleida. ⓘ Paseig de San Feliu 43
(Barruera). **Tel.** 973 69 40 00.

This small valley on the edge of the Parc Nacional d'Aigüestortes is dotted with tiny villages, many of which are built around magnificent Catalan Romanesque churches. Dating from the 11th and 12th centuries, these churches are distinguished by tall belfries, such as the Església de Santa Eulàlia at **Erill-la-Vall**, which has six floors. The two churches at **Taüll**, Sant Climent and Santa María, have superb frescoes. The originals are now in the Museo Nacional d'Art de Catalunya in Barcelona and replicas now stand in their place. Other churches worth visiting include those at **Coll**, **Barruera** and **Durro**.

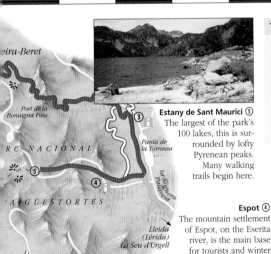

Estany de Sant Maurici ⑤
The largest of the park's 100 lakes, this is surrounded by lofty Pyrenean peaks. Many walking trails begin here.

Espot ④
The mountain settlement of Espot, on the Eserita river, is the main base for tourists and winter sports enthusiasts.

TIPS FOR TOURISTS

Tour length: Approximately 110 km (68 miles).
Stopping-off points: The larger villages, such as Espot and Esterri d' Àneu, have inexpensive hotels, bars and restaurants. Arties has an exclusive parador. There are campsites at the edge of the park, and refuges within it.

Esterri d'Àneu ③
This cultural hub of the Àneu valley features a Romanesque bridge. Here, you can also admire the park's vivid flora, which includes rhododendrons.

0 kilometres 5

0 miles 5

La Seu d'Urgell 25

Lleida. 🏛 *12,000.* 🛈 *Avenida Valles de Andorra 33; 973 35 15 11.* 🚍 *Tue and Sat.* 🎉 *Fiesta Mayor (last week in Aug).*

Set in a valley between the Segre and Valira rivers, this medieval town contains the only Romanesque cathedral in Catalonia – **Santa María d'Urgell**, dating from the 12th century. Ramón Llambard worked on the construction of the church until 1175, but it remains unfinished to this day.

The town's main thoroughfare is the **Carrer de Canonges**, lined with handsome houses, including the **Ca l'Armenter**, a property of the influential de los Luna family from Aragón, one of whose members was Pope Benedict XIII.

The town also has ski-lifts and former Olympic buildings.

The 12th-century Romanesque cathedral in La Seu d'Urgell

Cerdanya 26

www.cerdanya.net

This large, self-contained valley is situated on the borders of Catalonia, France and Andorra and is ringed by peaks over 2,000 m (6,560 ft) high. Cerdanya is also bordered on the south by Catalonia's largest nature park – **Cadí-Moixero**. From the popular observation point at Balcón de la Cerdanya extend views of the Cadí-Moixero mountain chain, La Tossa, and part of the Pyrenees' northern axis.

Because it is unusually sheltered, the valley has a special microclimate, with balmy

A street in Bellver, located in the verdant Cerdanya valley

summers and lush countryside known for its dairy produce.

The border between Spain and France, agreed in 1659, runs right across the valley. **Puigcerdà** is the main town on the Spanish side, and **Font-Romeu** on the French side. One village, **Llívia**, is Spanish but encircled entirely by French territory. Items from its historic pharmacy, one of Europe's oldest, are displayed at the Museo de Llívia.

Among the sites to be seen are Neolithic **dolmens** in Eina, Brangulí, Oren, Talltendre and Paborde. In **Talló** there is the Vía Ceretana – a Roman road, as well as a Romanesque cathedral. There are impressive churches in several villages, such as Ix, Planés, Dorres, Guils, Talltorta, Tarteras, Meránges, Ger, Saga, All,

Olopte, Mosoll and Bastanit. The village of **Bellver** still has its 13th-century town walls.

Cerdanya is a major winter sports area, especially around La Molina, which is one of the largest ski resorts in Catalonia. Other resorts include Masella and Aransa.

Puigcerdà 27

Girona. 🏛 *9,120.* 🛈 *Calle Querol 9; 972 88 05 42.* 🚍 *Sun.* 🎉 *Fiesta del Lago (third Sunday in Aug).* **www**.puigcerda.com

A popular ski centre in winter, and a magnet for walkers and climbers in summer, this is the main town of the Spanish side of the Cerdanya. It is set among hills at an altitude of 1,202 m (3,944 ft), next to the French border. The name of the town, which was established in 1177 by Alfonso II, king of Aragón, is derived from the Catalan word *puig* (hill). Territorial disputes, involving France and Spain, were settled by the Peace of the Pyrenees of 1659, under which Puigcerdà remained Spanish, although Cerdanya was divided by a new border.

In the town centre is a large man-made **lake** established in 1310 to channel water from Querol; it helped to popularize ice-skating in Spain.

The parish **church** of 1288 suffered damage during a fire; its present appearance dates from a partial reconstruction in 1938, though the interior contains medieval fragments.

CATALAN ROMANESQUE CHURCHES

Simple and beautifully proportioned, the Romanesque style flourished across western Europe from the 10th to the 13th centuries. The high valleys of the Catalan Pyrenees are especially rich in Romanesque building, with a distinctive style seen in the great monasteries of Ripoll and Sant Joan de les Abadesses or the village churches of the Vall de Boí or the Cerdanya. The churches display tall belfries, massive round apses and an extraordinary wealth of fresco painting, influenced by Byzantine art.

The Romanesque church in Taüll

The hilltop sanctuary of Queralt, with the town of Berga in the background

Berga and Serra del Cadí 28

C1411/E09. 👥 14,207. 🛈 Plaza de San Pedro 1 (town hall); 983 21 13 84. 🎉 La Patum (Corpus Christi).

This historic town, at the foot of the majestic Queralt mountain, is famous for La Patum, one of the wildest of Catalan fiestas. Just off the Calle Mayor, a street leads to the **Iglesia de San Joan**, built in 1220 by the Knights Hospitallers. Worth seeing are the former houses of the aristocracy, such as the modernist **Casa Barons** at nos 9–11 Calle Mayor, and opposite the church of San Joan, the **Palacio de los Peguera**. The palace was designed in 1905–8 by Ramon Cot. On its first floor is the Cal Negre café. Also on the main street is an 18th-century windmill – the **Molino de la Sal**.

A spectacular walk leads up from the town to the sanctuary of **Queralt**, high up above Berga, with fabulous views.

The Serra del Cadí has some of the best walking country in the eastern Pyrenees, and contains the lovely, lonely village of **Gosol**, where Picasso painted for several months in 1905.

Andorra 29

Principality of Andorra. 👥 76,900. 🛈 Plaza de la Rotonda (Andorra la Vella); 00 376 82 71 17.

Legend has it that Charlemagne established Andorra in 805 to thank local people for their help in fighting the Saracens.

For centuries, the principality fought for its independence from the Spanish dukedoms and France, which it gained in 1278. In 1993, it ratified its first-ever constitution.

Situated on the border between France and Spain, the principality occupies an area of 468 sq km (180 sq miles). It is divided into seven districts, characterized by typical mountain scenery and Mediterranean flora. The average altitude is 1,996 m (6,550 ft) above sea level, and the highest peak is Coma Pedrosa (2,946 m/ 9,665 ft). Winter sports play an important role, with the main ski centres in Arinsal, Pas de la Casa, Grau Roig and Soldeu.

Andorra is theoretically a constitutional monarchy, the ceremonial joint heads of state being the French Count of Foix (a title adopted by the French

A figure of the Virgin Mary, patron of Andorra

president) and the Spanish bishop of La Seu d'Urgell. The legislative branch of government is the General Council, comprising 28 elected members. The official language is Catalan, though French and Castilian are also spoken. Andorrans are a minority in their own country, accounting for barely 26 per cent of the population; the remainder is made up of Spanish, Portuguese and French.

For many years Andorra has been a tax-free paradise for shoppers, reflected in the crowded shops of the capital, **Andorra la Vella**. Almost every one of Andorra's 20,000 native residents owns a shop.

Andorra's charm lies not only in its beautiful landscapes, but also its Romanesque architecture. One of the oldest historic monuments is the **Iglesia de Santa Coloma**. It was built in the 9th century in a pre-Romanesque style, then remodelled several times thereafter. Of particular note is the 12th-century belfry with narrow double windows. The **Iglesia de Santa Eulalia** in Encamp, to the east of the capital, is an example of Pyrenean pre-Romanesque religious architecture. The stone **Iglesia de San Juan de Casello** has a typical Lombardy-style belfry.

At fiesta time, the streets of Andorra's towns are filled with people dancing the traditional *sardana, marratxa* and *el contrapes.*

The charming 9th-century Iglesia de Santa Coloma in Andorra

The magnificent portal of the monastery in Ripoll

Ripoll ⑳

Girona. 🏘 *11,000.* 🛈 *Plaza Abat Oliba; 972 70 23 51.* 🚌 *Sat.* 🎉 *Sant Eudald (11–12 May).*

Ripoll is known as the 'cradle of Catalonia', because it was the first part of Catalonia recovered from the Moors by Guifré El Pelos (Wilfred the Hairy), founder of the 500-year dynasty of the House of Barcelona. He made Ripoll his capital, and in 879 established here the Benedictine **Monestir de Santa María**, an important centre of culture and art. The monastery had a well-stocked library, a scriptorium and a highly regarded monastic school. Abbot Oliba (1008–46) raised a new double-aisled basilica, but this unfortunately suffered extensive damage during an earthquake in 1428. Romanesque cloisters, from the 12th to the 16th centuries, survive. The basilica was reconstructed during the 19th century in a simplified form.

Today, visitors can admire the magnificent Romanesque portal, with Christ Pantocrator occupying a central position above the entrance, flanked by angels, apostles and the 24 elders of the Apocalypse. The rich iconography also depicts scenes from the Old Testament, including the Judgement of Solomon and the Dream of Solomon, as well as Old Testament figures such as Moses and David.

Queralbs and Sanctuari de Núria ㉛

Girona. 🏘 *198.* 🚉 🛈 *Plaza Vila 3; 972 72 73 61.* **www**.ddgi.es/queralbs

For a favourite local day out, most people start in the little town of Ribes de Freser, in the Ribes valley. From here the Cremallera (Zipper Train) leads to the pretty village of **Queralbs**, at the halfway point, and Núria at the top. There are great views from the train.

Queralbs is home to the 12th-century Romanesque church of Sant Jaume. Lovely meadows spread across the hillsides around the **Sanctuari de Núria**. Set at an altitude of 1,967 m (6,453 ft), the shrine is an important place of pilgrimage. It was first mentioned in historical documents in 1162. St Gil, who sculpted the altar of the Virgin Mary of Núria, is said to have lived here in the 8th century; the feast of the Virgin is celebrated each year on 8 September.

The shrine was extended in 1449, and again in 1640 and 1648. In 1883, it acquired a neo-Romanesque church, consecrated in 1913 and completed in 1964. There are wonderful walks from here.

A colourful stained-glass window in the Sanctuari de Núria

Sant Joan de les Abadesses ㉜

Girona. 🏘 *3,800.* 🛈 *Plaza de Abadia 9; 972 72 05 99.* 🚌 *Sun.* 🎉 *Fiesta Mayor (second week in Sep).*

The beginnings of this pretty but unassuming market town date back to the establishment in 887 of a **monastery**. It was founded by Guifré El Pelos (Wilfred the Hairy), first count of Barcelona, as a gift to his daughter, the first abbess.

THE CATALAN LANGUAGE

Belonging to the Romance group of Indo-European languages, Catalan emerged as a literary language in the 13th century, although the first Catalan texts appeared as early as the 12th century. After a long period of Castilian (Spanish) dominance, Catalan experienced a renaissance in the mid-19th century. This revival was cut short by the Spanish Civil War; under Franco's dictatorship, the use of Catalan in public places was forbidden. Catalan has now re-emerged from this repression and is in everyday use all over Catalonia, Valencia and the Balearic Islands. It is spoken by around 7 million people.

The national emblem of Catalonia

Olot ☯

Girona. 🚍 *30,000*. 🛈 *Calle Hospici 8; 972 26 01 41*. 📅 *Mon*. 🎉 *Corpus Cristi, Fiesta del Tura (8 Sep)*.

This small market town, set in an odd landscape ringed by stumpy, extinct volcanoes and vast expanses of beech woods, lost most of its historic monuments during an earthquake in 1427. The buildings one sees today date largely from the 18th and 19th centuries. In 1783, a Public School of Drawing was founded in Olot, whose main aim was to train local craftsmen. In time, it became an important centre of religious art. Much of the school's work can be seen in the **Museu Comarcal de la Garrotxa**, housed in an 18th-century hospice with a large patio and arcades. The exhibition rooms have exhibits illustrating the development of the provincial economy and crafts.

🏛 **Museu Comarcal de la Garrotxa**
Calle Hospici 8. **Tel** *972 27 91 30*. 🕐 *Wed–Mon*. 🔵 *1 Jan, 25 Dec*. ♿ 🈸

Costa Brava ☯

Girona. ✈ Girona. 🛈 *Paseo Maritim s/n, L'Estartit; 972 75 19 10*. **www**.estartit.org 🛈 *Avda. del Pelegri 25 (Tossa de Mar); 972 34 01 08*. **www**.tossademar.com

The touristy "wild coast", stretching south from the French border for 200 km (124 miles), is a mix of pine-backed sandy coves, golden beaches and crowded resorts. **Lloret de Mar** is the busiest of these.

Trips can be made from **L'Estartit** to the **Illes Medes**, islands that once sheltered pirates and are now a marine reserve with clear waters for snorkelling, while in **Tossa de Mar** the main attraction is the fortified 12th-century Old Town and the golden beach. Inland, but within easy reach of the Costa Brava, is **Figueres**, the hometown of the Surrealist artist Salvador Dalí. The magnificent **Teatro-Museu Dalí**, founded by the artist in 1974, houses works by Dalí. Further south is **Girona**, whose cathedral has a superb silver altar. In the pre-Romanesque Església de Sant Pere de Galligants are fine mermaid sculptures.

Detail of *Rainy Taxi*, **Teatro-Museu Dalí**

🏛 **Teatro-Museu Dalí**
Pl. Gala-Salvador Dalí. **Tel** *972 67 75 00*. 🕐 *Oct–Jun: 10:30am–5:45pm Tue–Sun; Jul–Sep: 9am–7:45pm daily*. 🔵 *1 Jan, 25 Dec*. 🈸 🈂 **www**.salvador-dali.org

The church in Sant Joan de les Abadesses

The Benedictine monastery was in operation until 1076, when its activities were suspended by a papal bull due to a perceived lack of discipline.

The monastery **church** is unadorned, except for a superb wooden calvary depicting the Descent from the Cross. Made in 1150, it looks modern; part of it (one of the thieves crucified with Christ) was burnt in the Civil War and replaced with great skill. The monastery's **museum** contains a collection of beautiful Renaissance and Baroque altarpieces.

The town, which was encircled by walls with 24 towers and six gates, is approached by the fine 12th-century Gothic bridge that arches over the Ter river.

Vall de Camprodon ☯

C38, C26. 🛈 *Pl. de España 1 (Camprodon); 972 74 00 10*. **www**.valldecamprodon.org

Camprodon is the main town of this long valley, which is home to several charming villages. Nearby is tiny **Llanars**, with its beautiful Romanesque Església de Sant Esteve, tucked away in the old quarter among narrow winding streets. **Setcases**, further up the valley, is a famous beauty spot. Above it is **Vallter**, the easternmost ski resort in the Pyrenees.

View south along the Costa Brava from Tossa de Mar

TRAVELLERS' NEEDS

Castro Urdiales. The Harbour

WHERE TO STAY

Northern Spain offers an exceptional variety of visitor accommodation. There are places to suit all budgets, and even the most demanding visitor is bound to find something to satisfy them. Those searching for luxury will head straight for the exclusive hotels and paradors, while the family-run *casas rurales* are excellent places to escape the hustle and bustle of the city. There are also mountain refuges

Logo for a luxury 5-star hotel

with stunning views as well as campsites in the coastal areas. Weary pilgrims can find official accommodation and modest meals in towns and villages along the Road to Santiago. Regardless of the standard of accommodation, one thing is certain in Northern Spain: the region's inhabitants, famous for their hospitality, will give you a warm welcome and will be ready to help in the event of any problems.

Hotel de la Reconquista in Oviedo *(see p205)*

HOTEL GRADING AND FACILITIES

Hotels in Northern Spain are spacious, comfortable, clean and modern. All hotels are categorized and awarded stars by the regional tourist authorities. Hotels (indicated by an H on a blue plaque near the hotel door) are awarded from one to five stars. They usually have en-suite bathrooms, or at least a shower in the room. Hostels (Hs) and pensions (P) usually do not have en-suite facilities and have fewer comforts than hotels, so are a bit cheaper.

Spain's star-rating system reflects the number and range of facilities available, rather than the quality of service. One star is given to the most modest hotels, and five stars to the most elegant and expensive ones. The more exclusive hotels have all kinds of extra facilities, such as air-conditioning, on-site

parking, Internet access and rooms with televisions, as well as facilities for the disabled.

Two- and three-star hotels are the most popular, and their rates vary with the season.

A popular option in all the autonomous regions of Northern Spain are hostels *(hostales)* and guest houses

Reception desk in the cosy Minhotel Andria in La Seu d'Urgell *(see p211)*

(pensiones), which are cheaper than hotels. These are usually small, family-run establishments offering just a few beds.

There are in excess of 1,500 hotels, with a total of 92,000 beds, registered in the territory of 'Green Spain'– the Atlantic regions of Galicia, Asturias, Cantabria and the Basque Country.

The biggest hotel chains in Northern Spain are the **Grupo Sol-Meliá** and **NH**, with hotels in the main towns. Their facilities are of a high standard, and include Internet access. There is also now a growing number of small, individually run hotels with a distinctive character and charm, for a memorable and relaxing stay.

PARADORS

Paradors are government-run hotels, classified from three to five stars. Spain's first parador opened in 1928, and now there is a wide network of them throughout the country. They are located close together so that there is never more than a day's drive to the nearest one. The best, such as the Parador de los Reyes Católicos in Santiago de Compostela, are in former royal hunting lodges, monas-teries, castles and other monuments; some modern paradors have been purpose-built, often in spectacular scenery or in towns of historic interest.

A parador is not necessarily the best hotel in town, but it

can be counted on to deliver a predictably high level of comfort. The bedrooms are usually spacious and comfortable, and are furnished to a standard that varies little from parador to parador. Some also offer fine regional cuisine.

If you plan to tour in high season or to stay in the smaller paradors, it is wise to reserve a room. The paradors may be booked through the **Central de Reservas** in Madrid, or by calling a parador direct (they have English-speaking staff). Rates can be expensive; it is worth looking for special deals, especially in low season.

PRICES

Spanish law requires all hotel managements to display their prices behind reception and in every room. Rates for a double room can be as little as 20–25 euros a night for a cheap one-star hostel; a five-star hotel will cost more than 180 euros a night, but a room price higher than 300 euros a night is exceptional.

Prices vary according to room, region and season. High season *(temporada alta)* covers July and August, as well as major holidays (a couple of weeks around Easter, and between Christmas and New Year). Prices are slightly lower during the *temporada media* (off-season, from September to October, and April through June).

You'll find the best deals during the low season *(temporada baja)*, from November and March through May, although smaller hotels may close during this time.

Many of Spain's city hotels charge especially inflated rates for their rooms during fiestas.

At hotels in the Pyrenees, especially in the ski resorts, winter is high season; those hotels in the mountains that stay open year-round are much cheaper in the summer. A suite or a very spacious

Hall of the parador in Hondarribia *(see p207)*

room, or one with a view, a balcony or other special feature, may cost more than average. Rural and suburban hotels are less expensive than those in the city centre.

Most hotels quote prices per room and meal prices per person without including VAT (IVA), which is currently 7 per cent in Spain. Traditionally, hotel room rates in Spain have not included breakfast, which has been charged separately at about 7–12 euros per person. However, a growing number of hotels are now including breakfast, which comprises coffee, juice and pastries, or a more elaborate breakfast buffet.

BOOKING AND CHECK-IN

Off-season in rural or small towns you are unlikely to need to book ahead; but if you plan to travel in high season

or want to stay in a particular hotel, you should reserve a room by phone or e-mail or through a travel agent. You will need to reserve if you want a special room: one with a double bed (twin beds are the norm); on the ground floor; away from a noisy main road; or a room with a view.

The resort hotels often close from autumn to spring. Before you travel, it is always advisable to check that your preferred hotels will be open at that time of year.

You will not normally be asked for a deposit when you book a hotel room unless it is during a peak period or for a stay of more than a few nights. A credit card number is usually sufficient to hold a reservation. If you have to cancel, do so at least a week before the booking date or you may lose all or some of the deposit.

Most hotels will expect you to arrive by 8pm. If you are delayed, call the hotel to assure them that you are coming and to tell them when to expect you.

When checking into a hotel, you will be asked to show your passport or some other form of photographic ID to comply with Spanish police regulations. It will normally be returned to you promptly as soon as your details have been copied.

At most hotels you are obliged to check out of your room by noon on the last day of your stay, or to pay for another night. Sometimes it is earlier; remember to confirm the check-out time when you first check in.

The exclusive María Cristina hotel in San Sebastián *(see p208)*

La Oliva monastery in Navarra, overnight guests welcome

PAYING

The majority of hotels accept credit cards. The most frequently used cards are VISA and MasterCard, although JVC, Diner's Club and American Express are also widely accepted.

Eurocheques are accepted in some hotels, though they are on the decline. Personal cheques, on the other hand, are not accepted – even if they are backed up by a cheque guarantee card or drawn on a Spanish bank.

Cash is always welcome. When tipping hotel staff, the usual amount is 2–3 euros.

CASAS RURALES

Hotel accommodation in Northern Spain is supplemented by numerous family-run *casas rurales*. These country homes make ideal places for those seeking quiet relaxation in a family atmosphere rather than a large anonymous hotel in a bustling city centre. They usually offer accommodation to a dozen or so visitors. Regardless of the standard offered, guests of *casas rurales* can expect to find clean, well-kept rooms and a friendly atmosphere. In addition, many *casas rurales* offer excellent home cooking and traditional regional cuisine, though guests can also make their own dining arrangements.

Another major advantage of *casas rurales* is their affordable price. However, due to their popularity, especially in high season, it is always worth booking ahead by phone, Internet, or through local tourist agencies.

Casas rurales are especially popular in the regions of Asturias, Cantabria and Navarra. The number of *casas rurales* in Northern Spain is comparable to the number of hotels. There are more than 1,600 of them, offering a total of nearly 17,000 beds, and the majority of these are located in Galicia and Asturias. In Cantabria they are known as *casonas*, while in Catalonia they are called *cases de pagés*.

YOUTH HOSTELS AND MOUNTAIN REFUGES

To use the network of *albergues juveniles* (youth hostels) in Spain you need to show a YHA (Youth Hotel Association) card from your country or an international card, which you can buy from any hostel. Prices per person are much lower than in hotels or guest houses, but so, too, is the standard of accommodation – basic shared rooms with no bathrooms. There is no age limit for guests staying in youth hostels.

Youth hostels can be booked through the **Red Española de Albergues Juveniles** (Spanish Network of Youth Hostels).

Mountaineers heading for the more remote areas may use the *refugios* (refuges). These are shelters with a dormitory, cooking facilities and heating. Some are huts with about six bunks; others are mountain houses with up to 50 beds. The *refugios* are marked on large-scale maps of mountain areas and national parks and are administered by the regional mountaineering associations. The **Federación Española de Montañismo** and the local tourist offices will supply their addresses.

Pilgrims' hostels are also found along the Road to Santiago. They vary from basic to quite comfortable.

Sign of the pilgrims' hostel in Estella

MONASTERIES AND CONVENTS

Some Benedictine and Cistercian monasteries have rooms available for overnight guests to rent. Many pilgrims on the Road to Santiago stay at monasteries or convents along the way. The rooms are modest, with few amenities.

Guests are expected to tidy their rooms and to help with the washing-up; they are also expected to observe house rules. Some convents admit only women and some monasteries only men.

SELF-CATERING

In larger Spanish towns, particularly on the coast, it is possible to rent a holiday flat or villa. These are usually fully furnished lodgings with two bedrooms, a living room, bathroom, kitchen, and balcony or terrace. Some, especially those inland, have swimming pools. All you need to bring is your own bedding and towels, though these can also be rented for an extra charge. You are expected to keep your flat clean and tidy. A deposit is usually payable at the beginning of your stay, which will be returned to you when you leave.

A living room in a holiday flat

View from Cabina Verónica mountain refuge, the Picos de Europa

Be sure to book well in advance if you plan to stay in a monastery, as many are located in beautiful historic buildings and are consequently very popular.

CAMP SITES

Most camp sites throughout Northern Spain have electricity and running water; some also have launderettes, playgrounds, restaurants, shops, a swimming pool and other amenities.

Camping carnets can be used instead of a passport to check in at camp sites and they cover you for third-party insurance. Carnets are issued in the UK by the AA, RAC and **The Camping and Caravanning Club**.

An invaluable source of information about Spanish camp sites is the *Guía Oficial de Campings*, published each year by Tourespaña.

A lot of useful information can also be obtained from the **Federación Española de Clubes Campistas**. In Spain, camping is only permitted at official camp sites.

DISABLED TRAVELLERS

Hotel managers will advise on access for people in wheelchairs, and the staff will help, but disabled access is not widespread throughout Northern Spain. Gradually,

however, more and more hotels are introducing special facilities for disabled people, such as wheelchair ramps and adapted bathrooms.

COCEMFE (Confederación Coordinadora Estatal de Minusválidos Físicos de España). The Spanish Association for the Disabled and VIAJES 2000 travel agency advises on hotels in Northern Spain for guests with special needs.

Sign for a camp site

TRAVELLING WITH CHILDREN

Travelling with children in Spain is becoming increasingly easy. Many hotels allow small children to stay for free; others levy a special low rate. Cots or fold-out beds may be provided for a small fee, for kids to stay in the same room as their parents. Child-size portions are also available in some hotel restaurants.

DIRECTORY

HOTEL CHAINS

Grupo Sol-Meliá
Tel 902 14 44 44
www.solmelia.com

NH
Tel 902 115 116
www.nh-hoteles.com

HOTEL RESERVATIONS

www.innsofspain.com
www.rusticae.es
www.centraldereservas.com
www.muchoviaje.es

ACCOMMODATION

Asociación de Empresarios de Hostelería de Vizcaya
Calle Gran Vía 38–2
48009 Bilbao
Tel 944 35 66 60
www.asociacionhosteleria.com

Asociación de Empresarios de

Hostelería de Asturias
Alonso Quintanilla 3–1 f
33002 Oviedo
Tel 985 22 38 13
www.hosteleria.org

Asociación de Empresarios de Hostelería de Navarra
Calle Pedro I, 1 Entreplanta
31007 Pamplona
Tel 948 26 84 12
Fax 948 17 27 56
www.hostelerianavarra.com

Confederación Española de Hoteles y Alojamientos Turísticos
Calle Orense 32
28020 Madrid
Tel 91 556 71 12
www.cehat.com

Federación Española de Hostelería
Camino de las Huertas 18
28223 Pozuelo, Madrid
Tel 91 352 91 56
www.fehr.es

PARADORS

Central de Reservas
Calle Requena 3
28013 Madrid
Tel 915 16 66 66
www.parador.es

CASAS RURALES

www.toprural.com
www.guiarural.com
www.esgalicia.com
www.turismerural.com

YOUTH HOSTELS

Red Española de Albergues Juveniles
Tel 915 22 70 07
www.reaj.com

MOUNTAIN REFUGES

Federación Española de Montañismo
Calle Floridablanca 84
08015 Barcelona
Tel 934 26 42 67
www.fedme.es

CAMPING

Federación Española de Clubes Campistas
Calle Pizarro 60, 1ºA,
36204 Vigo.
Tel 986 47 22 73
www.campistasfecc.com

The Camping and Caravanning Club
Greenfields House,
Westwood Way,
Coventry CV4 8JH, UK
Tel 024 7669 4995 (UK)

DISABLED TRAVELLERS

COCEMFE
Calle Luis Cabrera 63
28002 Madrid
Tel 917 44 36 00
www.cocemfe.es

Viajes 2000
www.viajes2000.com

Northern Spain's Best Paradors

"Parador" is an old Spanish word for a lodging place for travellers of respectable rank. In the late 1920s a national network of state-run hotels called Paradores Nacionales was established. Many of the paradors are converted castles, palaces or monasteries, though some have been purpose-built in strategic tourist locations. They are generally well signposted and the prices are comparable with other luxury hotels. All offer a high degree of comfort and service, and have restaurants which offer excellent regional cuisine. Many are worth seeking out, even if you don't stay the night.

The Parador de Gijón *occupies a 100-year-old mill, situated in a park near the beach of San Lorenzo. All the rooms have sea views. The restaurant serves excellent seafood and fish* (see p204).

A Coruña

Gijón

Santander

Oviedo

Santiago de Compostela

Lugo

Ourense

Vigo

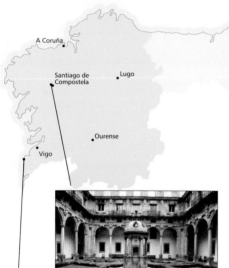

The Parador de los Reyes Católicos, *in the heart of Santiago de Compostela, was built at the end of the 15th century as a hospital for pilgrims* (see p203).

From the outside, the **Parador de Fuente Dé** *looks like a modern hostel. Inside, however, it is very cosy, with rooms painted in warm colours and featuring original décor* (see p204).

The Parador de Baiona *occupies a fortress on the Monterreal peninsula, with wonderful sea views from some rooms. It was built in the Galician* pazo *(manor house) style* (see p202).

The Parador de Hondarribia *is situated within the walls of a medieval castle. It boasts beautiful period rooms and salons as well as broad patios. The parador affords views of the French Atlantic coast* (see p207).

The Parador de Argomániz occupies a Renaissance palace with a colonnaded façade surrounded by lush gardens. The restaurant, with a wooden beamed ceiling, is also impressive (see p206).

The Parador de Bielsa *is a modern hotel in the Parque Nacional de Ordesa. The rooms, decked out in wood, are comfortable and elegant. Best of all are the beautiful views of Monte Perdido* (see p211).

0 kilometres 100

0 miles 50

San Sebastián (Donostia)

Vitoria (Gasteiz)

Pamplona (Iruña)

Logroño

Huesca

Girona

The Parador de Calahorra is a traditional brick building that forms a harmonious setting with the Ebro river and Cidacos valley. The interior decoration is inspired by medieval themes. Superb regional cuisine is served at the restaurant *(see p209).*

The Parador de Olite *is set in a 500-year-old castle, with historic touches in the décor, the stone walls and the lighting. The restaurant serves excellent asparagus dishes in season* (see p209).

The Parador de Santo Domingo de la Calzada *is housed inside a former 12th-century hostel, built by St Dominic for pilgrims heading to Santiago de Compostela. The hotel lobby features original Gothic arches* (see p210).

Choosing a Hotel

The hotels in this guide have been selected across a wide price range for their attractive location, high standard and excellent facilities. Many also have a highly recommended restaurant. The chart lists hotels by region, starting in the west and moving to the east. Within towns and cities, hotels are listed in ascending order of price.

PRICE CATEGORIES
Standard double room per night, with breakfast, tax and service charge included.

€ under 50 euros
€€ 50–75 euros
€€€ 75–100 euros
€€€€ 100–125 euros
€€€€€ over 125 euros

GALICIA

A CORUÑA Meliá María Pita   €€€€€

Avenida Ramón y Cajal 53, 15006 **Tel** *981 24 27 11* **Fax** *981 23 82 48* **Rooms** *181*

This elegant seafront hotel is situated next to the most beautiful city beaches of Orzán and Riazor, near the historic city centre and shopping district, as well as the port. The rooms at the Meliá María Pita have views of the Atlantic Ocean. **www.solmelia.com**

BAIONA Parador de Baiona   €€€€€

Carretera de Baiona, 36300 (Pontevedra) **Tel** *986 35 50 00* **Fax** *986 35 50 76* **Rooms** *122*

This is one of the most beautiful paradors in Spain, located inside an old fortress on the Monterreal peninsula, with breathtaking views of the Atlantic Ocean. The rooms, apartments, restaurants and corridors are furnished and decorated in a variety of styles. Among the many facilities is a tennis court. Rate includes lunch or dinner. **www.parador.es**

CAMBADOS Parador de Cambados   €€€€€

Paseo Calzada, 36630 (Pontevedra) **Tel** *986 54 22 50* **Fax** *986 54 20 68* **Rooms** *58*

This parador is situated in the centre of Cambados, facing the island of Toxa. It occupies an old Galician mansion – the Pazo de Bazán – dating from the 17th century. It has large bright rooms and a beautiful garden and pool. The speciality of the hotel restaurant is sole in Albariño wine. **www.parador.es**

FERROL Parador de Ferrol   €€€€€

Rúa Almirante Fernández Martín, 15401 (A Coruña) **Tel** *981 35 67 20* **Fax** *981 35 67 21* **Rooms** *37*

The building in which this spacious parador is located resembles a typical Galician mansion. It has glass-encased balconies and is surrounded by gardens. The rooms have views over the harbour. Regional cuisine is served at the hotel restaurant. **www.parador.es**

LUGO Gran Hotel Lugo   €€€€€

Avenida Ramón Ferreiro 21, 27002 **Tel** *982 22 41 52* **Fax** *982 24 16 60* **Rooms** *167*

Built in 1979, the centrally located Gran Hotel Lugo has elegantly arranged, comfortable and spacious guest rooms, just five minutes from the old quarter. Its list of distinguished guests over the years has included political luminaries and members of the Spanish royal family. **www.gh-hoteles.com**

MONTFORTE DE LEMOS Parador de Monforte de Lemos   €€€€€

Praza Luis de Góngora y Argote, 27400 (Lugo) **Tel** *982 41 84 84* **Fax** *982 41 84 95* **Rooms** *50*

This parador is housed inside a 17th-century Benedictine monastery. The rooms are elegant, though in deference to monastic tradition they are sparsely furnished. The same goes for the decoration of the restaurant, lounges and corridors. The facilities include a Jacuzzi, as well as an outdoor swimming pool. **www.parador.es**

O GROVE Gran Hotel de la Toja   €€€€€

Isla de la Toja, 36991 (Pontevedra) **Tel** *986 73 00 25* **Fax** *986 73 00 26* **Rooms** *199*

This majestic hotel, built at the start of the 20th century, stands on its own small island planted with palm and pine trees, and is reached from the mainland by a bridge. It has an old-fashioned feel to it, with a ballroom and a piano bar. Offers lovely sea views, and has good beaches nearby. It also has a spa. **www.granhotelhesperia-latoja.com**

NOIA Hotel Pesquería del Tambre   €€€€

Santa María de Roo, 15211 (A Coruña) **Tel** *981 05 16 20* **Fax** *981 05 16 29* **Rooms** *16*

In a lovely natural setting on the banks of the Ría Tambre, this hotel occupies the buildings of a former power station. With its stone walls, furnishings of natural materials, and crisp linens, the environment is calm and serene. Nature-lovers are drawn to the area for hiking, fishing and horse riding. **www.pesqueriadeltambre.com**

OURENSE Puente Romano   €€

Ramón Puga 56, 32005 **Tel** *988 23 15 20* **Fax** *98 823 15 20* **Rooms** *24*

The Puente Romano is an excellent place for those seeking peace and relaxation away from the bustle of city. The guest rooms, painted in pastel colours, are modestly but tastefully decorated. The restaurant serves delicious regional specialities. **www.hotelpuenteromano.com**

For key to symbols *see back flap*

PONTEVEDRA Madrid

Andrés Mellado 5, 36001 **Tel** *986 86 51 80* **Fax** *986 85 10 06* **Rooms** *28*

This hotel is located opposite the Plaza Galicia, the city's largest square, close to the train and bus stations. The rather small guest rooms are tastefully if modestly decorated in pastel colours. The Madrid does not offer many amenities, but this helps to keep the prices low. **www.hotelmadrid.org**

PONTEVEDRA Parador de Pontevedra

Rúa Barón 19, 36002 **Tel** *986 85 58 00* **Fax** *986 85 21 95* **Rooms** *47*

This parador is located inside a Renaissance palace dating from the 16th century. It offers guest rooms painted in warm colours, a beautiful garden, and patios with a fountain – everything is in very good taste. It is widely regarded as one of the most romantic paradors in Spain. **www.parador.es**

REBOREDO Hotel Bosque Mar

Reboredo, O Grove 36988 (Pontevedra) **Tel** *986 73 10 55* **Fax** *986 73 05 12* **Rooms** *52*

The Hotel Bosque Mar lies near the beach in the village of Reboredo, near O Grove. There are lovely gardens, and indoor and outdoor swimming pools and Jacuzzi, and a good restaurant. Self-catering apartments are also available. The area is good for active guests, with nearby golf, water sports and horse riding. **www.bosquemar.com**

RIBADEO Parador de Ribadeo

Rúa Amador Fernández 7, 27700 (Lugo) **Tel** *982 12 88 25* **Fax** *982 12 83 46* **Rooms** *47*

The Parador de Ribadeo lies at the mouth of the Eo river, on the border between Galicia and Asturias. It occupies a large, typical Galician house. The hotel restaurant serves regional dishes and has windows overlooking the river. The cosy rooms painted in warm colours are very welcoming. **www.parador.es**

SANTIAGO DE COMPOSTELA Girasol

Puerta Peña 4, 15704 (A Coruña) **Tel** *981 56 62 87* **Rooms** *12*

The Girasol is a small hotel frequented by pilgrims to Santiago. It is very near to the famous cathedral and the Praza do Obradoiro. Most of the rooms have bathrooms, although there are two that only have a wash basin (they share a bathroom). **www.hgirasol.com**

SANTIAGO DE COMPOSTELA Hespería Peregrino

Avenida Rosalía da Castro, 15706 (A Coruña) **Tel** *981 52 18 50* **Fax** *981 52 17 77* **Rooms** *148*

This quiet hotel is located close to the city centre. It has very attractive large rooms painted in bright colours. Other pluses at the Hespería Peregrino include the two swimming pools and the hotel restaurant, which serves Galician and international cuisine. **www.hesperia-peregrino.com**

SANTIAGO DE COMPOSTELA Parador de los Reyes Católicos

Praza do Obradoiro 1, 15705 (A Coruña) **Tel** *981 58 22 00* **Fax** *981 56 30 94* **Rooms** *137*

Built at the end of the 15th century as a hostel for poor pilgrims, the Parador de los Reyes Católicos is currently the most luxurious parador in Spain. Most of the rooms feature four-poster beds. Other highlights include the numerous patios and the royal chapel. **www.parador.es**

SANXENXO Hotel Rotilio

Avenida del Puerto 7 & 9, 36960 (Pontevedra) **Tel** *986 72 02 00* **Fax** *986 72 41 88* **Rooms** *40*

Between the fishing port and harbour, this attractive seaside hotel has modern, stylish rooms, most with a terrace. There is also a superb seafood restaurant. The same management also rents self-catering apartments (efficiency units) just down the road. **www.hotelrotilio.com**

TUI Parador de Tui

Avenida Portugal, 36700 (Pontevedra) **Tel** *986 60 03 00* **Fax** *986 60 21 63* **Rooms** *32*

Situated on the Portuguese border, this parador, occupying a Galician stone mansion, was reopened in April 2005 after a complete makeover. An ideal place for people wishing to engage in sport and active leisure pursuits, its facilities include a swimming pool and a children's playground in the beautifully maintained garden. **www.parador.es**

VERÍN Parador de Verín

Monterrei, 32600 (Ourense) **Tel** *988 41 00 75* **Fax** *988 41 20 17* **Rooms** *23*

This parador was converted from a Galician mansion, with a swimming pool and gardens. It offers tastefully furnished rooms and a restaurant with a beamed ceiling. There are beautiful views toward the castle and over the countryside. Bicycles can be rented on site. **www.parador.es**

VIGO Tres Luces

Cuba 19, 36204 (Pontevedra) **Tel** *986 48 02 50* **Fax** *986 48 33 27* **Rooms** *72*

Situated in the city's commercial district, close to El Corte Inglés department store and the Gran Vía, this hotel is perfect for business people. It features lovely modern bathrooms and elegant, well-lit guest rooms complete with desk and work area. **www.hotel3luces.com**

VILALBA Parador de Vilalba

Rúa Valeriano Valdesuso, 27800 (Lugo) **Tel.** *982 51 00 11* **Fax** *982 51 00 90* **Rooms** *48*

This luxury parador with a 15th-century medieval tower (containing six of the rooms) is situated in the historic quarter of Vilalba. The spacious, elegant rooms with beamed ceilings are decorated in neutral colours. The facilities include a gym, sauna and Turkish bath. **www.parador.es**

ASTURIAS AND CANTABRIA

ARRIONDAS Halcón Palace

Cofiño-Arriondas, 33548 (Asturias) Tel 985 84 13 12 Fax 985 84 13 13 Rooms 18

Situated on a hillside, this hotel occupies an 18th-century walled palace. The antique-filled rooms afford beautiful views of the nearby Picos de Europa. There is a terrace, garden and swimming pool for the use of guests. The Halcón Palace is considered to be one of the 20 best hotels in Spain. **www.halconpalace.com**

CABEZÓN DE LA SAL El Jardín de Carrejo

Carrejo, 39509 (Cantabria) Tel 942 70 15 16 Fax 942 70 18 71 Rooms 10

This small hotel, which occupies a late 19th-century stone manor house, has large bright rooms with tasteful furnishings. The ample gardens surrounding the building feature some unusual old trees: cedars, redwoods, maples, walnuts and lindens. **www.eljardindecarrejo.com**

CANGAS DE ONÍS Nochendi

Constantino González 4, 33550 (Asturias) Tel 985 84 95 13 Fax 985 84 95 14 Rooms 11

The Nochendi is located in the town centre, close to the confluence of the Sella and Güeña rivers, at the spot where, according to medieval chronicles, the area's settlement was built. The rooms are bright, clean and modern; most also have beautiful views of the river. **www.hotelnochendi.com**

CANGAS DE ONÍS Parador de Cangas de Onís

Villanueva, 33550 (Asturias) Tel 985 84 94 02 Fax 985 84 95 20 Rooms 64

From the 12th to the 18th centuries, this building functioned as a monastery. It is beautifully set on the banks of the Sella river, among greenery and hills; in the background are the soaring peaks of the Picos de Europa. This is an ideal place for visitors seeking a peaceful atmosphere, magnificent landscapes, and local fiestas and folklore. **www.parador.es**

CASTRO URDIALES Las Rocas

Paseo de la Playa, 39700 (Cantabria) Tel 942 86 04 00 Fax 942 86 13 82 Rooms 66

This comfortable modern hotel enjoys an attractive beachside location. Most of the rooms are furnished and decorated in warm colour schemes and overlook the sea. The hotel restaurant serves delicious fish and seafood. Bicycles are available for guests to rent. Not all rooms have air conditioning. **www.lasrocashotel.com**

COMILLAS Hotel Casal de Castro

Calle San Jerónimo, 39520 (Cantabria) Tel 942 72 00 36 Fax 942 72 00 61 Rooms 45

This agreeable hotel is located inside a 17th-century palace. The rooms are spacious and bright. Apart from the low prices, the main selling point of the Hotel Casal de Castro is the beach, lying some 700 m (770 yds) away. **www.acantabria.com/hotelcasaldecastro**

CUDILLERO La Casona de Pío

Riofrio 3, 33150 (Asturias) Tel 985 59 15 12 Fax 985 95 15 19 Rooms 11

The tiny La Casona de Pio features guest rooms with stone walls and antique furniture. The bathrooms have Jacuzzi bathtubs, while the restaurant serves superb *merluza del pincho* (hake) and local meat dishes. **www.lacasonadepio.com**

FUENTE DÉ Hotel El Rebeco

Carretera Fuente Dé, 39588 (Cantabria) Tel 942 73 66 01 Fax 942 73 66 00 Rooms 30

Situated below a rock face, the Hotel El Rebeco is an ideal base for making trips into the Picos de Europa. The rustic-style rooms, some with sloping ceilings and wooden balconies, are very cosy. Bicycles can be rented in the local area. **www.acantabria.com/hotelelrebeco/**

FUENTE DÉ Parador de Fuente Dé

Fuente Dé, 39588 (Cantabria) Tel 942 73 66 51 Fax 942 73 66 54 Rooms 78

Set at the foot of the Picos de Europa, this parador looks from the outside like a modern and rather spartan hostel. Inside, however, it is cosy, with rooms painted in warm colours and featuring original décor. Guests can take advantage of the many lounges, terraces and balconies with views of the mountains. **www.parador.es**

GIJÓN La Casona de Jovellanos

Plazuela de Jovellanos 1, 33201 (Asturias) Tel 985 34 20 24 Fax 985 35 61 51 Rooms 13

This small hotel occupies an 18th-century building overlooking a little square in the old part of the city, near San Lorenzo beach. The hotel restaurant contains fragments of the old city walls, which were uncovered here during renovation work. **www.lacasonadejovellanos.com**

GIJÓN Parador Molino Viejo (Parador de Gijón)

Parque de Isabel la Católica, 33203 (Asturias) Tel 985 37 05 11 Fax 985 37 02 33 Rooms 40

This parador is situated inside a converted watermill in a corner of one of Spain's prettiest parks, close to San Lorenzo beach and Cimadevilla – the city's fishing port. The large, stylish rooms have sea views. Gourmets come here for the excellent cuisine, which includes *fabada* (bean stew) and imaginatively prepared fish and seafood. **www.parador.es**

Price categories *see p202* **For key to symbols** *see back flap*

LEÓN París

Calle Ancha 18, 24003 (Castilla y León) **Tel** *987 23 86 00* **Fax** *987 27 15 72* **Rooms** *55*

This family-run hotel in the city centre has fairly large guest rooms that are comfortable, quiet and decorated in warm colours. The attractively designed restaurant serves regional dishes, and the hotel bar has a good choice of drinks. **www.hotelparisleon.com**

LEÓN Parador Hostal de San Marcos

Plaza de San Marcos 7, 24001 (Castilla y León) **Tel** *987 23 73 00* **Fax** *987 23 34 58* **Rooms** *226*

This parador was converted from one of Spain's loveliest Renaissance buildings into a luxury hotel. The Plateresque façade once concealed a convent. Today, the rooms are sumptuously furnished with four-poster beds, while the hotel restaurant serves excellent Spanish cuisine. **www.parador.es**

LIMPIAS Parador de Limpias

Fuente del Amor, 39820 (Cantabria) **Tel** *942 62 89 00* **Fax** *942 63 43 33* **Rooms** *65*

Set in mountain scenery, this newly opened parador occupies a 19th-century palace built as a country residence. The rooms are modest but stylish. Among the hotel's facilities are tennis and squash courts and two swimming pools. Bicycles can also be rented on site. **www.parador.es**

LLANES Cantábrico

Calle Gutiérrez de la Gándara 10, 33500 (Asturias) **Tel** *985 40 30 69* **Fax** *985 40 23 04* **Rooms** *16*

The Cantábrico is located inside a 20th-century building with typical wooden balconies. Due to its out-of-town setting, the hotel is an ideal place for visitors seeking peace and relaxation. It offers studio apartments with self-catering facilities. **www.llaneshotelcantabrico.com**

LUARCA Villa de Luarca

Calle Álvaro de Albornoz 6, 33700 (Asturias) **Tel** *985 47 07 03* **Rooms** *14*

Built in 1906, this hotel stands on one of the town's main streets. The guest rooms feature antique furnishings. There are many places to relax here, including a lounge with a fireplace, and a garden, patio and terrace. **www.hotelvilladeluarca.com**

NAVIA Blanco

La Colorada, 33710 (Asturias) **Tel** *985 63 07 75* **Fax** *985 47 32 01* **Rooms** *41*

The Blanco is situated close to the beaches of Frejulfe and Barayo. In 1999 it underwent a thorough modernization to upgrade the facilities. The guest rooms are fairly modest, and each one is decorated differently. There is a tennis court as well as a swimming pool on site. **www.hotelblanco.net**

OVIEDO Gran Hotel España

Jovellanos 2, 33003 (Asturias) **Tel** *985 22 05 96* **Fax** *985 22 21 40* **Rooms** *89*

This exclusive hotel is tucked away in the city's historic quarter, close to the Campoamor theatre and Gothic cathedral. The rooms are small but comfortable, and each has Internet access. The excellent restaurant specializes in Asturian as well as other Spanish dishes. There is a charge for parking. **www.hotelestrebol.com**

OVIEDO Hotel de la Reconquista

Calle Gil de Jaz 16, 33004 (Asturias) **Tel** *985 24 11 00* **Fax** *985 24 11 66* **Rooms** *142*

This luxury hotel in the centre of Oviedo occupies a magnificent 18th-century building that was once a hostel. The public rooms are arranged around several arcaded and balconied courtyards. Regional and Spanish cuisine is served in the elegant restaurants. **www.hoteldelareconquista.com**

PANES Covadonga

Plaza de la Iglesia, 33570 (Asturias) **Tel** *985 41 42 30* **Fax** *985 41 41 62* **Rooms** *22*

Situated at the foot of the Picos de Europa, the Covadonga was opened in 1999. It is a good base for visitors keen on active leisure pursuits. There are many attractions in the surrounding area, such as salmon fishing in the Cares river, canoeing and caving. **www.hotelcovadonga.net**

RIBADESELLA Gran Hotel del Sella

Ricardo Cangas 17, 33560 (Asturias) **Tel** *985 86 01 50* **Fax** *985 85 74 49* **Rooms** *81*

This luxury hotel is situated next to the broad sandy beach of Santa Marina. The hotel terraces overlook the sea. There are vast gardens and a swimming pool bordered by palm trees. Excellent seafood is served at the hotel restaurant. **www.granhoteldelsella.com**

SANTANDER Hotel Real

Paseo Pérez Galdos 28, 39005 (Cantabria) **Tel** *942 27 25 50* **Fax** *942 27 45 73* **Rooms** *123*

This elegant hotel is set on the city's highest hill and has balconies overlooking the bay. It was built in the early 20th century for nobility accompanying the Spanish royal family on holiday. All the rooms have Internet access. **www.hotelreal.es**

SANTILLANA DEL MAR Posada Araceli

Calle La Robleda 20, 39330 (Cantabria) **Tel** *942 84 01 94* **Fax** *942 81 80 83* **Rooms** *12*

The family-run Posada Araceli has delightful, friendly owners. Each room is arranged in a different way, while the furniture – wardrobes, beds and even hangers – is all handmade and comes from a local furniture workshop. The hotel is surrounded by a well-maintained garden. **www.posadaaraceli.com**

SANTILLANA DEL MAR Altamira 🖂📶🖨🅿🛗 €€€€

Calle Cantón 1, 39330 (Cantabria) **Tel** *942 81 80 25* **Fax** *942 84 01 36* **Rooms** *32*

This town-centre hotel occupies a restored 16th-century palace with stone walls and beamed ceilings. The windows look out onto the main street of Santillana del Mar and the 12th-century Colegiata de St Julián. **www.hotelaltamira.com**

SANTILLANA DEL MAR Parador de Santillana-Gil Blas 🖂📶🖨📋🅿 €€€€€

Plaza Ramón Pelayo 11, 39330 (Cantabria) **Tel** *942 02 80 28* **Fax** *942 81 83 91* **Rooms** *28*

One of two paradors in Santillana del Mar, the Santillana-Gil Blas occupies an 18th-century mansion in the town centre. Prices are fairly steep, but guests come for the period furnishings, spacious rooms, delightful patio and superb restaurant. **www.parador.es**

SAN VICENTE DE LA BARQUERA Villa de San Vicente 🖂📶🖨🅿 €€€€

Fuente Nueva 1, 39540 (Cantabria) **Tel** *942 71 21 38* **Fax** *942 71 51 52* **Rooms** *50*

This clean and cosy hotel lies close to the beach in the eastern part of the Cantabrian coast. The majority of the rooms are well lit on account of the huge windows. Many possibilities exist here for visitors seeking outdoor pursuits. There is limited parking only. **www.hotelvsvicente.com**

SOMIEDO Mirador del Parque 🖂🖨🅿 €€

Gua, 33840 (Asturia) **Tel** *985 76 36 29* **Fax** *985 76 36 29* **Rooms** *8*

Set in the mountainous landscape of the Parque Natural de Somiedo, this unassuming stone hotel building has rustic-style rooms. Regional dishes from Somiedo can be sampled at the nearby restaurants, and the attentive owners will make you feel very welcome. Minimum one-week stay during summer. **www.miradordelparque.com**

TARAMUNDI Taramundi 🖂📶🖨♿ €€

Mayor, 33775 (Asturias) **Tel** *985 64 67 27* **Fax** *985 64 68 61* **Rooms** *8*

This simple stone building contains cosy, rustic-style guest rooms that have been arranged with great attention to detail. The rooms also have Internet access. In the Taramundi's restaurant you can enjoy excellent grilled meats flavoured with delicious sauces. **www.hoteltaramundi.com**

VILLAVICIOSA Avenida Real 🖂🖨🅿 €€€€

Carmen 10, 33300 (Asturias) **Tel** *985 89 20 47* **Fax** *985 89 15 09* **Rooms** *8*

This new hotel in the town's historic centre features English colonial-style rooms, each decorated in a different way. With both the sea and the mountains close by, the location is ideal for nature-lovers. Several pre-Romanesque sites can be visited in the surrounding area. There is a charge for parking. **www.hotelavenidareal.com**

VILLAVICIOSA La Corte de Lugas 🖂📶🖨♿🅿🛗 €€€€€

Lugas, 33311 (Asturias) **Tel.** *985 89 02 03* **Fax** *985 89 02 03* **Rooms** *10*

This small hotel appeals to visitors primarily due to its location near several hiking trails and the pleasant beaches of Rodiles and España. Nearby, too, is the Costa de los Dinosaurios, where you can see dinosaur footprints from the Jurassic era. **www.lacortedelugas.com**

THE BASQUE COUNTRY

ARGOMÁNIZ Parador de Argomániz 🖂📶🖨♿🅿🛗 €€€€€

Carretera NI, 01192 (Álava) **Tel** *945 29 32 00* **Fax** *945 29 32 87* **Rooms** *53*

This parador is located inside a Renaissance palace with good views of the surrounding area. Napoleon lodged here before marching on Vitoria. The rooms are very elegant and complemented by a pleasant garden. Well worth trying are the traditional dishes served in the hotel restaurant. **www.parador.es**

BAKIO Hostería del Señorío de Bizkaia 🖂🖨📶🅿 €€€

José María Cirarda 4, 48130 (Vizcaya) **Tel** *946 19 47 25* **Fax** *946 19 47 25* **Rooms** *16*

A stone building with wooden balconies houses this hotel in the resort of Bakio on the Basque coast, not far from Bilbao. In summer, concerts are held in the garden. Guests can play the local racket game of pelota, take a guided tour or visit the nearby beach. The restaurant serves typical Basque cuisine. **www.hosteriasreales.com**

BILBAO (BILBO) Begoña 🖂🖨♿🛗 €€

Calle Amistad 2, 48001 (Vizcaya) **Tel** *944 23 01 34* **Fax** *944 23 01 33* **Rooms** *21*

This cosy little hotel is situated a few steps from Bilbao's main street, near public transport, shops and sights. It offers modest but inviting guest rooms. The main advantages at the Begoña are the low prices and Internet access. **www.hostalbegona.com**

BILBAO (BILBO) Iturrienea Ostatua 🖂🖨 €€€

Calle Santa María 14, 48005 (Vizcaya) **Tel** *944 16 15 00* **Fax** *944 15 89 29* **Rooms** *21*

A small hotel occupying the first and second floors of an old house in the lively old quarter of the city centre, the Casco Viejo. It is clean and welcoming, combining rustic decorations with some modern flourishes in its large bedrooms. Street-facing rooms, however, catch the noise from below. **www.iturrieneaostatua.com**

Price categories *see p202* **For key to symbols** *see back flap*

BILBAO (BILBO) Abba Parque

€€€€

Calle Rodríguez Arias 66, 48013 (Vizcaya) **Tel** *944 41 31 00* **Fax** *944 42 21 97* **Rooms** *176*

An excellent business hotel with large conference rooms and clean, bright and well-maintained guest rooms. Good standard of accommodation and amenities. The regional specialities served in the hotel restaurant are very enticing.
www.abbahoteles.com

BILBAO (BILBO) Barceló Hotel Nervión

€€€€

Paseo Campo de Volantín 11, 48007 (Vizcaya) **Tel** *944 45 47 00* **Fax** *944 45 56 08* **Rooms** *348*

Known as the "Hotel del Guggenheim", this vast, modern hotel opposite the Museo Guggenheim features soundproof rooms with large comfortable beds. It is situated close to the city's main sights. The modern and tastefully decorated hotel restaurant serves Basque cuisine. **www.barcelo.com**

BILBAO (BILBO) Sirimiri

€€€€

Plaza de la Encarnación 3, 48006 (Vizcaya) **Tel** *944 33 07 59* **Fax** *944 33 08 75* **Rooms** *28*

The Sirimiri enjoys a location close to Bilbao's Old Town. Its guest rooms are plain and simple, but very clean. There is a small on-site gym and sauna as well as hydromassage facilities. The simple dining room serves breakfast.
www.hotelsirimiri.com

GERNIKA-LUMO Akelarre Ostatua

€€

Barrenkale 5, 48300 (Vizcaya) **Tel** *946 27 01 97* **Fax** *946 27 06 75* **Rooms** *17*

This relatively inexpensive hotel in the centre of Gernika, opened in 2000, is close to the town's main attractions. The rooms are painted in lively colours and are very clean. The surrounding area offers a wide range of outdoor pursuits.
www.hotelakelarre.com

HONDARRIBIA (FUENTERRABÍA) Obispo

€€€€€

Plaza del Obispo 1, 20280 (Guipúzcoa) **Tel** *943 64 54 00* **Fax** *943 64 23 86* **Rooms** *16*

This hotel is housed in a palace dating from the turn of the 14th century. Each room is furnished in a different style and features fine views over Txingudi bay. Guests can enjoy breakfast in the Obispo's beautiful garden.
www.hotelobispo.com

HONDARRIBIA (FUENTERRABÍA) Pampinot

€€€€€

Kalea Nagusia 5, 20280 (Guipúzcoa) **Tel** *943 64 06 00* **Fax** *943 64 51 28* **Rooms** *8*

An atmosphere of warmth and elegance is achieved by the team who run this hotel in a 16th-century palace, which has been declared a national historic monument. It is located in the heart of old Hondarribia. The ceilings of the bedrooms are hand-painted with images of angels, birds and clouds. **www.hotelpampinot.com**

HONDARRIBIA (FUENTERRABÍA) Parador de Hondarribia

€€€€€

Plaza de Armas 14, 20280 (Guipúzcoa) **Tel** *943 64 55 00* **Fax** *943 64 21 53* **Rooms** *36*

An elegant parador in a 10th-century restored fortress that occupies the highest point of this historic town. It has a beautiful inner patio incorporating a ruined part of the castle and a terrace overlooking the Bidasoa estuary. Weapons and other memorabilia of its colourful history adorn the walls of the public rooms. **www.parador.es**

LAGUARDIA Posada Mayor de Migueloa

€€€€

Mayor de Migueloa 20, 01300 (Álava) **Tel** *945 62 11 75* **Fax** *945 62 10 22* **Rooms** *8*

This small hotel is located inside a 17th-century palace. The beamed ceilings, granite walls and tiled floors add to the atmosphere. In the restaurant you can sample wines from the hotel's own wine cellar. Garage parking is available for an additional charge. Pets are welcome. **www.mayordemigueloa.com**

LAGUARDIA Villa de Laguardia

€€€€€

Paseo de San Raimundo 15, 01300 (Álava) **Tel** *945 60 05 60* **Fax** *945 60 05 61* **Rooms** *80*

Set in beautiful surroundings, this hotel affords views of the Sierra de Cantabria. The rooms have elegant modern furnishings. There is a swimming pool, as well as a bodega and a library with a large selection of books on the art of wine-making. **www.hotelvilladelaguardia.com**

LEKEITIO Zubieta

€€€€

Calle Portal de Atea, 48280 (Vizcaya) **Tel** *946 84 30 30* **Fax** *946 84 10 99* **Rooms** *24*

This small hotel is located inside a fine 18th-century manor with a garden. Each room is differently furnished, while the general décor is dominated by wooden elements and warm colours. Not far from the hotel are some sandy beaches where sailing and windsurfing are popular. **www.hotelzubieta.com**

MUNDAKA El Puerto

€€€

Portu Kalea 1, 48360 (Vizcaya) **Tel** *946 87 67 25* **Fax** *946 87 67 26* **Rooms** *11*

A fisherman's house in one of the prettiest towns on the Basque coast. Located at the mouth of the Gernika estuary, which is renowned for its surfing beaches, the windows offer great views of the sea. Converted into a simple, cosy hotel, it is decorated in contemporary style. It has a cafeteria and a bar. Close to Bilbao.**www.hotelelpuerto.com**

MUNDAKA Mundaka

€€€

Calle Florentino Larrínaga 9, 48360 (Vizcaya) **Tel** *946 87 67 00* **Fax** *946 87 61 58* **Rooms** *19*

This hotel boasts a town-centre location, close to the beach. It offers modestly furnished but comfortable rooms, a friendly atmosphere, and wireless Internet access. Surfing and sailing are especially popular in the vicinity.
www.hotelmundaka.com

SAN SEBASTIÁN (DONOSTIA) Aida

€€€

Calle Iztueta 9, 20001 (Guipúzcoa) **Tel** *943 32 78 00* **Fax** *943 32 67 07* **Rooms** *9*

This cosy guest house is run by a very friendly family. Its location is excellent – close to Zurriola beach and the Kursaal auditorium and conference centre. The rooms are small, but nicely furnished. There are also facilities for children. Additional charge for parking. **www.pensionesconencanto.com**

SAN SEBASTIÁN (DONOSTIA) Abba de Londres y de Inglaterra

€€€€€

Calle Zubieta 2, 20007 (Guipúzcoa) **Tel** *943 44 07 70* **Fax** *943 44 04 91* **Rooms** *148*

Situated by the seafront promenade of Paseo de La Concha, this exclusive hotel was once a favoured summer haunt of aristocrats, politicians and diplomats. The grand Victorian hotel has been modernized, but is still plush. The chief selling points are the very elegant English-style rooms and the excellent cuisine. **www.hlondres.com**

SAN SEBASTIÁN (DONOSTIA) María Cristina

€€€€€

Calle Oquendo 1, 20004 (Guipúzcoa) **Tel** *943 43 76 00* **Fax** *943 43 76 76* **Rooms** *136*

The biggest stars of the silver screen stay at this luxurious hotel during San Sebastián's Film Festival in September. Guests have included Elizabeth Taylor, Charlie Chaplin, Orson Welles and, more recently, Pedro Almodóvar and Woody Allen. The hotel is in the city centre, close to the Kursaal and beautiful beaches. **www.westin.com/mariacristina**

SAN SEBASTIÁN (DONOSTIA) Mercure Monte Igueldo

€€€€€

Paseo del Faro 134, 20008 (Guipúzcoa) **Tel** *943 21 02 11* **Fax** *943 21 50 28* **Rooms** *125*

Superbly located on Monte Igueldo, this large hotel has panoramic views across San Sebastián and Bahía de la Concha. The luxurious rooms with glazed walls are fitted with elegant and very tasteful furnishings. Imaginatively prepared dishes are served at the hotel restaurant. **www.monteigueldo.com**

VITORIA (GASTEIZ) Páramo

€€

Calle General Alava 11 (Pasaje Postas), 01005 (Álava) **Tel** *945 14 02 40* **Fax** *945 14 04 92* **Rooms** *37*

This 1960s hotel was thoroughly revamped in 1997. It is situated in the city centre, not far from the Plaza España. The rooms have modest but tasteful furnishings. A buffet breakfast is served. The low prices at the Páramo are a definite plus. **www.hotelparamo.com**

ZARAUTZ Txiki Polit

€€

Musika Plaza, 20800 (Guipúzcoa) **Tel** *943 83 53 57* **Fax** *943 83 37 31* **Rooms** *29*

This small hotel has clean and pleasant rooms. At the café you can order delicious *pintxos* (open sandwiches) and excellent draught cider. Also good is the hotel bar, which offers a wide variety of drinks. Half- and full-board options are also available. **www.txikipolit.com**

ZARAUTZ Zarauz

€€€€

Nafarroa Kalea 26, 20800 (Guipúzcoa) **Tel** *943 83 02 00* **Fax** *943 83 01 93* **Rooms** *75*

The Zarauz owes its popularity largely to the sandy beaches on the nearby Basque coast. Guests can expect to find bright and elegantly furnished rooms, pleasant communal areas, superb food and a large choice of drinks at the hotel bar. **www.hotelzarauz.com**

NAVARRA AND LA RIOJA

ÁBALOS Hotel Villa de Ábalos

€€€€

Plaza Fermín Gurbindo 2, 26339 (La Rioja) **Tel** *941 33 43 02* **Fax** *941 30 80 23* **Rooms** *12*

This family-run hotel, in the heart of the Rioja wine-making country, is surrounded by vineyards and within easy reach of picturesque villages. The comfortable rooms are large and tastefully furnished, and the restaurant serves high-class regional dishes. The hotel also organizes wine tours for guests. **www.hotelvilladeabalos.com**

ANGUIANO Abadía de Valvanera

€€

Monasterio de Valvanera, 26323 (La Rioja) **Tel** *941 37 70 44* **Fax** *941 37 71 94* **Rooms** *26*

Ideal for those seeking a peaceful environment and beautiful views. This hotel is located inside a Benedictine monastery surrounded by extensive forests and the San Lorenzo mountain range. The modest rooms and serene atmosphere are perfect for quiet contemplation. Closed late Dec–early Jan. **www.abadiavalvanera.com**

LOS ARCOS Mónaco

€€€

Plaza del Coso 1, 31210 (Navarra) **Tel** *948 64 00 00* **Fax** *948 64 08 72* **Rooms** *14*

For the past 40 years, this town-centre hotel has been frequented by pilgrims heading to Santiago de Compostela. The rooms are sparsely furnished but clean and pleasant, with fine views onto the towers of the Iglesia de Santa María. **www.monacohotel.net**

ARNEDILLO El Molino del Cidacos

€€€

Carretera Arnendo km 14, 26589 (La Rioja) **Tel** *941 39 40 63* **Fax** *941 39 42 00* **Rooms** *8*

As its name suggests, this hotel is located inside a 17th-century water mill (*molino*). Each room is named after a different variety of grape and painted in the appropriate colour. The hotel also has a collection of wine-making equipment. Guest rooms have Internet access. **www.pegarrido.com**

Price categories *see p202* **For key to symbols** *see back flap*

BERA DE BIDASOA Churrut

€€€€€

Plaza de los Fueros 2, 31780 (Navarra) **Tel** *948 62 55 40* **Fax** *948 62 55 41* **Rooms** *17*

This family-run hotel has attractive, clean and inviting rooms, each furnished differently. The Churrut's spacious restaurant, featuring a beautiful beamed ceiling, serves local cuisine. A gym and a sauna can be found on the top floor. **www.hotelchurrut.com**

BURGOS Abba Burgos

€€€€€

Calle Fernán González 72, 09003 (Castilla y León) **Tel** *947 00 11 00* **Fax** *947 00 11 01* **Rooms** *99*

Built in 2003, this hotel is situated on the pilgrimage route to Santiago de Compostela, almost next door to Burgos Cathedral. It has good facilities, including a sauna, indoor and outdoor swimming pools, and raquetball courts. **www.abbahoteles.com**

CALAHORRA Zenit Calahorra

€€€

Carretera N – 232 km 363, 26500 (La Rioja) **Tel** *941 14 79 52* **Fax** *941 14 80 33* **Rooms** *30*

This small, well-located hotel near the centre of Calahorra is a good base for excursions into the surrounding area. It offers some business facilities, and the rooms are spacious, clean and well maintained. The restaurant serves delicious regional and traditional dishes. **www.zenithoteles.com**

CALAHORRA Parador de Calahorra

€€€€€

Paseo Mercadal, 26500 (La Rioja) **Tel** *941 13 03 58* **Fax** *941 13 51 39* **Rooms** *60*

This parador features medieval-style decoration and a beautiful garden full of roses and palms. Thanks to its spacious conference rooms and modern facilities, it is a popular venue for business meetings. The restaurant serves dishes made from local products, and tasty desserts, which include a dish of pears and peaches in wine. **www.parador.es**

CASALARREINA Hospedería Señorío de Casalarreina

€€€

Plaza Santo Domingo de Guzmán 6, 26230 (La Rioja) **Tel** *941 32 47 30* **Fax** *941 32 47 31* **Rooms** *15*

This hotel occupies part of a 16th-century Dominican monastery and is full of character. The individualized, spacious, rustic-style rooms are furnished with great attention to detail; some have bare stone walls, others have beamed ceilings. **www.hotelesconencanto.org**

ELCIEGO Hotel Marqués de Riscal

€€€€€

Calle Torrea, 01340 (Álava) **Tel** *945 180 888* **Fax** *945 180 881* **Rooms** *43 (all suites)*

Designed by Frank Gehry, architect of the Museo Guggenheim Bilbao, this prestigious hotel opened in autumn 2006. Its luxurious suites have marble bathrooms and fine views of La Rioja's extensive vineyards. The hotel has a top-notch gastronomic restaurant, and guests have easy access to leisure activities in the locality. **www.luxurycollection.com**

IZALZU Besaro

€€€

Irigoyen, 31689 (Navarra) **Tel** *948 89 03 50* **Fax** *948 89 00 86* **Rooms** *8*

An attractive *casa rural*, renovated in 2004, the Besaro is set among the wooded hills of Navarra. The rooms feature rustic-style decoration, and some have beamed ceilings. The hotel terrace makes an enjoyable spot from which to admire the surrounding area, and in the evenings it's pleasant to relax by the sitting-room fire. **www.besaro.es**

LEKUMBERRI Ayestarán

€€€

Calle Aralar 22, 31870 (Navarra) **Tel** *948 50 41 27* **Fax** *948 50 41 27* **Rooms** *91*

This typical *casa rural* is situated in a peaceful village at the foot of the Aralar mountains, half an hour's drive from Pamplona and San Sebastián. Its chief merits are the excellent cuisine, terrace and garden. There are also facilities for tennis and table tennis. **www.hotelayestaran.com**

LOGROÑO Husa Gran Vía

€€€€

Gran Vía Rey Juan Carlos I 71, 26005 (La Rioja) **Tel** *941 28 78 50* **Fax** *941 28 78 51* **Rooms** *93*

This town-centre hotel offers spacious accommodation decorated in lively colours. With its good facilities, the hotel is particularly popular among businesspeople. It is also a good starting point for a whistle-stop tour of Logroño's many tapas bars, the so-called *tapeo*. **www.hotelhusagranvia.com**

OLITE Parador de Olite

€€€€€

Plaza Teobaldos 2, 31390 (Navarra) **Tel** *948 74 00 00* **Fax** *948 74 02 01* **Rooms** *43*

The Parador de Olite is located inside a medieval castle with a slender tower and battlements. Its five centuries of history are evidenced by the period furnishings in the salons and by the rooms with bare stone walls. The restaurant is known for its excellent asparagus dishes in season. **www.parador.es**

PAMPLONA (IRUÑA) Navarra

€€€

Calle Tudela 9, 31002 (Navarra) **Tel** *948 22 51 64* **Fax** *948 22 34 26* **Rooms** *13*

The Navarra is located in the heart of Pamplona, close to the Old Town. It has bright and clean rooms, some of which are reserved for non-smokers. The facilities are modest, which is reflected in the rate, but be aware that rates jump to over 200 euros during the San Fermín fiesta in July. **www.hostalnavarra.com**

PAMPLONA (IRUÑA) Iruña Palace Hotel Tres Reyes

€€€€€

Jardines de la Taconera, 31001 (Navarra) **Tel** *948 22 66 00* **Fax** *948 22 29 30* **Rooms** *160*

This luxury hotel is located in the city centre. It was thoroughly revamped in 2002 and offers comfortable rooms and suites as well as whole floors reserved for non-smokers. With 18 conference rooms, this is an ideal hotel for business people. Other services include a squash court, sauna and solarium. **www.hotel3reyes.com**

SAN MILÁN DE LA COGOLLA Hospedería Monasterio San Millán   €€€€€

Monasterio de Yuso, 26226 (La Rioja) **Tel** *941 37 32 77* **Fax** *941 37 32 66* **Rooms** *25*

This hotel occupies a wing of the Monasterio de San Millán de Yuso, a UNESCO's World Heritage Site. Accommodation here ranges from elegant suites to royal apartments, with windows overlooking the monastery courtyard. All the rooms are filled with antiques and each is furnished differently. **www.sanmillan.com**

SANTO DOMINGO DE LA CALZADA Parador de Santo Domingo   €€€€€

Plaza del Santo 3, 26250 (La Rioja) **Tel** *941 34 03 00* **Fax** *941 34 03 25* **Rooms** *61*

In the 13th century, this building was a hostel for pilgrims heading to Santiago de Compostela. Today, the parador offers magnificently furnished rooms and salons. Excellent wines and fish dishes are served at the hotel's restaurant. Nearby is the newer Parador de Santo Domingo Bernardo de Fresneda, with 48 additional rooms. **www.parador.es**

URDAZUBI Irigoienea   €€€

Barrio Iribere 38, 31711 (Navarra) **Tel** *948 59 92 67* **Fax** *948 59 92 43* **Rooms** *11*

Situated in a village by the northern border of Navarra, this hotel offers rustic-style rooms, a romantic lounge with a fireplace, and a covered terrace with views of the mountains. Bicycles are available for hire – perhaps the best way of exploring the hilly, verdant surroundings. **www.irigoienea.com**

YESA Hospedería de Leyre   €€€

Monasterio de Leyre, 31410 (Navarra) **Tel** *948 88 41 00* **Fax** *948 88 41 37* **Rooms** *33*

This hotel occupies part of an 11th-century Benedictine monastery and is ideal for either a long or short stay. The rustic-style décor is dominated by wood and stone, and there is also a good restaurant. Group bookings are preferred. **www.hotelhospederiadeleyre.com**

CENTRAL AND EASTERN PYRENEES

AINSA Apolo   €€

Carrer Pineta 4, 22330 (Huesca) **Tel** *974 50 08 88* **Fax** *974 50 08 36* **Rooms** *27*

This small hotel, located in Aínsa, a village of medieval origins, is an excellent base for excursions into the nearby Pyrenees. The rooms are plain and basic, but very clean, and have television, mini-bar and air conditioning. The hotel restaurant offers a breakfast buffet. **www.apolo.com.es**

ANDORRA LA VELLA Andorra Park Hotel   €€€€€

Les Canals 24, AD 500 (Andorra) **Tel** *376 87 77 77* **Fax** *376 82 09 83* **Rooms** *40*

One of Andorra's most luxurious hotels, this modern structure is built into a steep, wooded hillside. There is a library, a swimming pool hewn out of rock, and a pleasant bar-restaurant. Rooms come with satellite TV and a mini-bar, and the hotel also provides a laundry and ironing service. **www.hotansa.com**

ARTIES Parador de Arties   €€€€€

Carretera Baqueira Beret, 25599 (Lleida) **Tel** *973 64 08 01* **Fax** *973 64 10 01* **Rooms** *57*

The Parador de Arties is the perfect place for apres-ski relaxation. Designed in a characteristic local mountain style, the building has comfortable and spacious rooms, all tastefully arranged. In summer you can relax by the hotel pool. Rates are highest during the winter sports season. **www.parador.es**

BAQUEIRA-BERET Chalet Bassibé   €€€€€

Carretera Beret, 25598 (Lleida) **Tel** *973 64 51 52* **Fax** *973 64 50 32* **Rooms** *36*

A pleasant hotel in the town centre, the Chalet Bassibé is frequented by skiers and winter-sports enthusiasts. The rooms, featuring beamed ceilings, are very cosy. Another attraction is the swimming pool, while gourmets will find lots of interesting choices on the restaurant menu. **www.valderuda-bassibe.com**

BARBASTRO Gran Hotel Ciudad de Barbastro   €€€

Plaça del Mercado 4, 22300 (Huesca) **Tel** *974 30 89 00* **Fax** *974 30 88 99* **Rooms** *41*

Opened in 2003, the Gran Hotel is located in the cultural and tourist area of Barbastro. It offers elegant rooms as well as four suites with king-size beds and terraces. The hotel restaurant serves Mediterranean and Aragonese cuisine. **www.ghbarbastro.com**

BELLVER DE CERDANYA Fonda Bianya   €€€

Carrer Sant Roc 11, 25720 (Lleida) **Tel** *973 51 04 75* **Fax** *973 51 08 53* **Rooms** *16*

This old family-run hotel, housed in a stately home in the centre of Bellver de Cerdanya, has comfortable rooms and a good restaurant serving local Catalan cuisine. The village itself is well located for hiking and horse riding excursions into the beautiful mountainous area. **www.fondabiayna.com**

BENASQUE Gran Hotel Benasque   €€€

Carretera de Anciles, 22440 (Huesca) **Tel/Fax** *974 55 10 11* **Rooms** *69*

The Gran Hotel Benasque has clean and comfortable rooms, some with sloping ceilings. Bicycles are available for rent, and guests can enjoy the sauna and the indoor and outdoor swimming pools. There is also a gym, tennis and squash courts, and massage is available. The hotel is closed in November. **www.hoteles-valero.com**

Price categories *see p202* **For key to symbols** *see back flap*

BIELSA Valle de Pineta

Los Cuervos, 22350 (Huesca) **Tel** *974 50 10 10* **Fax** *974 50 11 91* **Rooms** *26*

Located about 12 km (7 miles) from the Parque Nacional de Ordesa, this small hotel offers recently refurbished rooms, most with balconies. Thanks to the large windows in the hotel restaurant, you can enjoy the beautiful scenery while sampling the delicious local cuisine. **www.hotelvalledepineta.com**

BIELSA Parador de Bielsa

Valle de Pineta, 22350 (Huesca) **Tel** *974 50 10 11* **Fax** *974 50 11 88* **Rooms** *39*

The Parador de Bielsa is a modern hotel in the Parque Nacional de Ordesa. Designed in a typical mountain style, the building integrates harmoniously with its surroundings. The rooms, decked out in wood, are comfortable and elegant. From the hotel terrace extend beautiful views of the valley and Monte Perdido. **www.parador.es**

BROTO Pradas

Avinguda de Ordesa 7, 22370 (Huesca) **Tel** *974 48 60 04* **Fax** *974 48 63 96* **Rooms** *21*

This hotel, designed in a combination of wood and stone, is located in the town centre, almost at the gates to the Parque Nacional de Ordesa. The English-style rooms are painted in lively colours, and each one is arranged differently. Some rooms have air conditioning. There is also an on-site shop for the benefit of guests. **www.hotelpradas.com**

CANDANCHÚ Edelweiss

Carretera Francia km 189, 22889 (Huesca) **Tel** *974 37 32 00* **Fax** *974 37 30 46* **Rooms** *40*

The Edelweiss is a popular base for skiers, with a great location. From the balconies of its spacious rooms there are beautiful views of the nearby slopes, while its two restaurants serve tasty meals. The communal areas include a solarium. **www.edelweisscandanchu.com**

ESTERRI D'ÁNEU Esterri Park Hotel

Carrer Major 69, 25580 (Lleida) **Tel** *973 62 63 88* **Fax** *973 62 62 79* **Rooms** *24*

This small hotel, which is located in the town centre, offers plain but functional rooms, with the capacity for additional beds for families with children. Younger guests might be attracted by the games facilities – including billiards. **www.esterripark.com**

HUESCA Alfonso I

Carrer Padre Huesca 67, 22002 (Huesca) **Tel/Fax** *974 24 54 54* **Rooms** *11*

The Alfonso I has a central location in the heart of Huesca near the Praça Santa Clara, on a historic street. Although its rooms are modest, they come at affordable prices. The rooms are equipped with bathroom and television. **www.mercaragon.com/hostalalfonso1**

HUESCA Huesca

Carrer José Gil Cávez 10, 22005 (Huesca) **Tel** *974 23 99 45* **Fax** *974 22 27 99* **Rooms** *54*

This modern hotel in the city centre offers its guests the full range of facilities. The rooms are simple but very comfortable. Self-catering is an option for those on a more limited budget or those with families, and there are also small but functional conference rooms. **www.aparthotelhuesca.com**

HUESCA Pedro I de Aragón

Carrer del Parque 34, 22003 (Huesca) **Tel** *974 22 03 00* **Fax** *974 22 00 94* **Rooms** *120*

This stylish modern hotel, located in the city centre, is part of the Gargallo chain, which has more than a dozen hotels around Spain. The rooms are bright and spacious, and the hotel restaurant offers a wide range of tasty meals. Guests can relax by the pool. The hotel has a pet-friendly policy. **www.gargallohotels.es**

JACA Canfranc

Avinguda de Oroel 23, 22700 (Huesca) **Tel** *974 36 31 32* **Fax** *974 36 49 79* **Rooms** *20*

Located in an attractive street in the town centre, this small hotel has comfortable and quiet rooms – some with huge windows, others with sloping ceilings. Thanks to its proximity to excellent pistes, the Canfranc is an ideal base for skiers. **www.hotelcanfranc.com**

JACA Real

Carrer Membrilleras 7, 22700 (Huesca) **Tel** *974 36 30 08* **Fax** *974 36 30 75* **Rooms** *78*

The Real occupies a modern building that offers guests comfortable if plainly furnished rooms, some of which have skylights. Among the hotel's facilities are a Jacuzzi, sauna, swimming pool, gym and sun terrace. Garage parking is available for an additional charge. **www.hotelrealjaca.com**

LA SEU D'URGELL Minotel Andria

Passeig Joan Brudieu 24, 25700 (Lleida) **Rooms** *16*

This small hotel, occupying a modernist building with a beautiful patio and terrace, was established at the end of the 19th century. The rooms feature beamed ceilings and huge beds, while the restaurant serves traditional Catalan cuisine. Horse-riding and golf are among the sports on offer in the vicinity. **www.minotel.com**

VIELHA Parador de Vielha

Carretera del Túnel, 25530 (Lleida) **Tel/Fax** *973 64 01 00* **Rooms** *118*

This modern parador has spacious and tastefully furnished rooms. There are several swimming pools, both indoor and outdoor, and a well-equipped gym and spa facilities. From the hotel there extend pleasant views of the verdant Aran valley. **www.parador.es**

WHERE TO EAT

Every region of Northern Spain has its own cuisine and its own distinctive dishes. Eating establishments range from simple tapas bars – found even in the smallest villages – where you can drop in for a quick meal or a drink, to top-quality gourmet restaurants where you linger for hours. The Basque Country, in particular, is justifiably renowned for its outstanding culinary

Figure of a cook welcoming guests

tradition. *Bodegas* are good places to sample local wines, while in Asturias you'll find *sidrerías* serving, among other things, excellent cider. No matter what your culinary preferences, you're bound to find something to your taste in Northern Spain, with the wide variety of places to eat. Regardless of the category of establishment, you can always expect to find both friendly and professional service.

The Señorío de Alaiza – both a restaurant and a wine museum *(see p223)*

RESTAURANTS AND BARS

After a long day's sightseeing, there's no better place to visit than a tapas bar, where you can get quick, cheap snacks. Some bars, however, especially pubs (late-opening bars for socializing), serve no food.

If sand and sea are your aim, then *chiringuitos* are a good option. These beachside bars serve food as well as low-alcohol drinks. For an inexpensive, sit-down meal, try one of the family-run *ventas, posadas, mesones* or *fondas*, which offer simple but tasty food.

For something more substantial, choose from the wide array of restaurants across the price spectrum.

EATING HOURS

The Spanish breakfast *(desayuno)* is a light meal usually consisting of milky

coffee *(café con leche)* and a pastry, biscuits, or toast.

Many office workers step out to a café or tapas bar for a quick mid-morning snack between 10 and 11am.

The Spanish eat their main meal of the day at around 2pm, when restaurants fill up. Sunday lunch is a very busy time in restaurants, particularly in the countryside and on the coast.

Visitors looking for an earlier or lighter lunch can go to a tapas bar and order a few tapas *(see pp216–17)* – small

The Begoña restaurant *(see p222)*

snacks that range from cold meats, cheeses or salads to hot savoury dishes. Tapas are often accompanied by a beer *(cerveza)*, a glass of red wine *(vino tinto)* or juice.

Cafés, tea rooms *(salones de té)* and pastry shops *(pastelerías)* fill up between 5 and 6pm for afternoon snacks *(la merienda)*. By 8pm, the bars are crowded again with people having tapas accompanied by sherry, wine or beer.

Dinner *(la cena)* is eaten late in Spain – at 9pm or later, especially on Friday and Saturday nights. In the summer, people tend to eat their meal even later. Spanish restaurants will rarely serve meals earlier in the evening.

Most restaurants have a break between 4 and 8pm. They also usually close one day a week, and often on Sunday evening, too, as well as on some public holidays. Many close for an annual holiday, usually in August.

READING THE MENU

The Spanish term for menu is *la carta*. It usually features *sopas* (soups), *ensaladas* (salads), *entremeses* (starters or hors d'oeuvres), *huevos y tortillas* (eggs and potato omelettes), *verduras y legumbres* (vegetable dishes), *pescados y mariscos* (fish and shellfish), *carnes y aves* (meat and poultry) and *postres* (desserts).

Most restaurants offer a *menú del día*, or menu of the day, costing around 10 euros and consisting of: a starter *(entrada)*, bread *(pan)*, main course *(plato principal)*, dessert *(postre)* and something to drink *(bebida)*, usually water or wine; coffee, which is drunk at the end of the meal, after dessert, usually costs extra. This is by far the best-value way to eat, and considerably cheaper than ordering off the full menu *(carta)*. However, many restaurants only offer set *menús del día* for lunch. It's also nearly always cheaper to eat lunch in Spanish restaurants than it is to eat dinner.

Another type of menu is the *menú de degustación* – a gourmet menu or tasting menu, only found in upscale restaurants. It is a great deal more expensive than a *menú del día*, consisting of a selection of the chef's special dishes in smaller portions.

Sign for El Asesino in Santiago *(see p221)*

BOOKING

For popular and highly acclaimed restaurants, as well as all upscale restaurants, it's wise to book ahead for Friday and Saturday evenings, and for Sunday lunch. The rest of the week, restaurants are less busy and you can usually get a table. It's also worth booking ahead for any restaurant that has a particular regional speciality – and ordering the dish at the same time, because some specialities are only available with advance notice. Reservations can be usually made by phone.

CAFES

Cafés and pastry shops in Northern Spain, particularly in the Basque Country, enjoy a good reputation. Some make their own chocolate, which can include almonds *(almendras)*, hazelnuts *(avellanas)*, walnuts *(nueces)* or orange peel *(cáscara de naranja)*. Coffee is invariably

Outdoor dining in the Basque town of Hondarribia

excellent and aromatic. The most popular types are espresso *(café solo)*, espresso with a splash of milk *(cortado)* and milky coffee *(café con leche)*. Also popular are combinations, such as espresso with a dash of brandy *(carajillo)*.

PRICES AND TIPPING

VAT of 7 per cent is usually added to the bill. A growing number of Spanish restaurants also add a set service charge (indicated by *servicio incluído*), but in others it's normal to tip the staff, especially if they've been particularly helpful. There's no expectation of a set percentage, though, and many locals tip very little. It's reasonable to leave around 5–10 per cent of your bill.

Major debit and credit cards are now accepted in most restaurants. However, it is always best to have cash with you when visiting small cafés, bars or country taverns.

Prices depend on the category of restaurant and on what you order. The *menú del día* in a small restaurant will be priced at around 10 euros. For an evening meal in a comfortable, mid- to upper-range restaurant you can eat well for 30 euros. In an elegant city restaurant, you should expect to pay more than 40 euros.

CHILDREN AND VEGETARIANS

All eating places welcome children and will serve small portions if requested.

The choices for vegetarians are limited in Spanish cuisine, which relies heavily on fish, seafood and meat. Tapas can be a good choice for vegetarians, however, with a selection of salads, cheeses, potato, egg and vegetable dishes available.

DISABLED ACCESS

Few restaurants, especially those located inside historic buildings, are wheelchair-friendly. It is worth phoning in advance to check on access to tables and toilets.

DRESS

Casual wear is acceptable in almost all but the smartest city restaurants.

The charming interior of the Casa Conrado in Oviedo *(see p222)*

The Flavours of Northern Spain

The wild, wet north of Spain is as famous for its rain as it is for its culinary excellence. The rain keeps the pastures lush and green – perfect dairy farming terrain – and the Atlantic provides a wonderful variety of seafood. The Basques, in particular, are celebrated chefs, and the region boasts some of the finest restaurants in Europe, along with gastronomic societies (called *txokos*) in every village. Inland and in the remoter regions you'll find old-fashioned country cooking – roast lamb and tender young beef, slow-cooked stews – and traditionally made cheeses.

Idiazábal cheese

Goose-neck barnacles piled high for sale in a local market

GALICIA

The westernmost tip of Spain is famous for its extraordinary seafood – from staples like cod *(bacalao)* to delicacies like barnacles *(percebes)*, which look like tiny dinosaur feet. Every bar will serve up a plate of *pulpo a la gallega* (octopus with paprika and olive oil) or *pimientos de padrón* (small green peppers). Inland, you'll find tender veal, free-range chicken and delicate soft cheeses such as *tetilla*.

ASTURIAS AND CANTABRIA

The bay-pocked coastline provides delicious fresh fish, often served simply grilled or simmered in casseroles. Inland, the lush pastures form Spain's dairy country – most Spanish milk, cream and some of its finest cheeses come from this region. Try Asturian *cabrales*, a pungent blue cheese, accompanied by local cider. The mountains provide succulent meat and game, often stewed with beans, as in Asturian *fabada*.

BASQUE COUNTRY

The Basque Country is a paradise for gourmets, renowned throughout Spain for the excellence of its produce and

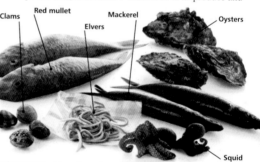

Clams   Red mullet   Mackerel   Oysters
Elvers   Squid

Fish and seafood from the waters of Northern Spain

REGIONAL DISHES AND SPECIALITIES

Unsurprisingly, seafood rules supreme along the coastline, from the ubiquitous octopus in a piquant sauce served in Galicia to the extraordinary spider crabs which are a sought-after delicacy in the Basque lands. The verdant pastures and rich farmland provide a wealth of fresh vegetables, including Navarra's justly famous asparagus, along with all kinds of wonderful cheeses. Slow-cooked stews, an Asturian speciality, are particularly good in the mountains, along with tender lamb and outstanding game in season.

Cherries

The renowned wines from La Rioja are excellent, but those of adjoining Navarra are less expensive and often equally interesting. The crisp whites of Galicia and the Basque lands are the perfect accompaniment to the fresh seafood, and throughout the North you'll find powerful liqueurs flavoured with local herbs.

Bacalao al Pil Pil *Salted cod is cooked slowly with olive oil, chilli and garlic to create this classic Basque dish.*

Array of *pintxos* laid out in a bar in the Basque Country

the creative brilliance of its chefs. Basque cuisine leans towards seafood, of which there is a dazzling variety: humble salted cod and hake (elevated to new heights with delicious sauces) are most common, but sought-after delicacies include elvers (baby eels) and spider crab. Basque wines, drunk young and tart, offer the perfect balance. Bar counters groan with platters of *pintxos* – the Basque variant of tapas, and the Basques also make wonderful cheeses, including delicate, smoky Idiazábal.

NAVARRA AND LA RIOJA

The fertile farmland of land-locked Navarra produces a spectacular array of fruit and vegetables such as asparagus, artichokes, cherries, chestnuts and peppers. In the Navarrese mountains, lamb is the most popular meat, as well as richly flavoured game in season, such as partridge and hare. *Trucha a la navarra* is the region's famous fish dish.

Tiny La Rioja is Spain's most famous wine region,

Red peppers – a speciality of La Rioja and popular in many dishes

producing rich, oaky reds and whites. The cuisine of La Rioja borrows from the neighbouring Basque Country and Navarra, with lamb a big feature, along with seafood and top-quality vegetables.

CENTRAL AND EASTERN PYRENEES

Hearty dishes with mountain-fresh ingredients typify Pyrenean cuisine, with a great variety of pork and poultry dishes such as *pollo al chilindrón* – chicken with onion, tomato, pepper and ham. For those who prefer fish, a good option is *bacalao al ajoarriero*, cod with potatoes and onions.

ON THE MENU

Trucha a la Navarra Trout, stuffed with ham and quickly grilled or fried.

Lacón con grelos Smoked pork shoulder joint with turnip leaves and potatoes.

Filloas queimadas Pancakes flambéed with *aguardiente*, cognac or whisky.

Sobaos, carajitos, casadielles Spongecakes filled with nuts.

Angulas a la Bilbaína Baby eels cooked in olive oil with garlic – a rare Basque delicacy.

Pimientos rellenos Peppers stuffed with meat or fish.

Vieiras Baked scallops.

Empanada Gallega *These golden pastries are stuffed with tuna and a wide choice of other fillings.*

Chilindrón de Cordero *Made with succulent lamb, this is a rich, hearty stew from the mountains of Navarra.*

Leche Frita *"Fried milk" is a delicious, custardy dessert from Cantabria. Simple but utterly delicious.*

Choosing Tapas

Tapas are small snacks that originated in Andalusia to
accompany sherry. Stemming from a bartender's practice
of covering a glass with a saucer or *tapa* (cover) to
keep out flies, the custom progressed to a chunk of
cheese or bread being used, and then to a few olives
being placed on a platter to accompany a drink. Choose
from a range of appetizing varieties, from cold meats to
elaborately prepared hot dishes of meat, seafood or vegetables. The Basque variant – *pintxos* – are like an open sand-
wich. Many bars also serve *raciónes*, which are larger portions.

Mixed green olives

Patatas bravas *is
a piquant dish of
fried potatoes
spiced with
chilli and
paprika.*

Albondigas *(meatballs)
are a hearty tapa, often
served with a spicy
tomato sauce.*

**Almendras
fritas** *are
fried, salted
almonds.*

Banderillas *are
canapés
skewered on
toothpicks.
The entire
canapé should
be eaten at once.*

Calamares fritos *are
squid rings and tentacles
which have been dusted with
flour before being deep fried in
olive oil. They are usually served
garnished with a piece of lemon.*

Jamón serrano *is salt-
cured ham dried in
mountain (serrano) air.*

ON THE TAPAS BAR

Alcachofas rellenas de carne
Meat-stuffed artichokes seasoned
with onion, tomato, garlic,
cheese and parsley.

Almejas a la marinera Clams
sautéed in a wine, onion and
garlic broth, garnished with
parsley.

Anchoas rellenas Anchovies
stuffed with onion and red or
green pepper.

Bacalao a la vizcaína Salt
cod served in a tomato sauce
seasoned with paprika, onion,
fried bread, garlic and almonds.

Berenjenas gratinadas Baked
aubergine (eggplant) stuffed

with *jamón serrano* and cheese,
served in an oregano-seasoned
tomato sauce.

Boquerones en vinagre
Small sardines in a vinaigrette.

Brochetas de verduras
Vegetable skewers, usually
consisting of marrow, aubergine
(eggplant), red peppers and
tomatoes.

Brochetas de marisco Seafood
skewers of lobster or mussels
with mushrooms and green
pepper.

Buñuelos de bacalao Fried
salt cod balls coated in
breadcumbs and beer.

Calamares a la romana Fried
squid rings.

Callos A serving of tripe.

Champiñones rellenos
Mushrooms stuffed with onion,
garlic, red pepper and *chorizo*
(sausage).

**Chuletitas de cordero con
alcaparras** Fried, breaded veal
served in a caper-flavoured
tomato sauce.

Empanadas gallegas Crispy
dumplings filled with fish,
seafood or meat.

Endivias al queso de Cabrales
Chicory leaves finished with a

TAPAS BARS

Even a small village will have at least one bar where the locals go to enjoy drinks, tapas and conversation with friends. On Sundays and holidays, favourite places are packed with whole families enjoying the fare. In the Basque Country and Asturias it is customary to move from bar to bar, sampling the specialities of each. A *tapa* is a single serving, whereas a *ración* is more substantial. Tapas are usually eaten standing or perching on a stool at the bar rather that sitting at a table, for which a surcharge is usually made.

Diners make their choice at a busy tapas bar

Chorizo, *a popular sausage flavoured with paprika and garlic, may be eaten cold or fried and served hot.*

Salpicón de marisco *is a luxurious cold salad of assorted fresh seafood in a zesty vinaigrette.*

Gambas a la plancha *is a simple but flavourful dish of grilled prawns (shrimp).*

Tortilla española *is the ubiquitous Spanish omelette of onion and potato bound with egg.*

Queso manchego *is a sheep's-milk cheese from La Mancha.*

Pollo al ajillo *consists of small pieces of chicken (often wings) sautéed and then simmered with a garlic-flavoured sauce.*

---

cheese and sour cream dressing.

Escalopines al queso de Cabrales Beef escalopes served with a Cabrales or some other blue cheese sauce.

Espárragos rellenos de salmón White asparagus stuffed with smoked salmon.

Espárragos verdes con jamón Green asparagus and ham, baked in a cheese sauce.

Gambas al ajillo Garlic prawns.

Mejillones a la vinagreta Mussels in a vinaigrette with onion, hard-boiled egg and parsley.

Patatas alioli Fried, cubed potates in a garlic mayonnaise sauce.

Pimientos rellenos de bacalao Red peppers stuffed with cod and seasoned with onion, salt and pepper.

Pimientos rellenos de chipirones Red peppers stuffed with seafood.

Pulpo a feira Octopus seasoned with hot and sweet paprika, bay leaves, olive oil and salt – a Galician speciality.

Revuelto de oricios Scrambled egg with sea urchins.

Riñones al jerez Kidneys served in dry sherry and seasoned with olive oil, onion and garlic.

Salpicón de marisco Baked sardines finished with a savoury vinaigrette flavoured with green pepper, onion, garlic, parsley and olive oil.

Sardinas asadas Roasted sardines.

Tortilla de patatas Traditional Spanish potato omelette, seasoned with salt, pepper and a little bit of cheese.

Vieiras gratinadas Fresh scallops served in a tasty béchamel sauce.

What to Drink in Northern Spain

Northern Spain is renowned as a wine-producing region. The best-known reds are from La Rioja, while the finest white wines are produced in Galicia and the sub-regions of Rías Baixas and Ribeira Sacra. When in Asturias, be sure to try the excellent cider, which can be sampled in special establishments known as *sidrerías*. Many other beverages – alcoholic and non-alcoholic – are served in bars and cafés, which provide an important focus for life in Spain. The Spanish are also great coffee drinkers. In summer a tempting range of cooling drinks is on offer, in addition to beer, which is always available.

Customers enjoying a drink at a café terrace in Haro

Café solo

Café con leche

Camomile   Lime flower

Hot chocolate

A plate of *churros* (batter sticks)

HOT DRINKS

The most popular hot drink is coffee *(café)*, which is drunk at all times of the day and served in a variety of ways. In the morning it is customary to drink *café con leche* – a large half-and-half measure of milk (warm or cold) and coffee. In the afternoon and evening, most common is *café cortado* – an espresso with a splash of milk. Strong plain espresso *(café solo)* is also popular. The Spanish have a taste for hot chocolate, which is served with batter sticks *(churros)*. Herbal teas include camomile *(manzanilla)* and lime flower *(tila)*.

COLD DRINKS

Spanish tap water is safe to drink, and many cities have convenient street-side water dispensers. Bottled mineral water, either still *(sin gas)* or sparkling *(con gas)*, is available from shops. A popular thirst-quenching drink is *horchata*, a non-alcoholic, sweet milky beverage made from ground tiger nuts *(chufas)*. *Zumo* is juice, sometimes from freshly squeezed fruit.

Sparkling mineral water

Horchata, made from *chufas*

Zumo, freshly squeezed juice

MIXED DRINKS

Sangria is a refreshing mixture of red wine, *gaseosa* (lemonade) and other ingredients including chopped fruit and sugar. Wine diluted with lemonade is called *vino con gaseosa*. Another favourite drink is Agua de Valencia, a refreshing blend of *cava* (sparkling wine) and orange juice. Young people will often order the popular *cuba libre*, cola with white rum.

Sangria

The popular cuba libre

Vino con gaseosa

SPIRITS AND LIQUEURS

The most common spirits drunk in Northern Spain are liqueurs. *Anís*, flavoured with aniseed, is popular; so, too, is *pacharán*, a richly coloured liqueur made from sloes and produced mainly in Navarra. The somewhat stronger *orujo* originates from Galicia; it is usually colourless, but there are also flavoured varieties: coffee, cherry or herb, with colours appropriate to the content.

Anís **Pacharán** **Orujo** **Herb liqueur**

WINE

No visit to Northern Spain is complete without sampling the local wines. The key standard for the industry is the Denominación de Origen (DO) classification, which guarantees the wine's origin and quality. The most renowned wine-producing region is La Rioja, where many vineyards established in the 19th century by émigrés from Bordeaux are still operating today. The best wines from this region are the dry red *tinto*. In Galicia, the most popular wines are *albariño*, *loureira* and *treixadura* from the sub-regions of Rías Baixas, Ribeiro, Valdeorras, Ribeira Sacra and Monterrei. In the Basque Country, it is well worth trying *txakolí*, a refreshing and slightly prickly white wine.

Montesierra **Tempranillo** **Galician** **Jarrero from**
white wine **red wine** **albariño** **La Rioja**

CIDER

Sidra, or cider, has been produced in Northern Spain since medieval times. There are several varieties of cider, including *colunga*, *porico* and *panquerina*. It is usually drunk in establishments known as *sidrerías*, or *chigres*. Traditionally, a thin stream of cider is poured into the glass from a great height; masters of this art manage not to spill a single drop.

Bottles of cider

Queimada being served

QUEIMADA

Queimada is a traditional Galician drink based on *orujo* – a fiery spirit made from grapes. The alcohol is poured into a special clay pot, to which sugar, coffee beans and slices of lemon or orange are added, and the mixture is then heated up over a fire. According to tradition, witches (*meigas*) would stay well away from anyone who had been drinking *queimada*.

BEER

As a rival of wine, beer is becoming increasingly popular in Spain, even in regions where there is no beer-drinking tradition. Most Spanish beer (*cerveza*) is bottled lager, but you can also find it on draught. Popular brands include San Miguel and Mahou, and in Galicia – Estrella. To order a bottled beer in a bar, ask for *"una cerveza"*; if you want a draught beer, ask for *"una caña"*.

Galician Estrella

Choosing a Restaurant

These restaurants have been selected across a range of price categories for their exceptional food, attractive decor and interesting location. This chart lists restaurants by region, and within each town or city by price category, from the least to the most expensive. Unless stated otherwise, restaurants are open for lunch and dinner daily.

PRICE CATEGORIES
For a three-course meal for one, including a half-bottle of house wine (or equivalent), tax and service:

€ under 20 euros
€€ 20–30 euros
€€€ 30–40 euros
€€€€ over 40 euros

GALICIA

A CORUÑA Pablo Gallego
€€€€

Praza María Pita 11 bajo **Tel** *981 20 88 88*

A stone wall and warm colours dominate this restaurant's rather dark interior. The Pablo Gallego offers traditional Galician dishes including fresh, high-quality seafood such as octopus and lobster, and a selection of more than 100 wines. The restaurant is close to the city's main tourist sites.

A CORUÑA Domus
€€€€

Ángel Rebollo (Casa del Hombre) **Tel** *981 20 11 36*

The huge windows of this spacious, modern restaurant afford beautiful views of A Coruña and Bahía de Orzán. Among the excellent starters served here are baby squid with lemon froth, dorada (sea bream), bacalao, and wild grouper with stewed tomatoes and rosemary; the meat dishes are also excellent. Closed Mon and evenings (except Fri & Sat).

BAIONA Pazo de Mendoza
€€€

Elduaien 1 (Pontevedra) **Tel** *986 35 50 12*

This spacious hotel restaurant is situated on Baiona's main street in a building dating from 1768. The Galician specialities include excellent beef fillet, fine fish and seafood. The chef uses fresh local ingredients and there is also an extensive wine list.

CAMBADOS María José
€€€

Rúa San Gregorio 2–1° (Pontevedra) **Tel** *986 54 22 81*

Situated opposite the Parador de Cambados (see p202), this restaurant offers cuisine combining tradition with modernity. A popular choice is the prawn and bacon salad. There is also a good selection of albariño wines. Closed Sun evening, Mon (in low season only) and 24 Dec–mid-Jan.

LUGO España
€€€

Rúa de Teatro 10 **Tel** *982 24 27 17 or 982 22 60 16*

The España stands adjacent to Lugo's medieval city walls. Bright colours dominate the spacious and elegant interior. The menu changes every week, but you'll usually find the highly recommended game, mushroom and rice dishes. The España is a good choice when dining out with friends or in a larger group.

LUGO Mesón de Alberto
€€€€

Rúa Cruz 4 **Tel** *982 22 83 10*

An institution of Galician cooking, located in a stone house in the monumental area of town. Award-winning chef Alberto García offers a selection of traditional delicacies and more modern creations. The fish and shellfish are excellent, including small squid and sea bass with baby eels. Wide selection of Galician cheeses and wines. Closed Sun.

O GROVE El Crisol
€€€

Rúa Hospital 10–12 (Pontevedra) **Tel** *986 73 00 29*

A restaurant renowned for its traditional Galician cooking as well as creative dishes. It serves mainly fish and seafood and is a good place to discover new kinds of fish such as sargo, dentón or pinto, or sample traditional ones such as sea bass and turbot. The dining room overlooks the sea. Closed Mon lunchtime in Jul–Aug, 13–31 Jan & 13–30 Nov.

OURENSE Adega do Emilio
€€

Avenida de las Caladas 11 **Tel** *988 21 91 11*

This delightful restaurant is located in an old building close to a Romanesque bridge. Fish dishes dominate the menu, including Galician-style bacalao and hake in green sauce. For dessert, you could try the coffee-flavoured flan, aniseed cake or apple pudding with raspberry sauce and cream. Closed Mon.

OURENSE San Miguel
€€€€

San Miguel 12–14 **Tel** *988 22 07 95*

The San Miguel is one of the best restaurants in Ourense. It has been in business for more than 50 years and has won many awards and distinctions. Earthy colours dominate the decor. The innovative Galician cuisine consists of fish and seafood dishes, including bonito (tuna) in a sheep's cheese sauce.

For key to symbols *see back flap*

PADRÓN Chef Rivera
Rúa Enlace Parque 7 (A Coruña) Tel 981 81 04 13

Chef José Antonio Rivera's varied menu offers fish, seafood, game specialities and traditional Galician cooking with a French touch. Especially good are his seasonal dishes, among them lamprey, a freshwater fish from the nearby Ulla river. There is also a remarkably wide choice of port wines and cigars. Closed Sun and Mon evenings (except in Aug).

PONTEVEDRA Alameda de Doña Antonia
Soportales de la Herrería 4 Tel 986 84 72 74

This pleasant restaurant overlooks the Plaza de la Herrería – one of the loveliest squares in Pontevedra. Elaborate regional cuisine is served in a refined and beautiful setting, and there's a choice of local wines. The monkfish salad, marinated sea bass salad, oven-cooked lamb and steamed fish are among the favourites. Closed Sun and Mon evening.

PONTEVEDRA Casa Román
Avenida Augusto García Sánchez 12 Tel 986 84 35 60

A busy restaurant with fast and efficient service serving traditional cuisine prepared with the best-quality produce. It specializes in rice dishes, and in eels from the Río Miño, when in season. The menu also offers traditional Galician cuisine, including the highly recommended Rías Baixas sole in *albariño* wine, quail, game, mussels, and home-made ice cream.

SANTIAGO DE COMPOSTELA El Asesino
Praza da Universidade 16 (A Coruña) Tel 981 58 15 68

El Asesino is run by three charmingly eccentric sisters. The name of the restaurant (The Assassin) is hardly promising – it used to be a place where chickens were slaughtered, as commemorated by the image on the street sign – but it is worth visiting. Galician cuisine and grilled food are served here, all at affordable prices.

SANTIAGO DE COMPOSTELA Casa Marcelo
Rúa Hortas 1 (A Coruña) Tel 981 55 85 80

You never know what to expect at Casa Marcelo, as the chef's creations change every day. Certainly worth trying are the mussels with mango in tomato sauce, and the excellent ice cream with fruit. There is also a large choice of local wines. In summer it is pleasant to dine outside. Closed Sun–Tue.

SANTIAGO DE COMPOSTELA Toñi Vicente
Rosalía de Castro 24 (A Coruña) Tel 981 59 41 00

Worshippers of Galician *haute cuisine* flock to Toñi Vicente's culinary temple, in an elegant and pretty venue. Among her creations are the marinated sea bass salad, the duck liver sautéed with apple, the red tuna fish in pickle and the carpaccio of venison with truffle oil, salad and parmesan. Booking recommended.

SANXENXO Pepe Vieira
Praza de la Constitución 2 (Pontevedra) Tel 986 69 17 49

A small, non-smoking restaurant run by the award-winning Torres Cannas brothers, who offer creative regional cooking. The dishes, which include *pulpo en su sangre* (octopus in its own blood) or *rape en emulsión de almendras* (monkfish in almond sauce), vary with the seasons. Closed Sun–Thu dinner (winter) & Mon lunch (summer).

SANXENXO La Taberna de Rotilio
Avenida del Puerto 7–9 (Pontevedra) Tel 986 72 02 00

Located in the cellar of the Hotel Rotilio, this restaurant is famous for its innovative approach to Galician cuisine. The chef's creations include monkfish *caldeirada* and delicious fried shrimp with vegetables, which is best accompanied by local wine. Wonderful home-made pies. Closed Sun evening (except in summer).

ASTURIAS AND CANTABRIA

AVILÉS La Cofradía del Puerto
Avenida Los Telares 11 (Asturias) Tel 985 56 12 30

La Cofradía del Puerto is a typical *sidrería*, where you can sample local Asturian cider and gorge on fresh seafood and fish caught off the Cantabrian coast. For a more substantial meal, you could try the well-seasoned meats cooked over embers or *frixuelos* (crêpes typical of the region). Closed Sun.

CANGAS DE ONÍS El Molín de la Pedrera
Calle Río Güeña 2 (Asturias) Tel 985 84 91 09

The spacious interior of El Molín is decked out in wood and stone with a preponderance of earthy colours. The owners specialize in traditional cuisine made from local produce. Among the specialities are excellent cheeses, hake with almonds, and Asturian cider. There is also a large terrace.

CANGAS DE ONÍS El Cenador de los Canónigos
Avenida Contranquil (Asturias) Tel 985 84 94 45 Fax 985 84 95 66

This modern and elegant restaurant is located inside La Cepada hotel. From its vast windows extend beautiful views over Cangas de Onís and the mountains surrounding the town. Asturian cuisine is served here – the speciality is succulent cod with rice and flavourful mushrooms. Closed Sun evening, Mon and Jan.

GIJÓN Ciudadela
🍴🅿 €€€

Capua 7 (Asturias) **Tel** *985 34 77 32*

As its name suggests, this restaurant is located underneath the old citadel. It serves excellent Asturian cheeses, game, and chestnut pudding. Equally enticing are the desserts – such as apple pie with pear sorbet – and the wines from the on-site cellar. Closed Sun evening.

GIJÓN Casa Victor
🍴♿ €€€€

Carretera Carmen 11 (Asturias) **Tel** *985 34 83 10*

The Casa Victor is practically a Gijón institution. It offers cuisine based on fish caught in the Cantabrian Sea, one of the specialities being *lomón de salmonete relleno de mariscos* (red mullet with shellfish). There is also a good selection of inexpensive dishes. Closed Sun.

LAREDO Casa Felipe
🍴🅿 €€€

Avenida José Antonio 5 (Cantabria) **Tel** *942 60 32 12*

A simple little restaurant in Laredo, one of Cantabria's most popular holiday resorts. It serves simple traditional food, emphasizing good fresh fish and seafood. It also specializes in local cheeses, mainly made from cow's milk, both fresh and semi-mature. Closed Mon and 20 Dec–15 Jan.

LEÓN Bodega Regia
🍴🅿♿V €€€€

Regidores 9 (Castilla y León) **Tel** *987 21 31 73* **Fax** *987 21 30 31*

Housed inside a 14th-century building in the city centre, the Bodega Regia has managed to preserve its traditional style. The decor is dominated by wood and dark colours. Among the many dishes on offer, the roast trout and the blancmange with walnuts stand out. Closed Sun.

LLANES El Jornu
🍴🅿♿V €€

Cuetu Molín 43, Pancar (Asturias) **Tel** *985 40 16 15*

El Jornu, located very near the centre of Llanes, is one of the most popular restaurants in the region due to its exceptionally good value. You can always expect to get hearty portions and home-made desserts. There is also a well-stocked wine cellar.

LUANCO Casa Nestor
🍴 €€€€

Conde del Real Agrado 6 (Asturias) **Tel** *985 88 03 15*

This small, unpretentious restaurant serves traditional, and at times innovative, Asturian cuisine. Especially good are Casa Nestor's fresh seafood dishes and oven-baked fish dishes, which can be washed down with one of several local wines. Closed Mon.

OVIEDO Casa Conrado
🍴 €€€

Argüelles 1 (Asturias) **Tel** *985 22 39 19*

Situated just next to the cathedral, the Casa Conrado has large mirrors on its walls, which make the interior look unusually spacious, but the numerous knick-knacks and paintings create a homely atmosphere. Traditional regional dishes are served here, such as *fabada, el pote* and hake in cider sauce. There is also a well-stocked bar. Closed Sun and Aug.

OVIEDO Casa Fermín
🍴V €€€€

San Francisco 8 (Asturias) **Tel** *985 21 64 52*

The walls of this restaurant are decked out in marble, and the interior is bright thanks to the large windows. If you need help with the menu, the friendly staff will oblige. Especially good are the salmon in yoghurt sauce and vanilla oil, and the hake in cider. Closed Sun.

POSADA DE VALDEÓN Begoña
€

Calle Los Llanos 2 (Castilla y León) **Tel** *987 74 05 16*

The Begoña guest house and restaurant occupies a charming wood-and-stone mansion in the Parque Nacional de los Picos de Europa. There are two dining rooms, each differently decorated, where you can sample regional cuisine – various roast meats, including veal, and home-made desserts. Group discounts are available.

POTES Casa Cayo
🍴 €€

Cantabra 6 (Cantabria) **Tel** *942 73 01 50* **Fax** *942 73 01 19*

This family-run hotel restaurant on the town's main street was established in 1936. The spacious interior, decked out in earthy colours, is lit by large windows. Among the tasty dishes on offer are tripe and stuffed peppers, which can be accompanied by local wine.

RIBADESELLA La Parrilla
🍴V €€€

Palacio Valdés 33 (Asturias) **Tel** *985 86 02 88*

Despite its modest decor, this is a very pleasant *sidrería* – a paradise for lovers of Asturian cider and wines. There is no menu as such, but the chef prepares different dishes each day. Fresh fish is always available, however, and is priced according to its weight. Save room for a home-made dessert.

SALINAS (Áviles) Real Balneario de Salinas
🍴🅿♿V €€€€

Avenida Juan Sitges 3 (Asturias) **Tel** *985 51 86 13*

Besides wonderful food, this seaside restaurant offers beautiful panoramic views. In summer it's very pleasant to dine outside, enjoying the best of both. The Real Balneario de Salinas serves excellent fish, seafood and meat dishes. Closed Sun evenings and Mon (both in winter only).

Price categories *see p220* **For key to symbols** *see back flap*

SAN VICENTE DE LA BARQUERA Maruja

Avenida del Generalísimo (Cantabria) **Tel** *942 71 00 77* **Fax** *942 71 20 51*

This restaurant, named after the current owner's grandmother, was established in 1941, and some of its original waiters continue to work here! Diners can expect to find fish and seafood dishes, as well as a large selection of foreign and domestic wines.

SANTANDER La Bombi

Casimiro Sáinz 15 (Cantabria) **Tel** *942 21 30 28* **Fax** *942 28 14 16*

Opened in 1936, La Bombi is one of Santander's best-known restaurants, frequented by cultural luminaries whose photographs adorn the walls. The menu focuses on fish and seafood dishes, including tasty fried mussels and marinated tuna.

SANTANDER El Serbal

Calle Andrés del Río 7 (Cantabria) **Tel/Fax** *942 22 25 15*

El Serbal is the only restaurant in Santander to have earned a Michelin star. Connoisseurs come here to savour the excellent cuisine and to sample some of the 300 Spanish wines on offer. Mouth-watering meat and fish dishes, and delicious desserts. Closed Sun evening and Mon.

SANTILLANA DEL MAR La Joraca

Los Hornos 20 (Cantabria) **Tel** *942 84 01 37*

This modest, unassuming restaurant in the Colegiata hotel is always busy because the dishes it serves are made with fresh local produce. The grilled monkfish with ham and onion salad is highly recommended. During summer tables are set up for outside dining. Closed Sun evening and Mon.

SANTILLANA DEL MAR Altamira

Calle Cantón 1 (Cantabria) **Tel** *942 81 80 25* **Fax** *942 84 01 36*

This town-centre restaurant is located inside the Altamira hotel (see p206). Decorated in a rustic style, complete with a fireplace, the restaurant specializes in traditional regional cuisine and also offers a large selection of wines – foreign, Spanish and Cantabrian.

SANTOÑA La Bodeguilla de la Tasca

Marqués de Robrero at the corner with Serna Occina (Cantabria) **Tel** *942 68 10 50* **Fax** *942 66 08 48*

This small, cosy restaurant, which has been in business since 1995, serves well-presented fish (anchovy is one speciality) and seafood dishes that combine traditional and modern cuisine. Tasty *tapas* are also available. Closed Mon.

VILLAVICIOSA Casa Pipa

Pedro Pidal Arroyo 8 (Asturias) **Tel** *985 89 02 59*

The owners of this restaurant base their cuisine on the following principle: eating is a necessity, but intelligent eating is an art form. Accordingly, the elegant Casa Pipa combines tradition with modernity. Highly recommended are the blood pudding with apples, homemade croquettes, seafood and, above all, the wines. Closed Sun evening and Wed.

THE BASQUE COUNTRY

ALAIZA Señorio de Alaíza

Alaiza 1, Alaiza-Araba (Álava) **Tel** *945 31 26 28*

Housed inside an old stone building in an out-of-the-way location, this restaurant doubles as a wine and antiques museum. Its interior, decorated in earthy colours, features a beamed ceiling. The restaurant serves typical Basque dishes and, unsurprisingly, has an exceptionally large selection of wines.

AZPEITIA Kiruri

Calle Loiola Hiribidea 24 (Guipúzcoa) **Tel** *943 81 56 08*

Located in front of the Santuario de Loiola, this family-run restaurant offers simple cooking and traditional Basque dishes such as txangurro (spider crab baked and served in the shell) and menestra de verduras (vegetable stew) and a choice of pies for dessert. The car park is convenient for visiting the shrine. Closed Mon evenings & 24 Dec–7 Jan.

BILBAO Etxanobe

Avenida Abandoibarra 4 (Palacio Euskalduna) (Vizcaya) **Tel** *944 42 10 71* **Fax** *944 42 10 23*

This cosy restaurant is situated on the third floor of the Palacio Euskalduna, one of Bilbao's most modern buildings. Large windows illuminate the dining area, and colourful murals adorn one wall. Despite the fairly high prices, the Etxanobe is well worth visiting if only to sample the anchovy lasagne, or cod in liquorice sauce. Closed Sun.

BILBAO Guría

Gran Vía 66 (Vizcaya) **Tel** *944 41 57 80* **Fax** *944 41 85 64*

Situated on one of the Bilbao's showpiece streets, the Guría has been running for several decades. In the attractive wood-and-stone interior you can sample traditional Basque dishes with elements of French cuisine. A good choice is the fried hake with red peppers. There is also a large selection of local wines.

BILBAO Restaurante Guggenheim Bilbao
Avenida Abandoibarra 2 (Vizcaya) **Tel** *944 23 93 33*

Set inside the Museo Guggenheim Bilbao (see pp124–5), the city's most famous landmark, this excellent restaurant is run by Martín Berasategui. There is an outstanding *menú de degustación* (tasting menu), which can be complemented by the good wine list. Exceptionally good-value lunch menu.

BILBAO Víctor
Plaza Nueva 2 (Vizcaya) **Tel** *944 15 16 78*

The Víctor has graced the Plaza Nueva since 1940. In its spacious, pastel-coloured interior, you can sample such traditional Basque dishes as green peppers stuffed with fish, or fried sole. Devotees of modern cuisine will also find some interesting choices on the menu. Closed Sun.

GERNIKA-LUMO Boliña
Barrenkale 3, (Vizcaya) **Tel** *946 25 03 00*

Traditional Basque cuisine with a modern twist is served at the Boliña. Among the especially good dishes are the seafood dishes, especially the octopus and crayfish, whose flavour is enhanced by the small selection of local Basque wines on offer.

GERNIKA-LUMO Zallo Barrí
Juan Calzada 79 (Vizcaya) **Tel** *946 25 18 00*

The Zallo Barrí is a spacious, elegant restaurant with white tones and beautifully laid tables. It can accommodate up to 140 people. Both traditional and modern versions of Basque cuisine are served here. A real treat for the palate is the sirloin served with walnut purée and roasted onions. Closed evenings from Sun–Wed.

GETARIA Kaia Kaipe
General Arnao 4 (Vizcaya) **Tel** *943 14 05 00*

With outstanding fresh fish and seafood dishes, delicious soups and an extensive wine list, including the local Basque wine *txakoli*, this harbourside restaurant has a fine reputation. Closed Wed evening, first two weeks in Mar, and last two weeks in Oct.

HONDARRIBIA Sebastián
Mayor 11 (Guipúzcoa) **Tel** *943 64 01 67*

This restaurant occupies a 16th-century Hondarribia house whose walls are decorated with murals. Among the items worth trying on the Sebastián's menu are the lobster salad with cured ham, or baked hake with mushroom cream. Closed Sun evening, Mon, and two weeks in Nov.

HONDARRIBIA Alameda
Minasoroeta 1 (Guipúzcoa) **Tel** *943 64 27 89* **Fax** *943 64 26 63*

This restaurant has a traditional interior of stone walls and large windows overlooking the garden. The delicious fish dishes include marinated scallops with artichokes, and fish with soya beans in a sweet and sour sauce. There is also a large selection of local wines.

LASARTE Martín Berasategui
Calle Loidi 4 (Guipúzcoa) **Tel** *943 36 64 71*

One of the top restaurants of Spain is located in a converted farmhouse, 7 km (4.5 miles) from San Sebastián. The specialities change with the season but Martín Berasategui, a trendsetter among chefs, always surprises with his creations. Reservations essential, especially for terrace tables. Closed Sun evenings, Mon, Tue and mid-Dec–mid-Jan.

PASAI DONIBANE Casa Camara
Calle San Juan 29 (Guipúzcoa) **Tel** *943 52 36 99*

A restaurant with wonderful views of Pasai Donibane port (just outside San Sebastián), where you can dine watching the boats and choose your own live lobster from the tank. Try the baked mushrooms with crunchy vegetables or the Basque speciality of *txangurro al horno*. Alternatively, there are steaks. Closed Sun evenings & Mon.

SAN SEBASTIÁN La Perla
Paseo de la Concha (Guipúzcoa) **Tel** *943 45 88 56*

With its enviable location on Bahía de la Concha, this restaurant has beautiful views of the sea and the island of Santa Clara. The owners experiment with new dishes and new flavours. Especially good are the fried *bacalao* in a sweet vegetable sauce and the vanilla dessert with caramel and yoghurt. Closed Mon, and Tue and Sun evenings (Mar–Oct).

SAN SEBASTIÁN La Muralla
Embeltrán 3 (Guipúzcoa) **Tel** *943 43 35 08*

Timber elements and earthy colours dominate the decor of this large modern restaurant, which is located close to the city's main tourist attractions. Among the tasty dishes on offer are octopus and mushroom risotto. There is also a good choice of local wines. Closed Sun and Wed in winter.

SAN SEBASTIÁN Akelarre
Paseo Padre Orcolaga 56, Barrio de Igueldo (Guipúzcoa) **Tel** *943 21 40 86*

One of the famous restaurants of Spain, a gourmet temple with great views of rolling hills which plunge into the sea. The safest option, if you have room for it, is to choose one of the two seven-course *menús de degustación* (tasting menus). Spectacular desserts. Closed Sun evenings and Mon, Tue (Jan–Jun;) Feb & 1–15 Oct.

Price categories *see p220* **For key to symbols** *see back flap*

SAN SEBASTIÁN Arzak
Av Alcalde José Elósegui 273 (Guipúzcoa) **Tel** *943 27 84 65*

Celebrity chef Juan Mari Arzak has earned a reputation beyond Spain for his perfectly presented, creative dishes. His daughter Elena works here as well. They even run a "laboratory" where a team of cooks experiment with new tastes and textures. Closed Sun evening and Mon, and Tue (Jan–Jun), 18 Jun–5 Jul, and Nov.

SAN SEBASTIÁN Rekondo
Paseo de Igueldo 57 (Guipúzcoa) **Tel** *943 21 29 07*

In a fine location on the flank of Monte Igueldo, this wonderful restaurant was opened in 1964 by Txomin Rekondo, and continues to be run by him and his daughters. It features an enormous wine list and classic Basque cuisine, such as artichokes with fresh páte or squid in their own ink. Closed last twqo week in June and first three weeks in Nov.

TOLOSA Frontón
San Francisco 4 (Guipúzcoa) **Tel** *943 65 29 41*

The Frontón serves simple, traditional food, such as tomato salad with goat's cheese and ham, bonito filet in black olive oil, and succulent veal. There is seating outside in summer. Closed Sun evening (winter), Sun and Mon evening (summer), 15–23 Aug and during the Christmas period.

VITORIA Marmitaco
Avenida Judizmendi 4 (Álava) **Tel** *945 12 03 84*

Marmitaco is a good place to sample good-quality cooking at reasonable prices. There are excellent rice and vegetable dishes, a variety of well prepared fish dishes, and fresh, tasty salads. Marmitaco also has a good wine list. Closed Tue.

VITORIA El Portalón
Correría 151 (Álava) **Tel** *945 14 42 01*

El Portalón occupies a 15th-century carriage house close to Vitoria's main historic sites. Timber elements and antique furniture dominate the decor of the six dining areas. The house speciality is stuffed quail. The restaurant has a very well-stocked wine cellar. There is also a contemporary art museum here.

ZARAUTZ Karlos Arguiñano
Mendilauta 13 (Guipúzcoa) **Tel** *943 13 00 00* **Fax** *943 13 34 50*

This town-centre restaurant is run by Karlos Arguiñano, a celebrated television chef. Its windows look out over Zarautz's beautiful sandy beach. The establishment features very tasteful rustic-style decoration and the well-stocked bar has a large terrace with additional seating for guests. Closed Wed and Sun evening.

NAVARRA AND LA RIOJA

BURGOS El 24 de la Paloma
Calle La Paloma 24 (Castilla y León) **Tel** *947 20 86 08*

This modest but stylishly decorated restaurant stands on one of the city's main streets, just next to the cathedral. It serves fish, seafood and meat dishes. The menu changes with the seasons, to ensure only the freshest ingredients are used. Closed Sun evening.

BURGOS Casa Ojeda
Calle Vitoria 5 – Plaza de la Libertad (Castilla y León) **Tel** *947 20 90 52*

This spacious city-centre restaurant occupies a building dating from 1912. The timber elements in the decoration add to the cosy, elegant atmosphere. Traditional Castilian cuisine, including excellent roast lamb, partridge salad, and *sopa castellana*, dominates the menu.

BURGOS Fábula
Calle de La Puebla 18 (Castilla y León) **Tel** *947 26 30 92*

This agreeable restaurant is situated in the city's historic quarter. It offers creative dishes, such as monkfish on sesame bread with a confit of green apple and onion, or flower-petal salad with a honey vinaigrette. Closed Sun evening, and Mon last two weeks in Jan and last two weeks in Sep.

ESTELLA Navarra
Calle Gustavo de Maeztu 16 (Navarra) **Tel** *948 55 00 40*

The Navarra is situated inside a grand house, with tiles depicting Navarra's former kings. It serves traditional regional cuisine, including asparagus and veal dishes. For dessert, the *blanca de Navarra* (lemon and honey ice cream served with fresh cream and nuts) is superb. Navarra is a no-smoking restaurant. Closed Sun evenings and Mon.

EZCARAY El Rincón del Vino
Calle Jesús Nazareno 2 (La Rioja) **Tel** *941 35 43 75*

Vino also has a shop selling local wines and other delicacies typical of the Rioja region. They serve traditional Riojan cuisine with an emphasis on seasonal produce including vegetables, mushrooms and truffles. During the hunting season, it offers good game dishes. Closed Mon–Thu evenings in winter & Wed except in Jun & Aug.

HARO Terete

Calle Lucrecia Arana 17 (La Rioja) **Tel** *941 31 00 23*

An ancient wood-burning oven has been roasting lamb here since 1877. Sit at the long wooden tables and savour the Riojan specialities, accompanied by a bottle of house wine. You can start with asparagus, and end the meal with traditional *cujada* that is served with walnuts and honey. Closed Sun evenings, Mon, 1–15 Jul & 15–31 Oct.

LOGROÑO El Cachetero

Calle Laurel 3 (La Rioja) **Tel** *941 22 84 63*

El Cachetero, established in the early 20th century, is the best restaurant in Logroño, with prices to match. It has an elegant cosy interior, where guests can choose from a large selection of dishes, including vegetable stews and peppers stuffed with a variety of fillings.

LOGROÑO Mesón Egües

Campa 3 (La Rioja) **Tel** *941 22 86 03*

This rustic-style restaurant, decorated in warm colour schemes, is very popular, so you are advised to book in advance. Excellent roasts and grilled food, superbly seasoned meats and well-prepared fish dishes are served here. There is also an enticing selection of desserts. Closed Sun.

OLITE Casa Zenito

Rúa Mayor 16 (Navarra) **Tel** *948 74 00 02*

The Casa Zenito is probably the best choice for those wishing to sample traditional Navarrese cuisine with a modern flourish. Tasty dishes such as fried artichoke salad with seafood can be rounded off with an excellent dessert, one of the favourites being apple pie with vanilla cream and cinnamon ice cream. Closed Mon and Tue in winter.

PAMPLONA Don Pablo

Navas de Tolosa 19 (Navarra) **Tel** *948 22 52 99*

The interior of this elegant restaurant, arranged in dark colours, is magnified by mirrors hung on the walls. On the menu are well-designed dishes as well as *pintxos* that have won several awards at the Pintxos Week in Pamplona. Other good options are the ravioli with snails and the sole stuffed with vegetables and pine nuts. Closed Sun and Tue evening.

PAMPLONA Enekorri

Tudela 14 (Navarra) **Tel** *948 23 25 47*

The Enekorri bases its meals on high-quality produce. Its specialities include artichoke salad with octopus and chopped parsley, fish with fruit, vegetables, nuts and almonds, as well as tasty desserts. Good vegetarian meals are served too. Closed Sun, Easter, and the second two weeks in Aug.

PAMPLONA Europa

Espoz y Mina 11 (Navarra) **Tel** *948 22 18 00*

This cosy hotel restaurant in the old centre of Pamplona serves typical Navarrese cuisine. The chef recommends chestnut soup and chateaubriand with mango. Connoisseurs of fish will not be disappointed either. For dessert, try the chocolate mousse with orange preserve or ice cream.

PAMPLONA Rodero

Emilio Arrieta 3 (Navarra) **Tel** *948 22 80 35*

The spacious and elegant interior of the Rodero – considered to be the best restaurant in Navarra – provides the perfect setting for the veritable feast that awaits guests. Among the sophisticated and highly original dishes served here are white and green asparagus with pistachios and shellfish, sweet paella, and fish with parmesan gnocchi.

PUENTE LA REINA Mesón del Peregrino

Irunbidea, Ctra N111 Pamplona-Logroño km 23 (Navarra) **Tel** *948 34 00 75*

This roadside restaurant is situated on the pilgrimage route to Santiago de Compostela. The chef imaginatively combines his own creations with elements of Mediterranean and Navarrese cuisine; pork with apple cream is the Mesón del Peregrino's signature dish.

SANTO DOMINGO DE LA CALZADA El Rincón de Emilio

Plaza Bonifacio Gil 7 (La Rioja) **Tel** *941 34 27 60*

This classic restaurant offers both traditional and modern cuisine from the La Rioja region. The favourite dishes include well-prepared fish, such as cod, and sirloin steak in a red wine sauce. A good dessert option is rice pudding with caramel ice cream or the warm chocolate cake.

TUDELA Restaurante 33

Calle Capuchinos 7 (Navarra) **Tel** *948 82 76 06*

A busy restaurant in the largest town of the Ribera region, where the menu reflects the local skill of growing vegetables. Try the *menú degustación de verduras*, a tasting menu consisting of several vegetable dishes, each one cooked in a different way. Closed Mon & Tue evenings, and first 3 weeks in Aug.

VIANA Borgia

Calle Serapio Urra (Navarra) **Tel** *948 64 57 81*

Situated in the historic centre of Viana, this small restaurant is open only at lunchtimes (except on Fridays and Saturdays, when it is open all day). It is named after Cesare Borgia, one of the town's most famous former inhabitants. The menu offers eclectic, light cuisine. Worth trying are the asparagus and the roast lamb in gin sauce.

Price categories *see p220* **For key to symbols** *see back flap*

CENTRAL AND EASTERN PYRENEES

AÍNSA Bodegón de Mallacan

Plaza Mayor 6 (Huesca) Tel 974 50 09 77

This restaurant occupies a beautiful 12th-century arcaded building on the town's main square. With its stone walls, wooden ceilings, and wooden tables placed alongside the walls, the interior resembles a medieval refectory. Classic cuisine is served here, including dishes of asparagus, *bacalao* (cod), game, mushroom and roast meat.

AÍNSA Bodega de Sobrarbe

Plaza Mayor 2 (Huesca) Tel 974 50 02 37

Get a taste of medieval history in the vaulted wine cellar of this 11th-century house, which is situated on the cobbled square of Aínsa, the medieval capital of the kingdom of Sobrarbe. Typical Pyrenean dishes and excellent chocolate desserts are served here.

AÍNSA Callizo

Plaza Mayor (Huesca) Tel 974 50 03 85

Situated on the town's main square, the Callizo serves local wines, Aragonese cheeses and well prepared and tasty regional dishes, including excellent *bacalao* with honey, currants, pine nuts and spinach leaves, as well as delicious game ragoût. Closed Sun evening and Mon (except in summer).

ANDORRA LA VELLA Borda Estevet

Carretera de la Comella 2 Tel (00) 376 86 40 26

This old country stable is still used for the traditional practice of drying tobacco from the nearby fields. The restaurant serves Pyrenean cuisine. Highly recommended are the delicate veal and beef dishes. The meat may be served on a hot slate, so that guests can cook it to their liking. Weather permitting, guests can sit outside.

BARBASTRO Flor

Calle Goya 3 (Huesca) Tel 974 31 10 56 Fax 974 31 13 18

This spacious restaurant in the town centre has a main dining room and several smaller salons. It specializes in Aragonese cuisine and meat dishes – various types of ham, sausage and blood pudding as well as excellent chicken dishes are served. There is also a good selection of wines from the on-site cellar.

BENASQUE El Fogaril

Avenida Los Tilos (Huesca) Tel 974 55 16 12

This spacious hotel restaurant, with rustic-style decoration and large windows, serves traditional Aragonese cuisine. Especially good are the game dishes with forest fruits, a large variety of pâtés (foie gras), and a wide range of regional dishes. The desserts include a delicate pineapple sorbet. Excellent local wines are also offered.

BERGA Sala

Passeig de la Pau 27 (Barcelona) Tel 938 21 11 85

The Sala prepares remarkably innovative and delicious food, but guests looking for local specialities won't be disappointed either. For a starter, try the marinated wild mushrooms. Tender game is available in season. The menu changes according to the season. Closed Sun evening and Mon.

HUESCA Las Torres

Calle María Auxiliadora 3 Tel 974 22 82 13

The owners of this stylish modern restaurant pay great attention to detail, with well-presented.dishes. Las Torres is one of very few restaurants in Northern Spain serving proper vegetarian food, including excellent asparagus and aubergine dishes. The local wines are a perfect accompaniment to the fish and meat specialities also served here. Closed Sun.

HUESCA Lillas Pastia

Plaza de Navarra 4 Tel 974 21 16 91

The Lillas Pastia has a different menu for each season, but the emphasis is always on well-prepared and flavourful Aragonese cuisine – meat and fish served in honey, as well as delicious desserts such as coconut with strawberries and rose petals. Closed Sun and Mon evening.

JACA Lilium

Avenida Primer Viernes de Mayo 8 (Huesca) Tel 974 35 53 56

Spread over three floors, this restaurant features avant-garde decor. The menu offers an array of meat, fish and seafood dishes. The Lilium's speciality is goat's cheese salad with a honey vinaigrette. There is also a good selection of local wines.

JACA La Cocina Aragonesa

Paseo de la Constitución 3 (Huesca) Tel 974 36 10 50

One of the attractions of this restaurant is the large glass-encased terrace, which affords beautiful views over the gardens. Aside from the main dining room, featuring stone walls and a fireplace, are a few smaller eating areas. Well worth trying are the cheese and egg-yolk salad served with mushroom sauce as well as the duck with red onions.

SHOPPING IN NORTHERN SPAIN

Spain has a thriving shopping culture, with many unique, family-run boutiques as well as a few reliable chain stores and big department stores. Staff are usually friendly and patient, and there is a vast selection of goods on offer. In the main shopping areas you'll find designer boutiques with high-end merchandise, though many offer seasonal discounts. Spanish shoes and clothes are elegant

Bobbin lace, popular in Galicia

and, compared to France or Italy, are good value for money. Food products, especially fish and seafood, are best bought at markets, where the quality is higher than in shops. Cider and wine are popular purchases with visitors to Northern Spain. Also popular are religious souvenirs connected with the pilgrimage route of St James, as well as local crafts including wicker baskets, hand-made lace and clogs.

A wide array of nuts for sale

OPENING HOURS

Supermarkets, hypermarkets and department stores are usually open from 10am to 9pm (also on Saturdays), and in larger cities they are sometimes open even longer.

Most small shops in Northern Spain open Monday to Saturday from 10am to 8 or 9pm, but they close for a long lunch break from 2 to 4:30 or 5pm. Service-related shops such as dry cleaners usually open an hour earlier and close an hour later. Bakeries open at 7:30 or 8am.

Traditionally, the only shops open on Sundays and holidays have been bakeries, *pastelerías* and newsstands, and most other small shops still close on Sundays, except in the run-up to Christmas. However, larger stores are allowed to open on at least a few Sundays each month, and a growing number of shops are open in resort towns.

PAYMENT METHODS

Cash is quicker to use for small purchases, and may be preferred in some small

shops. Credit cards are widely accepted, but cheques are not.

VAT

Value added tax (VAT), known as *IVA* in Spanish, is included in the price of nearly everything in Spain. Look for the words *IVA incluido* or *con IVA* (VAT included) and *sin IVA* (VAT not included) to see if tax is included on your hotel or restaurant bill.

Rates vary, depending on the type of purchase. For some basic items, such as children's clothes, it's 4%. For most services, including restaurant and hotel bills, it's 7%. For everything else, including most clothing and luxury and gift items, it's 16%.

Non-EU residents are eligible for a VAT refund if purchases exceed 90.15 euros worth of goods. These do not have to be one-off purchases.

For example, during your stay in Northern Spain you can collect receipts for purchases made from the same shop and then ask the sales assistant for one tax-free invoice at the end, detailing your transactions. You'll need to show your passport to receive a form. You must have the VAT refund form stamped at a Spanish customs office. Present the stamped form at a Spanish bank for a same-day refund, or mail it for the refund to be credited to your credit card.

SALES

Spain's twice-annual *rebajas* (sales) are a fantastic opportunity to find good deals on everything from shoes and clothes to linens, electronics and household goods. Some stores offer a reduction of 50% or more.

The first *rebajas* of the year begin on 7 January (the day after Epiphany) and continue

Colourful stalls on the promenade in Oviedo

until mid-February. Summer *rebajas* start in early July and continue until early August. Although January and August are the traditional sales periods, many shops now also have sales at other times of the year, offering goods at very attractive prices.

In large department stores, discounted goods are usually found on the top floor and less frequently in the basement.

LARGE STORES & SUPERMARKETS

Spain's leading department store is El Corte Inglés, with its characteristic triangular green, black and white logo. This mega-store, with a branch

A fruit and vegetable market in Santiago de Compostela

in every major city, sells internationally recognized brands of shoes, clothing, sports goods, furniture, accessories and cosmetics. There is usually also a well-stocked electronic goods department, selling everything from CDs, DVDs, televisions and audio devices to cameras. Various customer services, such as hairdressers and travel agents, can be found in every El Corte Inglés store. In the basement there is usually a large self-service grocery store – Hipercor.

Alcampo and Carrefour sell everything from groceries to clothing to household goods and appliances, are usually located out of town, and so are accessible only by car. FNAC stores have a wide range of music.

Entrance to a shop selling wine and liqueurs

SHOPPING ARCADES & MALLS

Spanish shopping arcades are elegant, brightly lit and tastefully designed; their displays change on a regular basis. The arcades are usually filled with designer boutiques, and the choice is truly vast. Although items are usually on the expensive side, you can often find goods at reduced prices as well as seasonal discounts in summer and winter.

Aside from clothes and shoe shops, every arcade has cafés, bars and restaurants, where you can enjoy a welcome break after a burst of shopping.

American-style malls, called *centros comerciales* in Spain, are gaining popularity and can be found on the outskirts of most large cities.

A local woven wicker basket

MARKETS

Every large town in Northern Spain has a daily food market, where you can buy bread, cheese, fruit, vegetables, meat, sausage, fish, seafood, as well as *frutos secos* (a variety of nuts, almonds and dried fruits) and honey. The smaller towns have designated market days, where stalls are set up, often on the town square. Most markets have a few cafés where you can grab a quick coffee or a snack. It's best to visit markets in the mornings, from 8am to 1pm. Most close around 2 to 3pm, and even if

they re-open after 4pm, many stalls remain shut. The earlier you arrive, the better chance you'll have of picking up the freshest, cheapest, and most attractive products.

Northern Spain has a strong crafts heritage, and the best places to buy authentic items are the artisan markets. The items on sale include basketware and leather goods – reasonably priced shoes, wallets and accessories. In Galicia you will find the popular bobbin lace and pottery, in La Rioja the region's famous wine, in Asturias clogs, and in the Pyrenees a range of wood products.

Bookstalls are also popular, selling cheap second-hand books. It's worth taking a look, as you can sometimes find rare books at bargain prices.

A range of goods outside the entrance to a souvenir shop

What to Buy in Northern Spain

Whether it's Basque berets or Galician pottery, each region of Northern Spain has its own unique handicrafts and souvenirs for sale, making shopping an enjoyable experience. Every town has a selection of souvenir shops and markets selling craft products and delicious foodstuffs. Especially popular are handmade goods such as wooden clogs, wicker baskets and Galician bobbin lace, as well as items connected with the pilgrimage route of St James. The region produces delicious wines and other alcoholic beverages – La Rioja wines, Galician *orujo* and *queimada*, and Asturian cider, are all good choices for gifts to take home.

Souvenirs in an antique shop in Santillana del Mar

SOUVENIRS OF THE PILGRIMAGE ROUTE OF ST JAMES

Northern Spain, and Galicia in particular, is strongly associated with the pilgrimage route to Santiago de Compostela, along which thousands of pilgrims travel each year. Religious artifacts, such as figures and paintings of St James, miniature models of Santiago Cathedral, and scallop shells, are available.

Scallop Shell
This white shell is a symbol of the route of St James — pilgrims would use these shells as spoons or cups.

A figure of St James
Figures of St James in various poses – sitting, standing, usually with a staff in hand – can be bought in practically every place along the pilgrimage route.

Pilgrim's Walking Stick
Wooden walking sticks and gourds for water were once indispensable items carried by every pilgrim. They are now popular souvenirs.

REGIONAL SOUVENIRS

Every region has its own typical souvenirs. Especially popular are ceramic plates decorated with images of important regional buildings. In Galicia, you can buy ceramic figures and utensils, as well as *azabache* – jet – jewellery. The Basque Country is famous for its berets and figures of the patron saints of Basque towns, while in Asturias you can buy tiny granaries and figures of the Virgen de Covadonga.

Dancing Basque
Dressed in a characteristic white outfit, with a red sash around his waist, the Dancing Basque is a popular purchase.

Basque Beret
Typical black berets (txapela or boina de Tolosa) are often adorned with the emblems of football clubs or the Basque national flag.

Tower of Hercules
A blue-and-white ceramic Tower of Hercules, a symbol of A Coruña, is a typical souvenir. In many towns you can buy ceramic miniatures of famous buildings.

Cantabrian candle holder, with windable wick

Ceramic plate from Santillana del Mar

CRAFTS

Every region has its own unique hand-made products. Galicia is famous for its bobbin lace; the Pyrenees region for its wooden spoons; and in Asturias you can buy clogs (*almadreñas* or *madrenyes*) with three heels – one at the front and two at the back – made from a single piece of willow or chestnut wood.

Wicker Baskets
Hand-woven wicker baskets, bread trays and wicker furniture can be bought all over Northern Spain.

Asturian clog

Bobbin Lace
Galician lace is called encaixes de Camariñas. *The designs were originally brought to Galicia from Flanders and were used at the royal court.*

POTTERY

Northern Spain is renowned for its beautiful pottery. Aside from ceramic figures and *olas* (typical earthenware containers, produced in three sizes), souvenir shops sell ceramic reproductions of bas-reliefs from Spanish churches.

Ceramic piggy bank

Bas-relief reproduction of The Last Supper

Vases from Buño
Beautiful earthenware containers are produced in many places in Galicia. Those from Buño are simple in form and are painted brown, blue and white.

FOOD

Natural produce reigns supreme at Spanish markets. In Galicia you can buy mixed-blossom honey and *pimientos de Padrón* (small spicy peppers), while markets in the Basque Country offer a magnificent variety of seafood and dried fish.

Cheeses
Northern Spain is known for its cheeses. In Cantabria you'll find Cabrales and Picón; in Galicia the mild Tetilla and San Simón; and in the Basque Country Idiazábal.

Jar of Galician honey

SPIRITS AND LIQUEURS

La Rioja and Navarra wines make good gifts. Galician *orujo* (grape spirit) and *queimada* pots (for mixing *orujo* with coffee) are also popular buys, while Asturias is famous for cider. Vessels for storing alcohol – such as wine-skins – are widely available.

A bottle of Viña Costeira

A bottle of white wine

A bottle of red wine

Wine-skin

Vessel for serving *queimada*

ENTERTAINMENT IN NORTHERN SPAIN

At the forefront of Northern Spain's diverse cultural life are the vibrant fiestas. Each town stages celebrations to honour its patron saint. Some events are small-scale and local in character; others, such as the *Los Sanfermines* festival in Pamplona, attract great crowds.

In summer there are festivals of jazz, film, theatre and folklore; many enjoy international status.

Figure of witch at a fiesta

All religious holidays are celebrated with great pomp and ceremony – Easter Week festivities include colourful processions, while at Corpus Christi the streets of towns and cities are carpeted with intricate designs made from brightly coloured flower petals. There is also a full calendar of entertainment options, from theatre and cinema to sport.

The magnificent lobby of the Teatro Arriaga in Bilbao

THEATRE, BALLET AND CONCERTS

One of the most beautiful theatre buildings is the eclectic **Teatro Arriaga** in Bilbao. Here you can see productions from around the world, as well as ballet performances and concerts. Bilbao is also home to the modern **Palacio Euskalduna**, where concerts, ballet, theatre and conventions are held. The **Kursaal**, a major music, dance and theatre venue, is located in San Sebastián

Oviedo's showpiece is the historic **Teatro Campoamor**, which was established in 1892. Top Spanish and foreign productions are staged here, as are classical music concerts and ballet productions.

The best-known theatre in Galicia is the **Teatro Rosalía de Castro** in A Coruña. In Asturias, the cultural hub of Gijón is the **Teatro Jovellanos**. This late 19th-century building hosts drama productions and symphony concerts, as well as rock and pop concerts. It is also the setting of the International Film Festival of Gijón.

CINEMA

Northern Spain has several reveting film festivals and is the home of some of the biggest names in Spanish cinema.

The great film director Carlos Saura was born in Huesca and Bilbao is the home of director Álex de la Iglesia; Imanol Uribe lived here, too.

Every September, the acclaimed **Festival Internacional de Cine de San Sebastián** takes place in the Basque city of San Sebastián. Stars of the silver screen converge on the **Kursaal arts centre** to attend the festival.

Other regions of Northern Spain also host important events.

The **Independent Film Festival** takes place in Ourense, and Spanish-American films are shown at the **Festival de Cine de Huesca**. In Gijón, films from around the world can be seen at the **Festival Internacional de Cine de Gijón**.

Towns and cities in Northern Spain have both small arts cinemas and large multiplexes. The leading major cinemas belong to the Yelmocineplex network – **Ocimax** in Gijón, **Yelmocineplex** in Lugo, and **IMAX Yelmocineplex** in Oviedo.

Foreign films are usually shown dubbed into Spanish or sometimes a local language, but an increasing number of cinemas, especially in cities, show films in their original language – most often English – with subtitles. This is indicated by the letters VO (for *versión original*) on cinema advertising and newspaper listings.

NIGHTLIFE

Spain's prodigious nightlife starts later than in most other countries, with 11pm

Classic cars during the Santiago pilgrimage

The exciting August regatta on the Sella river

considered an early start for most revellers. At weekends, in particular, the towns and cities of Northern Spain are buzzing with life late into the night. Social activities and entertainment are concentrated in the bars and clubs located primarily on the cities' main streets and squares – the Old Town in Bilbao, in Cañadío, the city center of Santander, along the Calle Mon in the university town of Oviedo, the old town of San Sebastián, which is known for bar-hopping, and at Orzán beach in A Coruña.

SPORT

Football is practically a religion for many Spanish men, and the top clubs attract thousands of spectators. The chief stadiums in the north, home to the first-division clubs, are Anoeta in San Sebastián (Real Sociedad club), **Estadio de Fútbol de San Mamés** in Bilbao (Athletic Bilbao), El Sadar in Pamplona (Osasuna), El Sardinero in Santander (Racing de Santander), **Estadio Municipal del Riazor** in A Coruña (Deportivo) and Balaídos in Vigo (Celta Vigo). Other popular spectator sports are cycling, tennis and Basque sports, such as *pelota*.

FIESTAS

Regardless of when you visit Northern Spain, you're bound to encounter some local festivities. The Spanish love fiestas, of which there are several kinds: religious, folkloric, or held in honour of a patron saint or commemorating a particular event. Every town celebrates the feast day of its patron saint by staging a colourful fiesta, comprising bands, parades, fireworks and other attractions.

Religious holidays are celebrated on a grand scale, with processions, fairs and other commemorative events taking place. The biggest fiesta in Galicia is held on St James's day (25 July), while in Asturias the main event is *La Santina* procession in Covadonga (8 September).

The most important religious holiday is Easter. During Easter Week, city streets throughout the region are filled with processions of monks carrying platforms bearing figures of saints and Passion scenes

Visitors in the glass tunnel in San Sebastián's aquarium

DIRECTORY

THEATRE, BALLET AND CONCERTS

Kursaal
Avda. De Zurriola 1
20002 San Sebastián
Tel 943 00 30 00
www.kursaal.org

Palacio Euskalduna
Abandoibarra 4, Bilbao
Tel 944 03 50 00
www.euskalduna.net

Teatro Arriaga
Plaza Arriaga 1, Bilbao
Tel 944 79 20 36
www.teatroarriaga.com

Teatro Campoamor
Calle Pelayo, Oviedo
Tel 985 20 75 90

Teatro Jovellanos
Calle Casimiro Velasco 23
33201 Gijón
Tel 985 18 29 29
www.teatrojovellanos.com

Teatro Rosalía de Castro
Rúa Riego de Agua 37
15001 A Coruña
Tel 981 18 43 49

FESTIVALS

Festival de Cine de Huesca
Avenida Parque 1, 2nd floor
22002 Huesca
Tel 974 21 25 82
www.huesca-filmfesival.com

Festival Internacional de Cine de Gijón
Alvarez Garaya 2
33201 Gijón
Tel 985 18 29 40
www.gijonfilmfestival.com

Festival Internacional de Cine de San Sebastián
P.O. Box 397

20080 San Sebastián
Tel 943 48 12 12
www.sansebastianfestival.com

International Independent Film Festival
Calle Isabel la Católica 1
32005 Ourense
Tel 988 22 41 27
www.ourencine.com

CINEMA

Ocimax Gijón
Maestro Amado Morán
33212 Gijón
Tel 985 30 81 36

IMAX Yelmocineplex
Calle Fernandez Ladreda
33010 Oviedo
Tel 985 11 99 01
www.imax-yelmocineplex.com

Kursaal
see Theatre, Ballet and Concerts (left)

Yelmocineplex Lugo
Plaza Viana do Castelo
27003 Lugo
Tel 982 21 79 86

SPORT

Estadio de Fútbol de San Mamés
Calle Luis Briñas
48013 Bilbao
Tel 944 24 08 77
www.athletic-club.net

Estadio Municipal de Riazor
Calle Manuel Murguía
15011 A Coruña
Tel 981 22 94 10

SPORTS AND OUTDOOR ACTIVITIES

Thanks to its diverse geography and temperate climate, Northern Spain is an ideal destination for outdoor enthusiasts. The Atlantic coast offers excellent opportunities for water sports, especially windsurfing, while inland, rafting and canoeing trips are organized along fast-flowing highland rivers. In the Pyrenees, spanning

A yachting club logo

Navarra, Aragón, Andorra and Catalonia, outdoor activities are possible all year round. Hiking and climbing are popular in summer, while in winter skiers can take advantage of the numerous well-maintained pistes. Northern Spain's verdant landscapes can also be explored on horseback or by bicycle, thanks to an extensive network of trails.

A trail through the Parc Natural d'Aigüestortes in the Pyrenees

WALKING AND TREKKING

The most accessible form of leisure activity in Northern Spain is walking, particularly mountain-walking. Its increasing popularity is due largely to the preponderance of well-marked trails, good accommodation and excellent guides. There are scenic trails throughout the mountains of Northern Spain, particularly in the Pyrenees, as well as in the Cantabrian Mountains, from the Ancares range on the border of Galicia, León and Asturias, through the Picos de Europa in the northern reaches of the Iberian Mountains.

The principal network of marked trails includes Major Trails (*Grandes Rutas* or *GR*, marked by red-and-white signs) and Minor Trails (*Pequeñas Rutas* or *PR*, marked by white-and-yellow signs). One of the most famous trails is GR 1, also known as the 'Historical

Trail', which starts at the ruins of Empúries, on the Mediterranean coast near Girona, and proceeds to Cabo Fisterra (Cape Finisterre) in Galicia, via the Pyrenees, the Basque Country, the northern part of Burgos province and the pilgrims' Road to Santiago. The GR 1 reflects the philosophy behind the planning of hiking trails in Spain, which is based on linking active leisure with culture and sightseeing. This philosophy is visible, too, in the GR 12 Euskal Herria (Basque Country) trail, which incorporates the most important places associated with Basque culture. Another trail well worth taking is the GR 11 (Pyrenean Trail), which goes from Hondarribia, through Elizondo, Roncesvalles, Ochagavía and Isaba in Navarra, the Ordesa valley, Andorra and Puigcerdà to Cap de Creus in Catalonia.

AERIAL SPORTS

The best way to take in Northern Spain's landscape is to view it from above, and this part of the country provides an excellent environment for aerial sports enthusiasts. For those who have forever been fascinated by birds' ability to fly, paragliding and hang-gliding are two excellent options. Paragliding is especially popular on account of the beautiful mountain scenery.

The **Real Federación Aeronáutico Española** will send information about Spanish airfields and clubs where visitors can practise flying, gliding and parachuting. The organization also provides information on the best locations for ballooning, hang-gliding and paragliding.

A foreign private pilot's licence is valid in Spain for a maximum of six months.

Paragliding above the Vall d'Aran in the eastern Pyrenees

Surfers in the Basque resort of Mundaka

WATER SPORTS

The Atlantic coast is great for both sunbathing and water sports, including windsurfing. In Galicia, windsurfers head for Pantin beach; in Asturias, the beaches in Salinas are popular; the Basque Country is home to the best surfing spots, such as the towns of Mundaka and Zarautz.

Many more beaches offer kitesurfing and bodyboarding all year round; kayaks and catamarans are also available. Sailing is popular, too, and you can rent a sailboat by the day or week, or sign up for a half- or full-day sailing excursion. Tourist offices at the coastal resorts provide information about local hire of boats and sailboards. Sailing information is also provided by the **Real Federación Española de Vela**.

The Galician coast is also excellent for snorkelling. A wonderful experience can be had exploring old shipwrecks on the ocean floor.

Speciality centres offer canoeing and white-water rafting in the mountains of Northern Spain. In Galicia, such centres can be found in the upper reaches of the Miño and Ulloa rivers; in Asturias on the Sella river; and in Cantabria on the Ebro and Asón. Pyrenean rivers, such as the Ara, Esera and Gállego, offer some of the best rafting.

NATURISM

Naturism is legal in Spain and is popular among local people and visitors alike. Specially designed nudist, or naturist beaches, are not hard to find. The beautiful beaches of the Atlantic coast, often concealed by bays, offer an ideal environment for nudists. The website of the **Federación Española de Naturismo** has descriptions of nudist beaches in various regions of Northern Spain and provides information on their location and facilities.

HUNTING AND FISHING

The Atlantic coast, as well as the hundreds of mountain streams, rivers and reservoirs, provide an attractive environment for fishing, particularly fly-fishing. The most common species caught are brown and rainbow trout, sea trout, and Atlantic salmon. In Galicia, the best fishing spots are located in the Eume, Tambre and Miño river basins. In Asturias, fishing is popular on the Sella, Narcea and Esva rivers. The Saja river basin is the best fishing ground in Cantabria. In the Basque Country, anglers head for Bayas and Zadorra, while in La Rioja, the Iregua river is considered to be the top spot.

In the Catalonian Pyrenees, the Noguera and Alto Segre rivers are excellent for fishing.

Each region of Northern Spain has its own strict fishing regu-lations. All the fishing grounds (for instance, the so-called "catch and release" grounds) are clearly marked. Permits for river or sea fishing from one day to one year, and for fishing competitions, are issued by the *comunidades* (regional governments). The

Fishing – a popular activity in the rivers of Northern Spain

Federación Española de Pesca gives information on licences, locations where fishing is permitted and the dates of open seasons. Fishing centres and many hotels in fishing areas will advise on permits, and will often obtain one for you.

If you want to hunt or shoot in Spain you must be licensed and insured. To obtain a licence you apply to the *comunidad* of the area where you want to hunt. Information about hunting and shooting is provided by the **Real Federación Española de Caza**.

Canoeists playing water football

A ski resort in Andorra

WINTER SPORTS

Spain's mountainous terrain makes it an excellent place for skiing, and resorts here are often cheaper than those in the Alps or other places in Europe. There are numerous winter resorts in Northern Spain, particularly in the Pyrenees. Especially popular is the huge ski resort of **Baqueira-Beret**, one of the largest in Spain. Skiers have at their disposal 72 pistes and more than 30 ski lifts, which ascend to between 1,520 m (4,987 ft) and 2,470 m (8,104 ft) above sea level. After a hard day's skiing, you can relax in nearby Arties' thermal springs.

Other popular Pyrenean resorts include Candanchú and Panticosa, in Huesca province, and Masella, in the province of Girona. There are also good resorts in the Cantabrian Mountains, such as **Manzaneda** in Galicia, San Isidro and Leitariegos in León, and **Alto Campoo** in Asturias. Here, skiers can enjoy several well-maintained and often picturesque runs, of varying length and difficulty. Andorra is another big destination for skiing and winter sports.

In recent years, an increasing number of people have been donning their snowshoes to explore the snow-covered mountainsides and valleys on foot.

Aside from snowboarding, downhill and cross-country skiing, Pyrenean spas offer numerous other attractions to keep visitors entertained. Most of the resorts have swimming pools, ice rinks, and a choice of restaurants, bars and nightclubs.

Every region of Northern Spain has its own winter sports association. The **Federación Española de Deportes de Montaña y Escalada** can

supply details about mountain sports and mountain conditions. Ski resorts themselves usually have good websites with up-to-date information.

CYCLING AND HORSE RIDING

Cycling and horse riding are both very popular activities in Northern Spain. The coastal areas, mountain valleys and picturesque inland trails provide terrain that is ideally suited to horse riding.

It is fairly easy to hire a horse, and many tour operators now specialize in equestrian holidays. The **Real Federación Hípica Española** can provide additional information on horse riding and pony trekking.

Information about cycle routes is provided by the **Real Federación Española de Ciclismo**. Bicycles can be

The La Toja golf course on an island in Galicia

rented in almost every town in Northern Spain. The whole region can be toured on any number of picturesque minor roads or special Vías Verdes routes *(see box)*.

GOLF AND TENNIS

The success of golfers such as Ballesteros, Olazábal, Jiménez and Sergio García is thanks in no small part to the excellent standard of Spanish golf courses. The number of golf courses is steadily increasing, too. From Galicia to northern Catalonia, visitors will find golf courses to suit all types

---

VÍAS VERDES

The Vías Verdes (Green Routes) programme was established in 1993 and enjoys huge popularity among both visitors and Spaniards alike. Its aim is to adapt old, disused railway lines so that they can be used for walking, cycling and horse riding. Many of the converted railway lines are also wheelchair-friendly. The picturesque routes

Cyclists on the Vía Verde del Río Oja route in La Rioja

lead through hills and lush meadows, passing historic towns and ancient monasteries. Among the best routes in Northern Spain are the Vía Verde del Plazaola in Navarra (40 km/25 miles) and the Vía Verde del Río Oja in La Rioja (28 km/ 17 miles).

of player – beginners, big hitters, technical masters. The majority of courses are 9-hole, but 18-hole ones are not uncommon. Apart from their purely sport-related qualities, golf courses in Northern Spain are also often set in beautiful landscapes. In this regard, the leading courses are in Galicia – the Ría de Vigo in the province of Pontevedra and La Toja in an island spa. A remarkable combination of sea and mountains can be found in Asturias and Cantabria; here, the best courses are La Rasa de Berbes in Ribadesella, La Cuesta in Llanes, Santa Marina in San Vicente de la Barquera (designed by Severiano Ballesteros) and Pedreña near Santander. In the province of Álava, the excellent Álava Izki Golf course in Urturi was also designed by Ballesteros.

Many admire Navarra's Zuasti course in Zuasti de Iza, designed by José María Olazábal, while in Catalonia the Aravell Golf Andorra is not to be missed. Most golf courses have their own websites where you can learn more about course specifications and the rules of various clubs. Information is also pro-

Ponies for hire – especially appealing to children

vided by the **Real Federación Española de Golf** or by www.golfspain.com

Tennis is also a popular sport. In most tourist areas there are tennis courts for hire. The local tourist information office can advise on the nearest court. Many travel agents arrange tennis holidays for enthusiasts. For more information, contact the **Real Federación Española de Tenis**.

OUTDOOR ACTIVITIES FOR CHILDREN

Northern Spain has many facilities that cater for children, and children can accompany their parents on outdoor holidays. Many beaches have special play areas with slides and paddling pools. Rental shops offer children's bicycles as well as bicycles with special chairs for carrying children. Stables often have ponies as well as horses for hire.

Skiing holidays are also suitable for children. All ski resorts have ski schools for children, with various events and competitions.

An excellent time can be had at aquariums, where children and parents alike can admire the Atlantic's many colourful species of fish.

DIRECTORY

AERIAL SPORTS

Real Federación Aeronáutica Española
Carretera de la Fortuna
28044 Madrid.
Tel 915 08 29 50.
www.rfae.org

WATER SPORTS

Real Federación Española de Vela
Luis de Salazar 9
28002 Madrid.
Tel 915 19 50 08.
www.rfev.es

NATURISM

Federación Española de Naturismo
www.naturismo.org

HUNTING AND FISHING

Federación Española de Pesca
Navas de Tolosa 3
28013 Madrid.
Tel 91 532 83 52.
www.fepyc.es

Real Federación Española de Caza
Calle Zurbano 76, 7
28010 Madrid.
Tel 913 95 04 60.
www.fedecaza.com

WINTER SPORTS

Alto Campoo
Zona Valle Campoo 39200
39200 Reinosa (Cantabria).
Tel 942 77 92 22 (pistes).
Tel 942 75 52 15 (info).
www.altocampoo.com

Baqueira-Beret
Tel 973 63 90 10.
Fax 973 64 44 88.
www.baqueira.es

Manzaneda
Estación de Manzaneda
32780 Puebla de Trives.
www.manzaneda.com

Federación Española de Deportes de Montaña y Escalada
Floridablanca 84
08015 Barcelona.
Tel 93 426 42 67.
www.fedme.es

CYCLING AND HORSE RIDING

Real Federación Hípica Española
Calle Menorca 3
28009 Madrid.
Tel 914 36 42 00
www.rfhe.com

Real Federación Española de Ciclismo
Ferraz 16, 28008 Madrid.
Tel 915 40 08 41.
www.rfec.com

Vías Verdes
www.viasverdes.com

GOLF AND TENNIS

Real Federación Española de Golf
Calle Provisional Arroyo del Fresno Dos 5
28035 Madrid.
Tel 91 555 26 82.
www.golfspainfederacion.com

Real Federación Española de Tenis
Avenida Diagonal 618, 2 B
08021 Barcelona.
Tel 93 200 53 55.
www.rfet.es

SURVIVAL GUIDE

PRACTICAL INFORMATION

Northern Spain has a solid tourist infrastructure, beyond the attractions of its coastline, bullfights and flamenco. Each of its regions has its own tourist information service, and there are tourist information offices in every city, and local offices in many smaller towns, especially on the coast. All offer help with finding accommodation, restaurants and activities in their area. In the last few years,

A weary pilgrim

the Spanish tourist authorities have intensively promoted "Green Spain" – the regions of Galicia, Asturias, Cantabria and the Basque Country that border the Cantabrian Sea. The Spanish themselves come here for their holidays to escape the busy and overcrowded south. August is Spain's main holiday month. Many businesses close for the month, and roads are busy at the beginning and end of this period.

A bilingual parking sign in Basque and Castilian

LANGUAGE

The main language of Spain is *castellano* (Castilian), which is spoken by almost everyone. In addition, there are three main regional languages: *gallego* (Galician), which is spoken in Galicia, *euskera* (Basque), spoken in the Basque Country and part of Navarra, and *catalá* (Catalan), spoken in Catalonia.

Galician, Basque and Catalan are not dialects of Castilian. They are wholly independent languages, and the Galicians, Basques and Catalans are very sensitive on this issue.

Visitors with a knowledge of Spanish or Portuguese will not have any difficulty understanding Galician. Knowledge of Spanish or French is useful for understanding Catalan. Workers who speak English are often employed in places that deal with tourists.

WHEN TO VISIT

The best time to visit Northern Spain depends on what you plan to do here. If your aim is a beach holiday on the Atlantic coast, then July and August are the best months. May, June and September are all good months to explore the historic sites of Northern Spain in relative peace and quiet. Galicia, Asturias, Cantabria and the Basque Country all have higher rainfall than other regions of Spain. Summer in Northern Spain is warm without being oppressively hot. Temperatures rarely exceed 30°C (86°F).

VISAS AND PASSPORTS

Visas are not required for citizens of EU countries, Switzerland, Norway or Iceland. A list of

entry requirements, which is available from Spanish embassies, specifies 35 other countries, including New Zealand, Canada, the USA and Australia, whose nationals do not need to apply for a visa if visiting Spain for less than 90 days. Thereafter they may apply to the *Gobierno Civil* (a local government office) for an extension. You need proof of employment or of sufficient funds to support yourself during a long stay. Visitors from other countries must obtain a visa before travelling.

If you know in advance that you will be staying longer than 90 days, you should

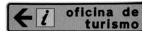

A Spanish tourist information office sign

apply to your nearest Spanish embassy for a visa. The process of issuing a visa can take from one to four months.

TAX-FREE GOODS

Non-EU residents can reclaim VAT (value-added tax) on purchases worth over 90.15 euros *(see p228)*. At certain airports, such as in Oviedo and Santander, you can get a cash refund on the spot.

TOURIST INFORMATION

All major towns and cities have a tourist information office *(oficina de turismo)*, which will provide you with

A café in Pamplona

◁ **Fishing boats in San Vicente de la Barquera**

Tourists on a sunny street in San Sebastián

maps, lists of hotels and restaurants, and information about the locality.

OPENING HOURS

Most museums, galleries and monuments close on Mondays. On other days they generally open from 10am to 2pm and from 5 to 8pm, although in some cases they are open all day. Admission is charged for most museums and monuments, as well as some cathedrals and churches. Admission for many museums is free on Sundays.

SPANISH TIME

In winter, Spain is one hour ahead of Greenwich Mean Time (GMT) and in summer one hour ahead of British Summer Time (BST), ie GMT + 2. Spain uses the 24-hour clock, so 1pm = 13:00.

FACILITIES FOR THE DISABLED

Spain's National Association for the Disabled, COCEMFE (*Confederación Coordinadora Estatal de Minusválidos Físicos de España*), publishes guides to facilities in Spain and will help plan a holiday to suit individual requirements. **Viajes 2000** travel agency specializes in holidays for disabled people (*see p199*).

In the UK, two organizations – Radar (www.radar.org.uk)

and Holiday Care Service (www.holidaycare.org.uk) – offer information on facilities for the disabled in Spain.

STUDENT INFORMATION

Holders of the International Student Identity Card (ISIC) are entitled to benefits, such as discounts on travel and reduced entrance fees to museums and galleries.

In Spain, you can obtain additional information from youth information centres (Centros de Información Juvenil – CIJ) in large towns (www.madrid.org/infojven).

The Viajes Educativos travel agency (TIVE) specializes in travel for students (www.madrid.org).

TRAVELLING WITH CHILDREN

Spain is a child-friendly country for the most part, and it's usual for children to accompany parents wherever they go. In the evenings, it's not uncommon to see children with their families in restaurants, even at midnight. By law, children travelling in a car must always sit on the back seat and wear a seatbelt; babies and small children should be secured in approved children's car seats. Nowadays, many airports, stations and restaurants have washing and nappy-changing facilities.

A disabled-access sign

WEIGHTS, MEASURES AND ELECTRICITY

Spain uses the metric system for weights and measures, including distances marked on road signs.

The electricity supply in Spain is 220 volts, but the 125-volt system still operates in some old buildings (usually only in the provinces). Plugs have two round pins. A three-tier standard travel converter enables you to use appliances from abroad on both supplies. Heating appliances should be used only on 220 volts.

DIRECTORY

EMBASSIES

United Kingdom
Paseo Recoletos 7 & 9, 28004 Madrid. *Tel* 91 524 97 00.
www.ukinspain.com

United States
C/ de Serrano 75, 28006 Madrid. *Tel* 91 587 22 00. www.embusa.es

SPANISH TOURIST OFFICES

Aragón
Tel 902 47 70 00.
www.turismodearagon.com

Asturias
Tel 902 30 02 02.
www.infoasturias.com

Basque Country
Tel 945 01 97 03.
www.euskaditurismo.net

Cantabria
Tel 901 11 11 12.
www.turismodecantabria.com

Catalonia
www.gencat.net/turistex_nou

Galicia
Tel 902 200 432.
www.turgalicia.es

La Rioja
Tel 941 29 12 60.
www.lariojaaturismo.com

Navarra
Tel 848 42 04 20.
www.turismo.navarra.es

in the United Kingdom
Tel 020 7486 8077 (London).
www.tourspain.co.uk

in the United States
Tel (212) 265 8822 (New York).
www.okspain.org

Personal Security and Health

In Spain, as in most European countries, rural areas are generally safe, but certain parts of cities are subject to petty crime. Carry cards and money in a belt and never leave anything visible in your car when you park it. Taking out medical insurance cover is advisable, but for minor health problems pharmacists are a good source of assistance. Northern Spain is well supplied with pharmacies, which are easy to find with their green neon signs. Emergency phone numbers vary – the most important ones are on the opposite page. If you lose your documents, contact your consulate or the local police.

The colourful window display of a pharmacy

IN AN EMERGENCY

Only the *Policía Nacional* operates a nationwide emergency phone number – **091**. Call it even if you need some other service, and they will assist you in getting help.

For emergency medical treatment, call the *Cruz Roja* (Red Cross), look under *Ambulancias* in the phone book, or go to the hospital casualty department (*Urgencias*).

MEDICAL TREATMENT

All EU nationals are entitled to Spanish social security cover. To claim, you must obtain the European Health Insurance Card from the UK Department of Health or from a post office before you travel. You give this card to anyone who treats you and it comes with a booklet, *Health Advice for Travellers*, which explains exactly what health care you are entitled to and where and how to claim. You may have to pay for treatment up front, and reclaim the money later.

Not all treatments are covered by the card and some are costly, so it is worth arranging separate medical insurance to cover the cost of, for instance, medication, home visits by a doctor, repatriation or an extended hospital stay. Visitors coming to Spain from non-EU countries should arrange cover through a private insurance company.

PHARMACIES

Spanish pharmacists (*farmacéuticos*) are well trained and have wide responsibilities. They can advise and, in some cases, prescribe medication without consulting a doctor. In a non-emergency a pharmacist is a good person to see first. It is easy to find one who speaks English.

The *farmacia* sign is a green illuminated cross. The addresses and telephone numbers of pharmacies open at night are listed in the windows of all the local pharmacies. Very basic medication, such as aspirin and painkillers, can be bought at a chemist (*droguería*). Do not confuse pharmacies with *perfumerías*, which sell toiletries only.

PERSONAL SECURITY

Violent crime is rare in Spain but visitors should avoid walking alone in poorly lit areas. Men occasionally make complimentary remarks (*piropos*) to women in public, particularly in the street. This is an old custom and not intended to be intimidating.

To protect yourself against theft, be sure to keep your credit cards, money and documents well hidden and close to your body. Wear a bag or camera strap across your body, not on your shoulder.

When visiting a café, restaurant or bar, keep your handbag on your knees – never leave it on the tabletop or the chair opposite.

A Spanish pharmacy sign

POLICE

There are three types of police in Spain. The Guardia Civil (national guard) are in charge of policing rural areas, and their responsibilities

Guardia Civil   **Policía Nacional**   **Policía Local**

A patrol car of the Policía Nacional, Spain's main urban police force

A patrol car of the Policía Local, mainly seen in small towns

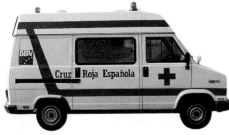

A Cruz Roja (Red Cross) ambulance

A fire engine with the emergency number painted on its side

include enforcing traffic restrictions on main highways.

The Policía Nacional (national police) are the main force charged with dealing with crime in towns of over 30,000 people. In addition, in two of Northern Spain's autonomous regions, many of the duties of the Policía Nacional and the Guardia Civil have now been taken over by regional forces, the red-uniformed Ertzainta in the Basque Country and the blue-uniformed Mossos d'Esquadra in Catalonia.

Local police forces (Policía Local, Policía Municipal or Guardia Urbana or Guardia Local), operate in each town,

with their own structure and uniforms. They are responsible for dealing with parking and associated town by-laws.

In the event of an incident, any of the three police services will either help or direct you to the relevant authority that deals with your problem.

PERSONAL PROPERTY

Before travelling to Spain it is worth arranging holiday insurance to protect you from the loss or theft of property. The moment you discover a loss or theft, report it to the local police station and obtain a report. To claim on insurance, you must act within 24 hours.

It's better and safer to pay by card, where possible, than to carry large amounts of cash.

PUBLIC CONVENIENCES

Public pay-toilets are rare in Spain. Department stores are often good places to find a toilet, as are petrol stations, cafés, bars and restaurants. Most cafés and restaurants will allow you to use their toilet (ask for *los aseos* or *los servicios*). Sometimes toilets are kept locked, in which case you should ask for the key *(la llave)*.

DIRECTORY

EMERGENCY NUMBERS

Emergency: all services
Tel 112 (toll-free).

Policía Nacional
Tel 091 (nationwide).

Fire Brigade (Bomberos)
Tel 080 (in all large cities).

Ambulance (Cruz Roja)
Tel 902 22 22 92.

HOSPITALS

Hospital Santa Teresa
Calle Londres 2, A Coruña (Galicia)
Tel 981 21 98 00, 902 32 22 33.

Hospital Nicolás Peña
Avenida de Las Camelias 109
Vigo (Galicia).
Tel 986 21 90 00.

Hospital Central de Asturias
Calle Celestino Villamil, Oviedo
(Asturias). *Tel* 985 10 80 00.

Clínica La Esperanza
Calle de La Esperanza 3
01002 Vitoria (Basque Country)
Tel 945 25 25 00.

Policlínica Guipúzcoa
Paseo Miramón 174
San Sebastián (Basque Country)
Tel 943 00 28 00.

Clínica Universitaria de Navarra
Avenida Pío XII 36
Pamplona (Navarra)
Tel 948 25 54 00.

Complejo Hospitalario San Millán-San Pedro
Autonomía de la Rioja 3
Logroño (La Rioja)
Tel 941 29 75 00.

Banking and Local Currency

The official currency of Spain is the euro. You may enter Spain with any amount of money, but if you intend to export more than 6,000 euros, you should declare it. Travellers' cheques may be exchanged at banks, *cajas de cambio* (foreign currency exchanges) as well as in some hotels and shops. Banks generally offer the most favourable exchange rates. The cheapest rates may be offered on your credit and debit card, which you can use in cash dispensers (ATMs), which are open 24 hours, but check before you travel on the charges made by your card provider for cash withdrawals.

A 24-hour cash dispenser

BANKING HOURS

Hours vary between Spanish banks, but most are open Monday to Friday from 8:30am to 1pm. In cities and larger towns, they may open at 8am and close at 2pm. A few banks open on summer Saturday mornings, but not the rest of the year.

CHANGING MONEY

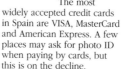

An ATM logo

Money can be exchanged in a bank *(banco)* or savings bank *(caja de ahorro)*. Most banks have a foreign exchange desk with the sign *Cambio* or *Extranjero*. Always take your passport as ID to effect any transaction.

In the tourist areas of Spanish towns and cities you'll find bureaux de change *(casas de cambio)*, which stay open later than banks. The exchange rates they offer can vary considerably, so it's best to shop around.

Some department stores, such as El Corte Inglés, have their own bureaux de change

that have the same opening hours as the store.

Avoid changing money in hotels, as they almost always levy heavier fees or have poorer rates than banks.

CHEQUES AND CARDS

Travellers' cheques in euros can be purchased at **American Express**, **Thomas Cook**, or your own bank before starting your trip. When cashing a cheque at a bank, you will need to show your passport or another form of photographic ID. The most widely accepted credit cards in Spain are VISA, MasterCard and American Express. A few places may ask for photo ID when paying by cards, but this is on the decline.

CASH DISPENSERS

If your card is linked to your home bank account, you can use it with your PIN to withdraw money from cash dispensers. Nearly all take VISA or MasterCard (Access);

cards with Cirrus and Maestro logos are also widely accepted throughout Spain.

When you enter your PIN, instructions are displayed in English, French, German and Spanish. Many ATMs are located inside buildings, and to gain access you will have to run your card through a door-entry system. This type of cash dispenser is the safest to use, especially at night or in crowded places.

DIRECTORY

BANKS

Banco de Galicia
www.bancogalicia.es
Tel 902 30 10 00.

Banco Santander
Tel 902 24 24 24.
www.gruposantander.es

Caixa Galicia
Tel 902 12 13 14.
www.caixgalicia.es

Kutxa
Tel 901 11 14 11.
www.kutxa.es

LOST CARDS AND TRAVELLERS' CHEQUES

American Express
Pl de Las Cortes 2, 28014 Madrid
Tel 902 37 56 37.

Diners Club
Tel 902 40 11 12.

MasterCard
Tel 900 97 12 31 (toll-free).

VISA
Tel 900 99 11 24 (toll-free).

The entrance to a branch of the Banco Pastor

THE EURO

Spain is among the 13 (out of 25) member states of the European Union that chose to join the euro. The new currency was introduced on 1 January 1999, but initially only for banking purposes.

Notes and coins came into circulation on 1 January 2002. After a transition period allowing for the use of both national currencies and the euro alongside each other, Spain's own currency, the *peseta*, was completely phased out on 28 February 2002.

All euro notes and coins can be used anywhere within the 13 participating member states: Austria, Belgium, Finland, France, Germany, Greece, Ireland, Italy, Luxembourg, The Netherlands, Portugal, Slovenia and Spain.

Bank Notes

Euro bank notes have seven denominations. The 5-euro note (grey) is the smallest, followed by the 10-euro note (pink), 20-euro note (blue), 50-euro note (orange), 100-euro note (green), 200-euro note (yellow) and 500-euro note (purple). All notes show the 12 stars of the European Union.

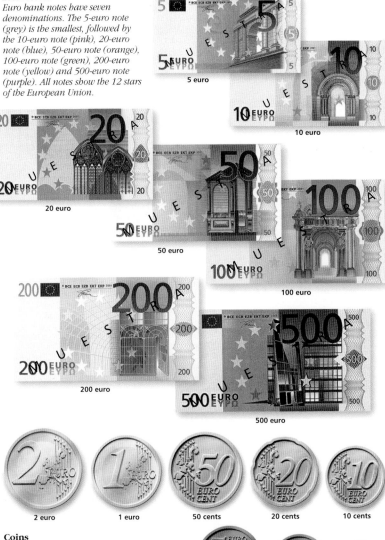

5 euro

10 euro

20 euro

50 euro

100 euro

200 euro

500 euro

Coins

The euro has eight coin denominations: 2 euros and 1 euro (silver and gold); 50 cents, 20 cents and 10 cents (gold); and 5 cents, 2 cents and 1 cent (bronze). The reverse side of euro coins is the same in all euro-zone countries, but the front varies by country.

2 euro   1 euro   50 cents   20 cents   10 cents

5 cents

2 cents

1 cent

Communications

Telefónica, the Spanish telecommunications company, has improved its service since it was digitized in 1995, and the state monopoly was removed in 1998. Public telephones are easy to find and most operate with cards *(tarjetas telefónicas)* instead of coins today, but international calls have a high charge.

The postal service (Correos) is identified by a crown insignia in red or white on a yellow background. Registered post and telegrams can be sent from all post offices. They sell stamps as well, but most people buy them from state-run tobacconists *(estancos)*. There are no public phones in Correos offices.

Public payphone booths, with their characteristic blue tops

USING A COIN AND CARD TELEPHONE

1 Lift the receiver, and wait for the dialling tone and for the display to show *Inserte monedas o tarjeta*.

2 Insert either coins *(monedas)* or a card *(tarjeta)*.

3 Key in the number firmly, but not too fast – pause between each digit.

4 As you press the digits, the number you are dialling will appear on the display. You will also be able to see how much money or how many units are left. The display will indicate when you need to deposit more coins.

5 When your call is finished, replace the receiver. The phone card will then re-emerge automatically or any excess coins will be returned.

A Spanish phonecard

TELEPHONING IN SPAIN

Public payphones accept phonecards *(tarjetas telefónicas)*, which can be bought from tobacconists *(estancos)* and from some newsstands. Aside from public telephone boxes *(cabinas telefónicas)*, there are nearly always payphones in bars, which accept coins, though their connection charge is high. Payphones can be found in the reception areas of guest houses, hostels and hotels, but it's best to avoid making telephone calls direct from your hotel room, as the hotel usually adds a surprisingly high surcharge.

There are also public telephone offices *(locutorios)*, where you can phone to anywhere in the world and pay for the call afterwards.

There are four charge bands for international calls. The cheapest calls are to numbers within the European Union; slightly more expensive are calls to non-EU countries and

USEFUL SPANISH DIALLING CODES

- Within Spain, you must always dial the area code; a list of area codes can be found in the A–K phone directory.
- Numbers beginning with 900 are toll-free, with 902 are inexpensive information lines, and with 906 are the most expensive lines. Those beginning with 6 are mobiles (cell).
- To make a call to Andorra, dial 00 376 followed by the full number (omit initial 0).
- To make an international call from Spain, dial 00, then the country code, area code (omitting the initial 0) and phone number.
- Country codes are: Spain (34), UK 44,

Eire 353; France 33; USA and Canada 1; Australia 61; New Zealand 64; South Africa 27.
- To make a collect (reverse-charge) call within Spain dial 1009.
- To make an international call dial 1005.
- Spanish directory enquiries – 11818.
- International directory enquiries – 11825.
- Speaking clock – 093.
- Weather information – 807 17 03 65.
- Road conditions – 900 12 35 05.
- Wake-up calls – 096.
- To report a technical fault, dial 1002.

North Africa, followed by calls to North and South America; the most expensive calls are to the rest of the world.

UK and Irish mobiles will work in Spain if they have a roaming facility, but check on current charges on foreign calls with your service provider, as they can be high. US and Canadian cell phones will only work in Europe if they have a multiband facility.

POSTAL SERVICE

Correos, the Spanish postal service, has a network of more than 6,000 post offices. There are often post offices at railway stations and airports. Most post offices also have telegram and fax facilities.

Although you can buy stamps in Correos offices, it is quicker and easier to buy them in an *estanco* (tobacconist).

The Spanish postal service is not the fastest in the world, so urgent post should be sent by express *(urgente)* or registered *(certificado)* mail. Main post offices open Monday to Friday from 8am to 8pm and on Saturday from 8am to 7pm. Branches in the suburbs and small towns and villages open 9am to 2pm Monday to Friday and 9am to 1pm Saturday.

If you want to receive post while you are in Spain, *poste restante* letters should be addressed care of the *Lista de Correos* in the relevant town. You can collect them from main post offices.

LETTERS AND PARCELS

Letters posted at a central post office usually arrive quicker than if posted in a postbox *(buzón)*. Spanish postboxes are painted bright yellow; in larger towns and cities there are separate slots for local *(ciudad)* and other destinatioins *(otros destinos)*.

To send money by post, ask for a *giro internacional*

Spanish daily papers

Spanish magazines

(for abroad) or a *giro nacional* (when sending within Spain).

INTERNET

The Internet is extremely popular in Spain, and you will find Internet cafés *(cibercafés)* in every town, where you can check your e-mail. They are usually open from 10am till late (often until 2 or 3am, especially in summer). The charges for using the Internet vary from a few cents to 1–1.50 euros per hour.

An ornate Spanish postbox

TELEVISION AND RADIO

Televisión Española, Spain's state television company, broadcasts on two national channels, TVE and TVE 2. Almost all *comunidades* (cultural groups) have their own television channels (for instance, TVG – Televisión Gallega – in Galicia, and ETB – Euskal Telebista – in the Basque Country), which broadcast in the language of the region. There are also five national independent television stations: Antena 3, Cuatro, Tele-5, La Sexta and Canal+. Most foreign films shown on Spanish television (and in cinemas) are dubbed but films

A yellow postbox

are sometimes shown in their original language with Spanish subtitles, indicated by VO *(versión original)* in newspaper listings.

The state radio company, Radio Nacional de España, has four stations. The various *comunidades* also have their own radio stations, which broadcast in the language of the region (Radio Galega, for instance, broadcasts in Galician). There are hundreds of private radio stations, too.

NEWSPAPERS AND MAGAZINES

Spanish national dailies *(periódicos)*, such as *El País*, *ABC* or *El Mundo*, are of a high standard.

As well as the national press, the various *comunidades* have their own local newspapers. Some of these are entirely written in regional languages (for instance, *Berria* – a Basque newspaper), while other local papers have non-Spanish sections (such as *La Voz de Galicia)*.

Newspapers usually cost 1 euro. Weekend newspapers that have colour supplements are more expensive, costing from 2 to 2.50 euros.

Newsagents and kiosks in town centres often stock periodicals in English. Many foreign newspapers, such as the *International Herald Tribune, Financial Times* and *Guardian*, as well as German, French and Italian newspapers, are widely available in Spain.

TRAVEL INFORMATION

Spain has an increasingly efficient transport system. All the major cities have airports, and many international flights arrive at Madrid and Barcelona. One third of visitors to Spain arrive by air. Aside from scheduled flights, and charter flights in summer, budget airlines fly to many Spanish cities throughout the year. Within Spain, too, especially when travelling long distances, flights are the

The logo of Iberia, Spain's national airline

best option – comfortable, fast, and increasingly cheap. Both the road and rail networks were greatly improved during the 1980s and 90s. Intercity rail services are efficient, but coaches are a faster and more frequent option between smaller towns. In much of rural Spain, however, public transport is limited and a car is the most practical solution for getting about. Ferries connect mainland Spain with the UK.

ARRIVING BY AIR

Spain is served by most international airlines. Iberia, the national airline, has scheduled flights daily into Madrid and Barcelona from all western European capitals, and once or twice weekly from most east European capitals.

All the major European airlines (Alitalia, Air Europa, Air France, British Airways, CSA, Iberia, KLM, LOT, Lufthansa, Malev, Spanair and Swiss) fly direct to Madrid and Barcelona, Spain's two main international airports. British Airways offers scheduled flights to Madrid and Barcelona daily from London Heathrow and London Gatwick; and Madrid from Manchester, and Barcelona from Birmingham. Low-cost airlines run many additional services. Easyjet has direct flights from London Stansted to Bilbao and Oviedo (Asturias), Ryanair flies from London Stansted, Frankfurt and

Rome to Santander, Santiago de Compostela, Valladolid, Vitoria and Zaragoza, while Air Berlin and Hapag-Lloyd Express have connections from Germany's major cities to Santiago de Compostela and Bilbao. In recent years, competition among the budget airlines has forced all carriers to lower their prices, allowing passengers more choice.

Of the US airlines serving Spain, Delta Air Lines flies to both Madrid and Barcelona, and American Airlines flies to Madrid. Iberia has a comprehensive service from the USA, as well as an indirect service from Canada.

INTERNATIONAL AIRPORTS

Most international services operate from Madrid and Barcelona. Barajas airport in Madrid, serving 42 million passengers each year, is located 12km (8 miles) from

the city centre, which can be reached by metro or the shuttle bus service leaving every 12 minutes. A taxi from the airport to the city centre costs around 20–25 euros.

Terminal 1 operates some international flights (British Midland Airways, Delta and easyJet, among many others); Terminal 2 operates domestic flights; Terminal 3 is for Lagun Air (with flights to León); and the new Terminal 4, designed by British architect Richard Rogers, operates most international and some domestic flights (including Iberia, American Airlines, British Airways and Virgin Express). Terminal 4 is a long way from the others, but a free shuttle bus runs between it and the Metro station next to Terminals 1 and 2. Allow an extra 30 minutes if you are travelling by public transport to Terminal 4.

Barcelona's El Prat international airport is located 12km (7.5 miles) from the city centre, to which train services run every 30 minutes and buses every 15 minutes. Terminal A deals with all international arrivals and departing flights on foreign airlines, while terminals B and C operate departures on Spanish airlines and arrivals from EU countries.

Altogether Spain has 47 airports. Of those located in the north, the following have the status of international airports: Oviedo (Asturias), Bilbao, A Coruña, Pamplona, San Sebastián, Santander, Vigo

Bilbao's modern international airport

A Brittany Ferries service from Plymouth to Santander

DIRECTORY

Info on Spanish airports
Tel 902 404 704. www.aena.es

AIRPORTS IN NORTHERN SPAIN

A Coruña
Tel 981 18 73 15.

Asturias
Tel 985 12 75 00.

Bilbao
Tel 944 86 96 64.

Pamplona
Tel 948 16 87 00.

Santander
Tel 942 20 21 00.

San Sebastián
Tel 943 66 85 00.

Santiago de Compostela
Tel 981 54 75 01.

Vigo
Tel 986 26 82 00.

Vitoria
Tel 945 16 35 91.

SPANISH AIRLINES

Air Europa
Tel 902 40 15 01.
www.aireuropa.com

Iberia
Tel 902 40 05 00.
www.iberia.com

Spanair
Tel 902 13 14 15.
www.spanair.com

FERRIES

P&O FERRIES
Calle Cosme Etxebarrieta 1
48009 Bilbao. **Tel** 944 23 44 77,
0870 598 0333 (UK).
www.poferries.com

Brittany Ferries
Estación Marítima, 39002 Santander
Tel 942 21 45 00.
Tel 942 36 06 11 (Spain).
Tel 0870 536 0360 (UK).
www.brittany-ferries.com

FERRY TICKET RESERVATIONS

www.brittanyferries.com
www.aferry.co.uk
www.directferries.co.uk
www.poferries.com

and Vitoria. However, most international flights go through Madrid or Barcelona. The biggest international airport in Northern Spain is Bilbao, which has direct flights to several major European cities.

There are also domestic airports in León and Logroño. Iberia flies from Madrid and Barcelona to Oviedo (Asturias), Bilbao, A Coruña, Logroño, León, Pamplona, San Sebastián, Santiago de Compostela, Vigo and Vitoria. **Spanair** has flights from Madrid and Barcelona to Asturias, Bilbao, Vigo, Santander and Santiago de Compostela. Low-cost Spanish airline Vueling flies daily between Madrid and Santiago de Compostela.

Air Europa has regular flights to Oviedo (Asturias), Bilbao, Santiago de Compostela, Vigo, Valladolid and Zaragoza. Domestic flight times vary from 50 minutes (Madrid-Bilbao) to 90 minutes (Barcelona-A Coruña).

AIR FARES

The price of air tickets to Spain depends on the time of year, whether the trip includes a weekend, and how far in advance the booking is made. The prices fluctuate according to demand. Air fares are typically highest during the summer months. Special deals, particularly for weekend city breaks, are often offered in the winter and may include a number of nights at a hotel.

Generally, the earlier you book, the cheaper your fare. The lowest fares are available

A self-ticketing machine

only when you book direct with the airline via its website. Look out for **Iberia**'s reduced air fares, and check easyJet and Ryanair for competitive deals. Christmas and Easter flights are often booked up well in advance.

Charter flights from the UK are sometimes available. These can be very cheap, but less flexible, and often fly at inconvenient times. Make sure your agent is ABTA bonded before booking. Local car hire companies may offer good deals at resort airports, but read rental terms carefully.

FERRIES

The British company **P&O Ferries** sails regularly between Portsmouth and Bilbao in the Basque Country. The *Pride of Bilbao* ferry leaves two to three times weekly from Santurce (Santurtzi) harbour and offers passengers a luxurious journey lasting 30 hours. The return crossing from the UK to the Basque Country is longer by three hours.

Brittany Ferries has regular connections between Plymouth and Santander in Cantabria. The *Pont-Aven* ferry leaves two to three times weekly, the crossing lasting 18 hours. Tickets are best purchased in advance, on the Internet if possible. It is wise to book early if you plan to travel in summer or around big public holidays.

Ferries are equipped with cabins, restaurants, cafés, casinos, cinemas, disco and gym, beauty parlours and other facilities for passengers.

Travelling by Train

Logo of the Spanish state railways

The Spanish state railway, RENFE *(Red Nacional de Ferrocarriles Españoles)*, operates a service that is continually improving, particularly between cities. The fastest intercity service is operated by TALGO – with high-speed, luxury trains. *Intercity* trains, between major destinations, are quick and comfortable. *Largo recorrido* (long-distance) and *regionales y cercanías* (regional and local) trains operate slower services, many stopping at every station, but they are much cheaper than the high-speed trains.

ARRIVING BY TRAIN

There are several direct train services from France to Northern Spain. The main western route runs from Paris through Hendaye in the Pyrenees to San Sebastián. The eastern route from Paris runs via Cerbère and Port Bou to Barcelona. The trains from London, Amsterdam, Brussels, Geneva, Zurich and Milan all reach Barcelona via Cerbère. There is also a direct rail connection between Lisbon and Madrid.

EXPLORING BY TRAIN

Spain offers many options for train travellers, and the TALGO services make it possible to travel the long distances betwen the main cities quickly. These luxury trains run at speeds of up to 200 km/h (124 mph). Journeys are comfortable, with a high level of service. Ticket prices compare favourably with the cost of high-speed train fares in other European countries. Long-distance trains *(largo recorrido)* are significantly cheaper. Those that run at night offer a *cochecama* (a compartment with two *camas* or beds) or a *litera*, a compartment with six seats that convert into bunk beds.

The logo of FEVE regional railways

In both cases you reserve these when booking your ticket, and you will need to pay a supplement. Tickets for overnight trains should be booked well in advance.

Regional trains *(regionales)* and local trains *(cercanías)* are frequent and cheap. Their main drawback is that they stop at almost every station, which lengthens journey time.

Train tickets can be bought on the **RENFE** website and from station ticket offices and ticket machines.

Most RENFE lines converge on Madrid, so if you want to get from one part of Northern Spain to another (such as the Basque Country to Galicia),

you have to head inland and change trains. A faster option is to take the FEVE *(see Regional Railways, opposite)*.

DIRECTORY

REGIONAL RAILWAYS

ET
Tel 902 54 32 10.
www.euskotren.es

FEVE
Tel 902 10 08 18. **www**.feve.es

FGC
Tel 932 05 15 15. **www**.fgc.es

TICKET RESERVATIONS

RENFE
Tel 902 24 02 02, 902 24 34 02 (international tickets).
www.renfe.es

MAIN TRAIN STATIONS

A Coruña
Calle Joaquín Planelles Riera.

Bilbao
Estación de Abando, Plaza Circular 2.

Burgos
Avda. Conde Guadalhorce.
Tel 947 20 35 60.

León
Calle Astorga.

Logroño
Plaza de Europa.

Oviedo
Avda. Santander. *Tel* 985 98 12 52.

Pamplona
Avda. San Jorge. *Tel* 948 13 02 02.

San Sebastián
Estación del Norte, Paseo de Francia
Tel 943 28 30 89, 943 28 35 99.

Santander
Plaza de las Estaciones.

Santiago de Compostela
Rúa de Hórreo *Tel* 981 59 60 50.

TRAIN STATIONS

Most large cities in Northern Spain have train stations served by all categories of train. Some cities have two stations.

The main RENFE routes from Madrid to Northern Spain are: Madrid to A Coruña route via Ávila, Medina del Campo, Zamora, Ourense and Santiago de Compostela; Madrid to

The Estación Santander de Bilbao

The railway station in Padrón

Santander via Ávila, Medina, Valladolid and Palencia; Madrid to Bilbao via Burgos and Miranda; and finally Madrid to San Sebastián via Guadalajara and Pamplona.

REGIONAL RAILWAYS

As well as the RENFE services there are also three separate local rail companies in Northern Spain. Two are run by different regional governments, the **FGC** (Ferrocarrils de la Generalitat) in Catalonia and the Basque **ET** (Eusko Tren), while another, the FEVE, is a private company with a very useful and attractive line right along the north coast from San Sebastián to Santiago, linking towns that are otherwise only served by separate RENFE rail lines from Madrid.

Eusko Tren includes not only trains but also trams, buses, cable cars and even a steam train *(tren de vapor)* which departs from the Basque Railway Museum (Museo Vasco del Ferrocarril) in Azpeitia.

Ferrocarriles de Vía Estrecha, or FEVE, is a railway network in Northern Spain with more than 1,200 km (745 miles) of track. Its main services go from Ferrol to Bilbao. FEVE lines are especially important in Asturias and Cantabria, where they are heavily used.

FARES

Spanish railways offer a 10 per cent discount on specified days to encourage people to travel. They are *días azules* (blue days) and are indicated

in the timetables in blue. Fares for rail travel in Spain are structured according to the speed and quality of the service. Tickets for the TALGO and AVE are most expensive.

Interrail tickets for people under 26, and Eurodomino tickets for people over 26, are available from major travel agencies in Europe and from RENFE ticket offices in Spain. Always take photographic proof of your identity and age when booking.

BOOKING TICKETS

TALGO, AVE and any other tickets for long-distance trains *(largo recorrido)* may be booked and bought on the RENFE website or at any of the major railway stations from the ticket office *(taquilla)*. Reservations

can be made up to 59 days prior to the date of travel. Tickets for regional services *(regionales)* and local services *(cercanías)* cannot be reserved. You can buy them on the RENFE website or from the station *taquilla*. In large stations there are ticket machines *(cajeros automáticos)*.

For a one-way ticket ask for a *billete de ida*; for a return ask for a *billete de ida y vuelta* (sold at 20 per cent discount).

TIMETABLES

RENFE timetables, available from RENFE offices, change in May and October each year. Most timetables are broken down into the various types of journey: intercity, *largo recorrido* and *regionales*. *Cercanías* timetable are posted on boards at local train stations. Timetables can be accessed in English via the RENFE website. FEVE timetables are available at www.feve.es or by calling 944 25 06 15.

A regional FEVE train

ENJOYABLE TOURIST TRAINS

In addition to daily service, rail companies also offer tourist routes. In Northern Spain, FEVE (Ferrocarriles de Vía Estrecha) runs the luxurious Transcantábrico, a splendid eight-day journey along Spain's north coast between Santiago de Compostela and León, passing important sights along the way. Passengers on this train travel in style in 14 period carriages built between 1900 and 1930, and restored

to their former glory, giving a feel of days gone by. For more information, visit www.transcantabrico. feve.es

For a much shorter, but still stunning journey, the Catalan FGC runs the Cremallera mountain train up to Nuria and Queralbs, with beautiful views.

Cremallera mountain train in the Pyrenees

Travelling by Road

Sign for motorway toll booths ahead

Spain's fastest roads are its *autopistas*. They are normally dual carriageways and are subsidized by *peajes* (tolls). *Autovías* are similar but have no tolls. The *carretera nacional* is the countrywide network of main roads or highways with the prefix N. Smaller minor roads are generally less well kept but provide a more leisurely and enjoyable way to see rural areas of Spain. These pages tell you how to use the roads, tolls and parking meters, and explain important driving regulations.

Red de Carreteras del Estado

CARRETERA N-110

A national highway sign

ARRIVING BY CAR

Many people drive to Spain via the French motorways. The most direct routes across the Pyrenees, using the motorways, pass through Hendaye on the western flank (Basque Country) and Port Bou in the east (Catalonia). Other, rather more tortuous routes may be used, from Toulouse through the Vall d'Aran, for instance. The mid-Pyrenees route through Puerto de Somport to Jaca is beautiful, for those with time to spare. From the UK there are car ferries from Plymouth to Santander and from Portsmouth to Bilbao in the Basque Country (*see p249*).

WHAT TO TAKE

Spanish law requires you to carry with you at all times your vehicle's registration document, a valid insurance certificate and your driving licence. You must always be able to show a passport or a national identity card as ID. You must also display a sticker with the car's country of registration on the rear of the vehicle.

The headlights of right-hand-drive vehicles will have to be adjusted or deflected. This is done with stickers that can be bought at ferry ports and on ferries. You risk on-the-spot fines if you fail to carry two red warning triangles, spare light bulbs, a first-aid kit and a reflective vest. In winter you should carry chains if you intend to drive in mountain areas. In summer, it is a good idea to take drinking water with you if you are travelling in a remote area.

BUYING PETROL

In Spain petrol stations (*gaso-lineras*) sell both unleaded petrol (*gasolina sin plomo*) and diesel (*gasóleo*). Petrol stations are usually self-service. Automatic card-operated pumps often reject foreign credit cards. It's better to fill up at a staffed station. You will need to show ID if you pay by credit card.

RULES OF THE ROAD

Spain has a few road rules and signs that may be unfamiliar to some drivers from other countries. To turn left at a busy junction or across oncoming traffic you may have to turn right first and cross a main road, often across traffic lights, over a bridge or through an underpass. If you are going the wrong way on a motorway or a main road with a solid white line, you are allowed to do a u-turn where you see a sign for a *cambio de sentido*.

At any crossing you must give way to traffic on the right unless a sign indicates otherwise. It is compulsory always to wear seat belts if they are fitted in front and rear seats. Oncoming drivers may flash their headlights at you, which means they are claiming the right of way and you should let them go first.

Sign for an *autovía*, a fast toll-free road

SPEED LIMITS AND FINES

The speed limits on Spanish roads for cars without trailers are as follows: 120 km/h (75 mph) on motorways, 100 km/h (62 mph) on dual carriageways, 90 km/h (56 mph) on main or secondary roads, and 50 km/h (31 mph) in built-up areas. Speed traps and tests for drink-driving are increasingly common. The latter are especially frequent at weekends by motorway exit roads.

The legal limit for blood alcohol is 30 mg per millilitre (0.05%).

MOTORWAYS

Spanish motorways are among the best in Europe – well maintained and signposted. They are expensive, with tolls calculated per kilometre. There are service stations every 40–50 km (25–30 miles) marked by a blue and white parking sign or

A petrol station belonging to the Repsol chain

The toll-booth barrier at the entrance to a motorway

a sign indicating the services available. Most have fuel, shops and toilets. There are emergency telephones every 2 km (1.2 miles) on motorways.

CAR HIRE

International car hire companies operate all over Spain. **Hertz**, **Avis** and **Europcar** are the most popular, and they have branches at airports and in most large towns. The best-known Spanish car hire company is **National-Atesa**. When signing a car hire agreement, you will be required to show your driving licence, credit card, and passport or other ID.

The logos of the larger car hire companies

PAYING TOLLS

When you join a motorway you pick up a ticket from a toll booth (*peaje*, also called *peaxe* in Galicia and *peatge* in Catalan); when you leave the motorway, you surrender the ticket along with the fee. Over some short stretches of motorway, a fixed price is charged; otherwise you pay according to the distance you have travelled.

There are three types of toll booths: *telepago* (avoid this lane – only for motorists who subscribe to a special pre-paid credit system), *automático* (for motorists who can pay the exact amount by credit card or coins) and *manual* (for motorists who require change from an attendant).

OTHER ROADS

Spain's main roads (*carreteras nacionales*) have black and white signs and are designated N plus a number. Those with Roman numerals (N-III) start at the Puerta del Sol in Madrid. The distance from the Kilómetro Zero mark at the Puerta del Sol appears on kilometre markers. Those with ordinary numbers (N-3, N-12 etc.) have kilometre markers giving the distance from the provincial capital. Some *carreteras nacionales* are dual carriageways, but most are single-lane roads. Secondary roads (*carreteras comarcales*) have a number preceded by the letter C. Other minor roads have numbers preceded by the letters representing the name of the province, such as the

LE-1313 in Lleida. In winter, especially in the Pyrenees and around Burgos, minor roads may be closed.

TRAVEL BY COACH

The cheapest way to travel to Spain is by coach. **Eurolines** operates routes throughout Europe and runs services to Madrid and Barcelona.

Asturias-based **Alsa** and **Continental** are two other coach companies operating in Northern Spain.

Coach services within Spain are comfortable and efficient. Coach companies operate many long-distance routes, as well as short routes and special sightseeing trips for tourists. Spanish coaches are clean and usually air-conditioned.

HITCHHIKING

Hitchhiking in Spain is not recommended as a safe method of transport, though young people, mainly tourists, are often seen hitchhiking around, especially during the summer.

DIRECTORY

Alsa
Tel 902 42 22 42 www.alsa.es

National-Atesa
Tel 902 10 01 01 www.atesa.es

Avis
Tel 902 13 55 31
www.avis.com
www.avis.es

Continental
www.continentalautos.es

Eurolines
Tel 934 90 40 00 (Barcelona)
Tel 0158 250 4511 (UK)
www.eurolines.es

Europcar
Tel 902 10 50 30
www.europcar.com
www.europcar.es

Hertz
Tel 901 10 10 01 (toll-free)
www.hertz.com www.hertz.es

Traffic Information
Tel 900 12 35 05 www.dgt.es

Weather Forecast
Tel 807 17 03 65

A long-distance coach, part of the fleet run by Alsa

Getting Around Cities

A pedestrian crossing sign

As ever more people in Spain move from the countryside to the towns and cities, they are becoming increasingly crowded. Getting around the cities by car can be challenging, with many one-way streets, pedestrianized streets, and heavy traffic during rush hour. It's generally far better to use the very efficient local transport systems, which comprise buses, trams, the metro and taxis. The historic centres of towns and cities in Northern Spain are best explored on foot, as they are compact enough to see easily.

ON FOOT

Most of the sights are clustered together within walking distance of each other, so exploring on foot is the best option. Many of the streets are closed to traffic *(calles peatonales)*, and even if they are not, finding a parking space can be difficult.

TAXIS

There is no central system for taxis in Spain. Every city and/or region has its own operation and tariffs for its taxis. All display a green light if they are available.

Taxis are a comfortable means of transport. Most taxis are metered, and at the start of the journey a minimum fare will be shown on the meter. Ask at the hotel reception or in a nearby shop for the name and number of a local taxi company. Only in the smallest villages is it possible that you'll encounter

Signs to a city's historic sites and accommodation

unmetered taxis, in which case you should negotiate the fare before setting off.

In cities there are taxi ranks at the airports, the railway and bus stations and usually in the main shopping areas.

Visitors with luggage have to pay an additional charge of approximately 1–2 euros per item. You should remember this, especially when travelling to or from an airport. An average fare from an airport to a city centre is around 20–30 euros. To travel an average distance by taxi within a city you should expect to pay around 7–12 euros. Tips of about 1 euro will be acceptable.

BICYCLES, MOPEDS AND MOTORBIKES

Bicycles are becoming more common on Spanish streets, but be very careful if you cycle in traffic, as many drivers do not make allowances for cyclists. An increasing number of Spanish cities have excellent cycle lanes.

Motorbikes and scooters – much loved by the Spanish – continue to be a fashionable way to avoid traffic jams and also reach one's destination quickly.

Cycling trips through the Spanish countryside are also popular. Visitors can easily hire one from an *alquiler de bicicletas*.

Bicycles may be carried on local trains *(cercanías*, after 2pm only)*, on all regional trains *(regionales)* with goods compartments, and on all overnight long-distance trains *(largo recorrido)*. Sometimes you may have to send your bicycle as luggage and pay a baggage charge.

BUSES

Local bus routes and timetables are posted at bus stops. Single tickets can be bought from the driver when you board the bus (always through the front doors), but in most cities multijourney tickets *(bonobus* or *tarjeta)* valid for 10 journeys on local buses and – where there is one – the Metro system are preferable. You buy these in advance from bus offices, automatic machines or *estancos* (tobacconists). They work out a lot cheaper, and save a lot of time whenever you board a bus.

TRAMS

Tram systems are a rarity in Spanish cities (Valencia has one), but one of the most modern tram services in Northern Spain is the Basque **EuskoTran**, part of the EuskoTren company, which operates trains and trams in and around Bilbao. There is a fast and elegant service within and beyond the borders of the city, for instance, to the

The modern green EuskoTran in Bilbao

The futuristic entrance to a metro station in Bilbao

town of Hendaia (Hendaye) on the French-Spanish border, to the spa of San Sebastián, as well as to several beach resorts, including Zarautz and Bermeo.

METRO

Bilbao's excellent new metro system is a pleasure to use. It enables you to reach your destination quickly, providing a good alternative to overground transport. The station entrances, especially in the city centre, are very impressive. Viewed from afar, both during daytime and at night, they resemble giant shrimps and are among the boldest examples of modern design to be seen in Bilbao. The stations, which perfectly complement the city's showpiece Museo Guggenheim, were designed by Norman Foster.

DRIVING

Driving in Spanish cities is not a pleasant experience, especially for visitors unfamiliar with the surroundings. In the more crowded cities motorists tend to drive aggressively. Signs are often misleading or missing, service stations are few and parking is usually difficult. Read the map before setting off, but watch out for one-way systems, tunnels and overpasses. In rush hour, traffic often comes to a standstill. If you get lost while driving, hail a taxi, shout the address and follow the driver.

50

Speed limit sign
in an urban area

PARKING

Parking spaces are especially scarce in the summer season. Free parking is almost impossible to find, while metered parking is expensive. To park on the street, you normally need to find a blue pay-and-display parking space. Be sure to remember when your time-limit expires. In most cities in Northern Spain, parking is free between 8pm on Friday evening and 8am on Monday morning.

Underground car parks provide an alternative to metered on-street parking. You collect a ticket when you enter, retain it, and then pay the attendant, or at the machine, as you drive out. Underground parking is convenient, but tends to be expensive. Parking your car for just a few hours may cost more than 10 euros.

A sign with information on parking regulations

PARKING PENALTIES

Be sure to park in designated spaces only. Exceeding your pay-and-display time-limit may incur a penalty of up to 20 euros. When a vehicle receives a penalty ticket it is automatically registered on the computer system. Any further infringements or traffic violations may result in the car being clamped or towed.

Parking is controlled by the local police in each town, and it is to them you have to go to pay a fine or retrieve your car if it's been towed away.

DIRECTORY

TAXI COMPANIES

Oviedo
Radio Taxi Ciudad de Oviedo
Tel 985 25 00 00.

A Coruña
Tele Taxi
Calle Rafael Alberti 18
Tel 981 28 77 77.

Santander
Tele Taxi
Tel 942 36 91 91.
Radio Taxi
Tel 942 33 33 33.

Bilbao
Radio Taxi Nervión
Tel 944 26 90 26.
Radio Taxi Bilbao
Tel 944 44 88 88.
Radio Taxi Getxo
Tel 944 91 53 53.

San Sebastián
Radio Taxi Donostia
Tel 943 46 46 46.

Logroño
Radio Taxi
Tel 941 22 21 22.
Tele Taxi
Tel 941 50 50 50.

TRAMS

Bilbao
EuskoTran
Tel 900 15 12 06.
www.euskotren.es/euskotran

METRO

Bilbao
Calle Navarra 2
Tel 944 25 40 00.
www.metrobilbao.net
e-mail info@metrobilbao.net

General Index

Acknowledgments

Dorling Kindersley and Hachette Livre Polska would like to thank the following people and institutions, whose contributions and assistance have made the preparation of this guide possible:

PUBLISHING MANAGER Vivien Antwi, Kathryn Lane
MANAGING ART EDITOR Kate Poole, Jane Ewart
PUBLISHER Douglas Amrine
SENIOR CARTOGRAPHIC EDITOR Casper Morris
SENIOR DTP DESIGNER Jason Little
DTP DESIGNER Jenn Hadley, Natasha Lu
EDITORIAL ASSISTANCE Alexandra Farrell
PRODUCTION COORDINATOR Louise Minihane
JACKET DESIGN Tessa Bindloss
SENIOR PICTURE RESEARCHER Ellen Root
ASSISTANT PICTURE RESEARCHER Rachel Barber
CONSULTANT Nick Ryder
FACTCHECKER Lola Carbonell
PROOFREADER Stewart J Wild
INDEXER Hilary Bird

Additional Photography
Max Alexander, Frank Greenaway, Zuzanna Jakubowska, Krzysztof Kur, Ian O'Leary, Grzegorz Micuła, Małgorzata Omilanowska, Ewa Szwagrzyk.

Special Assistance
The publisher would like to thank the following for their kind assistance and permission to photograph at their establishments, and to reproduce photographs from their collections and archives:

Ayuntamiento de Oviedo and Carmen López; Aranecie Sacristan and Miren Begoñe; Centro de Atracción y Turismo de San Sebastián; Centro Información Turística del Principado de Asturias El Camino Real; Federación Internacional de Pelota Vasca and Fundación de los Ferrocarriles Españoles union; Amaya Asiain and Vias Verdes programme - www.viasverdes.com; La Rioja Alta S.A. and Gabriela Rezoli; Museo de Altamira and Eusebio Dohijo; Museo de Bellas Artes de Álava and Itziar Ruia de Erentxun; Museo Provincial de Lugo; Josi Martinez; the staff of www.ordesa.com; Sahatsa Basque Dance Group and Juan Luis Izabe; Santuario de Loyola and Txakel Urarte; Teatro Arriaga; Turgalicia; Turismo Rural de Cantabria and Francisco Javier San Jóse from www.cantabriarural.com.

Picture Credits

t = top; tr = top right; tl = top left; ftr = far top right; tlc = top left centre; tc = top centre; trc = top right centre; c = centre; cl = centre left; cla = centre left above; clb = centre left below; cb = centre below; cr = centre right; crb = centre right below; b = bottom; bcl = bottom centre left; bc = bottom centre; bcr = bottom centre right; bl = bottom left; br = bottom right.

Works of art have been reproduced with the permission of the following copyright holders: Eduardo Chilida © DACS, London 2007 127cl, 130-1; Salvador Dali © Kingdom of Spain, Gaia – Salvador Dali Foundation and DACS, London 2007 193tc; Benjamin Palencia © DACS, London 2007 8-9; © Succession Picasso/DACS, London 2007 22bl; Richard Serra © ARS, NY and DACS, London 2007 124br; Zubiaurre © DACS, London 2007 143cla.

The publisher would like to thank the following individuals, companies and picture libraries for permission to reproduce their photographs:

AGENCE VU: Christina Garcia Rodero 17bc; AISA - ARCHIVO ICONOGRAFICO S.A., Barcelona: 36br, 38t, 65br, 117cb; Catedral de Sevilla *Ignacio de Loyola* Alonso Vazquez 138br; AJUNTAMIENTO DE OVIEDO: 88bcl; ALAMY IMAGES: Adams Picture Library/Eric Farrelly 231tc; Alan Copson City Pictures/Alan Copson 154cla, 155bl; Arcaid/Inigo Bujedo Aguirre 248bl; Sébastien Baussais 28tr; Mark Baynes 143bl; Bildarchiv Monheim GmbH/Markus Bassler 39crb, 238-9; Chris Cameron 155cr; Cephas Picture Library/Mick Rock 2–3, 44–5; Cephas Picture Library/Neil Phillips 32bl; Ashley Cooper 103crb; Jean Dominique Dallet 36tl; Andrew Darrington 184bc; Roger Day 28bl, 228cl; Elizabeth Whiting & Associates 103bl; Paul Hobson 184cb; John Warburton-Lee Photography/Ian Aitken 230cra; John Warburton-Lee Photography/John Warburton-Lee 231crb; Christian Kober 236tl; Mike Lane 184bl; M. J. Mayo 231cr, 233tl; Melba Photo Agency 154t, 155tl, 197br; Philip Mugridge 184clb; Point-of-view 129ca; Robert Harding World Imagery 28cr; Ray Roberts 233cr; Carmen Sedano 27; Alex Segre 22cl, 214cl, 215tc, 217tr; Stephen Saks Photography 120cl; © TNT Magazine 154bl, 154clb; Dave and Sigrun Tollerton 184tc; Andrew Watson 155tr; WildPictures 185bl; ARCAID: Paul Rafferty 124bl; AMAYA ASIAIN: 236b.

BAQUEIRA-BERET: 189t.

CARLOS VIANA: 219ftr; CASA DE JUNTAS DE GERNIC: 22–23c; CENTRO DE ARTE REINA SOFIA: *Bertsolaris* Zubiaurre 143cla; CENTRO INFORMACIÓN TURÍSTICA DEL PRINCIPADO DE ASTURIA: 88b; CEPHAS PICTURE LIBRARY: Mick Rock 24tr; CORBIS: Oriol Alamany 26trc, 26bl, 27c, 184tlc; © Archivo Iconografico S.A. 36br, 39t, 41t; Philip de Bay 41b; © Bettmann 40t, 42b, 155br; Michael Busselle 19tr, 53b, 57bl; © Christie's Images 38bl; Dusko

Despotovic 43t, 43tr, 140bl; Owen Franken 15c, 215c; Darrel Gulin 29bl, 29br; © Hulton-Deutsch Collection 42t; Maurizio Lanini 26cr, 103cl; George D. Lepp 185tl; Lothar Lenz 29cr; George McCarthy 185bl; Tania Midgley 26bcl; © Francesca Muntada 180–81, 184-5c; Gianni Dagli Orti 34; Jacques Pavlovsky 23cr; Ruggero Vanni 40b; Nick Wheeler 31t, 54b, 80; Martin B. Withers 29cl; Adam Woolfitt 19t; Joe Cornish: 168tr; COVER: Quim Llenas 22tr.

Edilesa: 113br; El Camino Real: 93trc.

Federación Internacional de Pelota Vasc: Josean Iraundegui 23br; Francisco Javier San Jóse: 198b.

Darrio Garrido: 33bl, 133trc, 143cr; Germán Limeres: 76tlc; Gert Voor in't Holt: 141b; © Guggenheim Museum Bilbao: Erica Barahona Ede 124tr, 124br, 125br, 125tc.

Imagestate: AGE Fotostock 172br, 183cra, 183crb, 199tl, 235cra; Incafo: J A Fernandez 47clb; JA Fernandez & Cde Noriega 143br; Index Fototeca: 42bc, 42br; X. Correa 35crb; Nick Inman: 243cb.

Humberto Bilbao: 75b, 143cl.

Ines Jauregi: 232tc.

La Rioja Alta S.A.: 164b.

Pasqualino Marchese: 219cr, 219br; Mary Evans Picture Library: 9c, 45c, 195c, 239c; Museo de Altamira: 108–9; Museo de Bellas Artes de Alva, Vitoria: 141bc; Museo Provincial de Lugo: 76cla.

Natural Science Photos: Nigel Charles 100tl; C. Dani & I. Jeske 94br; Naturpress: Jose Martinez 27cla.

Omega Foto: 30br; Oronoz: 37tr, 117br, 166bc; Biblioteca National. Madrid *Isabel la Catolica* Luiz

Madrazo 40bc; Museo Lazaro Galdiano, Madrid *Santiago Matamoros Guerrea en 1500* Juan de Flandes 20tl; Museo Prado 41bl; *Alrededores de Bilbao* Benjamín Palencia 8–9; *Interior de la Catedral de Santiago* Villaamil Perez 20-21; *Guernica* Pablo Picasso 22bl.

Paradores de Turismo de España S.A.: 200t, 200trc; 201tl, 201bl; Parque Nacional Ordesa: 185tr, 185cr; Paweł Pasternak: 219tr, 230bl, 231tcl; Photoshot/NHPA: Manfred Daneggar 27tc; Pictures Colour Library: 26br; Prisma, Barcelona: 43tl; *Diputacion de Madrid* Enrique Segura 43tl; Museo de Bellas Artes, Zaragoza *Principe de Viana* Jose Moreno Carbonero 152bc.

Reuters: Jim Hollander 31c; Pablo Sanchez 135bc; Javier Anton Riestra: 213b.

Sahatsa Basque Dance Group: 23tcl, 143t; Maria Angeles Sanchez: 25t, 33cr; Santuario de Loiola: 138bcl; Science Photo Library: geospace 10cl; Anna Skrzyńska: 27trc; Stockphotos: Heinz Hebestein 31bc; Mikael Helsing 234br.

Teatro Arriaga: 232cla; Turgalicia: Juan A Mascareñas Cid 30tlc.

Alan Williams: 24br.

JACKET
Front – Corbis: Francesc Muntada main image; DK Images: Frank Greenaway clb.
Back – DK Images: Max Alexander clb; Malgorzata Omilanowska bl; Kim Sayer tl; Getty Images: Robert Harding World Imagery/Duncan Maxwell cla. Spine – Corbis: Francesc Muntada t; DK Images: Max Alexander b.

All other images © Dorling Kindersley. For further information see www.dkimages.com

Phrase Book – Spanish

In an Emergency

Help!	¡Socorro!	soh-koh-rob
Stop!	¡Pare!	pab-reb
Call a doctor!	¡Llame a un médico!	yab-meb ab oon meb-dee-koh
Call an ambulance!	¡Llame a una ambulancia!	yab-meb ab oonab abm-boo-labn-thee-ab
Call the police!	¡Llame a la policía!	yab-meb ab lab pob-lee-thee-ab
Call the fire brigade!	¡Llame a los bomberos!	yab-meb ab lohs bohm-beb-robs
Where is the nearest telephone?	¿Dónde está el teléfono más próximo?	dohn-deb ebs-tah ebl teb-leb-foh-noh mabs probx-ee-moh
Where is the nearest hospital?	¿Dónde está el hospital más próximo?	dohn-deb ebs-tah ebl obs-pee-tabl mabs probx-ee-moh

Communication Essentials

Yes	Sí	see
No	No	nob
Please	Por favor	pobr fab-vobr
Thank you	Gracias	grab-thee-abs
Excuse me	Perdone	pebr-dob-neb
Hello	Hola	ob-lab
Goodbye	Adiós	ab-dee-obs
Goodnight	Buenas noches	bweb-nahs nob-chebs
Morning	La mañana	lab mab-nyah-nah
Afternoon	La tarde	lab tabr-deb
Evening	La tarde	lab tabr-deb
Yesterday	Ayer	ab-yebr
Today	Hoy	oy
Tomorrow	Mañana	mab-nya-nab
Here	Aquí	ab-kee
There	Allí	ab-yee
What?	¿Qué?	keb
When?	¿Cuándo?	kwabn-dob
Why?	¿Por qué?	pobr-keb
Where?	¿Dónde?	dohn-deb

Useful Phrases

How are you?	¿Cómo está usted?	koh-mob ebs-tah oos-tebd
Very well, thank you	Muy bien, gracias.	mwee bee-ebn grab-thee-abs
Pleased to meet you	Encantado de conocerle.	ebn-kahn-tab-dob deb kob-nob-thebr-leb
See you soon	Hasta pronto.	abs-tab probn-tob
That's fine.	Está bien.	ebs-tah bee-ebn
Where is/are . . .?	¿Dónde está/están . . .?	dohn-deb ebs-tah/ebs-tabn
How far is it to . . .?	¿Cuántos metros/ kilómetros hay de aquí a . . .?	kwahn-tobs meb-trobs/kee-loh-meb-trobs eye deh ab-kee ab
Which way to . . .?	¿Por dónde se va a . . .?	pobr dohn-deb seb bab ab
Do you speak English?	¿Habla inglés?	ab-blab een-glebs
I don't understand	No comprendo	nob kobm-prebn-dob
Could you speak more slowly please?	¿Puede hablar más despacio por favor?	pweb-deb ab-blabr mabs debs-pab-thee-oh pobr fab-vobr
I'm sorry	Lo siento.	loh see-ebn-tob

Useful Words

big	grande	grabn-deb
small	pequeño	peb-keb-nyob
hot	caliente	kab-lee-ebn-teb
cold	frío	free-ob
good	bueno	bweb-nob
bad	malo	mab-lob
enough	bastante	babs-tabn-teb
well	bien	bee-ebn
open	abierto	ab-bee-ebr-tob
closed	cerrado	thebr-rab-dob
left	izquierda	eeth-key-ebr-dab
right	derecha	deb-reb-chab
straight on	todo recto	toh-dob rebk-tob
near	cerca	thebr-kab
far	lejos	leb-bobs
up	arriba	ab-ree-bab
down	abajo	ab-bab-bob
early	temprano	tehm-prah-nob
late	tarde	tahr-deb
entrance	entrada	ebn-trab-dab
exit	salida	sab-lee-dab
toilet	lavabos, servicios	lab-vab-bobs sehr-bee-thee-obs
more	más	mabs
less	menos	meb-nobs

Shopping

How much does this cost?	¿Cuánto cuesta esto?	kwahn-toh kwebs-tah ebs-toh
I would like . . .	Me gustaría . . .	meb goos-ta-ree-ab
Do you have?	¿Tienen?	tee-yeb-nebn
I'm just looking, thank you	Sólo estoy mirando, gracias.	soh-loh ebs-toy mee-rabn-dob grab-thee-abs
Do you take credit cards?	¿Aceptan tarjetas de crédito?	ab-thebp-tahn tabr-heb-tabs deh kreb-dee-toh
What time do you open?	¿A qué hora abren?	ah keb ob-rab ab-brebn
What time do you close?	¿A qué hora cierran?	ah keb ob-rab thee-ebr-rahn
This one	Éste	ebs-teb
That one	Ése	eb-seb
expensive	caro	kabr-ob
cheap	barato	bab-rab-tob
size, clothes	talla	tab-yab
size, shoes	número	noo-mebr-ob
white	blanco	blabn-kob
black	negro	neb-grob
red	rojo	rob-bob
yellow	amarillo	ab-mab-ree-yob
green	verde	bebr-deb
blue	azul	ab-tbool
antiques shop	la tienda de antigüedades	lah tee-ehn-dah deb abn-tee-gweb-dab-debs
bakery	la panadería	lab pab-nab-deb-ree-ab
bank	el banco	ebl babn-kob
book shop	la librería	lah lee-breb-ree-ab
butcher's	la carnicería	lab kabr-nee-theb-ree-ab
cake shop	la pastelería	lab pabs-teb-leb-ree-ab
chemist's	la farmacia	lab fabr-mab-thee-ab
fishmonger's	la pescadería	lab pebs-kab-deb-ree-ab
greengrocer's	la frutería	lah froo-teb-ree-ab
grocer's	la tienda de comestibles	lab tee-yebn-dab deb kob-mebs-tee-blebs
hairdresser's	la peluquería	lab peb-loo-keb-ree-ab
market	el mercado	ebl mehr-kab-dob
newsagent's	el kiosko de prensa	ebl kee-obs-koh deb prebn-sab
post office	la oficina de correos	lah ob-fee-thee-nah deb kobr-reb-obs
shoe shop	la zapatería	lab thab-pab-teb-ree-ab
supermarket	el supermercado	ebl soo-pebr-mebr-kab-dob
tobacconist	el estanco	ebl ebs-tabn-kob
travel agency	la agencia de viajes	lah ab-hebn-thee-ab deb bee-ab-hebs

Sightseeing

art gallery	el museo de arte	ebl moo-seb-ob deb abr-teb
cathedral	la catedral	lab kab-teb-drabl
church	la iglesia	lah ee-gleb-see-ab
	la basílica	lab bab-see-lee-kab
garden	el jardín	ebl babr-deen
library	la biblioteca	lab bee-blee-ob-teb-kab
museum	el museo	ebl moo-seb-ob
tourist information office	la oficina de turismo	lab ob-fee-thee-nab deb too-rees-mob
town hall	el ayuntamiento	ebl ab-yoon-tab-mee-ebn-tob
closed for holiday	cerrado por vacaciones	thebr-rab-dob pobr bab-kab-cee-ob-nebs
bus station	la estación de autobuses	lab ebs-tab-see-ob deb owtoh-boo-sebs
railway station	la estación de trenes	lab ebs-tab-thee-ohn deb treb-nebs

Staying in a Hotel

Do you	¿Tienen	tee-eb-nebn
have	una	oo-nah
a vacant	habitación	ab-bee-tah-thee-
room?	libre?	obn lee-breh
double	habitación	ab-bee-tah-thee-
room	doble	obn dob-bleb
with double	con cama de	kobn kab-mab deb
bed	matrimonio	mab-tree-moh-nee-oh
twin room	habitación	ab-bee-tah-thee-
	con dos camas	obn kobn dobs
		kab-mabs
single room	habitación	ab-bee-tah-thee-
	individual	obn een-dee-vee-
		doo-abl
room with	habitación	ab-bee-tah-thee-
a bath	con baño	obn kobn bab-nyoh
shower	ducha	doo-chab
porter	el botones	ebl bob-toh-nebs
key	la llave	lah yab-veb
I have a	Tengo una	tehn-gob oo-na
reservation	habitación	ab-bee-tah-thee-
	reservada.	obn reb-sehr-bab-dah

Eating Out

Have you got	¿Tienen	tee-eb-nebn
a table for . . .?	mesa para . . .?	meb-sah pah-rah
I want to	Quiero	kee-eb-rob
reserve	reservar	reb-sehr-bahr
a table	una mesa.	oo-nah meb-sah
The bill	La cuenta	lah kwebn-tah
please	por favor.	pobr fah-vobr
I am a	Soy	soy beb-beb-tab-
vegetarian	vegetariano/a	ree-ab-no/na
waitress/	camarera/	kab-mab-reb-rah
waiter	camarero	kab-mab-reb-rob
menu	la carta	lah kahr-tah
fixed-price menu	menú del día	meb-noo debl dee-ab
wine list	la carta de	lah kabr-tah deb
	vinos	bee-nobs
glass	un vaso	oon bab-sob
bottle	una botella	oo-nah bob-teb-yah
knife	un cuchillo	oon koo-chee-yob
fork	un tenedor	oon teb-neb-dobr
spoon	una cuchara	oo-nah koo-chab-rah
breakfast	el desayuno	ebl deb-sab-yoo-nob
lunch	la comida/	lah kob-mee-dab/
	el almuerzo	ebl abl-mwebr-tboh
dinner	la cena	lah tbeb-nah
main course	el primer plato	ebl pree-mebr plab-tob
starters	los entremeses	lohs ebn-treb-meb-sebs
dish of the day	el plato del día	ebl plab-tob debl
		dee-ab
coffee	el café	ebl kab-feb
rare	poco hecho	pob-kob eb-chob
medium	medio hecho	meb-dee-ob eb-chob
well done	muy hecho	mwee eb-chob

Menu Decoder

baked	al horno	abl obr-nob
roast	asado	ab-sab-dob
oil	el aceite	ab-thee-eb-teb
olives	las aceitunas	ab-tbeb-toon-abs
mineral water	el agua mineral	ab-gua meb-neb-rabl
still/sparkling	sin gas/con gas	seen gas/kobn gas
garlic	el ajo	ab-bob
rice	el arroz	abr-robth
sugar	el azúcar	ab-tboo-kabr
meat	la carne	kabr-neb
onion	la cebolla	tbeb-bob-yab
beer	la cerveza	tbebr-beb-tbab
pork	el cerdo	tberb-dob
chocolate	el chocolate	chob-kob-lab-teb
red sausage	el chorizo	chob-ree-tbob
lamb	el cordero	kobr-deb-rob
cold meat	el fiambre	fee-abm-breb
fried	frito	free-tob
fruit	la fruta	froo-tab
nuts	los frutos secos	froo-tobs seb-kobs
prawns	las gambas	gabm-babs
ice cream	el helado	eb-lab-dob
egg	el huevo	oo-eb-vob
cured ham	el jamón serrano	bab-mobn
		sebr-rah-nob
sherry	el jerez	beb-rebz

lobster	la langosta	lahn-gobs-tab
milk	la leche	leb-cheb
lemon	el limón	lee-mohn
lemonade	la limonada	lee-moh-nab-dab
butter	la mantequilla	mabn-teh-kee-yab
apple	la manzana	mabn-tbab-nab
seafood	los mariscos	mab-rees-kobs
vegetable stew	la menestra	meb-nebs-trab
orange	la naranja	nab-rabn-bab
bread	el pan	pabn
cake	el pastel	pabs-tebl
potatoes	las patatas	pab-tab-tabs
fish	el pescado	pebs-kab-dob
pepper	la pimienta	pee-mee-yebn-tab
banana	el plátano	plab-tab-nob
chicken	el pollo	pob-yob
dessert	el postre	pobs-treb
cheese	el queso	keb-sob
salt	la sal	sabl
sausages	las salchichas	sabl-chee-chabs
sauce	la salsa	sabl-sab
dry	seco	seb-kob
sirloin	el solomillo	sob-lob-mee-yob
soup	la sopa	sob-pab
pie/cake	la tarta	tabr-tab
tea	el té	teb
beef	la ternera	tebr-neb-rah
toast	las tostadas	tobs-tab-dabs
vinegar	el vinagre	bee-nab-greb
white wine	el vino blanco	bee-nob blabn-kob
rosé wine	el vino rosado	bee-nob rob-sab-dob
red wine	el vino tinto	bee-nob teen-tob

Numbers

0	cero	tbeb-rob
1	uno	oo-nob
2	dos	dobs
3	tres	trebs
4	cuatro	kwa-trob
5	cinco	tbeen-kob
6	seis	says
7	siete	see-eb-teb
8	ocho	ob-chob
9	nueve	nweb-veb
10	diez	dee-ebtb
11	once	obn-tbeb
12	doce	dob-tbeb
13	trece	treb-tbeb
14	catorce	kab-tobr-tbeb
15	quince	keen-tbeb
16	dieciséis	dee-eb-thee-seb-ees
17	diecisiete	dee-eb-thee-see-eb-teb
18	dieciocho	dee-eb-thee-ob-chob
19	diecinueve	dee-eb-thee-nweb-veb
20	veinte	beb-een-teb
21	veintiuno	beb-een-tee-oo-nob
22	veintidós	beb-een-tee-dobs
30	treinta	treb-een-tab
31	treinta y uno	treb-een-tab ee
		oo-nob
40	cuarenta	kwab-rebn-tab
50	cincuenta	tbeen-kwebn-tab
60	sesenta	seb-sebn-tab
70	setenta	seb-tebn-tab
80	ochenta	ob-cbebn-tab
90	noventa	nob-vebn-tab
100	cien	tbee-ebn
101	ciento uno	thee-ebn-tob oo-nob
102	ciento dos	thee-ebn-tob dobs
200	doscientos	dobs-tbee-ebn-tobs
500	quinientos	kbee-nee-ebn-tobs
700	setecientos	seb-teb-tbee-ebn-tobs
900	novecientos	nob-veb-tbee-ebn- tobs
1,000	mil	meel
1,001	mil uno	meel oo-nob

Time

one minute	un minuto	oon mee-noo-tob
one hour	una hora	oo-na ob-rab
half an hour	media hora	meb-dee-a ob-rab
Monday	lunes	loo-nebs
Tuesday	martes	mabr-tebs
Wednesday	miércoles	mee-ebr-kob-lebs
Thursday	jueves	boo-web-vebs
Friday	viernes	bee-ebr-nebs
Saturday	sábado	sab-bab-dob
Sunday	domingo	dob-meen-gob

Phrase Book – Basque

In an Emergency

Help!	Lagundu!	lah-goon-doo!
Stop!	GeldItu!	gehl-dee-too!
Call a doctor!	Sendagile bati deitu!	sehn-dah-gee-leh bah-tee deh-ee-too!
Call an ambulance!	Anbulantzia bati deitu!	ahn-boo-labn-tzee-ah bah-tee deh-ee-too!
Call the police!	Poliziari deitu!	pob-lee-zee-ah-ree deh-ee-too!
Call the fire brigade!	Suhiltzaileei deitu!	suh-eel-tzah-ee-leh-ee deh-ee-too!
Where is the nearest telephone?	Non dago telefonorik gertuena?	nohn dah-goh teb-leh-phob-noh-reek gehr-too-eh-nah?
Where is the nearest hospital?	Non dago ospitalerik gertuena?	nohn dah-goh obs-pee-tah-leh-reek gehr-too-eh-nah?

Communication Essentials

Yes	Bai	bab-ee
No	Ez	ehs
Please	Mesedez	meh-seh-debs
Thank you	Eskerrik asko	ehs-keh-reek ahs-koh
Excuse me	Barkatu	babr-kah-too
Hello	Kaixo	kah-ee-sho
Goodbye	Agur	ah-goor
Good night	Gabon	gab-bohn
Morning	Goiza	gob-ee-sah
Afternoon	Arratsaldea	ah-rah-tsabl-deb-ah
Evening	Arratsaldea	ah-rah-tsabl-deb-ah
Yesterday	Atzo	ab-tzoh
Today	Gaur	gah-oor
Tomorrow	Bihar	bee-ahr
Here	Hemen	eh-mehn
There	Hor	obr
What?	Zer?	zebr?
When?	Noiz?	nob-ees?
Why?	Zergatik?	zebr-gah-teek?
Where?	Non?	nohn?

Useful Phrases

How are you?	Zer moduz?	zebr moh-dooz?
Very well, thank you.	Ondo, eskerrik asko	obn-dob, ehs-keh-reek ahs-koh
Pleased to meet you.	Pozten nau zu ezagutzeak	pobz-tebn nah-oo zoo eh-zah-goo-tzeh-ahk
See you soon.	Gero arte	geb-rob abr-teb
That's fine.	Ados	ah-dobs
Where is/are...?	Non dago/daude ...?	nohn dah-goh/dah-oo-deh ...?
How far is it to...?	Ze tarte dago hemendik ...-ra?	seb tahr-teb da-goh eh-mehn-deek ... -rah?
Which way to...?	Nondik joaten da ...-ra?	nohn-deek joh-ab-tebn dah ... -rah?
Do you speak English?	Ingelesez badakizu?	een-geb-leh-sebs bah-dah-kee-zoo?
I don't understand	Ez dut ulertzen	ehs doot oo-lehr-tzebn
Could you speak more slowly please?	Mantsoago hitz egin dezakezu, mesedez?	mahn-tsoh-ab-gob ee-tz eh-geen deh-sah-keh-zoo, meh-seh-debs?
I'm sorry.	Barkatu	babr-kah-too

Useful Words

big	Handia	ahn-dee-ah
small	Txikia	txee-kee-ah
hot	Beroa	beb-rob-ah
cold	Hotza	ob-tzab
good	Ona	ob-nab
bad	Txarra	txab-rah
enough	Nahiko	nah-ee-koh
well	Ondo	obn-doh
open	Zabalik	sab-bab-leek
closed	Itxita	ee-txee-tah
left	Ezkerra	ehs-keh-rah
right	Eskuina	ehs-koo-ee-nah
straight on	Zuzen	zoo-zebn
near	Gertu	gebr-too
far	Urrun	oo-roon
up	Goian	gob-ee-abn
down	Behean	beb-eb-abn
early	Goiz	gob-eez
late	Berandu	beb-rahn-doo

Shopping

How much does this cost?	Zenbat balio du honek?	zebn-baht bab-lee-ob dub ob-nehk?
I would like...	... gustatuko litzaidake	... guhs-tab-too-kob lee-tzab-ee-dah-keh
Do you have?	Ba al daukazue ...-rik?	bah abl dah-oo-kah-zoo-eh ... -reek?
I'm just looking.	Begiratzen nago, besterik ez.	beb-gee-rah-tzebn nah-gob, behs-teb-reek ehs
Do you take credit cards?	Txartelik onartzen al duzue?	txabr-teh-leek obn-nahr-tzebn abl doo-zoo-eh?
This one.	Hau	ab-oo
That one.	Hori	ob-ree
expensive	Garestia	gah-rehs-tee-ah
cheap	Merkea	mehr-keb-ah
size, clothes	Neurria, arropa	neb-oo-ree-ah, ab-rob-pab
size, shoes	Neurria, oinetazkoak	neb-oo-ree-ab, ob-ee-neh-tabz-koh-abk
white	Zuria	zoo-ree-ab
black	Beltza	bebl-tzah
red	Gorria	gob-ree-ah
yellow	Horia	ob-ree-ab
green	Berdea	bebr-deb-ab
blue	Urdina	oor-dee-nab
antiques shop	Antigoaleko gauzen denda	abn-tee-gob-ab-leh-kob gab-oo-zebn debn-dab
bakery	Okindegia	ob-keen-deb-gee-ab
bank	Bankua	babn-koo-ab
book shop	Liburu-denda	lee-boo-roo debn-dab
butcher's	Harategia	ab-rah-teb-gee-ab
cake shop	Gozotegia	gob-zob-teb-gee-ab
chemist's	Farmazia	far-mab-zee-ab
fishmonger's	Arrandegia	ab-rahn-deb-gee-ab
greengrocer's	Frutategia	froo-tab-teb-gee-ab
grocer's	Janari-denda	jab-nab-ree debn-dab
hairdresser's	Ile-apaindegia	ee-leh ab-pab-een-deb-gee-ab
market	Azoka	ab-zob-kah
newsagent's	Kioskoa	kee-obs-koh-ab
post office	Postetxea	pobst-eb-txeb-ah
shoe shop	Zapata-denda	zab-pab-tab debn-dab
supermarket	Supermerkatua	soo-pebr-mehr-kab-too-ab
tobacconist	Tabako-denda	tab-bak-kob debn-dah
travel agency	Bidaia-agentzia	bee-dab-ee-ab ab-gbehn-tzee-ab

Sightseeing

art gallery	Arte-galeria	abr-teb gab-leb-ree-ab
cathedral	Katedrala	kab-teb-drab-lab
church	Eliza	eb-lee-zah
garden	Lorategia	loh-rah-teb-gee-ab
library	Liburutegia	lee-boo-roo-teb-gee-ab
museum	Museoa	moo-seb-ob-ab
tourist information office	Turismo bulegoa	too-rees-mob boo-leb-gob-ab
town hall	Udaletxea	oo-dbal-eb-txeb-ab
closed for holiday	Oporretan gaude	ob-pob-reh-tabn gab-oo-deb
bus station	Autobus-geltokia	ab-oo-tob-boos gebl-tob-kee-ab
railway station	Tren-geltokia	trebn gebl-too-kee-ab

Numbers

0	Zero	zeb-rob
1	Bat	baht
2	Bi	bee
3	Hiru	ee-roo
4	Lau	lab-oo
5	Bost	bobst
6	Sei	seb-ee
7	Zazpi	zabz-pee
8	Zortzi	zobr-tzee
9	Bederatzi	beb-deb-rab-tzee
10	Hamar	ab-mabr

entrance	Sarrera	sab-reb-rah
exit	Irteera	eer-teb-eh-rah
toilet	Komunak	koh-moo-nahk
more	Gehiago	geb-ee-ah-gob
less	Gutxiago	guh-txee-ab-gob

Phrase Book – Galician

In an Emergency

Help!	¡Axuda!	ah-shu-dah
Stop!	¡Deténase!	deh-teh-nyah-seh
Call a doctor!	¡Chamen a un médico!	chab-mebn ab oon meh-dee-koh
Call an ambulance!	¡Chamen a unha ambulancia!	chab-mebn ab oon-ah abm-boo-labn-thee-ah
Call the police!	¡Chamen á policía!	chab-mebn ab pob-lee-thee-ah
Call the fire brigade!	¡Chamen ós bombeiros!	chab-mebn obs bohm-beh-ee-robs
Where is the nearest telephone?	¿Onde está o teléfono máis próximo?	onb-deh ebs-tab ob teb-leb-foh-nob mah-ees probx-ee-mob
Where is the nearest hospital?	¿Onde está o hospital máis próximo?	onb-deh ebs-tab ob obs-pee-tabl mab-ees probx-ee-mob

Communication Essentials

Yes	Sí	see
No	Non	nobn
Please	Por favor	pobr fab-bohr
Thank you	Gracias	grab-thee-abs
Excuse me	Desculpe	Debs-kool-peb
Hello	Ola	ob-lab
Goodbye	Adeus	ab-deb-oos
Good night	Boas noites	bob-abs nob-ee-tebs
Morning	Mañá	mab-nya
Afternoon	Tarde	tabr-deb
Evening	Serán	seb-rabn
Yesterday	Onte	obn-teb
Today	Hoxe	ob-sheb
Tomorrow	Mañá	mab-nya
Here	Aquí	ab-kbee
There	Alí	ab-lee
What?	¿Que?	keb
When?	¿Cando?	kabn-dob
Why?	¿Por que?	pobr-keb
Where?	¿Onde?	obn-deb

Useful Phrases

How are you?	¿Como está vostede?	kob-mob ebs-tab bobs-teb-deh
Very well, thank you.	Moi ben, gracias.	mob-ee bebn grab-thee-abs
Pleased to meet you.	Encantado de coñecelo.	ebn-kabn-tab-doh deb kob-nye-teb-lob
See you soon.	Ata pronto.	ab-tab probn-tob
That's fine.	Está ben.	ebs-tab bebn
Where is/are...?	¿Onde está/están...?	obn-deh ebs-tab/ebs-tban
How far is it to...?	¿Canto hai de aquí a...?	kabn-tob eye deb ab-kee ab
Which way to...?	¿Cal é o camiño para ir a...?	kabl eb ob kab-mee-nyo pab-ra eer ab
Do you speak English?	¿Fala inglés?	fab-lab een-glebs
I don't understand	Non comprendo.	nobn kobm-prebn-dob
Could you speak more slowly please?	¿Podería falar máis amodo?	pob-deb-reeab fab-labr mab-ees ab-mob-dob
I'm sorry.	Síntoo.	seen-tob-ob

Useful Words

big	grande	grabn-deb
small	pequeno	peb-keb-nob
hot	quente	kebn-teb
cold	frío	free-ob
good	bo	bob
bad	malo	mab-lob
enough	abondo	ab-bobn-dob
well	ben	bebn
open	aberto	ab-bebr-tob
closed	pechado	peb-cha-dob
left	esquerda	ebs-kebr-dab
right	dereita	deb-reb-eb-tab
straight on	cara adiante	kab-rab ab-dee-abn-teb
near	preto	preb-tob
far	lonxe	lobn-sheb
up	arriba	ab-ree-bab
down	abaixo	ab-bab-ee-shob
early	cedo	tbeb-dob

late	tarde	tabr-deb
entrance	entrada	ebn-trab-dab
exit	saída	sab-ee-dab
toilet	baño	bab-nyo
more	máis	mab-ees
less	menos	meb-nobs

Shopping

How much does this cost?	¿canto custa?	kabn-tob koos-tab
I would like...	quero...	keb-rob
Do you have?	¿teñen...?	teb-nyebn
I'm just looking.	estou a mirar.	ebs-tob-oo ab mee-rabr
Do you take credit cards?	¿aceptan tarxetas de crédito?	ab-tbep-tan tabr-sbeb-tabs deb kreb-dee-tob
What time do you open?	¿a que hora abren?	ab keb ob-rab ab-brebn
What time do you close?	¿a que hora pechan?	ab keb ob-rab peb-cbabn
This one.	este.	ebs-teb
That one.	ese.	eb-seb
expensive	caro	kab-rob
cheap	barato	bab-rab-tob
size, clothes	talla	tab-yab
size, shoes	número	noo-meb-rob
white	branco	brabn-kob
black	negro	neb-groh
red	vermello	bebr-meb-yob
yellow	amarelo	ab-mab-reb-lob
green	verde	bebr-deb
blue	azul	ab-tbool
antiques shop	tenda de antigüidades	tebn-dab deb abn-tee-gwib-dab-debs
bakery	forno	fobr-nob
bank	banco	babn-kob
book shop	librería	lee-breb-ree-ab
butcher's	carnicería	kabr-nee-tbeb-ree-ab
cake shop	pastelería	pabs-teb-leb-ree-ab
chemist's	farmacia	fabr-mab-tbee-ab
fishmonger's	peixería	pey-sbeb-ree-ab
greengrocer's	froitería	frob-ee-teb-ree-ab
grocer's	tenda	tebn-dab
hairdresser's	barbería (men) / perruquería (women)	babr-beb-ree-ab / pebr-roo-keb-ree-ab
market	mercado	mebr-kab-dob
newsagent's	quiosco de prensa	kee-obs-kob deb prebn-sab
post office	correos	kobr-reb-obs
shoe shop	zapatería	tbab-pab-teb-ree-ab
supermarket	supermercado	soo-pebr-mebr-kab-dob
tobacconist	estanco	ebs-tabn-kob
travel agency	axencia de viaxes	ab-sbebn-tbee-ab deb bee-ab-sbebs

Sightseeing

art gallery	galería de arte	gah-leb-ree-ab deb abr-teb
cathedral	catedral	kab-teb-drabl
church	igrexa	ee-greb-sbab
garden	xardín	sbar-deen
library	biblioteca	bee-blee-ob-teb-kab
museum	museo	moo-seb-ob
tourist information office	oficina de turismo	ob-fee-tbee-nab deb too-rees-mob
town hall	casa do concello	kab-sab dob kobn-tbeb-yob
closed for holiday	pechado por vacacións	peb-chab-dob pobr bab-kab-tbee-obns
bus station	estación de autobuses	ebs-tab-tbee-obn deb ab-oo-tob-boo-sebs
railway station	estación de trens	ebs-tab-tbee-obn deb trebns

Numbers

0	cero	tbeb-rob
1	un	oon
2	dous	dob-oos
3	tres	trebs
4	catro	kab-trob
5	cinco	tbeen-kob
6	seis	saybs
7	sete	seb-teb
8	oito	ob-ee-tob
9	nove	nob-beb
10	dez	debtb

FOR PEACE OF MIND ABROAD,
WE'VE GOT IT COVERED

DK INSURANCE PROVIDES YOU WITH QUALITY WORLDWIDE INSURANCE COVER

For an instant quote
go to **www.dk.com/travel-insurance**

Organised by Columbus Travel Insurance Services Ltd, 17 Devonshire Square, London EC2M 4SQ, UK. Underwritten by certain underwriters at Lloyd's and Professional Travel Insurance Company Ltd.

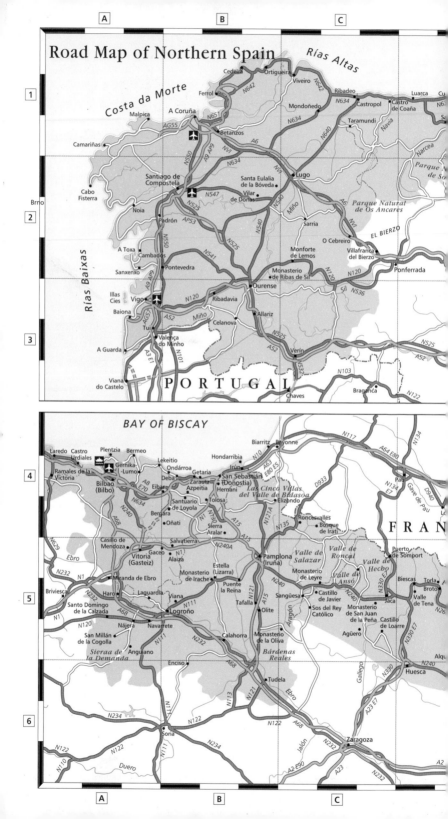